CORIOLIS GROUP BOOK

Advanced Graphics Programming Using C/C++

Loren Heiny

John Wiley & Sons, Inc.

New York • Chichester • Brisbane • Toronto • Singapore

Library of Congress Cataloging-in-Publication Data

Heiny, Loren.
  Advanced graphics Programming using C/C++ / Loren Heiny.
      p.   cm.
  "Coriolis Group book."
  Includes index.
  ISBN 0-471-57159-8
  1. Computer graphics. 2. C++ (Computer program language)
  I. Title.
  T385.H437 1993
  006.6'7--dc20

Printed in the United States of America

5721

10 9 8 7 6 5 4 3 2 1

Contents

Preface   **xiii**

  Who This Book Is For   xiii
  A Glance Inside   xiv
  What You'll Need   xiv
  About the Code   xv

Chapter 1 Introduction to Ray Tracing   **1**

  Capturing Images with Ray Tracing   1
    Tracing Light Rays   2
    Using a Camera Model   2
    From Rays to Images   5
    Representing a Scene   5
  A Simple Ray Tracing Program   5
    The Major Data Structures   6
    Specifying Colors   6
    Specifying Light Sources   6
    Specifying Objects   7
    Specifying Vectors and Points   8
    Describing the World   9
  Overview of SIMPLRAY   9
    The Main Function   10
    Generating Rays   10
    Getting Oriented   11
    Calculating a Ray   12
    Determining What a Ray Hits   16
    Working with Planes   16
    Representing a Ray   17
    Intersecting a Ray and a Plane   18
    Representing a Sphere   20
    Finding the Closest Object   22
    Calculating the Normal   23

Chapter 2 Adding a Lighting Model   **25**

  A Good Lighting Model   25
    Ambient Intensity   26
    Diffuse Light   26
    Specular Light   28

                                     v

Adding the Light Components   29
Multiple Light Sources   30
Back to Tracing Rays   30
Applying the Lighting Model   32
Calculating the Ambient Color   32
Calculating the Diffuse Color   32
Scaling the Light   34
Adding the Specular Component   34
Calculating the Reflecting Ray   36
Handling Shadows   36
Tracing the Ray   38
Setting the Pixel   40
Compiling SIMPLRAY for DOS   40
Compiling for Windows   41
Choosing a Video Mode   42
Setting the Video Mode   43
DOS Versus Windows Applications   43
Modifying SIMPLRAY   44
Computing Power and Ray Tracing   45

Chapter 3 An Enhanced Ray Tracer   **55**
Using C++ Effectively   55
Overview of the RAY Program   56
The New Objects   57
Deriving Rectangles   59
Triangle Objects   63
Supporting Spheres   67
Ellipsoids   68
Cylinder Objects   69
Managing Objects   72
An Enhanced Lighting Model   73
New Light Sources   73
Point Light Sources   74
Directed Light Sources   75
Cone Light Sources   76
Scaling Light   77
Adding Fog   78
Managing Light Sources   80
Translucent Objects   80
Antialiasing   81
Bounding Boxes   83

Building a Hierarchy of Objects 85
    Supporting Bounding Boxes 86

Chapter 4   Creating a World   133

The Scene Description Language 133
The Parser 136
    Reading Tokens 136
    Parsing a File 137
    Processing Parameters 138
    Handling Nested Commands 138
Creating an Object 139
Grouping Objects 139
Handling Parser Errors 140
Using the Scene Description Language 140
    Setting the Display Parameters 140
    Setting the Viewing Parameters 141
    Specifying Lights 142
Specifying Objects 142
    Nesting Files 143
    Saving an Image 143
Compiling and Using RAY 144
Sample Scenes 145
Things Are Shaping Up 145
Generating Swept Surfaces 146

Chapter 5   Textures and Patterns   173

Rendering a Pattern 173
    Setting the Texture 174
    Mapping onto Three-Dimensional Objects 175
Rendering a Checker Pattern 176
    Mapping the Checker Pattern 177
Rendering Non-Checker Patterns 177
    Mapping to Planar Objects 178
    Mapping to a Rectangle 178
    Mapping to a Sphere and Ellipse 180
    Mapping to a Cylinder 181
Defining a Checker Pattern 182
Mapping Images 183
    Managing Images 184
    From Point to Pixel 185
    Defining an Image Map 186

Blended Colors 187
A Textured Scene 189
Constructing the Room 189
Constructing the Cabinets 190
Making the Soup Can 192
Making a Pot 192
Using Bounding Boxes 193
Nothing's Perfect 193

Chapter 6 Adding Animation **199**
Animation Overview 199
Supporting Animation 200
The Animating Structure 201
Animating Objects 202
Going the Next Step 204
The Animation Language 204
Specifying the Number of Frames 205
Specifying a Motion Path 205
Moving the Viewer 205
Saving the Image Sequence 206
Playing Back an Image Sequence 207
An Animation Example 207

Chapter 7 Rendering Water and Clouds **215**
Designing a Model of Water 215
The Essence of Water 216
Animating Waves 217
Using Normals to Make Waves 218
A Water Object 218
Creating Waves 219
Adding Water to a Scene 221
Sample Water Scene 221
A Watery Glass 222
Extending the Water Model 224
Rendering Clouds 224
A Two-Dimensional Sky 225
Implementing A Sky Plane 226
Calculating the Texture 227
Defining Two-Dimensional Clouds 227
Cloudy Marble 228

Three-Dimensional Clouds   229
    Creating Three-Dimensional Clouds   229
    The Three-Dimensional Cloud Function   231
Defining Clouds   233
    Sample Clouds   233
Tips on Constructing Clouds   236

Chapter 8 Rendering Fractal Mountains   **237**
Rendering Natural Objects   237
    How Fractals Work   238
    Using Triangles   238
Generating Mountains   239
    Reading the Initial Triangles   240
    Setting the Fractal Parameters   241
    Subdividing Triangles   242
    Writing the Triangles   243
    Setting the Color   244
    Generating a Random Number   245
    Using Bounding Boxes   246
Compiling and Running GENMTN   247
Designing Your Mountains   249
Making More Interesting Images   250

Chapter 9 A PCX Toolkit   **271**
Overview of PCX Files   271
    The PCX File Format   272
    The PCX File Header   272
    Run-Length Encoding   274
    Decoding a PCX File   275
The PCX Toolkit   275
    Processing the Header   276
    Initializing a Header   277
    Writing the Header   278
    Writing an Image   278
    Processing the Palette   279
Reading a PCX File   279
    Reading a Header   280
    Reading the Image   280
    A Sample Read Function   281
Testing PCXTOOL.C   282

Chapter 10 TIFF: A Flexible Image File Format   **293**

TIFF Overview   293
   Working with Classes   294
   The Pieces of a TIFF File   294
   Working with Tags   296
   The Image Format   299
The TIFF.C Toolkit   299
   Reading a TIFF File   300
   Processing the Tags   302
   Determining an Image's Size   303
   Reading the Image   303
   A High-Level Read Function   304
   Writing a TIFF File   305
   Writing the Image Data   306
Testing the TIFF Tools   306
Compiling and Running TESTTIFF   308

Chapter 11 Image Processing Essentials   **331**

Working with Images   331
An Image Processing Toolkit   332
   Using Histograms   333
   Contrast Enhancement   334
   Brightness Adjustment   335
   Reducing Noise   336
   Sharpening an Image   336
   Zooming and Resizing Images   338
   Mirroring and Rotating Images   339
   Converting a Color Image to Grayscale   340
   Colorizing an Image   340
   Gamma Correction   341
Testing IMTOOLS.C   342

Chapter 12 Morphing Magic   **355**

How Morphing Works   355
   Warping Images   355
   Mapping Images   356
Creating a Simple Morphing Program   357
   Controlling the MORPH Program   357
   Initializing the Morphing Process   358
   Generating Images   359
   Moving the Triangle Patches   359

Morphing the Images   360
Determining a Point in a Triangle   361
Generating the Output Color   362
Compiling MORPH   363
Using MORPH   363
Morphing Tips   365

Appendix A Vector Operations   **377**
Working with Vectors   377
Vector Operations   379

Appendix B A Graphics Toolkit   **385**
Setting the Mode   385
Setting a Pixel   386
Working with Colors   387
Supporting C and C++ Compilers   388

Appendix C Working with Windows   **395**
Overview of WINSHELL   395
Using WINSHELL   396
Preparing for Windows   396
Displaying an Image   396
Working with Colors   397
Compiling for Windows   397

Index   **401**

Preface

Like many aspects of the personal computer revolution, the standards of graphics performance are constantly changing. Each month as hardware prices drop and technology improves, graphics techniques that were once restricted to high-end workstations become more practical on PCs. The goal of this book is to show you how to implement the most popular of these techniques on your PC.

Inside, you'll learn how to create your own computer-generated worlds, complete with clouds, mountains, and rippling water. You'll also learn the secrets behind morphing—an imaging technique popularized by Michael Jackson's "Black or White" music video—that transforms an image of one object into another.

This is a hands-on book and includes lots of code for you to experiment with. Each concept is introduced in a stepwise manner and presented so that you can easily follow along. I've tried to strike a balance between programs that are loaded with features, and code that is easy to follow and modify.

One feature I think you'll find useful is that several of the programs are designed so that you can compile them as either DOS or Windows applications. You can take your pick between the simplicity of DOS programming and the flexibility of Windows. By using Windows, for instance, you won't have to deal with the low-level graphics details of supporting different graphics adapters or the limitations of DOS's 640K ceiling.

Here are some of the book's highlights:

- A feature-packed ray tracing application written in C++
- Toolkits for reading and writing PCX and TIFF graphics files
- A morphing program
- A collection of useful image-processing tools

WHO THIS BOOK IS FOR

This book is written for the curious programmer who wants to experiment with today's state-of-the-art graphics techniques. If you're like me, you want to know how things work and you want code that you can run and modify. And this book includes lots of C and C++ code.

You'll need at least a working knowledge of C and a basic understanding of C++. If you are an experienced C programmer and you are making the step up to C++, you may want to seek help from other books such as Bryan Flamig's *Turbo C++ Step-by-Step*.

A GLANCE INSIDE

The first part of this book focuses on ray tracing. Chapters 1 and 2 introduce you to the fundamentals of ray tracing, and present a simple ray tracing program. Chapters 3 through 8 take ray tracing further, and develop a more sophisticated ray tracing application that is written in C++. Chapters 3 and 4 describe the major enhancements included in the new ray tracing program, and Chapters 5 through 8 show you how to use the program to render a variety of scenes.

The remaining chapters focus on other graphics topics. Chapters 9 and 10 present useful tools for reading and writing PCX and TIFF graphics files. Chapter 11 discusses several image processing techniques, including techniques for stretching, zooming, and enhancing images. Finally, Chapter 12 presents a simple, but entertaining morphing program that you can use to create short movies of one object turning into another.

WHAT YOU'LL NEED

To run the programs in this book, minimally you'll need an IBM AT or clone equipped with a VGA display. To compile the programs, you must also have a C/C++ compiler. I wrote and tested the code using Borland C++ V3.1; however, you can use other C/C++ compilers with little or no modifications.

Although you can run the programs presented here on just about any PC, several of the programs perform extensive floating point calculations. Therefore, a math coprocessor is a necessity—unless you are a *very* patient person. Of course, this also implies that the faster your computer is, the better.

In addition, if you want to display the best looking images, you'll want a graphics adapter that can display a large number of colors, such as a Super VGA equipped with a Sierra Hicolor DAC, which can simultaneously display 32,768 colors. The new 24-bit color cards—capable of millions of colors—produce the best images. However, if you use a 24-bit graphics adapter with the programs in the book, you must compile and run the code in Windows. This, of course, means that you must have Windows and a Windows-capable compiler.

I developed most of the code on a 486 33MHz clone equipped with 16Mb RAM and a Radius Multiview 24-bit graphics adapter running Windows 3.1.

About the Code

If you've already thumbed through this book, you've probably noticed that there is a great deal of code. If you don't want to type it in, you can order a disk that contains all the source code and the images used throughout the book. A disk order form is located at the back of the book. If you don't want to order the disk, but want the image files used in the book, you can download the image files from the BBS listed on the disk order page. The BBS is also where you'll find any updates to the code.

Introduction to Ray Tracing

After working through this book, you're sure to see your computer more as a camera or electronic darkroom than you ever have before. In fact, one of the most common goals of computer graphics is to render photo-realistic images—images that appear as if you had captured them on film.

Although we can strap a camera onto a computer and digitize actual photographs, the computer enables us to go beyond a camera's field of view. We can write programs to capture images of things that we can't see or that don't even exist.

Of course, we don't need a computer to create pictures of scenes we can't see. We can paint them ourselves using an old-fashioned brush and canvas. But for most of us, the results would be dismal. It's not that our imaginations are lacking, it's just that when it comes to the mechanics of drawing or painting, we're no threat to the Pablo Picassos of this world.

With computer graphics, we can separate the skills of rendering an image from those of designing the scene, leaving the exacting painting to the computer and instead focusing on the overall composition. While we still need a touch of artistic skill, editing scenes is a lot easier to do with a computer than a brush.

CAPTURING IMAGES WITH RAY TRACING

One of the most popular image rendering techniques and the focus of the first part of this book is *ray tracing*. With ray tracing, you can generate impressive images of computer-based, three-dimensional worlds, like those shown in color

1

plates 1 through 8. The term ray tracing comes from the fact that rays are projected into the computer's model of the world to determine what color to display at each point in the image.

Ray tracing is not new; the basic idea dates back to the 1960's when it was an expensive technique. But with the arrival of faster computers and math coprocessors, it has become a practical imaging tool for desktop computers.

In this chapter and Chapter 2, we'll explore the fundamentals of ray tracing. We'll begin with an overview of ray tracing and describe in general terms how a ray tracer works. Later, we'll develop a simple ray tracing program so that you can see how one is put together and begin creating your own eye-catching images.

In Chapters 3 and 4, we'll develop a much more sophisticated ray tracer program, which will include, among many other changes, support for texture mapping, animation, and a larger database of objects. Before we get ahead of ourselves, however, let's get back to the basics of ray tracing.

Tracing Light Rays

What we see depends on the light that reaches our eyes. It makes sense, therefore, to model an image rendering program around the way that light behaves. Ray tracing does exactly this by modeling light as individual rays. Light rays are a ray tracer's mechanism for determining what objects should appear in an image and what colors they should be.

In the real world and your computer's version of it, light rays originate from light sources, such as table lamps, flashlights, and the sun. These light rays streak through the world like an explosion of billiard balls, colliding with objects, bouncing off in new directions, and sometimes reaching the viewer, as shown in Figure 1.1. As the light rays collide with objects, some of their energy is absorbed and some of it is reflected. The reflected light carries the color of the object. It may in turn reflect off of other objects contributing to their colors, or make its way to the viewer enabling the viewer to see the object.

Actually, since most light rays bounce in directions that miss the viewer, ray tracing is typically performed backwards—starting from the viewer and projecting rays backwards to determine where they came from and therefore what color they should be transmitting.

Using a Camera Model

Ray tracing uses a model of a camera, as shown in Figure 1.2, to determine how to initially project the backward-directed rays into the computer's internal representation of the world. The *from* point is the location of the camera or

Figure 1.1 A ray tracer models light as rays.

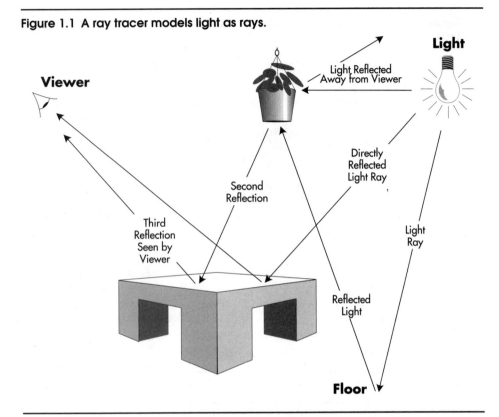

viewer; the *at* point is the spot that the camera is aimed toward. The *image plane*, which conceptually lies between the viewer and the world model, contains the image being synthesized. The *up* vector specifies how the image plane is oriented with respect to the camera. Finally, the extent of the world that is captured in one image depends on the *viewing angle*.

Like your computer's screen, the image is made up of small dots or *pixels*. The resolution of the image depends on how many pixels and colors are used, both of which are typically programmable.

An important aspect of our camera model is that it renders objects using *perspective projection*, which enhances the sense of depth in a two-dimensional image. Perspective projection makes objects appear distorted when they are close to the viewer and parallel lines converge farther away as illustrated in Figure 1.3. The amount of distortion is related to the viewing angle. Generally, the larger the viewing angle, the greater the distortion.

Figure 1.2 A ray tracer uses a camera model to determine how to initially project light rays.

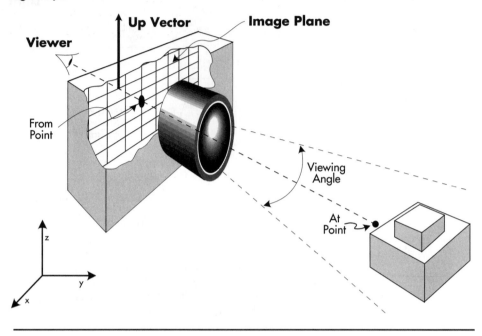

Figure 1.3 Perspective projection adds a sense of depth to a scene.

Looking at a Long Box from Above

With Perspective Projection

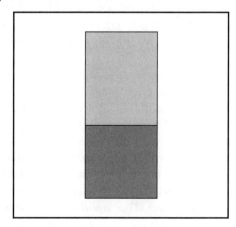

Without Perspective Projection

From Rays to Images

Ray tracing projects light rays from the viewer through each pixel in an image using the constraints of the camera model. The ray tracer sets the pixel to the color of the object that the ray hits. Well, almost. Ray tracing is more complicated than this for one key reason: Merely plotting an object's physical color doesn't generate a realistic image. If this approach were implemented, a red box would have the same shade of red all over.

To render realistic scenes the computer must account for reflections, shadows, highlights, and various surface properties of the object. The parameters and equations that support these lighting contributions are part of the ray tracer's *lighting model*.

We'll reveal the full details of the lighting model in Chapter 2. For now it's only important for you to understand that the color we attribute to a point on an object depends on the properties of the object and how the light interacts with them.

Representing a Scene

A ray tracer renders an image of whatever is in its world model. But what does the world model look like? Usually, it is a collection of constants and parameters that describe each object. The constants specify the size, location, and surface properties of the object such as whether it is glossy, its color, and so on. These constants are plugged into equations that specify how to render a particular type of object. For instance, the ray tracer may supply one equation to display a triangle, one for an ellipse, another for a cylinder, and so on.

A SIMPLE RAY TRACING PROGRAM

For the rest of this chapter, we'll explore ray tracing by looking at SIMPLRAY.C— a simple ray tracing program. The minimalist program will give you an easy-to-understand platform from which you can begin experimenting with ray tracing.

The complete source code for SIMPLRAY.C is located at the end of Chapter 2. In this chapter, we'll focus on the mechanics of the ray tracer up to the point where the ray tracer determines what object to display. Chapter 2 completes the picture with an exploration of the lighting model.

The ray tracing program is written in C and intended to be compiled and linked with several other files presented elsewhere in this book. If you want to jump right in and run the SIMPLRAY program, skip ahead to the section *Compiling SIMPLRAY for DOS*, in Chapter 2.

As you'll learn later, you can compile SIMPLRAY to run as a DOS or Windows application. To keep things simple, however, for now we'll focus on using SIMPLRAY in DOS.

The Major Data Structures

When encountering a new program like SIMPLRAY it's a good idea to get an overview of its major data structures. At the top of the SIMPLRAY.C source file you'll find the definitions for three types of structures: **COLOR**, **LIGHT**, and **OBJECT**. The next sections discuss each of these in detail.

Specifying Colors

The **COLOR** type specifies the color of something, such as an object or a light source. Its definition looks like the following example:

```
typedef struct {      // A color value is represented by a red,
  float r, g, b;      // green, and blue component. Components
} COLOR;              // have values between 0 and 1, where a
                      // value of 1 is fully "on."
```

The **r**, **g**, and **b** fields specify the red, green, and blue intensities of a particular color. Specifically, each component is a floating point value between 0 and 1. If a component is 1, its color is considered fully on. If it is 0, it's off—meaning it doesn't contribute anything to the final color. Therefore, if all three components are 0, the resulting color is black. If all three components are 1, the structure represents a bright white. Many times we'll refer to colors as *triples* with the notation *(r,g,b)*. For instance, the triple (.2,0,0) represents a dark red and (0,.9,0) specifies a bright green.

Specifying Light Sources

A **LIGHT** structure defines the location of a light source and its color, as shown in the following example:

```
typedef struct {      // Represents the light
  VECTOR LFw;         // Location of light in world coordinates
  COLOR Color;        // r, g, and b intensities of light
} LIGHT;
```

Although a light source can take several different forms, for now we'll restrict ourselves to *point* light sources. A point source is unique in that its light emanates equally in all directions from a point in space. This type of source contrasts with a flat fluorescent light panel that you may have in your kitchen or office where the source of light is spread out over a region. Figure 1.4 illustrates the difference.

Figure 1.4 Point light sources are more like the sun than a fluorescent lamp.

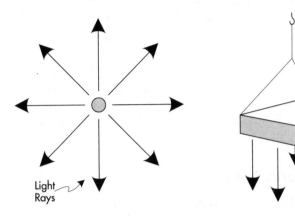

Specifically, SIMPLRAY creates a single, white light source fixed at the world coordinate (100,60,40), as shown here:

```
LIGHT Light = {{100.0, 60.0, 40.0},    // x, y, z
               {1.0, 1.0, 1.0}};       // r, g, b
```

The units of the world coordinates are arbitrary; they represent inches, feet, or millimeters. It's not that important. However, what *is* important is that the measurements used in the world model are consistent in relation to one another.

Specifying Objects

We'll use the third data type, **OBJECT**, to represent objects that the program is to display. The **OBJECT** type contains the location, size, and orientation of a single object, as well as its surface properties, such as its color and how reflective it is, as shown in the following example:

```
typedef struct {         // Contains information about an object
  unsigned int Shape;    // The type of object represented
  float ka, kd, ks;      // Ambient, diffuse, and specular constants
  int NO;                // Controls size of specular highlights
  COLOR Ia;              // Object's color
  float A, B, C, D;      // Used to represent object
} OBJECT;
```

The topmost field in the **OBJECT** structure, **Shape**, specifies the type of object being represented. The SIMPLRAY program only supports two types of objects: *planes* and *spheres*. The **PLANE** and **SPHERE** constants, defined at the top of SIMPLRAY.C, select the desired object type.

The next five fields specify various attributes of the object. As you'll learn in Chapter 2, these fields control the object's color and how shiny, smooth, or metallic its surface appears.

The **A**, **B**, **C**, and **D** fields are generic labels that we'll use to specify the location and size of an object. The exact meanings of these fields depend on whether the object is a plane or a sphere, as shown in Figure 1.5. For instance, in the case of a sphere, **A**, **B**, and **C** specify the center of the sphere and **D** its radius.

Specifying Vectors and Points

One other data type we'll use is **VECTOR**, which is defined in the VECTOR.H header file as:

```
typedef {
  float x, y, z;
} VECTOR;
```

More information about VECTOR.H and its companion file, VECTOR.C, are included in Appendix A. Briefly, the **VECTOR** type specifies the three-dimensional

---

Figure 1.5 The constants used in planes and spheres.

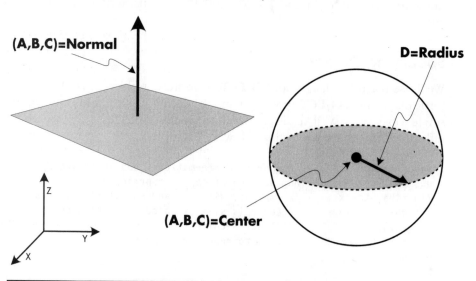

coordinates of a point or the endpoint of a ray or vector. You may have noticed it was used earlier in the **LFw** field of the **LIGHT** structure in order to specify the position of a light source. (The VECTOR.C source file also contains a handful of functions for manipulating these vectors.)

Describing the World

The **Objects** array, which is a collection of **OBJECT** structures, contains the objects that make up the program's world model. Each **OBJECT** structure represents one of the objects in the scene. Altogether SIMPLRAY has six objects: three planes and three spheres. You can find the specifications for these objects in the declaration for **Objects**, as shown here:

```
// This array contains the objects to display
OBJECT Objects[OBJECTNUM] =
  {{SPHERE, 1.0, 0.5, 0.5, 4, {1.0, 0.0, 1.0},
   2.5, 5.0, 1.0, 0.75},              // Rightmost sphere
   {SPHERE, 0.7, 0.0, 0.9, 4, {0.1, 0.1, 0.1},
   3.5, 1.25, 1.5, 1.0},              // Leftmost sphere
   {PLANE, 0.7, 0.6, 0.0, 4, {0.5, 0.5, 0.0},
   0.0, 0.0, 1.0, 0.0},               // Bottom plane
   {PLANE, 0.7, 1.0, 0.0, 4, {0.0, 0.0, 1.0},
   1.0, 0.0, 0.0, 0.0},               // Plane on right
   {SPHERE, 1.0, 1.0, 0.0, 4, {0.0, 1.0, 1.0},
   2.0, 3.0, 1.0, 1.0},               // Middle sphere
   {PLANE, 0.7, 1.0, 0.0, 4, {1.0, 0.0, 0.0},
   0.0, 1.0, 0.0, 0.0}};              // Plane on left
```

OVERVIEW OF SIMPLRAY

Now that we have the basic data types out of the way, let's explore how the details of the ray tracer are implemented in SIMPLRAY. It's helpful to think of SIMPLRAY in terms of four distinct components, shown here. This chapter covers the first three.

- The **main** function, which gives a high-level, skeletal view of SIMPLRAY.
- The **GenImage** function, which projects the initial rays into the world model to determine what objects to display, then plots the resulting pixels.
- The set of functions **ComputeTForPlane**, **ComputeTForSphere**, and **FindClosestIntersection**, which determine if and where a light ray hits an object.
- The **ComputeLight** function, which applies the lighting model to determine what color to display for an object.

The Main Function

Compiled as a DOS application, the ray tracer begins with the following rather simple main function:

```
int main()
{
  Setup("");
  if (SetupDisplay(M320x200x256 | COLORPALETTE)) {
    GenImage(0);
    EndDisplay();
    Cleanup();
  }
  return 0;
}
```

The topmost routine, **Setup**, initializes several of the ray tracer's variables to default values. Next, the program calls **SetupDisplay** to initialize the graphics mode in preparation for displaying the image. **SetupDisplay**'s sole parameter selects the desired graphics mode. The parameter is a combination of two constants defined in GRPHICS.H. The **M320x200x256** constant specifies the display resolution and the **COLORPALETTE** constant selects a color palette rather than a grayscale one. These constants are explained further in Appendix B. As long as the graphics initialization is successful, the **GenImage** function is called to perform the actual ray tracing. After rendering and displaying an image, **EndDisplay** and **Cleanup** wait for a keypress, return the display adapter to text mode, and release any memory and close any open files.

Generating Rays

The **GenImage** routine launches light rays originating from the viewer's *from* point into the object list. As Figure 1.6 illustrates, each ray passes through a single image pixel and is used to determine what object appears at that pixel.

GenImage consists of two parts. The first set of statements initializes various variables that calculate the directions of the rays. The second set consists of two **for** loops that actually project the rays into the scene. The **TraceRay** function located in the inner **for** loop determines what color to plot at each ray's position. The following pseudocode highlights what is going on here:

```
Set up coordinate system
For each row in the image
  For each pixel in the row
    Calculate the ray that extends from the eye through the pixel
      in the image
    Determine what the projected ray hits in the world model and
      determine that object's color
    Display the pixel's color
```

Figure 1.6 GenImage projects light rays through each image pixel.

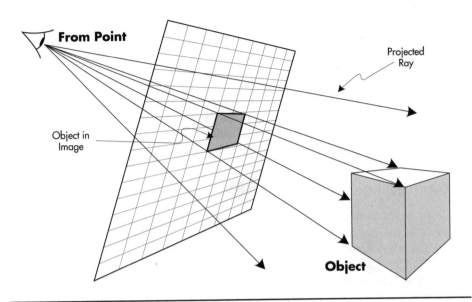

Getting Oriented

The projected light rays are expressed using two vectors. One of the vectors specifies the starting coordinate of the ray. We'll often refer to this as the *base* of the ray. The second vector specifies the direction of the ray. Therefore, we'll call it the *direction* vector.

The initial light rays all start at the from point. Therefore, all the light rays in **GenImage** have a base equal to the **From** vector. The base vectors are set to the from point by passing **From** to the **TraceRay** function.

How are the direction vectors for the light rays determined? The process is a little convoluted, but conceptually quite simple. We'll begin by calculating a set of vectors that define the perimeters of the world model that appear in the image. We'll then express the direction of the projected rays relative to these bounding vectors. To simplify the light ray calculations, we'll introduce a new eye-based coordinate system, shown in Figure 1.7. This coordinate system places the viewer at its origin and aligns the camera's image plane with its axes.

The program uses three unit vectors—**A1**, **A2**, and **A3**—to partially prescribe how world coordinates relate to this eye-based coordinate system. The values for these vectors are calculated in the **SetEye** function, as shown here:

```
void SetEye()
{
   DVal = cos(VuAngle/2.0) / sin(VuAngle/2.0);
```

```
    A3 = Subtract(&At, &From);
    A1 = Cross(&A3, &Up);
    A2 = Cross(&A1, &A3);
    Normalize(&A1);
    Normalize(&A2);
    Normalize(&A3);
}
```

The **SetEye** function calculates values for the unit vectors **A1**, **A2**, and **A3** using the current *from*, *at*, and *up* vectors, and a specified viewing angle. It's a bit beyond this book to explain the theory behind these vectors, however, the next section explains how **GenImage** uses them to render an image.

Calculating a Ray

Our objective here is to project rays starting at the from point through each pixel in the image. We have to perform a few calculations here since we have the coordinate systems of the image, the world model, and now the eye-based coordinate system to deal with.

The coordinate system of the image, shown in Figure 1.8, has a width of **ImWd** pixels and a height of **ImHt** pixels. The image dimensions are defined at the top of SIMPLRAY.C to be 128 and 128.

Figure 1.7 An eye-based coordinate system is used in the ray tracer.

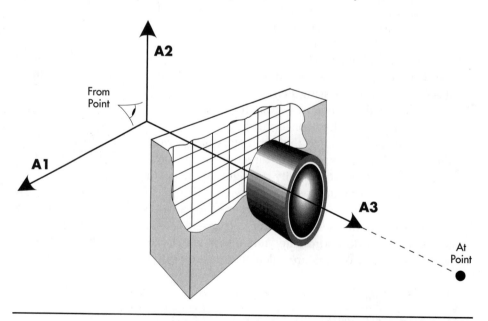

Figure 1.8 The coordinate system of the image.

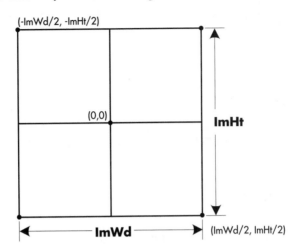

We'll use the three vectors **RightV**, **UpV**, and **CenterV**, which are based on the vectors **A1**, **A2**, and **A3**, to help calculate the positions of the rays in terms of world coordinates.

You can think of these three vectors this way: The **CenterV** vector points to the location of the world model that is to be placed at the center of the image. The **RightV** vector points to what is to become the right edge of the image. And, similarly, **UpV** points to the portion of the world model that will become the top of the image. Therefore, the code sends out rays within the bounds of the vectors **RightV**, **-RightV**, **UpV**, and **-UpV**, as shown in Figure 1.9. The image displays whatever is in this bounded region.

Recall, we want one ray to project through each pixel in the image. Since we know the bounds of the world model that coincide with the bounds of the image, we merely need to take an appropriate proportion of the **RightV** and **UpV** vectors to specify a vector that goes through each pixel in the image. The **UInc** and **VInc** variables are used for this purpose. The **UInc** variable specifies the relative difference, in eye-coordinates, between two neighboring light rays in an image row. The **VInc** variable contains the difference between two pixels on consecutive rows. These two variables are calculated by the statements shown here:

```
VInc = 2.0 / (ImHt - 1) * AspectRatio;
UInc = 2.0 / (ImWd - 1);
```

Why do these statements divide the number of pixels in the image into the number 2.0? Recall that the eye coordinate system is designed so that its extents

---

Figure 1.9 The RightV, UpV, and CenterV vectors define the bounds of the image in relation to the world model.

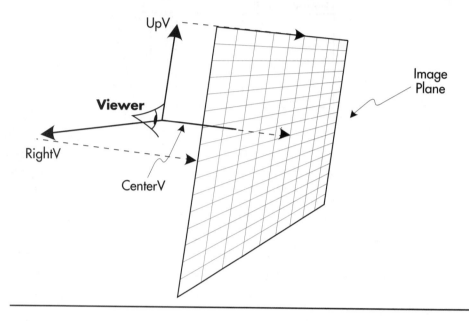

are demarcated by the *unit* vectors **A1** and **A2**. Since each of these vectors has a length of one, by definition, and the image fits within their bounds as shown in Figure 1.10, the image must be two units high and two units wide. This is where the value of 2.0 comes into play.

The **AspectRatio** variable scales the vertical spacing of the rays to compensate for screens that do not have square pixels. For instance, in a 320x200 mode, pixels are taller than they are wide. Therefore, **AspectRatio** is precalculated in GRPHICS.H so that it effectively divides the image height, **ImHt**, by 1.33 so that the objects won't appear stretched in height. Keep in mind, however, that the **AspectRatio** calculation does not change the resolution of the image. The image is still **ImWd** by **ImHt** in size.

Now we're ready to calculate the direction for each ray. The two **for** loops in **GenImage** simply step through each pixel in the image, calculating the direction of a ray that passes through it. The direction of the ray is stored in the **VECTOR** variable **Dir**, as shown here:

```
for (Y=ImHt/2; Y>-ImHt/2; Y--) {
  v = Y * VInc;
  for (X=-ImWd/2; X<ImWd/2; X++) {
    u = X * UInc;
    Dir.x = CenterV.x + u * RightV.x + v * UpV.x;
    Dir.y = CenterV.y + u * RightV.y + v * UpV.y;
```

Figure 1.10 The vectors A1, A2, and A3 help to determine the light rays in an image.

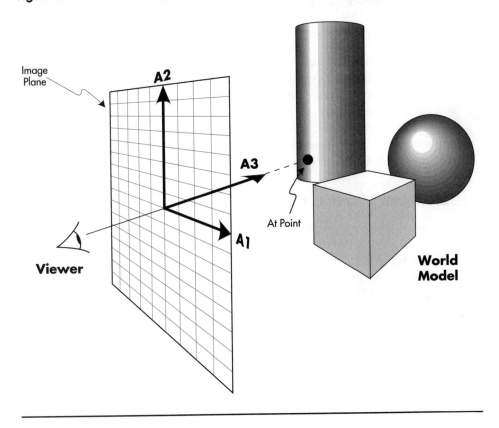

```
Dir.z = CenterV.z + u * RightV.z + v * UpV.z;
TraceRay(1, &From, &Dir, &I);
if (I.r > 1.0) I.r = 1.0;
if (I.g > 1.0) I.g = 1.0;
if (I.b > 1.0) I.b = 1.0;
// Color pixel at (x,y) with I.r, I.g, I.b.
// The values in I range between 0 and 1.
PutPixel(hDC, X+ImWd/2, -Y+ImHt/2,
  I.r*255, I.g*255, I.b*255);
  }
}
```

The **GenImage** function calls **TraceRay** to perform the ray tracing for the ray calculated. It returns the color to display at the current pixel in the variable **I**, as shown here:

```
TraceRay(1, &From, &Dir, &I);
```

The last step in **GenImage**'s inner **for** loop is to plot the color of the pixel using the **PutPixel** function, as shown here:

```
PutPixel(hDC, X+ImWd/2, -Y+ImHt/2, I.r*255, I.g*255, I.b*255);
```

Where is **PutPixel** defined? You won't find it in SIMPLRAY.C. The **PutPixel** function is a high-level graphics primitive included in GRPHICS.C that supports both DOS graphics mode and Windows. Chapter 2 and Appendix B cover the routine in greater detail.

So far we've looked at the main function in SIMPLRAY and **GenImage**, which generates the initial rays. Now we're ready to take a closer look at how the program determines what objects the rays intersect.

Determining What a Ray Hits

Once we know the direction of a ray, the next question becomes: What is the closest object that the ray intersects with, if any? This object's color is assigned to the image pixel that the ray passes through.

As you'll soon discover, a typical ray tracing program spends most of its time testing for intersections. The problem is that generally you don't know which object to test. In the worst case, you'll have to test every object to determine that the ray doesn't intersect any of them. In this situation, the light ray's color is set to the scene's background color.

How does the ray tracer determine whether a ray intersects a particular object? The solution involves a little bit of math and a clever choice of objects. We'll use simple object types, such as planes and spheres, where every point on the object can be determined from a single equation. To test for an intersection point, the ray tracer substitutes the equation of the ray into the equation for the object and looks for a solution. If there is one, that coordinate is the location where the ray intersects the object. If there isn't a solution, the ray missed that object and the remaining objects are tested.

Working with Planes

The ray tracer uses the following equation to represent a plane:

```
ax + by + cz + d = 0
```

The variables (x,y,z) represent the coordinates or points on the plane. The coefficients a, b, c, and d specify its orientation and location. In particular, the coordinate (a,b,c) specifies a vector that is perpendicular to the plane's surface, called its *normal*. To help make sure you're comfortable with how the plane equation operates, Figure 1.11 presents several planes and their corresponding equations. Take a few minutes to go over them before going on. (Although the

Figure 1.11 Several sample planes and their equations.

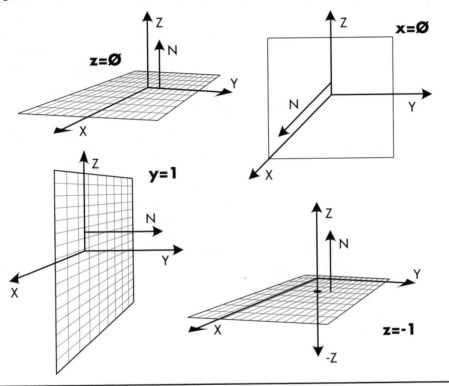

figure does not illustrate this, remember that the surface of a plane extends in all directions.)

Representing a Ray

So far we have an equation that enables us to calculate the points on a plane. We also need an equation to determine the points along a light ray. It turns out that the best way to represent a ray is not the most obvious. To reduce the number of calculations in the ray tracer and avoid problems with handling the slope of the ray, we'll use a parametric equation for rays. What does a parametric equation look like? The trick is to enlist an additional variable, or *parameter*, that specifies the relative position between two points on a line. The parametric equation of a line is given by the following set of equations:

$$x = x_0 + t(x_1 - x_0)$$
$$y = y_0 + t(y_1 - y_0)$$
$$z = z_0 + t(z_1 - z_0)$$

where (x_0,y_0,z_0) and (x_1,y_1,z_1) are two points on the line. The value of t, which is the new parameter, changes as you move along the line, as Figure 1.12 illustrates. When t is 0, for instance, the equations yield the point (x_0,y_0,z_0); when t is 1, they resolve to (x_1,y_1,z_1). Values of t between 0 and 1, on the other hand, represent points between (x_0,y_0,z_0) and (x_1,y_1,z_1). Finally, values of t greater than 1 lie to the right of (x_1,y_1,z_1) and those that are negative lie to the left of (x_0,y_0,z_0).

Intersecting a Ray and a Plane

A principle question in the ray tracer is whether a particular light ray intersects a plane. To answer, all we need to do is plug the ray equation into the plane's equation and solve for t. This yields the intersection point in terms of t. We can plug t back into the ray equation to get the actual intersection coordinate.

Before going any further, however, let's adapt the parametric ray equation to our needs. The coordinate (x_0,y_0,z_0) represents the base of the light ray. Inside **TraceRay**, this vector is stored in the variable **Base**. (Recall that the initial rays in **GenImage** originate from the *from* point.) Similarly, we can replace the quantities x_1-x_0, y_1-y_0, and z_1-z_0 with the normalized direction vector, **Dir**, calculated in **GenImage** and passed to **TraceRay**. Therefore, a modified version of the parametric ray equation is:

```
x = Base.x + t * Dir.x
y = Base.y + t * Dir.y
z = Base.z + t * Dir.z
```

Now we're ready to substitute the parametric equation of the ray into the plane equation:

```
a * (Base.x + t * Dir.x) + b * (Base.y + t * Dir.y) +
  c * (Base.z + t * Dir.z) + d = 0
```

Figure 1.12 **The parametric equation of a line.**

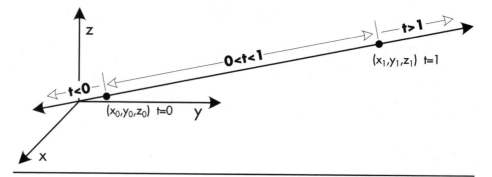

The first step in solving for t is to multiply everything out:

```
a * Base.x + a * t * Dir.x + b * Base.y + b * t * Dir.y +
  c * Base.z + c * t * Dir.z + d = 0
```

Next, we'll factor together all of the t terms and move them to one side of the equation:

```
t * (a * Dir.x + b * Dir.y + c * Dir.z) = -(a * Base.x +
  b * Base.y + c * Base.z + d)
```

Solving for t we get:

```
t = -(a * Base.x + b * Base.y + c * Base.z + d) /
  (a * Dir.x + b * Dir.y + c * Dir.z)
```

That's all there is to it. We now have an equation that can tell us where a ray intersects a plane. You'll find it implemented in SIMPLRAY's **ComputeTForPlane** function, as shown here:

```
float ComputeTForPlane(OBJECT *Obj, VECTOR *Base, VECTOR *Dir)
{
  float denom;

  denom = Obj->A * Dir->x + Obj->B * Dir->y + Obj->C * Dir->z;
  if (denom != 0)
    return -(Obj->A * Base->x + Obj->B * Base->y +
      Obj->C * Base->z+ Obj->D) / denom;
  return -1;
}
```

The **ComputeTForPlane** function returns the t value for a specific ray and plane. The value of t tells us where along the ray that the intersection occurs. A negative value means the line containing the ray intersects the plane behind the base of the ray or is parallel to the plane. This latter case occurs when the denominator is equal to 0.

Realize that **ComputeTForPlane** only calculates the intersection point in terms of the parametric t value. To determine where the intersection point actually is, we'll later plug t back into the parametric equation for the ray along with the base of the ray and the ray's direction vector. Why not calculate the intersection point in **ComputeTForPlane**? It turns out that we can organize the code so that we only need to perform this additional calculation for the closest intersecting object rather than all objects. You'll see where this takes place later.

Representing a Sphere

Now let's turn our attention to the other type of object that SIMPLRAY supports: spheres. The general equation for a sphere that is centered at the origin (x_c, y_c, z_c) and has a radius r is:

$$(x-x_c)^2 + (y-y_c)^2 + (z-z_c)^2 = r^2$$

The point (x,y,z) that solves this equation falls on the surface of the sphere.

To determine where a light ray intersects a sphere, substitute the parametric form of the ray equation into the sphere equation:

$$(x_0 + tx_d - x_c)^2 + (y_0 + ty_d - y_c)^2 + (z_0 + tz_d - z_c)^2 = r^2$$

Multiplying everything out and rearranging the terms you get:

$$(x_d^2 + y_d^2 + z_d^2)\, t^2 + 2\,(x_d(x_0-x_c) + y_d(y_0-y_c) + z_d(z_0-z_c))\, t + (x_0-x_c)^2 + (y_0-y_c)^2 + (z_0-z_c)^2 - r^2 = 0$$

Hidden in this complex looking equation is really something of the form:

$$A_q t^2 + 2B_q t + C_q = 0$$

which is a quadratic equation in terms of t. The variables A_q, B_q, and C_q represent the following more complex expressions:

$$A_q = (x_d^2 + y_d^2 + z_d^2)$$
$$B_q = x_d(x_0-x_c) + y_d(y_0-y_c) + z_d(z_0-z_c)$$
$$C_q = (x_0-x_c)^2 + (y_0-y_c)^2 + (z_0-z_c)^2 - r^2$$

Since we have a quadratic equation, we can use the quadratic formula to solve for t. Recall from your high school algebra class that the quadratic formula is:

$$t = \frac{-B_q \pm \sqrt{B_q^2 - 4A_q C_q}}{2A_q}$$

Realize that there will either be no solution or two solutions, as shown in Figure 1.13. There's no solution if the determinate (what is in the square root) is negative, indicating that the ray misses the sphere. Otherwise, there are two solutions for t. However, we want the closest intersection point that is in front of the ray's base. Therefore, we'll select the smaller value of t that is greater than 0. Recall that values of t that are less than 0 are behind the base of the ray.

The code to determine the intersection of a light ray and sphere are located in the function **ComputeTForSphere**. The rest of this section walks through its code.

Figure 1.13 A ray may intersect a sphere in several different ways.

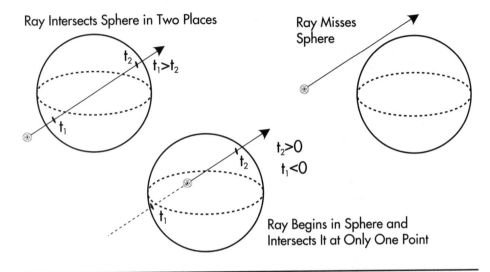

The first thing **ComputeTForSphere** does is to subtract the origin of the sphere from the base location of the light ray and store the result in the vector **Base2**, as shown here:

```
Base2 = Subtract(Base, &Obj->Loc);
```

This calculation helps to reduce the number of calculations later. Next, the code calculates the values for **Aq**, **Bq**, and **Cq**:

```
Aq = Dot(Dir, Dir);
Bq = 2 * Dot(Dir, &Base2);
Cq = Dot(&Base2, &Base2) - Obj->D * Obj->D;
```

Notice that the **Dot** vector function (in VECTOR.C) is used to make the calculations for **Aq**, **Bq**, and **Cq** appear a little cleaner. You may want to convince yourself that these function calls are equivalent to the functions listed earlier.

Recall that **Obj->D** is the radius of the sphere. Since the radius of the sphere never changes, we could precompute the **Obj->D * Obj->D** term of the **Cq** equation. As a result, we could save one multiplication at run time. In fact, this is one of the optimizations we will use in our enhanced ray tracer discussed in Chapters 3 and 4.

The next sequence of statements determines which t value, specified by the variables **First** and **Second**, is the closer t greater than 0:

```
Det = Bq * Bq - 4 * Aq * Cq;
if (Det >= 0) {
  Det = sqrt(Det);
  First = (-Bq + Det) / (2 * Aq);
  Second = (-Bq - Det) / (2 * Aq);
  if (First < TOL && Second < TOL)
    return -1;
  if (First < Second) {
    if (First < TOL)
      return Second;
  }
  else if (Second > TOL)
    return Second;
  return First;
}
return -1;
```

If the determinate is negative, **ComputeTForSphere** returns -1, indicating that the ray misses the sphere.

As you look at the code, you'll notice the constant **TOL** used in several of the **if** expressions. What is it? **TOL** is a small value, defined as 0.001, that compensates for inaccuracies in floating point calculations. It enables the code to treat values that are extremely close to a point—in this case 0—as actually being on the point. Without **TOL**, we'd miss some intersections.

Finding the Closest Object

In the previous sections, we discussed how the ray tracer can determine whether a ray intersects a plane or sphere. When **GenImage** projects rays through the image and into the world model, however, we want to find the *closest* object to the viewer. This object is the one we want to display. How can we tell which object is closest? Using the t value it's simple. We only need to find the smallest value of t that is greater than 0 for all objects.

The function **FindClosestIntersection** makes this test and calculates the actual intersection point. It loops through all of the objects, calling the **ComputeTForPlane** or **ComputeTForSphere** function to find the closest t, as shown here:

```
int FindClosestIntersection(VECTOR *Base, VECTOR *Dir, VECTOR *Q)
{
  int I, Closest = -1;
  float NearInt = 100000000000.0, t;
```

```
// Calculate the intersection with the ray and each object
for (I=0; I<OBJECTNUM; I++) {
  switch (Objects[I].Shape) {
    case PLANE:
      t = ComputeTForPlane(&Objects[I], Base, Dir);
      break;
    case SPHERE:
      t = ComputeTForSphere(&Objects[I], Base, Dir);
      break;
  }
  if (t < NearInt && t > TOL) {
    NearInt = t;
    Closest = I;
  }
}
```

After the **for** loop is done, **Closest** contains the index of the closest object that the ray intersects, if there is one. Only then does the code calculate the actual intersection point of the ray and the object, as shown here:

```
// Calculate the actual intersection point
if (Closest >= 0) {
  Q->x = Base->x + Dir->x * NearInt;
  Q->y = Base->y + Dir->y * NearInt;
  Q->z = Base->z + Dir->z * NearInt;
}
return Closest;
```

Calculating the Normal

Before ending this chapter, there is one more calculation we'll need to support for the objects in the world model. The lighting model is going to need the normal of the object at the intersection point. (Remember, the normal is a vector perpendicular to the surface of the object.) This vector is used to determine the direction in which reflected light travels and partially define how much light strikes the object's surface.

You'll find these calculations in the function **DetermineNormal**. Calculating the normal for a plane is quite simple: it's merely the **A**, **B**, and **C** coefficients of the plane equation, as shown here:

```
switch (Obj->Shape) {
  case PLANE:
    N->x = Obj->A;
    N->y = Obj->B;
    N->z = Obj->C;
    break;
```

The normal of a sphere is only slightly more complex. If the point **Q** is where we want to find the normal, all we need to do is subtract the sphere's origin from **Q**, as shown in Figure 1.14.

```
case SPHERE:
  N->x = Q->x - Obj->A;
  N->y = Q->y - Obj->B;
  N->z = Q->z - Obj->C;
  break;
```

The call to the **Normalize** function at the end of **DetermineNormal** normalizes **N** so that it's values range from 0 to 1. This removes unwanted effects of the vector's magnitude from the normal. Again, the lighting model we'll be using is only interested in the direction of the normal vector, not its magnitude.

Figure 1.14 Calculating the normal of a sphere.

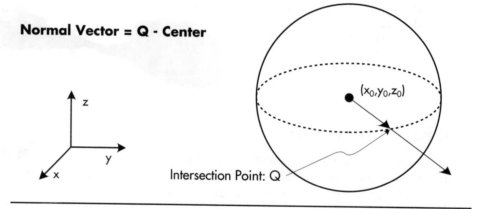

2

Adding a Lighting Model

In ray tracing there are two important questions: What objects should appear in an image and what colors should these objects appear as? Chapter 1 covers the first question; this chapter answers the second.

Selecting realistic colors for objects requires that our ray tracer account for a number of factors, including each object's physical color, surface properties, reflecting rays, shadows, and more. Together these components make up the ray tracer's *lighting model.*

The first part of this chapter describes the lighting model we'll be using and explains how it is implemented in SIMPLRAY. Once these details are out of the way, we'll round out the SIMPLRAY program so that you can get it up and running and begin rendering your own scenes.

A GOOD LIGHTING MODEL

The lighting model we'll use consists of a series of equations and a handful of constants that you adjust for each object to make the image appear as realistic as possible. Realize that the lighting model does not faithfully implement the physics of light, but rather it's an approximation that creates results that are quite good.

For instance, although the model is based on light rays, it does not attempt to account for every ray bouncing around in a scene. Instead, it follows critical ones that show where objects are and those that generate highlights, reflections, and shadows. In a similar fashion, the model divides light into *ambient*, *diffuse*, and *specular* lighting. An object's color is determined one point at a time by adding up how each of these forms of light influence its appearance.

25

Ambient Intensity

Ambient lighting is the general illumination in a scene and gives an object its base color. There's no specific source for ambient light. Therefore, an object's ambient color is the same all over the object and doesn't change with different vantage points.

Each object has an ambient color represented by the **Ia** field in SIMPLRAY's **OBJECT** structures. The **OBJECT** structure also contains the **ka** field that specifies how much of the ambient color to add to the overall color seen. The following equation, therefore, gives the color for an object if it were to only have ambient lighting:

```
I = Ia * ka
```

The value of **ka** ranges between 0 and 1; therefore, a low value of **ka** renders a darker object. For many objects in a typical room, the ambient constant is set to around 0.7.

Diffuse Light

The diffuse portion of the lighting model represents the light that matte objects reflect. As Figure 2.1 illustrates, matte surfaces scatter light evenly in all directions. Therefore, for a given surface point, you see the same amount of diffuse, reflected light no matter where you view the point from.

Figure 2.1 Matte surfaces scatter light evenly in all directions.

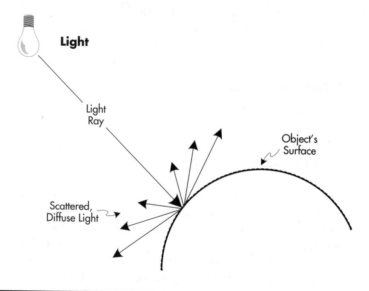

The intensity of this light, however, does depend on the angle between the direction of the light source and the surface's normal, as shown in Figure 2.2. The greater the angle, the smaller the resulting light. It's as if at these greater angles more light is skimming past the object's surface and not being reflected. If the angle is small, on the other hand, more light directly hits the surface and, therefore, is scattered.

We'll calculate the amount of diffuse lighting using the equation:

```
I = I  * kd * cosθ * Ia
     L
```

where θ is the angle between a ray to the light source (L) and the normal (N) of the surface point.

The **OBJECT** structure in SIMPLRAY contains the **kd** constant to specify how much diffuse lighting influences the color of an object. As was the case with ambient lighting, the **kd** constant is a value between 0 and 1, where larger values of **kd** give the object more shading.

Notice from the earlier equation that the diffuse color partially depends on the color of the light source, indicated here by the variable I_L. This makes sense since the diffuse lighting is based on the light from the light source. In the case of SIMPLRAY, the light's color is given by the **Color** field in the **LIGHT** structure.

Notice also that the equation implies that diffuse lighting does not change with changing vantage points. In other words, the equation does not involve the viewer's position. It only depends on the light's position relative to the object's surface.

Figure 2.2 Diffuse lighting varies with the angle between the surface normal and the direction of the light source.

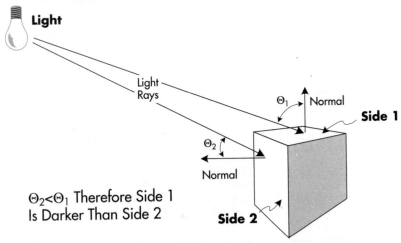

Specular Light

The specular component of an object's color reproduces the bright highlights you expect to see on shiny objects such as billiard balls. Expressed in terms of light rays, specular light is the light from a light source that is reflected by an object *directly* toward the viewer. Unlike diffuse lighting, specular highlights move as the viewer moves.

Figure 2.3 gives a pictorial view of the vectors we'll use to calculate specular highlights. The highlight appears as a spot and is brightest along the reflected direction (R), which has the same angle with the surface normal as the incoming light ray. Its brightness falls off rapidly as the viewer moves to the side of the reflected ray. To get this rapid fall off, we'll raise the cosine of the angle between the line of sight vector and the reflecting vector to a constant defined for each object.

Mathematically, the specular light is represented as:

$$I = I_L * ks * \cos^{NO}\alpha$$

Let's go over the variables in this equation. The ks constant is a field in the **OBJECT** structure and specifies how much the specular light contributes to the object's final color. Its value ranges between 0 and 1. Larger values of ks

---

Figure 2.3 The vectors used to model specular highlights.

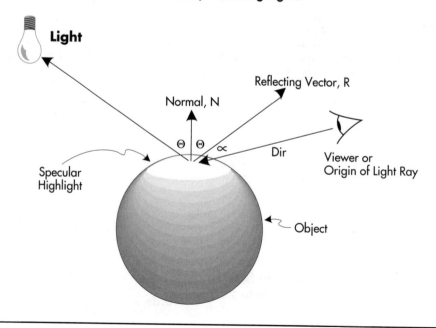

Figure 2.4 The size of a specular highlight depends on the NO constant.

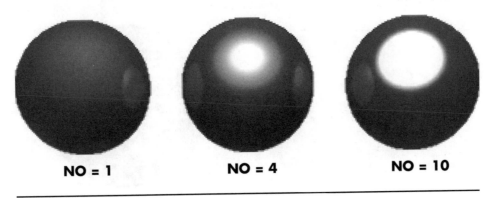

produce stronger specular highlights. The variable NO specifies how rapidly the specular highlight falls off. It's also in **OBJECT** and is a positive integer that does not have to be very large. The *larger* the number, the *smaller* the specular highlight, as illustrated in Figure 2.4.

Notice that, as with diffuse lighting, the color of the specular light depends on the color of the light source.

Adding the Light Components

How do ambient, diffuse, and specular light work together in an image? Figure 2.5 shows four versions of the same sphere, each rendered with a different combination of lighting. For instance, the top-left sphere uses only ambient lighting. Notice that it doesn't have any shading. The top-right sphere has only diffuse lighting; therefore, it has some shading, but the sphere is not complete. The bottom-left sphere has only specular lighting and is even less complete. The bottom-right sphere, on the other hand, shows the same sphere using all three components of light.

The overall color, in fact, is given by the equation:

$$I = Ia * ka + I_L (kd * \cos\theta + ks * \cos^{NO}\alpha)$$

We can control how an object appears by varying the object's color and the four constants ka, ks, kd and NO. Determining the correct lighting parameters can require a lot of trial and error.

A mirrored object, for instance, has a high specular component. A matte surface, such as a typical office room wall, scatters light diffusely; therefore, it would have higher ambient and diffuse lighting components.

Figure 2.5 Ambient, diffuse, and specular lighting contribute to the final image of an object.

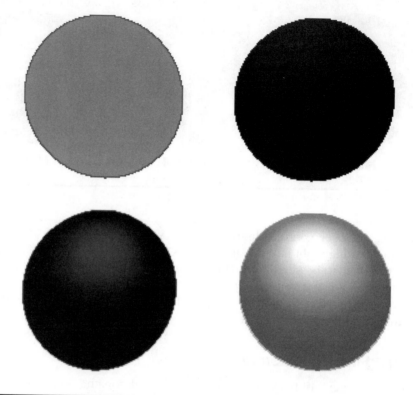

Multiple Light Sources

The diffuse and specular components of light represent the rays reflected from a light source. What happens if there are several light sources? Simple: The same calculations are made for each light source and the values are totaled up to determine the final color for the object's surface point.

BACK TO TRACING RAYS

So far we've been talking about the lighting model in general terms. How does it fit into a ray tracing program? First, we need to finish outlining how light rays bounce around in a scene and accumulate the colors we see. Then, we'll show how SIMPLRAY implements the equations of the lighting model. Let's begin with the light rays.

We ended our discussion of ray tracing in Chapter 1 at the point where the ray tracer has determined what object should appear in an image pixel. Let's call the point to display Q. To determine what color to plot for point Q we need to apply the following steps:

1. Test whether point Q is in a shadow. If it is, set the color of point Q to the object's ambient color. Otherwise, apply the complete lighting model equation that we described in the previous sections.

2. Follow the reflecting ray R from point Q and see what object it intersects. Call this point Q_1. Compute the color of the object at point Q_1 by starting at Step 1.

3. Add the colors for Steps 1 and 2 together and plot this color for point Q.

Figure 2.6 shows a pictorial view of this process for one ray. Realize that the process of following reflected rays can be repeated for many levels. From a programming standpoint, this is usually implemented with a recursive call to

Figure 2.6 The process of determining the color of a point.

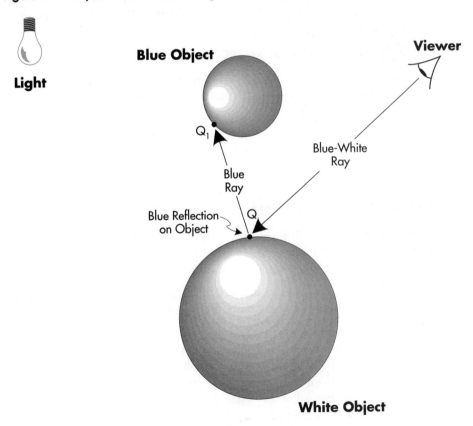

the function computing Steps 1 and 2. Therefore, ray tracers usually put an upper limit on how many reflected rays are followed. In Figure 2.6, for instance, only one reflected ray is calculated. Generally, the more levels calculated, the longer the ray tracing will take. For most cases, you'll only need to follow two or three reflected rays to achieve a realistic image. On less reflective objects, fewer levels of rays will suffice.

APPLYING THE LIGHTING MODEL

Now let's see how the SIMPLRAY program implements the lighting model equations to determine the color of an object.

The **ComputeLight** function is the primary routine that determines the color of a single point on an object. When SIMPLRAY calls **ComputeLight**, the ray tracer already knows what object a ray intersects with and its exact location. At this stage, the program is attempting to determine what color to display for the object at the intersection point **Q**. Since the lighting model is at the heart of the ray tracer, we'll take a detailed tour through **ComputeLight**'s code.

Table 2.1 gives a description of each of **ComputeLight**'s parameters.

Calculating the Ambient Color

ComputeLight's first step is to determine the ambient portion of the object's color. This is calculated by multiplying the ambient constant **ka**, stored in the **OBJECT** structure for the object, with the object's ambient color, **Ia**.

```
I->r = Obj->ka * Obj->Ia.r;
I->g = Obj->ka * Obj->Ia.g;
I->b = Obj->ka * Obj->Ia.b;
```

Calculating the Diffuse Color

Next, the code adds the diffuse component to the running sum of the color. To do this, it first calculates the vector from the intersection point **Q** to the light source, as illustrated in Figure 2.7.

Table 2.1 The parameters of the ComputeLight function.

Parameter	Description
Level	The number of levels into the ray tracing
Index	The index of the object which the ray intersects
Q	The intersection point of the ray and the object
NormalN	The normal of the object at point Q
Dir	The direction vector of the light rays that hit the object
I	The color of the object at point Q

Figure 2.7 Calculating the light vector, L.

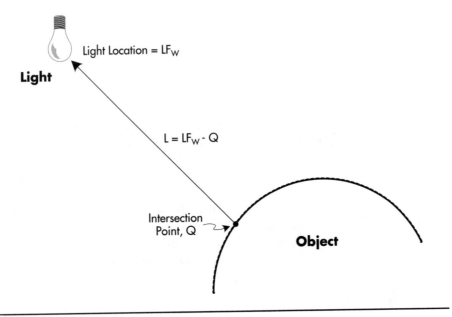

```
L.x = Light.LFw.x - Q->x;    // Calculate the vector from
L.y = Light.LFw.y - Q->y;    // the intersection point to
L.z = Light.LFw.z - Q->z;    // the light source
```

The code uses the vector **L** to determine the intensity of the diffuse lighting and whether the point **Q** is in a shadow.

ComputeLight tests whether **Q** is in a shadow by calling the function **InShadow**, which we'll discuss later in this chapter. For now, all you need to know is that it returns non-zero if point **Q** is not in a shadow cast by another object.

If an object is in a shadow, we want the point **Q** to be slightly darker than the rest of the scene. Specifically, we won't give the object any diffuse or specular shading. Remember, both of these components of light require that the point be visible to the light—which isn't the case when a point is in a shadow.

The following code adds in the diffuse lighting as long as the point is not in a shadow:

```
// Calculate the diffuse portion of the point's color
if (!InShadow(Index, &L, Q)) {
  LightDist = Mag(&L) / LIGHTSCALE;
  DiffScale = sqrt(LightDist);

  Normalize(&L);
```

```
NDotL = Dot(&L, NormalN); // Calculate angle between light
if (NDotL > 0) {
  I->r += Obj->kd * Obj->Ia.r * Light.Color.r * NDotL /
    DiffScale;
  I->g += Obj->kd * Obj->Ia.g * Light.Color.g * NDotL /
    DiffScale;
  I->b += Obj->kd * Obj->Ia.b * Light.Color.b * NDotL /
    DiffScale;
}
```

The variable **NDotL** is the result of the dot product of the object's normal at **Q**, given by **NormalN**, and the normalized direction of the light source, **L**. The dot product of these two normalized vectors is equivalent to the cosine of the angle between them. Recall that this angle is what adjusts the diffuse lighting across an object's surface.

The code makes sure that **NDotL** is positive before adding the diffuse lighting. In other words, the angle between the light source and normal must be smaller than 90 degrees. If the angle were other than this, the light would be on the other side of the surface and therefore not visible.

Scaling the Light

As you look at the code in the previous section, you'll notice that it divides the diffuse lighting by the value in **DiffScale**. If you trace the code back, you'll see that **DiffScale** is a value proportional to the distance from the point **Q** to the light source:

```
LightDist = Mag(&L) / LIGHTSCALE;
DiffScale = sqrt(LightDist);
```

In other words, the larger the distance to the light source, the larger the value of **DiffScale** and, hence, the smaller the diffuse lighting contribution. This makes sense because light weakens the farther that it must travel.

Adding the Specular Component

The specular color is based on the reflecting vector **R** shown in Figure 2.8. The code uses the following three statements, which we won't derive here, to calculate the vector **R**:

```
R.x = -L.x + 2 * NDotL * NormalN->x;
R.y = -L.y + 2 * NDotL * NormalN->y;
R.z = -L.z + 2 * NDotL * NormalN->z;
```

Figure 2.8 Calculating the reflecting vector.

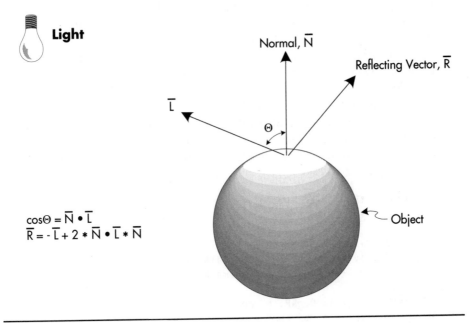

The final step is to add in the specular portion of the lighting. Recall that the lighting model raises the cosine of the angle between the reflecting vector and sight vector to some power. Therefore, first the code calculates the cosine of this angle:

```
CosAlpha = -Dot(&R, Dir);
```

The negative sign adjusts for the positions of the vectors. A quick glance at Figure 2.8 illustrates why it is needed.

As long as the angle is positive—meaning that the reflecting vector is visible—the specular component is added in, as shown by the following code:

```
if (CosAlpha > 0) {
    // Add in the specular portion of the point's color
    I->r += Light.Color.r * Obj->ks * pow(CosAlpha, Obj->NO) /
        LightDist;
    I->g += Light.Color.g * Obj->ks * pow(CosAlpha, Obj->NO) /
        LightDist;
    I->b += Light.Color.b * Obj->ks * pow(CosAlpha, Obj->NO) /
        LightDist;
}
```

Calculating the Reflecting Ray

At this point in **ComputeLight**, the program has a fairly good value for the color of point **Q**. However, to make it better we must add in the reflecting rays. This corresponds to Step 2 that we outlined earlier.

We'll only add in reflecting rays if the program has not traced too many levels of reflecting vectors already. Therefore, the code tests whether the **Level** variable, which is incremented with each recursive call to **TraceRay**, has reached the limit defined by **MAXLEVEL**.

If the test succeeds, **ComputeLight** calculates the reflecting vector, calls **TraceRay** to compute the color of the object that the reflecting ray hits, and adds this amount to the running total of point **Q**'s color, as shown here:

```
if (Level+1 < MAXLEVEL) {
  // Add in the reflecting color
  DotProd = -Dot(Dir, NormalN);

  R.x = Dir->x + 2 * DotProd * NormalN->x;
  R.y = Dir->y + 2 * DotProd * NormalN->y;
  R.z = Dir->z + 2 * DotProd * NormalN->z;
  Normalize(&R);
  TraceRay(Level+1, Q, &R, &TempI);
  I->r += TempI.r * Obj->ks;
  I->g += TempI.g * Obj->ks;
  I->b += TempI.b * Obj->ks;
```

After the ambient, diffuse, specular, and reflecting colors are added together, the value of **I** is returned as the color to display for point **Q**.

Handling Shadows

Determining whether a point is in a shadow is easy. The ray tracer simply projects a ray from the point in question to each light source. If the ray intersects with any other object, as shown in Figure 2.9, the original point must be blocked from the light and is therefore in a shadow. This procedure is repeated for each light. In SIMPLRAY, however, there is only one light source, therefore the test only needs to be done once for each point.

The **InShadow** function performs the shadow test just outlined. It calls the intersection-test functions for each object to determine if the parametric value for the intersection point is between 0 and 1. If so, the function returns non-zero immediately, signaling that the object is between the base of the ray and the light source. In other words, the object is casting a shadow on **Q**. If no obscuring object is found, **InShadow** returns 0. The complete function is shown here:

```
unsigned char InShadow(int Index, VECTOR* Ray, VECTOR* Q)
{
  int I;
  float T;

  // Test whether the ray is blocked by another object
  for (I=0; I<OBJECTNUM; I++) {  // Check for intersection
    if (I != Index) {           // Don't check against itself
      switch (Objects[I].Shape) {
        case PLANE:
          T = ComputeTForPlane(&Objects[I], Q, Ray);
          break;
        case SPHERE:
          T = ComputeTForSphere(&Objects[I], Q, Ray);
          break;
      }
      if (T > TOL && T < 1)
        return 1;
    }
  }
  return 0;
}
```

Figure 2.9 A ray is projected toward the light source to determine whether a point is in a shadow.

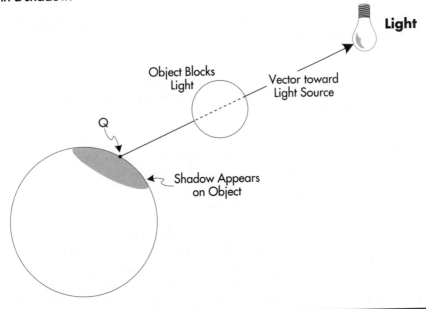

Notice that the code below compares the parametric value, **T**, with the constant **TOL**:

```
if (T > TOL && T < 1)
    return 1;
```

The value of **TOL**, which is slightly larger than 0, ensures that the code won't accidentally believe that the object is intersecting with itself. Actually, there are some types of objects that can cast a shadow on themselves, however, we'll ignore these cases.

Tracing the Ray

Recall that the purpose of **TraceRay** is to determine the color that corresponds to a particular light ray. It accomplishes this by first calling **FindClosestIntersection** to determine which is the closest object in the world model that the ray intersects. Then it calls a series of functions to determine what color to return for that object.

The function begins by determining the array index of the closest object found. If this index value is positive, it contains the index of the object and the vector **Q** contains the intersection point:

```
Index = FindClosestIntersection(Base, Dir, &Q);
if (Index >= 0) {              // If some intersection found
```

If no intersection is found, the background color is returned and the function ends, as shown here:

```
else {
    I->r = Background.r;    // The ray didn't hit any of the
    I->g = Background.g;    // objects. Use the backdrop's color.
    I->b = Background.b;
}
```

If there is an intersection, however, the code proceeds by determining the normal, **N**, of the object at point **Q**, as shown here:

```
DetermineNormal(&Objects[Index], &N, &Q);
```

Before we go any further, we must take special note of the normal vector **N**. If you think about it, the normal may be pointing on either side of the surface, as illustrated in Figure 2.10. Since we want to render the surface that we see, we'll flip the sign of the normal if it is pointing the wrong way. How can we tell which way the normal is pointing? The code computes the dot product of the normal at **Q** and the direction vector **Dir**. This is equivalent to

Figure 2.10 The ray tracer uses only the normal facing the viewer.

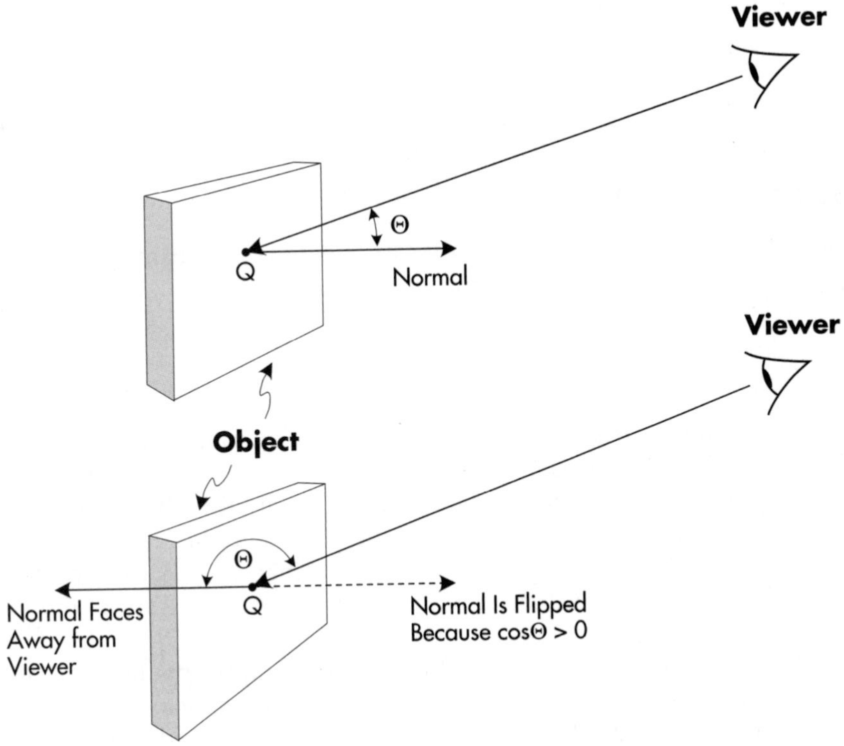

the cosine of the angle between the two vectors. The normal must be flipped if its angle with the direction vector is greater than 90 degrees. The code that performs this test is shown here:

```
if (Dot(&N, Dir) > 0) {
    N.x = -N.x;
    N.y = -N.y;
    N.z = -N.z;
}
```

Now we're ready to determine the color of the object at **Q**. We know the index of the object that the ray intersects, the intersection point **Q**, its normal (**N**), and the direction of the intersecting ray (**Dir**). To compute the color of **Q**, we call **ComputeLight**, as shown here:

```
ComputeLight(Level, Index, &Q, &N, Dir, &Iq);
```

ComputeLight returns the color of **Q** in the **COLOR** variable **Iq**. We'll assign this value to the parameter **I** passed into **TraceRay**, then exit the function, as shown here:

```
I->r = Iq.r;
I->g = Iq.g;
I->b = Iq.b;
```

Setting the Pixel

Once **TraceRay** determines the color for a light ray, **GenImage** can display it with the following call to **PutPixel**:

```
PutPixel(hDC, x+ImWd/2-1, -y+ImHt/2-1,
  I.r*255, I.g*255, I.b*255);
```

You'll find **PutPixel** packed with several other graphics support functions in the source file GRPHICS.C.

PutPixel's second and third parameters specify the pixel coordinate to be set. Their seemingly awkward calculations are required because of the coordinate systems that the code uses. Recall from Chapter 1 that the center of the image is the coordinate (0,0) and positive x and y values are in the top-right portion of the image.

Notice that the red, green, and blue color components in **I** are multiplied by 255. Remember, the color fields in a **COLOR** structure normally range between 0 and 1. **PutPixel** accepts 8-bit red, green, and blue color values, therefore the color fields in **I** are scaled by 255. Together, **PutPixel**'s last three parameters enable you to specify a 24-bit color. Your graphics hardware may only support a lower color resolution, however this is a detail that **PutPixel** handles.

You may have noticed that we skipped past **PutPixel**'s first parameter, **hDC**. What is it? If you're a Windows programmer, you probably can guess. If you're not, you're probably scratching your head. The key thing to understand about **hDC** is that it tells Windows what to draw on—in this case the screen. When compiled for DOS, **hDC** is ignored. Either way, you don't really have to worry about it because the GRPHICS.C file takes care of it for you.

COMPILING SIMPLRAY FOR DOS

The SIMPLRAY program and most of the other programs in this book are designed so that you can compile them as DOS or Windows applications. To create a DOS version of one of these programs, you merely need to compile the program using a DOS-based compiler.

To build SIMPLRAY you must compile and link the files SIMPLRAY.C, VECTOR.C, and GRPHICS.C together. You can use any memory model.

A grayscale version of SIMPLRAY's output is shown in Figure 2.11. By default, the program displays a color image in a 256-color mode. For details on how to select another video mode, see *Choosing a Video Mode* later in this chapter.

COMPILING FOR WINDOWS

Creating an application for Windows requires a few special steps. Appendix C describes in detail what these are. Essentially, you'll need to:

1. Define the macro constant **FORWINDOWS**.
2. Compile and link the main program with the Windows shell (WINSHELL.C) listed in Appendix C. It becomes the new "main" source file.
3. Compile the source files with a Windows-capable compiler such as Turbo C++ for Windows or Quick C for Windows.

As you may have already noticed, the graphics programs in this book are sprinkled with **#ifdef** using **FORWINDOWS**. They select between graphics output for DOS and Windows.

The Windows shell, WINSHELL.C, takes care of setting up the color palette and managing the image in the window.

Figure 2.11 Output of the Windows version of SIMPLRAY.

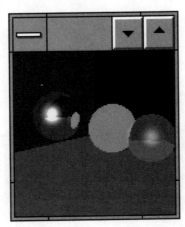

Choosing a Video Mode

To create nice looking images you'll want to run your program in a video mode, which provides as many simultaneous colors as possible. The minimum mode you'll probably want to use is a 256-color mode. The standard VGA, for instance, provides a 320x200, 256-color mode, although this is not available in Windows. To get 256 colors in Windows you must step up to an SVGA display that supports 256 colors in resolutions of 640x480 or better.

The drawback to a 256-color mode is that many ray traced images require more than 256 colors. In these situations, the additional colors are mapped to similar existing colors. You can avoid this problem if you have a 15-bit SVGA that is capable of displaying 32,768 simultaneous colors. The extra colors are quite valuable, but there is a catch. Although a 15-bit color card gives you more colors, you'll have fewer shades of each. For instance, you'll only have 32 shades of gray, rather than the 64 you'd get in a 256-color mode. How can this be? The 15-bit color standard is a special display mode that encodes each red, green, and blue component with only 5-bits of resolution. The 256-color modes use 6 bits of resolution.

Unfortunately, neither the 256-color modes and 32K graphics adapters provide photo-quality images. The 5 or 6 bits of resolution they provide is simply not sufficient. As a result, you'll see banding or contouring of slowly changing shades of colors, as illustrated in Figure 2.12. This is particularly evident on spheres or large planes. The best way to get rid of contouring is to step up to a 24-bit graphics card.

Figure 2.12 Contouring occurs if there aren't enough shades of a color.

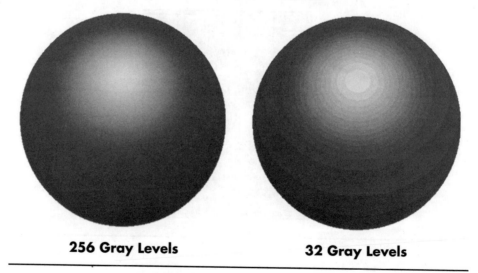

256 Gray Levels　　　　　**32 Gray Levels**

Since there currently is not a widespread 24-bit standard, we'll rely on Windows to access this mode.

Finally, you should realize that the display mode you select has an impact on how fast your programs will display an image. Generally, if you're looking for the most speed, the 320x200 256-color mode in DOS is the fastest.

Setting the Video Mode

To set the video mode for a DOS version of the program, you must pass the desired constant listed in Table 2.2 to the **SetupDisplay** function. Each of these constants are defined in GRPHICS.H and explained further in Appendix A.

In Windows, you must set the video display driver that Windows uses with Windows' SETUP program. Note that in Windows a 256-color mode actually limits your program to 236 colors; the other 20 colors are used for displaying the windows, scroll bars, and so on.

DOS Versus Windows Applications

One of the drawbacks to developing a graphics program for Windows is that it generally runs slower than a comparable DOS application. On the plus side, you can easily display multiple images on the screen at once.

Another advantage of Windows is that your programs can work on several different display adapters since Windows manages the low-level details of the screen so your program doesn't have to. As a result, the same code will run on a standard 16-color VGA and a 24-bit color card. Of course, 24-bit color cards generate far superior images.

Because of these differences, you may want to do much of your debugging and trial-and-error work in DOS. Once you have your application working well, recompile it for Windows and enjoy the flexibility it provides.

Table 2.2 Display modes available in DOS.

Constant	Description
M320x200x256	320x200x256-color mode
M800x600x32K	800x600 32K-color mode
M640x480x256	640x480x256-color mode
M640x480x32K	640x480 32K-color mode
COLORPALETTE	Use a color palette
GRAYSCALEPALETTE	Use a gray scale palette (default)

Modifying **SIMPLRAY**

After you get SIMPLRAY running, you'll probably want to begin experimenting with it. Here are some ideas you might try:

1. Modify the values for the from and at points, up vector, and viewing angle. You can change each of these in the **Setup** function. Figure 2.13 shows the objects and the coordinate system used in the world model.

2. If you want a larger image, set the **IMWD** and **IMHT** macro constants to the desired pixel width and height, respectively.

3. Change the locations and properties of the objects in the **Objects** array. To do this, you must alter the declaration of **Objects** near the top of the program. If you change the number of objects in the list, make sure you update the **OBJECTNUM** constant to the new number of objects in the world model.

Figure 2.13 The world coordinates used in SIMPLRAY.

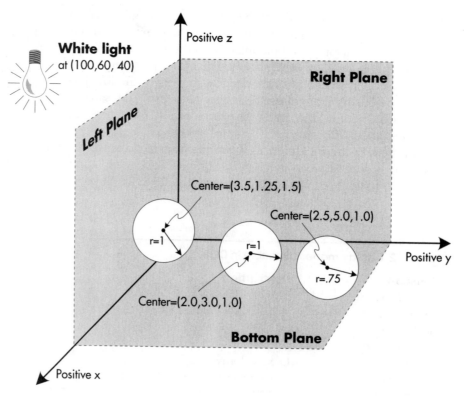

4. Modify the location and color of the light source. Notice how the shading and specular highlights change.

5. Try different levels of recursion by altering **MAXLEVEL**. If you set **MAXLEVEL** to 1, for instance, none of the objects will show reflections. Alternatively, if **MAXLEVEL** is large, the ray tracing takes longer, but the quality of the image is not improved.

6. You may also want to try different values for the light attenuation factor that is represented by the **LIGHTSCALE** constant. Similarly, you can change the background color by modifying the declaration for the **Background** variable. Currently the background is set to black.

COMPUTING POWER AND RAY TRACING

You can run a ray tracing program such as SIMPLRAY on just about any PC equipped with a VGA graphics display. However, the faster the computer, the more enjoyable the experience will be. Ray tracing is *time consuming*. Therefore, a 486 is better than a 386, and a 386 much better than a 286. Actually, what really bogs down the computer are all the floating point operations. So a math co-processor is almost a necessity.

We could modify the routines to use all integer arithmetic, but unfortunately doing so obfuscates some of the code and makes it a bit more difficult to modify later. Using floating point arithmetic may be expensive, but looking into the crystal ball of computers, it appears like raw computing power is a lot cheaper than your programming time.

• SIMPLRAY.C

```
// SIMPLRAY.C: A simple ray tracing program that displays planes
// and spheres. The objects are hard-coded into the program. You
// can compile SIMPLRAY for DOS or Windows. When compiled for
// DOS, SIMPLRAY runs under VGA's 320x200 256-color mode.
// The scenes are displayed using up to 256 colors.
//
// To compile for DOS: Link with VECTOR.C and GRPHICS.C.
//
// To compile for Windows: Link with VECTOR.C, GRPHICS.C
// and WINSHELL.C. You must define the compilation constant
// FORWINDOWS. You can do this with Borland C++'s IDE by
// adding "FORWINDOWS" to the Defines section of the
// Options\Compiler\Code Generation dialog. If you use
// a command-line compiler, add FORWINDOWS to its list of
// options or define FORWINDOWS in each of the files.
//
// #define FORWINDOWS 1 // Uncomment this to compile for Windows
```

```c
#include <math.h>
#include "grphics.h"
#include "vector.h"

#define PLANE 1          // Code for a plane object
#define SPHERE 2         // Internal code for a sphere object
#define IMWD 128         // Horizontal resolution of image created
#define IMHT 128         // Vertical resolution of image created
#define OBJECTNUM 6      // Number of objects displayed
#define MAXLEVEL 2       // Maximum levels of ray tracing recursion
#define TOL 0.001        // Tolerance for floating point numbers
#define LIGHTSCALE 6     // Scales light's drop-off rate

typedef struct {         // A color value is represented by a red,
  float r, g, b;         // green, and blue component. Components
} COLOR;                 // have values between 0 and 1, where a
                         // value of 1 is fully "on."

typedef struct {         // Contains information about an object
  unsigned int Shape;    // The type of object represented
  float ka, kd, ks;      // Ambient, diffuse, and specular constants
  int NO;                // Controls size of specular hightlights
  COLOR Ia;              // Object's color
  float A, B, C, D;      // Used to represent object
} OBJECT;

typedef struct {         // Represents the light
  VECTOR LFw;            // Location of light in world coordinates
  COLOR Color;           // r, g, and b intensities of light
} LIGHT;
LIGHT Light = {{100.0, 60.0, 40.0},    // x, y, z
               {1.0, 1.0, 1.0}};       // r, g, b

// This array contains the objects to display
OBJECT Objects[OBJECTNUM] =
  {{SPHERE, 1.0, 0.5, 0.5, 4, {1.0, 0.0, 1.0},
    2.5, 5.0, 1.0, 0.75},              // Rightmost sphere
   {SPHERE, 0.7, 0.0, 0.9, 4, {0.1, 0.1, 0.1},
    3.5, 1.25, 1.5, 1.0},              // Leftmost sphere
   {PLANE, 0.7, 0.6, 0.0, 4, {0.5, 0.5, 0.0},
    0.0, 0.0, 1.0, 0.0},               // Bottom plane
   {PLANE, 0.7, 1.0, 0.0, 4, {0.0, 0.0, 1.0},
    1.0, 0.0, 0.0, 0.0},               // Plane on right
   {SPHERE, 1.0, 1.0, 0.0, 4, {0.0, 1.0, 1.0},
    2.0, 3.0, 1.0, 1.0},               // Middle sphere
   {PLANE, 0.7, 1.0, 0.0, 4, {1.0, 0.0, 0.0},
    0.0, 1.0, 0.0, 0.0}};              // Plane on left

COLOR Background = {0, 0, 0};          // Background's color
VECTOR From, At, Up, A1, A2, A3;
```

```
float DVal, VuAngle;
int ImWd = IMWD, ImHt = IMHT;

// Function prototypes:
float ComputeTForPlane(OBJECT *Obj, VECTOR* Base, VECTOR* Dir);
float ComputeTForSphere(OBJECT *Obj, VECTOR* Base, VECTOR* Dir);
int FindClosestIntersection(VECTOR *Base, VECTOR *Dir, VECTOR *Q);
void DetermineNormal(OBJECT *Obj, VECTOR *N, VECTOR *Q);
unsigned char InShadow(int Index, VECTOR* Ray, VECTOR* Q);
COLOR *ComputeLight(int Level, int Index, VECTOR *Q,
  VECTOR *NormalN, VECTOR *Dir, COLOR* I);
void TraceRay(int Level, VECTOR *Base, VECTOR *Dir, COLOR *I);
unsigned char Intensity(int Level, VECTOR *Base, VECTOR *Dir,
 COLOR* I);
void SetEye(void);

///////////////////////////// main \\\\\\\\\\\\\\\\\\\\\\\\\\\
//
// Main program entry point for the program when it is compiled
// as a DOS application. It's not used when compiled for Windows.
//
#if !defined(FORWINDOWS)
int main()
{
  Setup("");
  if (SetupDisplay(M320x200x256 | COLORPALETTE)) {
    GenImage(0);
    EndDisplay();
    Cleanup();
  }
  return 0;
}
#endif

///////////////////////////// Setup \\\\\\\\\\\\\\\\\\\\\\\\\\\
//
// Initialize various variables for the program
//
void Setup(char far* Str)
{
  // Set the positions of the from, at and up vectors
  From.x = 7.5;    From.y = 7.5;    From.z = 2.3;
  At.x = 0.0;      At.y = 0.0;      At.z = 0.0;
  Up.x = 0.0;      Up.y = 0.0;      Up.z = 1.0;
  VuAngle = 50.0 * 0.017453293;  // Use a 50 degree view
  ImWd = IMWD;    ImHt = IMHT;   // Set the dimesions of image
}
```

```
//////////////////////////// Cleanup \\\\\\\\\\\\\\\\\\\\\\\\\\
//
// In this program, no special actions are required here. This
// function is provided so that the source code can be combined
// with WINSHELL.C.
//
void Cleanup(void)
{
}


//////////////////////////// GenImage \\\\\\\\\\\\\\\\\\\\\\\\\\
//
// This is the main entry point for the ray tracing code. If
// compiled as a DOS application, the hDC parameter is not used.
// In Windows, hDC is a handle to the device context to draw on.
//
void GenImage(int hDC)
{
  COLOR I;
  int X, Y;
  float UInc, VInc, u, v;
  VECTOR RightV, CenterV, UpV, Dir;

  SetEye();        // Set up for calculating eye coordinates

  VInc = 2.0 / (ImHt - 1) * AspectRatio;
  UInc = 2.0 / (ImWd - 1);
  RightV.x = A1.x;  RightV.y = A1.y;  RightV.z = A1.z;
  UpV.x = A2.x;     UpV.y = A2.y;     UpV.z = A2.z;
  CenterV.x = A3.x * DVal;
  CenterV.y = A3.y * DVal;
  CenterV.z = A3.z * DVal;
  for (Y=ImHt/2; Y>-ImHt/2; Y--) {
    v = Y * VInc;
    for (X=-ImWd/2; X<ImWd/2; X++) {
      u = X * UInc;
      // Compute the direction vector
      Dir.x = CenterV.x + u * RightV.x + v * UpV.x;
      Dir.y = CenterV.y + u * RightV.y + v * UpV.y;
      Dir.z = CenterV.z + u * RightV.z + v * UpV.z;
      TraceRay(1, &From, &Dir, &I);   // Determine the color
      if (I.r > 1.0) I.r = 1.0;        // for the image pixel
      if (I.g > 1.0) I.g = 1.0;
      if (I.b > 1.0) I.b = 1.0;
      // Color pixel at (x,y) with I.r, I.g, I.b.
      // The values in I range between 0 and 1.
      PutPixel(hDC, X+ImWd/2, -Y+ImHt/2, I.r*255, I.g*255, I.b*255);
    }
```

```
  }
}

///////////////////////// ComputeTForPlane  \\\\\\\\\\\\\\\\\\\\\
//
// Computes the intersection point between the ray and a plane
// in terms of t. The value of t must be greater 0. If t is
// negative then the intersection is "behind" the base of the
// ray. Returns -1 if no intersection exists.
//
float ComputeTForPlane(OBJECT *Obj, VECTOR *Base, VECTOR *Dir)
{
  float denom;

  denom = Obj->A * Dir->x + Obj->B * Dir->y + Obj->C * Dir->z;
  if (denom != 0)
    return -(Obj->A * Base->x + Obj->B * Base->y +
      Obj->C * Base->z+ Obj->D) / denom;
  return -1;
}

///////////////////////// ComputeTForSphere  \\\\\\\\\\\\\\\\\\\\\
//
// Determine where the ray intersects a sphere. It returns
// a value of t that can be used with the parametric equation
// of the ray to determine where the intersection point is.
// A ray can intersect a sphere in two places. Therefore,
// the code finds the closest intersection (smallest t value).
// Returns -1 if there isn't an intersection.
//
float ComputeTForSphere(OBJECT *Obj, VECTOR *Base, VECTOR *Dir)
{
  float Det, Aq, Bq, Cq, First, Second;
  VECTOR Base2, Loc;

  Loc.x = Obj->A;  Loc.y = Obj->B;  Loc.z = Obj->C;
  Base2 = Subtract(Base, &Loc);
  Aq = Dot(Dir, Dir);
  Bq = 2 * Dot(Dir, &Base2);
  Cq = Dot(&Base2, &Base2) - Obj->D * Obj->D;
  Det = Bq * Bq - 4 * Aq * Cq;
  if (Det >= 0) {
    Det = sqrt(Det);
    First = (-Bq + Det) / (2 * Aq);
    Second = (-Bq - Det) / (2 * Aq);
    if (First < TOL && Second < TOL)
      return -1;
    if (First < Second) {
```

```
      if (First < TOL)
        return Second;
    }
    else if (Second > TOL)
      return Second;
    return First;
  }
  return -1;
}


/////////////////// FindClosestIntersection \\\\\\\\\\\\\\\\\\
//
// Finds the closest object that intersects the ray. Finds the
// smallest parametric t value for the objects. Returns -1
// if no intersection is found.
//
int FindClosestIntersection(VECTOR *Base, VECTOR *Dir, VECTOR *Q)
{
  int I, Closest = -1;
  float NearInt = 100000000000.0, t;

  // Calculate the intersection with the ray and each object
  for (I=0; I<OBJECTNUM; I++) {
    switch (Objects[I].Shape) {
      case PLANE:
        t = ComputeTForPlane(&Objects[I], Base, Dir);
        break;
      case SPHERE:
        t = ComputeTForSphere(&Objects[I], Base, Dir);
        break;
    }
    if (t < NearInt && t > TOL) {
      NearInt = t;
      Closest = I;
    }
  }
  // Calculate the actual intersection point
  if (Closest >= 0) {
    Q->x = Base->x + Dir->x * NearInt;
    Q->y = Base->y + Dir->y * NearInt;
    Q->z = Base->z + Dir->z * NearInt;
  }
  return Closest;
}


/////////////////////// DetermineNormal \\\\\\\\\\\\\\\\\\\\\\\
//
// Return the normal N at the point Q for the object
//
```

```c
void DetermineNormal(OBJECT *Obj, VECTOR *N, VECTOR *Q)
{
  switch (Obj->Shape) {
    case PLANE:
      N->x = Obj->A;
      N->y = Obj->B;
      N->z = Obj->C;
      break;
    case SPHERE:
      N->x = Q->x - Obj->A;
      N->y = Q->y - Obj->B;
      N->z = Q->z - Obj->C;
      break;
  }
  Normalize(N);
}


///////////////////////////  InShadow  \\\\\\\\\\\\\\\\\\\\\\\\\
//
// Determine whether the point Q (which is assumed to be on
// the Index object) is in a shadow cast by another object.
//
unsigned char InShadow(int Index, VECTOR* Ray, VECTOR* Q)
{
  int I;
  float T;

  // Test whether the ray is blocked by another object
  for (I=0; I<OBJECTNUM; I++) {  // Check for intersection
    if (I != Index) {            // Don't check against itself
      switch (Objects[I].Shape) {
        case PLANE:
          T = ComputeTForPlane(&Objects[I], Q, Ray);
          break;
        case SPHERE:
          T = ComputeTForSphere(&Objects[I], Q, Ray);
          break;
      }
      if (T > TOL && T < 1)
        return 1;
    }
  }
  return 0;
}


///////////////////////////  ComputeLight  \\\\\\\\\\\\\\\\\\\\\\\\\
//
// Given the point (x,y,z) calculate its intensity scaled
// between 0 and 1. For now, only assume 1 point light source.
```

```
//
COLOR *ComputeLight(int Level, int Index, VECTOR *Q,
  VECTOR *NormalN, VECTOR *Dir, COLOR* I)
{
  VECTOR L;             // Vector to light source
  VECTOR R;             // Reflecting vector
  float NDotL;          // Angle between ray and normal
  float DotProd;
  float CosAlpha;
  OBJECT *Obj;
  COLOR TempI;
  float LightDist, DiffScale;

  Obj = &Objects[Index];

  // Calculate the ambient portion of the point's color
  I->r = Obj->ka * Obj->Ia.r;
  I->g = Obj->ka * Obj->Ia.g;
  I->b = Obj->ka * Obj->Ia.b;

  L.x = Light.LFw.x - Q->x;   // Calculate the vector from
  L.y = Light.LFw.y - Q->y;   // the intersection point to
  L.z = Light.LFw.z - Q->z;   // the light source

  // Calculate the diffuse portion of the point's color
  if (!InShadow(Index, &L, Q)) {
    LightDist = Mag(&L) / LIGHTSCALE;
    DiffScale = sqrt(LightDist);

    Normalize(&L);

    NDotL = Dot(&L, NormalN); // Calculate angle between light

    if (NDotL > 0) {
      I->r += Obj->kd * Obj->Ia.r * Light.Color.r * NDotL /
        DiffScale;
      I->g += Obj->kd * Obj->Ia.g * Light.Color.g * NDotL /
        DiffScale;
      I->b += Obj->kd * Obj->Ia.b * Light.Color.b * NDotL /
        DiffScale;
    }

    R.x = -L.x + 2 * NDotL * NormalN->x;
    R.y = -L.y + 2 * NDotL * NormalN->y;
    R.z = -L.z + 2 * NDotL * NormalN->z;

    CosAlpha = -Dot(&R, Dir);
    if (CosAlpha > 0) {
      // Add in the specular portion of the point's color
```

```
        I->r += Light.Color.r * Obj->ks * pow(CosAlpha, Obj->NO) /
          LightDist;
        I->g += Light.Color.g * Obj->ks * pow(CosAlpha, Obj->NO) /
          LightDist;
        I->b += Light.Color.b * Obj->ks * pow(CosAlpha, Obj->NO) /
          LightDist;
      }
    }
    if (Level+1 <= MAXLEVEL) {
      // Calculate the amount that the reflecting vector adds
      // to the point's color
      DotProd = -Dot(Dir, NormalN);

      R.x = Dir->x + 2 * DotProd * NormalN->x;
      R.y = Dir->y + 2 * DotProd * NormalN->y;
      R.z = Dir->z + 2 * DotProd * NormalN->z;
      Normalize(&R);

      TraceRay(Level+1, Q, &R, &TempI);
      I->r += TempI.r * Obj->ks;
      I->g += TempI.g * Obj->ks;
      I->b += TempI.b * Obj->ks;
    }
    return I;
}


//////////////////////////// TraceRay \\\\\\\\\\\\\\\\\\\\\\\\\\
//
// Performs the ray tracing. Given a ray, it returns the
// intensity to plot in the image.
//
void TraceRay(int Level, VECTOR *Base, VECTOR *Dir, COLOR *I)
{
  int Index;
  COLOR Iq;
  VECTOR Q, N;

  Index = FindClosestIntersection(Base, Dir, &Q);
  if (Index >= 0) {              // If some intersection found

    DetermineNormal(&Objects[Index], &N, &Q);

    // Flip the normal vector if it is facing away from the
    // viewer
    if (Dot(&N, Dir) > 0) {
      N.x = -N.x;
      N.y = -N.y;
      N.z = -N.z;
    }
```

```
      ComputeLight(Level, Index, &Q, &N, Dir, &Iq);

    I->r = Iq.r;
    I->g = Iq.g;
    I->b = Iq.b;
  }
  else {
    I->r = Background.r;    // The ray didn't hit any of the
    I->g = Background.g;    // objects. Use the backdrop's color.
    I->b = Background.b;
  }
}


/////////////////////////// SetEye \\\\\\\\\\\\\\\\\\\\\\\\\\\
//
// Calculate the matrix values that are used when calculating
// the locations of the rays in eye coordinates.
//
void SetEye(void)
{
  DVal = cos(VuAngle/2.0) / sin(VuAngle/2.0);
  A3 = Subtract(&At, &From);
  A1 = Cross(&A3, &Up);
  A2 = Cross(&A1, &A3);
  Normalize(&A1);
  Normalize(&A2);
  Normalize(&A3);
}
```

3

An Enhanced Ray Tracer

T he SIMPLRAY program, discussed in Chapters 1 and 2, is ideal for exploring the basics of ray tracing. However, you're probably eager for more. Over the next several chapters, we'll develop a more sophisticated ray tracing application, which we'll call RAY. Some of the ray tracer's new features are that it:

- is written with an object-oriented style
- saves ray traced images to files
- provides more object types
- includes an enhanced lighting model
- supports new types of light sources
- supports animation
- defines scenes in a separate text file so that you can easily modify them

In this chapter, we'll introduce each of the new object types and focus on the extensions to the lighting model. In Chapters 4 through 8, we'll explore RAY's other components and show you how to use them to create a variety of impressive images.

USING C++ EFFECTIVELY

One change we'll make is to write the new ray tracing program using C++. If you're a C programmer, however, you'll be pleased to know that the code is designed so that you can readily port it to C.

In fact, we'll only use features that are specific to C++ where they really make sense. For instance, we'll use C++ objects to represent the objects in the world model, but we won't try to force all of the ray tracer's code into an object-oriented style.

One other C++ feature we will exploit occasionally are inline functions. They'll enable us to write modular code, without the overhead of function calls. You may want to go further and rewrite the vector support functions in VECTOR.C so that they use inline functions. This change may help to make your programs run faster, however, at the expense of making the code size bigger.

If you look at the code, you'll notice that we did not overload operators, such as the plus sign to add two vectors, to support vector operations. Although C++ allows us to overload operators, there really isn't a good set of operators to use. For instance, what should we use to represent a dot product? Besides, the overloaded operators really won't make the code more readable—especially as you take your first steps through the code.

OVERVIEW OF THE RAY PROGRAM

The ray tracer is split between the eight principle source files listed in Table 3.1. This chapter focuses on the files RAY.CPP, LIGHTS.CPP, and OBJECTS.CPP, which implement the core of the ray tracer. In later chapters, we'll concentrate on the remaining portions of the code. Along the way, we'll give special attention to the differences between RAY and SIMPLRAY.

If you want to jump right in and begin running the RAY program, you should skip ahead to the section *Compiling and Running RAY* in Chapter 4. You'll find there an explanation of how to compile RAY and begin putting it to use. If you plan on modifying RAY, however, you'll want to read through these next several chapters.

Table 3.1 The source files for the RAY program.

Filename	Discussed in	Description
RAY.CPP	Chapters 3-8	Contains main entry point for program and most of the lighting model
LIGHTS.CPP	Chapter 3	Provides support for light sources
OBJECTS.CPP	Chapters 3, 5-8	Support for each of the object types
PARSER.CPP	Chapter 4	Reads files that control which screen to display
TIFF.C	Chapter 10	TIFF image file tools
VECTOR.C	Appendix A	C++ version of the vector operations
GRPHICS.C	Appendix B	Graphics support functions
WINSHELL.C	Appendix C	Enables the program to support Windows

THE NEW OBJECTS

The enhanced ray tracer supports several new object types. The list now includes:

- cylinders
- ellipsoids
- rectangles
- spheres
- triangles

You'll find the code that supports these objects in the source file OBJECTS.CPP and its header file OBJECTS.H. Both of these files are listed at the end of this chapter.

Recall that SIMPLRAY only supports two object types. The program uses **switch** statements to select between statements that support them. In the RAY program, we'll implement each object type as a class and let C++ select the correct functions for us. The code derives each type of object, as shown in Figure 3.1, from the base class **Object**. You'll notice that the object hierarchy is not very complex; it doesn't need to be. In fact, there is great virtue in keeping things simple.

Figure 3.1 The object hierarchy used in RAY.

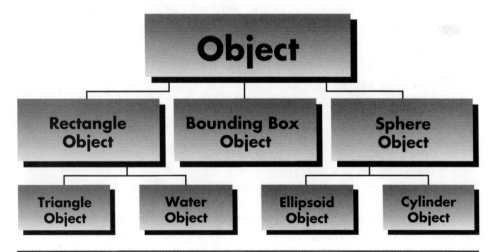

The **Object** base class, located in OBJECTS.H, has the following definition:

```
class Object {
public:
  unsigned int Shape;      // The object's type
  int ImageNdx;            // Index of the image mapped to the object
  int Sibling, Group;      // Indexes of sibling and grouped objects
  float MaxT0;
  float ka, kd, ks, kt;    // Lighting model constants
  int NO;                  // Specular reflection constant
  COLOR Ia1, Ia2;          // Object's color
  VECTOR Loc;              // Object's location
  Object();                // Constructor
  virtual float ComputeT(VECTOR* From, VECTOR* Dir) { return 0; }
  virtual void ComputeNormal(VECTOR *Q, VECTOR *N) { }
  virtual void MapToUV(VECTOR* Q, float& U, float& V) { }
  COLOR (*DeterminePattern)(Object *Obj, VECTOR *Q);
};
```

The **Object** class defines the common variables and the basic functions that are used to process each object. You'll recognize many of these variables and functions from the SIMPLRAY program. For example, the **Shape** field specifies the object's type and the **Loc** vector specifies where the object is located. The fields **ImageNdx**, **Ia2**, and **MaxT0** are new and are used to apply a texture to the object. The **Sibling** and **Group** fields, which we'll discuss later in this chapter, are used to group object's together.

The **Object** class contains five functions. The topmost function is the class constructor that initializes several of the object's fields to default settings. For instance, it sets the object's color to white and the ambient constant, **ka**, to 0.7, as shown here:

```
Object::Object()
{
  Ia1.r = 1; Ia1.g = 1;  Ia1.b = 1;
  Ia2.r = 0; Ia2.g = 0;  Ia2.b = 0;
  ka = .7;   kd = .6;    ks = .3;    kt = 0;   NO = 4;
  Sibling = -1;
  Group = -1;
  MaxT0 = 0;
  DeterminePattern = NoPattern;
}
```

The **ComputeT** and **ComputeNormal** functions supply the object-specific code to render the figure. Notice that they are both defined as virtual functions that don't do anything. We're doing this because derived object types will supply their own ray tracing functions.

The **MapToUV** and **DeterminePattern** functions are used to map a pattern to the object's surface. Notice that the **DeterminePattern** function is not a virtual function, but only a pointer to a function. We'll set the **DeterminePattern** pointer to a function that supplies the object's color or a pattern to be painted on it. For instance, we might set **DeterminePattern** to a function that paints a checker pattern or woodgrain effect on the object. By default, the constructor sets the function pointer to the **NoPattern** routine that is also defined in OBJECTS.CPP and always returns the object's **Ia1** color, as shown here:

```
COLOR NoPattern(Object* Obj, VECTOR*)
{
  return Obj->Ia1;
}
```

Why not make **DeterminePattern** a virtual function and derive a class for each type of pattern desired? We could, however, it would require extra code. The function pointer approach is simpler. It also demonstrates an important technique. We could use the exact same strategy to replace the constructor and virtual functions **ComputeT**, **ComputeNormal**, and **MapToUV** with function pointers and assign the pointers to the desired routines. This is, in fact, what you'd want to do if you were to implement the code in C or remove the C++ objects altogether.

Deriving Rectangles

The **Object** class defines a common base for all the objects in the RAY program. We'll derive classes from **Object** that support specific types of objects. For instance, the **RectangleObj** class, defined here, contains all the code for rendering rectangles.

```
class RectangleObj : public Object {  // Rectangle object
public:
  VECTOR Normal;
  float D;
  VECTOR V1, V2;
  float Len1, Len2;
  float MinX, MaxX, MinY, MaxY, MinZ, MaxZ;
  float T0, T1;
  RectangleObj(VECTOR *LocV, VECTOR *Vect1, VECTOR *Vect2);
  virtual float ComputeT(VECTOR* From, VECTOR* Dir);
  virtual void ComputeNormal(VECTOR *Q, VECTOR *N);
  virtual void MapToUV(VECTOR* Q, float& U, float& V);
};
```

The **RectangleObj** class introduces a dozen new variables. Most of these are used to hold precomputed values to speed up the rendering process and are not strictly required. The key fields are the three vectors **V1**, **V2**, and **Normal**, as well as the variable **D**. The **Loc** vector, which is inherited from the **Object** class, specifies the location of one of the rectangle's corners; the vectors **V1** and **V2** specify the lengths of the two connecting sides. These vectors are assumed to be perpendicular to each other, although no test is made to verify this. Figure 3.2 shows a sample rectangle located at coordinate (3,2,1) with sides four units long.

The vector **Normal** holds the normal of the rectangle. It is calculated in **RectangleObj**'s constructor by taking the cross product of the vectors **V1** and **V2**, as shown here:

```
Normal = Cross(&V1, &V2);
```

Keep in mind that the normal also gives us the a, b, and c constants for the equation of the plane that contains the rectangle. The constructor calculates the remaining d term and stores the result in the field **D**. We'll use the plane equation when testing for intersections in **ComputeT**.

The **RectangleObj** constructor also assigns the fields **MinX**, **MaxX**, and their related fields to the bounds of the rectangle, as shown in Figure 3.3 and given by the statements:

```
MinX = MinOf(Loc.x, Loc.x+V1.x, Loc.x+V2.x, Loc.x+V1.x+V2.x);
MaxX = MaxOf(Loc.x, Loc.x+V1.x, Loc.x+V2.x, Loc.x+V1.x+V2.x);
MinY = MinOf(Loc.y, Loc.y+V1.y, Loc.y+V2.y, Loc.y+V1.y+V2.y);
MaxY = MaxOf(Loc.y, Loc.y+V1.y, Loc.y+V2.y, Loc.y+V1.y+V2.y);
MinZ = MinOf(Loc.z, Loc.z+V1.z, Loc.z+V2.z, Loc.z+V1.z+V2.z);
MaxZ = MaxOf(Loc.z, Loc.z+V1.z, Loc.z+V2.z, Loc.z+V1.z+V2.z);
```

Figure 3.2 The Loc, V1, and V2 vectors define a rectangle.

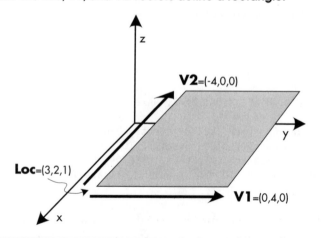

You can find the **MinOf** and **MaxOf** routines in the OBJECTS.CPP file. The bounding variables are used in the **ComputeT** member function when calculating the intersection of a light ray and the rectangle. Let's take a look at it.

The process of determining whether a ray hits a rectangle is performed in two parts. First, it tests whether the light ray intersects the plane that contains the rectangle. Remember, the plane equation, represented by the **Normal** vector and the variable **D**, is calculated in the **RectangleObj** constructor. The calculations, shown here, are similar to those that we used in SIMPLRAY:

```
float A=Normal.x, B=Normal.y, C=Normal.z;

// Determines where the ray intersects the plane that contains
// the rectangle, if the intersection exists.
denom = A * Dir->x + B * Dir->y + C * Dir->z;
if (denom == 0)
  return -1;
t = -(A * Base->x + B * Base->y + C * Base->z+ D) / denom;
if (t < 0) return -1;    // Intersection is behind the viewer
```

These statements determine the intersection point in terms of the parametric t. If there isn't an intersection, the **ComputeT** function returns -1. If there is an intersection point, the location is calculated as:

```
Pt.x = Base->x + Dir->x * t;
Pt.y = Base->y + Dir->y * t;
Pt.z = Base->z + Dir->z * t;
```

Figure 3.3 The bounds of a rectangle object.

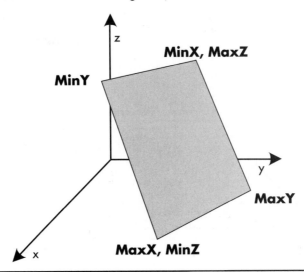

This calculation tells us where the ray intersects the plane containing the rectangle. However, it doesn't tell us whether the point **Pt** is inside the rectangle. How can we do this rapidly? We'll use a simple mathematical trick. The point **Pt** is inside the rectangle if it also is inside the bounds of the rectangle projected onto its major axis, as shown in Figure 3.4. The major axis is the one that produces the largest two-dimensional projection. We can tell which way to project the rectangle by looking for the largest term in the plane's normal. For example, if the x coordinate of the normal vector (represented in **ComputeT** by the variable **A**), is larger than the y or z terms, then the rectangle is projected onto the x axis. All this means is that we can ignore the x terms of the rectangle's bounds and point **Pt**. As a result, the code compares the y and z bounds of the rectangle, stored in **MinY**, **MaxY**, and so on, with the y and z fields of **Pt**. If the point is between these bounds, the light ray must have intersected the rectangle and **ComputeT** returns the parametric value, t. Here's the portion of the code that makes these tests:

```
if (fabs(A) > fabs(B) && fabs(A) > fabs(C)) {
  // X axis plane equation is greatest. Project the rectangle
  // on to the X axis.
  if ((MinZ < Pt.z && Pt.z < MaxZ) &&
      (MinY < Pt.y && Pt.y < MaxY))
    return t;
}
```

Similar operations are performed for projections on the y and z planes.

Figure 3.4 Projecting a rectangle onto its major axis.

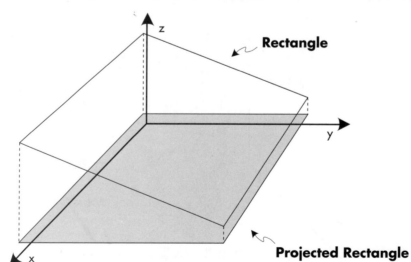

Recall, the lighting model in the ray tracer needs the normal of the rectangle. The **RectangleObj** class defines **ComputeNormal** for this purpose. Actually, for the case of a rectangle, determining the normal is not that complicated. The normal is, in fact, the normal of the plane that contains the rectangle—the same values calculated in the constructor. Therefore, **ComputeNormal** merely returns the value of **Normal** when it is called, as shown here:

```
void RectangleObj::ComputeNormal(VECTOR*, VECTOR *N)
{
  N->x = Normal.x;    // The normal is normalized in the constructor
  N->y = Normal.y;
  N->z = Normal.z;
}
```

Triangle Objects

Another planar object that RAY supports is the triangle object. The **TriangleObj** class, defined here, encapsulates all the logic we need to render a triangle.

```
class TriangleObj : public RectangleObj {
public:
  TriangleObj(VECTOR* LocV, VECTOR* Vect1, VECTOR* Vect2);
  virtual float ComputeT(VECTOR* From, VECTOR* Dir);
};
```

The simplicity of this class is a little deceiving. It derives much of its power from the **RectangleObj** class. For instance, the variables **Loc**, **V1**, and **V2** that specify the location and size of a triangle are inherited from the **RectangleObj** class and its parent object. Figure 3.5 shows how these fields represent the coordinates of a triangle.

The process of rendering a triangle is similar to that for a rectangle, but a little more complicated. The **ComputeT** function, for instance, begins by determining whether the light ray intersects the plane that contains the triangle. If it does, the code tests whether the intersecting point falls within the bounds of the projected triangle. This second step is more complicated than that for a rectangle.

We can tell if a point is inside or outside of a triangle by counting the number of times a ray that is projected from the intersection point crosses the sides of the triangle. If the projected ray crosses the sides of the triangle an odd number of times, the point is inside the triangle. Otherwise, the point is outside the triangle. Figure 3.6 illustrates this for two different points, one inside a triangle and the other outside the triangle.

How can we count the number of times a ray intersects the sides of a triangle? First, we'll translate the triangle and intersection point so that the

Figure 3.5 The Loc, V1, and V2 vectors specify the location and dimensions of a triangle.

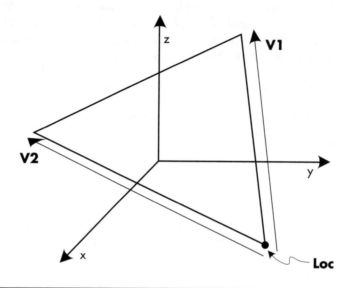

Figure 3.6 A ray crosses a triangle's edges an odd number of times only if it begins inside the triangle.

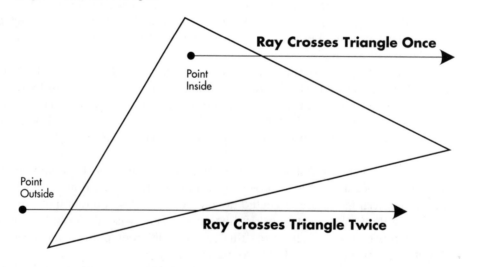

intersection point serves as the origin of a new (U,V) coordinate system. Specifically, the triangle is translated by the amount calculated in **Delta**, as shown here:

```
Delta = Subtract(&Pt, &Loc);
```

Actually, we'll only translate a projection of the triangle. As we did with rectangles, we'll only work with the largest projection. The following code, for instance, projects the triangle onto the x axis, then translates the triangle by the amount in **Delta**, as illustrated in Figure 3.7.

```
if (fabs(A) > fabs(B) && fabs(A) > fabs(C)) {
  // Project the triangle onto the x axis, where x = 0
  U[0] = -Delta.y;
  V[0] = -Delta.z;
  U[1] = V1.y - Delta.y;
  V[1] = V1.z - Delta.z;
  U[2] = V2.y - Delta.y;
  V[2] = V2.z - Delta.z;
}
```

Figure 3.7 The triangle is projected and translated so that the intersection point is at the origin of the two-dimensional (U,V) coordinate system.

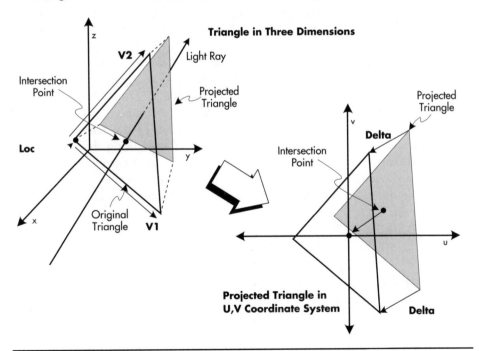

As a result, the first array locations in **U** and **V** store the translated **Loc** vector and the remaining ones store the locations of the triangle's other two vertices.

Next, the code projects a ray out from the intersection point—which is now the origin of the (U,V) coordinate system—and counts the number of times the ray crosses the edges of the triangle. The choice of the projected ray's direction is arbitrary; therefore, we'll project it along the positive U axis.

The following **for** loop, therefore, steps through the **U** and **V** arrays testing for cases where the vertices of the triangle cross over the positive U axis:

```
for (i=0, j=1; i<3; i++, j++) {
  if (j == 3) j = 0;
  if ((V[i] < 0 && V[j] >= 0) ||
      (V[i] >= 0 && V[j] < 0)) {
    if (U[i] >= 0 && U[j] >= 0)
      CrossCount++;
    else if (U[i] >= 0 || U[j] >= 0)
      if (U[i] - V[i] * (U[j] - U[i]) / (V[j] - V[i]) > 0)
        CrossCount++;
  }
}
```

The **i** and **j** variables sequence through the **U** and **V** coordinate arrays. Notice that the **j** value is essentially equivalent to **i+1**. The code divides into three tests. The first test checks whether two neighboring V coordinates have different signs. If they do, then we know that those two vertices must be on opposite sides of the U axis. The next **if** statement determines if the U coordinates of these two points are both positive. If so, the triangle must cross the positive side of the U axis, as shown in part *(A)* of Figure 3.8. As a result, the **CrossCount** variable is incremented. Even if this test fails, the triangle may still cross the positive U axis, as shown in part *(B)* of Figure 3.8, if one of the **U** values is positive. The calculation at the bottom of the **for** loop determines where the triangle would cross the U axis. If it is along the positive U axis, **CrossCount** is incremented. You may want to read over this last paragraph again to convince yourself that the technique really works.

The final step is to check whether the **CrossCount** variable is odd or even:

```
if (CrossCount%2 == 0)
  return -1;      // No intersection
return t;
```

If **CrossCount** is odd, the intersection point must be inside the triangle and the parametric t value is returned. Otherwise, the intersection point is outside of the triangle and the light ray must have missed the triangle. In this situation, **ComputeT** returns a -1.

Figure 3.8 Testing whether a ray crosses a triangle's edge.

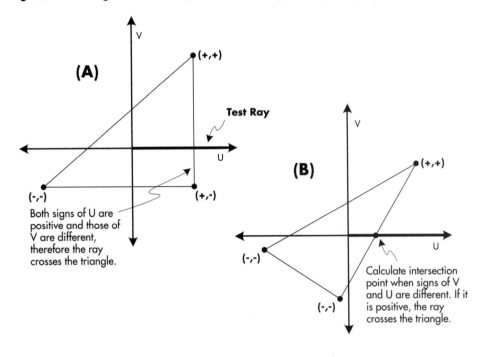

You can generalize this technique quite easily to support polygons as well as triangles. You'll have to modify the routine, however, to handle the variable number of vertices. Since we won't be using polygons in the scenes later in this book, we'll leave polygons out.

What about calculating the normal of the triangle? The code that computes the normal is inherited from the **RectangleObj** class. The process is identical as that for a rectangle. The **ComputeNormal** function returns the normal of the plane that contains the triangle.

Supporting Spheres

The **SphereObj** class contains the code to render spheres. Most of it is identical to that in SIMPLRAY. The few changes were made to speed up the code. If you look carefully, you'll notice a handful of statements rearranged to minimize the calculations that may be required. The modifications bloat the code a little, however, if speed is the goal, these changes are worthwhile.

Ellipsoids

An *ellipsoid* is a three-dimensional elliptical shape, like that shown in Figure 3.9. The class that supports ellipsoids is **EllipsoidObj**, shown here:

```
class EllipsoidObj : public SphereObj {
public:
  float A, B, C, D;
  VECTOR V1, V2;
  EllipsoidObj(float X, float Y, float Z, float AVal,
    float BVal, float CVal, float DVal);
  virtual float ComputeT(VECTOR* From, VECTOR* Dir);
  virtual void ComputeNormal(VECTOR *Q, VECTOR *N);
};
```

An ellipsoid centered at the origin has an equation of the form:

$$\frac{X^2}{X_a^2} + \frac{Y^2}{Y_a^2} + \frac{Z^2}{Z_a^2} = 1$$

where X_a, Y_a, and Z_a are the ellipsoid's axes lengths. For convenience, we'll multiply this expression out so that we can come up with an equation that looks like:

```
A * X² + B * Y² + C * Z² + D = 0
```

Figure 3.9 An example of an ellipsoid and its equation.

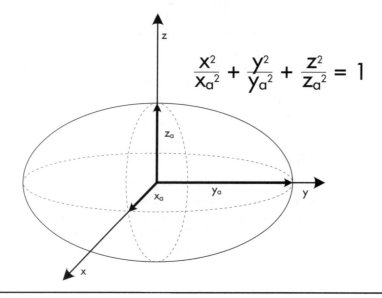

$$\frac{X^2}{X_a^2} + \frac{Y^2}{Y_a^2} + \frac{Z^2}{Z_a^2} = 1$$

The process of testing whether a light ray intersects an ellipsoid is similar to that for a sphere. We'll plug the parametric equation of the light ray into the equation of an ellipsoid and solve for the parametric t. This leads to a quadratic equation with the coefficients:

$$A_q = A * X_d^2 + B * Y_d^2 + C * Z_d^2$$
$$B_q = 2 * (A * X_0 * X_d + B * Y_0 * Y_d + C * Z_0 * Z_d)$$
$$C_q = A * X_0^2 + B * Y_0^2 + C * Z_0^2 - D$$

These values are plugged into the quadratic formula that is solved for its roots. The remaining steps are the same as those we used to render a sphere.

What about calculating the normal for an ellipsoid? You might guess that determining the normal for a point on an ellipsoid is difficult, but it really isn't. We can get the normal of the surface by taking the partial derivative of the ellipsoid's equation, which yields:

$$X_n = 2 * A * X$$
$$Y_n = 2 * B * Y$$
$$Z_n = 2 * C * Z$$

Since the magnitude of the normal is not important, we can drop the constant of 2 in these calculations. Other than this, you'll recognize these expressions in the ellipsoid's **ComputeNormal** function. Realize, however, that the function must subtract the location of the ellipsoid from the surface point **Q**, because we want an object-oriented coordinate system. Here's the complete **ComputeNormal** routine:

```
void EllipsoidObj::ComputeNormal(VECTOR *Q, VECTOR *N)
{
  VECTOR Pos = Subtract(Q, &Loc);

  N->x = A * Pos.x;
  N->y = B * Pos.y;
  N->z = C * Pos.z;

  Normalize(N);
}
```

Cylinder Objects

The **CylinderObj** class provides all the object-specific code that RAY needs for ray tracing cylinders. The class, which is derived from **SphereObj**, looks like:

```
class CylinderObj : public SphereObj {
public:
  float Radius, Height;
```

```
VECTOR V1;
CylinderObj(VECTOR LocV, VECTOR Vect1, float R);
virtual float ComputeT(VECTOR* From, VECTOR* Dir);
virtual void ComputeNormal(VECTOR *Q, VECTOR *N);
virtual void MapToUV(VECTOR* Q, float& U, float& V);
};
```

Figure 3.10 shows how **CylinderObj** uses the fields **Loc**, **V1**, and **Radius** to specify a cylinder.

The equation of a cylinder centered at the origin is:

$$AX^2 + BY^2 = C$$

Once again, we'll substitute in the parametric equation of a light ray to determine where the ray intersects the cylinder, if at all. We'll solve the resulting equation, which is a quadratic, using the quadratic formula:

$$(AX_d^2 + BY_d^2)t^2 + 2(AX_0X_d + BY_0Y_d)t + (AX_0^2 + BY_0^2) - C = 0$$

In terms of code, the **ComputeT** function requires a few extra steps compared with **EllipsoidObj** and **SphereObj**. The reason is that we must

---

Figure 3.10 A cylinder object.

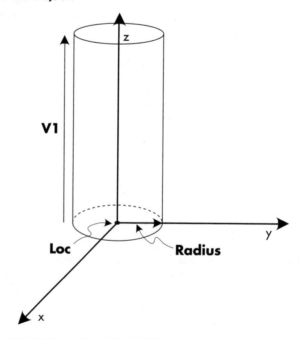

restrict the cylinder to some height. Other than this, however, the code is much like what you've seen earlier.

Computing the normal of the point, **Q**, on a cylinder is a three step process. First, the **ComputeNormal** function calculates the parametric value where the center line of the cylinder intersects the plane that contains point **Q**. This relationship is illustrated in Figure 3.11 and executed by the statements:

```
C = V1;
Normalize(&C);

// Compute the parametric t value where the center line of
// the cylinder intersects the plane that contains the point Q
VECTOR Tmp = Subtract(Q, &Loc);
t = Dot(&Tmp, &C) / Dot(&C, &V1);
```

Next, **ComputeNormal** determines where the cylinder's axis intersects this plane. This point is stored in the vector **Pt**, as shown here:

```
Pt.x = Loc.x + t * V1.x;
Pt.y = Loc.y + t * V1.y;
Pt.z = Loc.z + t * V1.z;
```

Figure 3.11 Three vectors are used to determine the equation of the plane that contains Q.

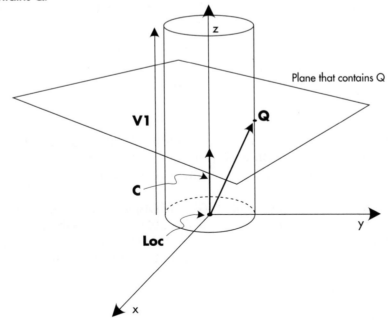

With point **Pt** in hand, we calculate the normal by subtracting point **Q** on the cylinder's surface with point **Pt**. This value is normalized before returning:

```
*N = Subtract(Q, &Pt);
Normalize(N);
```

MANAGING OBJECTS

The RAY program does not hard-code its world model like SIMPLRAY does. Instead, it reads the objects to display from a file and adds them one at a time to the internal array, **Objects**, which is defined as:

```
Object *Objects[MAXOBJECTS];  // List of objects in the world model
```

The value of **MAXOBJECTS**, specified in RAY.H, is currently set to 500 objects. You'll want to customize this value to your system's memory resources. If you're running RAY in DOS, for instance, you may not be able to set **MAXOBJECTS** any greater than several hundred. Anything bigger than this will require too much memory. In Windows, however, you'll be able to have many thousands of objects. Some of the more complex scenes discussed in later chapters, for instance, require that you run under Windows to gain the additional memory and allow for more objects.

Adding an object to the **Objects** array is a two step process. First, you must construct the desired object. For instance, if you want to add a triangle object located at the point (10,5,1) with the sides (0,5,0) and (10,0,0), you could use:

```
VECTOR Loc = {10,5,1};
VECTOR V1 = {0,5,0};
VECTOR V2 = {10,0,0};
TriangleObj *Obj = new TriangleObj(&Loc, &V1, &V2);
if (Obj < 0)
  ObjNdx = AddObject(Obj);
```

The **AddObject** function, defined in OBJECTS.CPP, adds the new object to the **Objects** array. If the **Objects** list is full, the function returns -1. If there is room, however, the function returns the index location where the object was inserted into the list.

Where are the objects de-allocated? The OBJECTS.CPP source file supplies the **FreeObjects** function to free all the objects in the **Objects** array. The **Cleanup** function in RAY.CPP calls the **FreeObjects** function as the RAY program is terminating. Here's the complete **FreeObjects** routine:

```
void FreeObjects()
{
  int i;
```

```
  for (i=0; i<LastObj; i++)
    delete Objects[i];
}
```

The **LastObj** variable maintains the count of the number of objects in the **Objects** array, starting at 0. The **AddObject** function increments the number each time an object is added to the **Objects** array. Therefore, **LastObj** always points to the next index location to add an object.

AN ENHANCED LIGHTING MODEL

The lighting model gives ray traced images their realism. Although SIMPLRAY enables us to render objects with shadings, shadows, and highlights, we can do better. The RAY program introduces five extensions to the lighting model:

- Three different types of light sources
- Multiple light sources in a scene
- Translucent objects
- Fades light that travels long distances
- Objects with textures and patterns

Chapter 5 discusses how RAY supports surfaces with textures and patterns. In the rest of this chapter, we'll focus on the first four items listed.

New Light Sources

Recall that the SIMPLRAY program only allows a scene to contain a single point light source. A point source is fine for illuminating a scene evenly in all directions. However, sometimes it's useful to illuminate only a portion of a scene. To solve this problem, the RAY program introduces *directed* and *cone* light sources.

A directed light source is unique in that it is brightest along a single ray. The light gradually fades away as the light rays deviate from the light's main direction. A cone light source is even more restrictive. Like a flashlight or spot light, a cone source only illuminates a scene within a well defined cone.

What differences do these light sources make in an image? Figure 3.12 shows three versions of the same scene, each illuminated with a different type of light source. The left image uses a single point source, the middle image uses a directed light source, and the right image uses a cone light source. The latter two have their lights aimed at the box in the image.

Figure 3.12 The same image rendered with a point, directed, and cone light source.

Point Light Sources

You'll be in control of the light sources in RAY.CPP. For each scene you must define where and of what type the light sources are. The next chapter details how to do this. Here, we'll focus on how the code below manages these light sources.

In SIMPLRAY, we used the **LIGHT** structure to support light sources. Now we'll use classes. We'll supply one class for each type of light source, as shown in Figure 3.13. The point source class, **PointLight**, defined here, serves as the base class.

```
class PointLight {
public:
  VECTOR LFw;          // Location of light in world coordinates.
  COLOR Color;         // r, g, and b intensities of light.
  PointLight(VECTOR* Loc, COLOR* I) {
    LFw = *Loc;
    Color = *I;
  }
  float W(float CosTheta, float K);
  virtual float LightFactor(VECTOR*) { return 1.0; }
};
```

Figure 3.13 The hierarchy of light sources.

The **PointLight** class, which is similar to SIMPLRAY's **LIGHT** structure, is defined in LIGHTS.H and LIGHTS.CPP. The class contains two variables: the **LFw** field holds the location of the light source and the **Color** field holds the light's color. Both of these are set in the class' constructor. Other than the constructor, the class contains the functions, **W** and **LightFactor**. Both control the magnitude of the light, however, **LightFactor** is not really used by **PointLight**. It's used by derived classes.

Directed Light Sources

A directed light source shines brightest along a single ray and grows dimmer at rays that deviate from its direction. The **DirectedLight** class supplies the code that supports directed light sources, as shown here:

```
class DirectedLight : public PointLight {
public:
  int DirectPow;
  VECTOR Direction;   // Direction of light source. Not
                      // used by point light sources.
  DirectedLight(VECTOR* Loc, COLOR* I) : PointLight(Loc, I) {
    // The smaller the number (0 or greater), the more widespread
    // a cone or directed light source's light will be
    DirectPow = 10;   // Default to power of 10
    // By default, directed and cone light sources are
    // pointed toward the at point. The at point should already
    // be defined.
    Direction = Subtract(&At, Loc);
    Normalize(&Direction);
  }
  void SetLightDirection(VECTOR *D);
  virtual float LightFactor(VECTOR* L) {
    float CosBeta = -Dot(L, &Direction);
    if (CosBeta > 0)
      return pow(CosBeta, DirectPow);
    return 0.0;
  }
};
```

The **DirectedLight** class introduces two new variables and two functions. The new **Direction** vector holds the direction of the light source. By default, the light is directed toward the **At** point:

```
Direction = Subtract(&At, Loc);
```

The other new field, **DirectPow**, specifies how rapidly the light falls off away from the **Direction** vector. It can be any integer value greater than 0. The larger it is, the more focused the light is along the **Direction** vector.

One key to the **DirectedLight** class is the **LightFactor** function. It returns a scale factor that is to be multiplied against the intensity of the light. The scale factor is, in part, based on a vector that points to the light source, **L**, and the direction of the light source. Here's the complete **LightFactor** function:

```
virtual float LightFactor(VECTOR* L) {
  float CosBeta = -Dot(L, &Direction);
  if (CosBeta > 0)
    return pow(CosBeta, DirectPow);
  return 0.0;
}
```

The scale factor is actually the angle between **L** and **Direction** raised to the value in **DirectPow**. Since the cosine of this angle, stored in **CosBeta**, is always between 0 and 1, the scale factor decreases as the vector **L** makes larger angles with **Direction**. Notice that **LightFactor** returns a 0 for the scale factor when the light ray is pointing behind the location of the light source.

Cone Light Sources

A cone light source projects light rays within a cone. As Figure 3.14 shows, objects within the light cone are brightly illuminated and those outside don't get any light at all. Cone light sources are represented by the **ConeLight** class that is defined in LIGHTS.CPP as:

```
class ConeLight : public DirectedLight {
public:
  float CosGamma;     // cosine of half angle if cone light source
  ConeLight(VECTOR* Loc, COLOR* I) : DirectedLight(Loc, I) {
    CosGamma = .9397; // Default to 20 degrees
  }
  virtual float LightFactor(VECTOR* L) {
    float CosBeta = -Dot(L, &Direction);
    if (CosBeta > 0 && CosBeta <= CosGamma)
      return pow(CosBeta, DirectPow);
    return 0.0;
  }
  void SetConeLightAngle(float Angle);
};
```

The **ConeLight** class overrides the **LightFactor** routine to generate the cone effect. As in the **DirectedLight** class, **LightFactor** returns a scale factor that is based on the angle between the current light ray and the light source's direction. However, the **ConeLight** class adds one more restriction. The angle between the light ray, **L**, and the direction vector must be less than a prescribed angle. This angle, stored in **CosGamma**, is assigned in **SetConeLightAngle**.

Figure 3.14 A cone light source illuminates a scene within a cone.

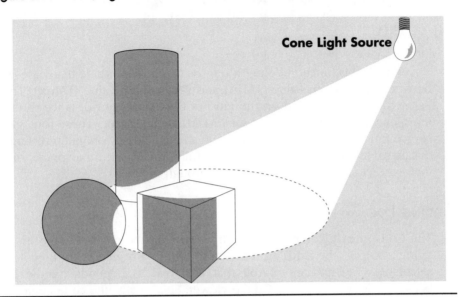

By default, the constructor sets it to 20 degrees. This means that the cone light will have a radius of 20 degrees.

Scaling Light

The scale factor returned by the **LightFactor** function, discussed in the previous section, controls how much a light's intensity is added into the current color being calculated. For instance, RAY multiplies the specular light contribution by the scale factor:

```
Temp = Lights[i]->LightFactor(&L) * WValue *
  pow(CosAlpha, Obj->NO) / DistScale;
I->r += Temp * Lights[i]->Color.r;
I->g += Temp * Lights[i]->Color.g;
I->b += Temp * Lights[i]->Color.b;
```

Notice that these statements in **ComputeLight** also divide the specular light by the value in **DistScale**. This variable holds yet another scale factor. It is based on the distance between the point being rendered and the light source. The **ScaleLight** function makes the calculation:

```
float ScaleLight(float PointToLight)
{
  float LightScale = (LMax - LMin) * (PointToLight - DMin) /
```

```
    (DMax - DMin) + LMin;
  if (LightScale < LMin) return LMin;
  else if (LightScale > LMax) return LMax;
  else return LightScale;
}
```

What is this function doing? It returns a light scale value that varies linearly between a minimum value (**LMin**) and a maximum value (**LMax**). The scale value calculated is based on the ratio of the actual light distance to the minimum and maximum distances set in **DMin** and **DMax**. These four variables, shown in Figure 3.15, are used to diminish the intensity of light traveling longer distances. In all, this somewhat successfully models the atmospheric distortion that light experiences when it travels through the air.

ADDING FOG

The **ComputeLight** function, which determines the color of a specific surface point, also calls the **AddFog** function to add in a fog color to the color being calculated. The amount of fog that is added in depends on the distance between the surface point and the viewer. Specifically, the code begins adding in the fog at distances greater than **FogMin**. The fog linearly increases until

---

Figure 3.15 Scaling light based on the distance it travels.

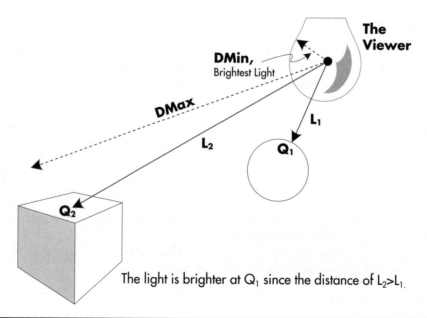

The light is brighter at Q_1 since the distance of $L_2 > L_1$.

distances greater than or equal to **FogMax** are reached at which case only the fog appears. You can control the fog's color by setting the variable **FogColor**. By default, it is set to white. To disable it, you must set **FogMax** to 0. Here's the complete **AddFog** function:

```
inline void AddFog(COLOR* I, float Dist)
{
  float LightScale = 1.0;

  if (FogMax > 0) {
    if (Dist > FogMin) {
      // Don't apply fog if the distance is too small
      if (Dist < FogMax)
        LightScale = (Dist - FogMin) / (FogMax - FogMin);
      I->r = FogColor.r * LightScale + I->r * (1 - LightScale);
      I->g = FogColor.g * LightScale + I->g * (1 - LightScale);
      I->b = FogColor.b * LightScale + I->b * (1 - LightScale);
    }
  }
}
```

How does the fog affect an image? Figure 3.16 shows two versions of the same scene. The image on the left has the fog mechanism enabled and the one on the right doesn't. Notice how the fog increases in density at larger distances.

Figure 3.16 **The effect of fog in an image.**

 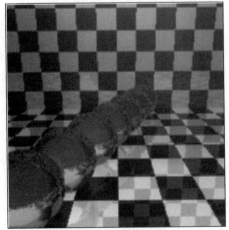

MANAGING LIGHT SOURCES

The RAY program maintains a list of the lights in a scene in the array **Lights**. It's defined in LIGHTS.CPP as:

```
PointLight* Lights[MAXLIGHTS];// List of lights in the scene
```

The array is declared as an array of pointers to **PointLight** objects so that it can hold any of the three types of light sources. Currently, the RAY.H header file sets the maximum number of lights allowed to 5. If you want to have more lights, simply redefine **MAXLIGHTS**.

The LIGHTS.CPP file includes the **AddLight** function to add a light source to the **Lights** array. The function doesn't actually allocate the light itself, however. You must do this yourself and pass **AddLight** a pointer to the new light source. For example, to add a red point light source that is located at (100,100,10), you'd use the statements:

```
VECTOR Loc = {100,100,10};
COLOR I = {1,0,0};
PointLight* L = new PointLight(&Loc,&I);
int i = AddLight(L);
```

The **AddLight** function returns the index location where the light source is placed in the **Lights** array. You can use it to help access the fields in the light object. If the **Lights** array is full, however, **AddLight** doesn't append the object to the array and returns a -1.

TRANSLUCENT OBJECTS

Another twist that RAY introduces is its ability to render transparent objects. Each object now contains the variable **kt** that controls how transparent an object is to appear. The value of **kt** can range between 1 and 0. If **kt** is 0, then the object is solid. Larger values of **kt** render more transparent objects.

How does the code render a transparent object? When a ray intersects a translucent surface, the code takes note of its color and then sends the ray on to see what else it may hit. The color of this intersection point is added into the color of the translucent surface by the amount specified in **kt**. Actually, the second intersection point might be transparent too, in which case its penetrating ray is followed also.

You can find these details in the **Transparency** function. The routine follows a light ray through an object by recursively calling **Intensity** to determine how much light passes through an object, as shown here:

```
Intensity(Level, Q2, Dir2, &I2);
```

The light that is seen through the object is returned in the variable **I2** and is added to the running sum of the object's color in **Iq**:

```
Iq->r = (1-kt) * Iq->r + kt * I2.r;
Iq->g = (1-kt) * Iq->g + kt * I2.g;
Iq->b = (1-kt) * Iq->b + kt * I2.b;
```

As you look at the **Transparency** function, notice that it saves the transparency constant in the temporary variable **kt** before calling **Intensity**. This extra step is required to properly render the clouds we will be working with in Chapter 8.

The **Intensity** function calls **Transparency** to add in the light that passes through a translucent object. As a timesaver, however, **Intensity** only calls **Transparency** if the **kt** constant is greater than 0. After all, it doesn't make sense to follow a light ray through an object if it is solid. Here's how this test appears:

```
if (Objects[Index]->kt > TOL)
   Transparency(Level, Index, &Q, &Dir, &Iq);
```

You may want to modify the transparency routine so that it accounts for refraction. You must model refraction, for instance, if you want to realistically render scenes of objects partially submerged in water. Basically, you'll want to bend light rays as they pass from one translucent medium to another. The amount that you bend the rays depends on the material they pass through.

ANTIALIASING

If you've been using the SIMPLRAY program to render images in a low-resolution mode, such as a 320x200 mode, you've probably noticed the jagged edges along the perimeters of the spheres, as shown in Figure 3.17. You can

Figure 3.17 Objects in ray traced images may have jagged edges.

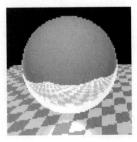

reduce the impact of these jagged edges by increasing the resolution of the image, but if you look closely, they'll still be there. This problem, called *aliasing*, is quite common in computer-generated images. In simple terms, aliasing is caused by the fixed resolution of the ray tracing. If we had an infinite resolution display, we could eliminate the problem. Otherwise, there will always be some surface oriented in such a way that it appears jagged.

Techniques for reducing the jaggedness are called *antialiasing*. In RAY, we'll employ a simple antialiasing technique that requires a minimum of code. The program calculates the image's color for the four corners of a pixel, then plots the average of these four values.

You may be thinking that we'll have to perform four times as many operations to make this antialiasing technique work. We don't. Realize that the top two corners of a particular pixel coincide with the bottom two corners of the pixel above it. Therefore, if we save the results for the bottom corners of the previous row of pixels, we can use them for the top corners of the current row. This, in fact, is what RAY does. The **GenImage** function defines the **LastRow** variable to contain the previous row of pixel values. The **PrevColor** variable stores the right bottom edge of the previous pixel. The current color is stored in the variables **Red**, **Green**, and **Blue**. Therefore, the pixel that is displayed is the average of these variables together, as shown here:

```
Red = ((int)LastRow[sp].r + (int)LastRow[sp+1].r +
   (int)PrevColor.r + (int)Red) / 4.0;
Green = ((int)LastRow[sp].g + (int)LastRow[sp+1].g +
   (int)PrevColor.g + (int)Green) / 4.0;
Blue = ((int)LastRow[sp].b + (int)LastRow[sp+1].b +
   (int)PrevColor.b + (int)Blue) / 4.0;
```

The left image in Figure 3.18 shows a scene rendered without antialiasing; the image on the right has antialiasing employed. Although the jaggedness has not been completely removed, the problem is minimized. One extension to the

Figure 3.18 A scene without antialiasing, then with antialiasing.

antialiasing technique is to compare the four color values for a pixel. If they differ by more than some preset amount, the pixel is divided into four equal pieces and the ray tracing is recursively performed on these smaller components to yield a better pixel value.

BOUNDING BOXES

Scenes that have a dozen or so objects take much less time than one with thousands of objects. Unfortunately, you usually need a large number of objects to make a scene interesting and realistic. How can we get around this dilemma? Recall that a ray tracer spends a great deal of its time testing whether a ray intersects an object. Therefore, to reduce the ray tracing time we should minimize these calculations.

We can improve the performance a bit by optimizing the intersection code. However, this only gets us so far. Another technique is to group objects together, as illustrated in Figure 3.19. The ray tracer then can ignore those objects in bounding boxes that the ray does not intersect. The ray tracer goes through a process of first testing whether a ray intersects the bounded region. If it doesn't, the ray can skip the objects that the bounded region contains. If, on the other hand, the ray intersects the bounded region, the code goes on to check each object within it. Time can be saved further by allowing bounded regions to be placed inside of one another. The results can be dramatic.

Figure 3.19 Grouping objects will speed ray tracing.

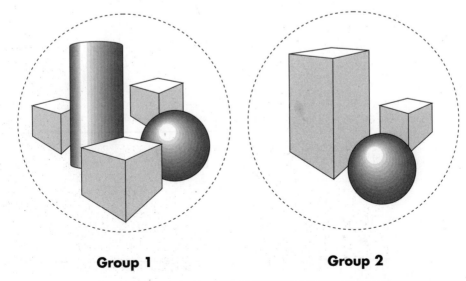

Group 1   **Group 2**

There are several different types of bounding regions that we can use. The goal is to avoid as many calculations as possible. For this reason, many ray tracers employ bounding boxes, as shown in Figure 3.20. The boxes are aligned so that their planes are parallel to the axes of the world coordinate system. Although, this means that the bounding box will not always form a tight fit around the object, the ray tracer will more than make up for this by being able to use very simple intersection calculations.

A bounding box object is much like the other objects in the ray tracer. However, it never displays anything. The bounding box class is derived from the **Object** base class as:

```
class BoundingBoxObj : public Object {
public:
  float MinX, MaxX, MinY, MaxY, MinZ, MaxZ;
  BoundingBoxObj(float XMin, float XMax,
    float YMin, float YMax, float ZMin, float ZMax);
  virtual float ComputeT(VECTOR* From, VECTOR* Dir);
};
```

Figure 3.20 Grouping objects using bounding boxes helps to minimize calculations.

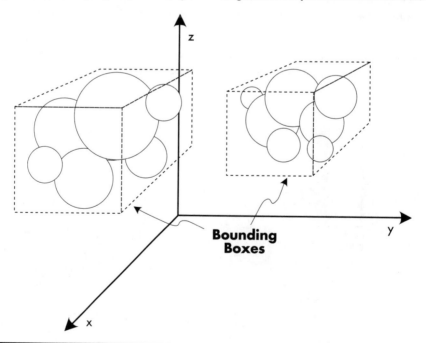

The **MinX**, **MaxX**, and similar variables specify the sides of the bounding box. The **ComputeT** function determines whether a light ray intersects the box. It's a little different than its object counterparts. The routine returns -1 if the light ray intersects the bounding box and 1 otherwise.

Let's take a quick look at **ComputeT**. The function checks for an intersection between the light ray and each side of the bounding box. The following code, for instance, tests whether the light ray intersects the side of the bounding box parallel to the y plane:

```
if (fabs(Dir->y) < TOL) {
  if (Base->y < MinY || Base->y > MaxY)
    return 0;
}
else {
  T1 = (MinY - Base->y) / Dir->y;      // Calculate the intersection
  T2 = (MaxY - Base->y) / Dir->y;      // distances with the y planes
  TMinY = (T1 < T2) ? T1 : T2;
  TMaxY = (T1 < T2) ? T2 : T1;
  if (TMaxY < 0) return 0;             // Box is behind ray
}
```

The first part of the **if** statement eliminates the case where the light ray is parallel to the y plane and its base is outside of the box. Clearly, the ray misses the bounding box in this case, so the function returns 0. The else part determines the two locations where the ray intersects the planes that make up the bounding box. Similar values are computed for the other bounding planes. The function then compares these intersection points to determine whether the ray intersects the bounding box or not.

BUILDING A HIERARCHY OF OBJECTS

Grouping objects helps to speed up ray tracing, but often the only way to get dramatic improvements in speed is to *nest* the groups and create a hierarchy. This is particularly true for complex scenes where there are many objects.

To understand how nesting works, we must go back to the **Sibling** and **Group** fields contained in the **Object** class. The **Sibling** pointer points to the next object in the **Objects** array that is at the same level as the current object. The **Group** index is used only by bounding box objects and points to the list of objects that the bounding box contains. For instance, the scene in Figure 3.21 contains seven objects—two of which are bounding boxes. The objects are organized into two major groups. A bounding box is placed around each of these groups. The tree shown in Figure 3.21 gives you an idea of how this nesting works. Pay close attention to how the **Group** and **Sibling** pointers coincide with the grouping of the objects.

Figure 3.21 A collection of objects grouped together to improve ray tracing performance.

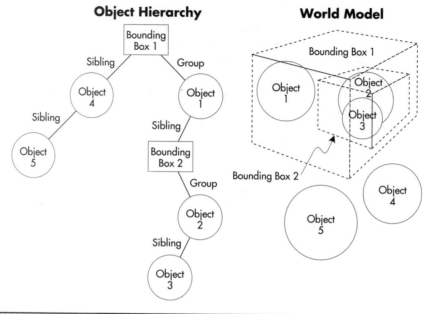

Supporting Bounding Boxes

To accommodate the bounding box objects, we must first alter the **FindIntersection** and **InShadow** routines. The code now recursively calls these routines when an intersection occurs with a bounding box. If the current object being tested is not a bounding box, all of the objects in the **Sibling** list are followed. As the code processes these lists, the code maintains the closest intersection point in the variable **NearestT**.

For example, the top of the **FindIntersection** function, which processes bounding boxes, looks like:

```
if (Objects[I]->Shape == BOUNDINGBOX) {
  if (Objects[I]->ComputeT(Base, Dir) == 1) {
    // Bounding boxes have at least one child
    J = Objects[I]->Group;
    while (J != -1) {
      T = *NearestT;
      Tmp = FindClosestIntersection(Objects, J, Base, Dir, Q, &T);
      if (Tmp != -1) {
        if (T < *NearestT && T > TOL) {
          *NearestT = T;
```

```
        Closest = Tmp;
      }
    }
    J = Objects[J]->Group;
  }
}
}
```

The inner **while** loop processes each of the objects in the bounding box. Notice that it recursively calls **FindIntersection** since each object might be another bounding box.

If the current object is not a bounding box, the intersection point is computed and the **NearestT** variable is incremented if necessary, as shown here:

```
else {
  T = Objects[I]->ComputeT(Base, Dir);
  if (T < *NearestT && T > TOL) {
    *NearestT = T;
    Closest = I;
  }
}
```

• RAY.H

```
// RAY.H: Header file for RAY.CPP.

#ifndef RAYH
#define RAYH

#include "vector.h"
#include "objects.h"

#define TRUE 1
#define FALSE 0
#define MAXOBJECTS 500
#define MAXLIGHTS 5        // Maximum number of light sources allowed
#define MAXLEVEL 4         // Maximum levels of ray tracing recursion
#define TOL 0.001

extern int x, y;           // The current image pixel being displayed
extern Object *Objects[MAXOBJECTS];
extern int LastObj;        // Next open space in Objects array
extern int PrevObj;        // Last sibling added to Objects array
extern int GroupObj;       // Last group object added to Objects array

#define MAXIMAGES 4        // Maximum number of images in Images array
```

```
#define GRAYSCALEIMAGE 1   // Signals a grayscale image
#define RGBIMAGE 2         // The image is a color RGB image

struct IMAGE {
  char Filename[13];          // Image's filename
  int ImWd, ImHt;             // Pixel width and height of image
  unsigned char ImType;       // Type of image: RGB or grayscale
  unsigned char huge *Image;  // Pointer to image data
};
extern IMAGE Images[MAXIMAGES];
extern int NumImages;


extern VECTOR From, Up, At;  // Viewing parameters
extern COLOR Background;     // Background color
extern int ImWd, ImHt;
extern char OutFilename[];    // Save generated image to this file
extern unsigned char SaveTo; // Nonzero if image is to be saved
extern unsigned char Antialiasing;
extern int VMode;            // Display mode in DOS
extern int MaxLevel;         // Number of recursive calls
extern int FogMin, FogMax;   // Controls fog effect
extern COLOR FogColor;
extern float HorizonOffset;  // Location of a horizon on a
                             // rectangle with blended colors
struct STEP {                // Describes a move to make
  int T0, T1;                // Start and stop frame numbers
  float x0, y0, z0;          // Beginning value or location
  float x1, y1, z1;          // Ending value or location
  STEP *Next;                // Next step in the animation sequence
};


#define ANIMATEOBJLOC 1      // Animate an object's location
#define ANIMATEFROM 2        // Animate the from point
#define ANIMATEAT 3          // Animate the at point
#define ANIMATELIGHTLOC 4    // Animate a light's location
#define MAXANIMATEOBJ 10     // Can't animate more than 100 objects

struct ANIMATE {
  unsigned char Type;        // Type of "object" to animate
  int Ndx;                   // The object's index in array
  STEP *Steps;               // List of steps in animation
  STEP *CurrStep;            // Current step in animation
};
// List of objects and/or values to animate
extern ANIMATE Animate[MAXANIMATEOBJ];
extern int NumObjToAnimate; // Number of "objects" to animate
extern int FrameNum;         // Current frame number in sequence
extern int NumFrames;        // Number of frames in sequence
```

```
// Functions defined in RAY.CPP:
void InitializeObjects();
int FindClosestIntersection(Object *Objects[],
  VECTOR *Base, VECTOR *Dir, VECTOR *Q, float NearestT);
unsigned char InShadow(Object *Objects[], int Index,
  VECTOR* Q, VECTOR *LRay);
COLOR *ComputeLight(int Index, VECTOR *Q, VECTOR *NormalN,
  VECTOR *From, VECTOR *R, COLOR* I, COLOR *ObjColor, VECTOR *Dir);
void Transparency(int Level, int Index,
  VECTOR *Q, VECTOR *Dir, COLOR *Iq);
void Intensity(int Level, VECTOR Base, VECTOR Dir, COLOR *I);
void SetEye();
void RepositionObjects(int FrameNum);
int AddImage(char *Filename);
void FreeImages();
void WorldToScreen(VECTOR& V, float& X, float& Y);
inline void AddFog(COLOR* I, float Dist);
void Usage();
void AppendFrameNumber(char *Filename, char *OutFilename,
  int Frame);

#endif
```

• RAY.CPP

```
// RAY.CPP: Ray tracing code. Compile and link with OBJECTS.CPP,
// PARSER.CPP, LIGHTS.CPP, VECTOR.CPP, TIFF.C, and GRPHICS.C.
//
#include <stdio.h>
#include <stdlib.h>
#include <math.h>
#include <conio.h>
#include <string.h>
#include "ray.h"
#include "vector.h"
#include "objects.h"
#include "tiff.h"
#include "lights.h"
#include "grphics.h"


Object *Objects[MAXOBJECTS];   // List of objects in the world model
int LastObj;            // The index of the last object+1 in the world model
PointLight* Lights[MAXLIGHTS]; // List of lights in the scene
float LMin, LMax;              // These four variables are used
float DMin, DMax;              // to control the lighting
int NumLights;                 // Number of light sources used
int FrameNum;                  // Current frame in an animation sequence
int NumFrames;                 // Number of frames in an animation sequence
```

```c
char OutFilename[80];              // Output filename used to save image
unsigned char Antialiasing;        // Nonzero if antialiasing performed
IMAGE Images[MAXIMAGES];           // Images used in texturing
int NumImages;                     // Number of texturing images
int x, y;                          // Current image pixel being rendered
VECTOR RightV, UpV;                // World to image coordinate
VECTOR CenterV, Dir;               // version
VECTOR From, At, Up, A1, A2, A3;   // Viewing parameters
float DVal, OffsX, OffsY, OffsZ;
float VuAngle;
COLOR Background;                  // Background color of image
int ImWd, ImHt;                    // Image width and height
int VMode;                         // Display mode
int MaxLevel;                      // Level of ray tracing
unsigned char SaveTo;              // Nonzero when saving image to a file
int FogMin, FogMax;                // Controls depth of fog
COLOR FogColor;                    // Fog color
float HorizonOffset;               // Horizon used in blending colors
FILE *OutputFile;                  // Output image file pointer

struct BYTECOLOR {                 // Color structure that has byte
  unsigned char r, g, b;           // values
};

ANIMATE Animate[MAXANIMATEOBJ];    // List of objects to animate
int NumObjToAnimate;               // Number of objects to animate

int ReadSceneFile(char *filename);

//////////////////////////// main \\\\\\\\\\\\\\\\\\\\\\\\\\\

#if !defined(FORWINDOWS)
int main(int argc, char *argv[])
{
  if (argc != 2)
    Usage();

  // Sets the default video mode to 320x200x256 so that
  // it uses a color palette. This field only affects the
  // program if it is compiled as a DOS application.
  VMode = M320x200x256 | COLORPALETTE;
  Setup(argv[1]);  // Process command-line arguments

  if (SetupDisplay(VMode)) {
    GenImage(0);
    EndDisplay();
    Cleanup();
  }
```

```
    return 0;
}
#endif

////////////////////////////////// Setup  \\\\\\\\\\\\\\\\\\\\\\\\\\\
//
// Sets up default values for variables
//
void Setup(char far *Str)
{
  randomize();

  Antialiasing = 0;       // Disable antialiasing
  ImWd = 128; ImHt = 128; // Default output image dimension
  LastObj = 0;            // No objects in Objects array
  NumLights = 0;          // No default lights
  NumFrames = 1;          // By default, render one frame
  NumObjToAnimate = 0;    // By default, no objects to animate
  NumImages = 0;          // By default, no images to map
  MaxLevel = MAXLEVEL;    // Recursive levels for ray tracing
  strcpy(OutFilename,""); // Output filename for image
  SaveTo = 0;             // By default, don't save image to a file
  LMin = 1;  LMax = 10;   // These four variables scale
  DMin = 1;  DMax = 100;  // the light's intensity
  From.x = 15;  From.y = 15;  From.z = 0;   // Default
  At.x = 0.0;   At.y = 0.0;   At.z = 0.0;   // viewing
  Up.x = 0.0;   Up.y = 0.0;   Up.z = 1.0;   // parameters
  VuAngle = 50.0 * 0.017453293;
  // The fog begins 50 units away and is maximum at 1000 units.
  // The fog color defaults to white. To turn off the fog
  // set FogMax to 0.
  FogMin = 50;     FogMax = 1000;
  FogColor.r = 1.0;  FogColor.g = 1.0;  FogColor.b = 1.0;
  HorizonOffset = 0; // Blend colors equally if the blend function is used
  if (Str[0] == '\0') return;  // No SDF filename specified

  ReadSceneFile(Str);  // Read the scene description file
}

////////////////////////////////// Cleanup \\\\\\\\\\\\\\\\\\\\\\\\\\\
//
// Performs any clean actions
//
void Cleanup()
{
  RemoveLights();
  FreeObjects();
  FreeImages();
}
```

```
//////////////////////////// ClampTo \\\\\\\\\\\\\\\\\\\\\\\\\\\
//
// Clamps a fields in the COLOR structure to the specified number
//
inline void ClampTo(COLOR* I, float Max)
{
  if (I->r > Max) I->r = Max;
  if (I->g > Max) I->g = Max;
  if (I->b > Max) I->b = Max;
}


//////////////////////////// GenImage \\\\\\\\\\\\\\\\\\\\\\\\\\\
//
// This is the main entry point for the ray tracing code. If
// compiled as a DOS application, the hDC parameter is not used.
// In Windows, hDC is a handle to the device context to draw on.
//
void GenImage(int hDC)
{
  COLOR I;
  int Red, Green, Blue, sp;
  char Filename[13];
  float UInc, VInc, U, V;
  BYTECOLOR C;              // Color of a pixel
  BYTECOLOR *LastRow;      // Last row of the image
  BYTECOLOR PrevColor;     // Previous pixel's color

  if (LastObj <= 0) return;  // Nothing to draw

  // Allocate a row of COLOR structures to hold the image's
  // previous row of colors
  LastRow = new BYTECOLOR[ImWd+1];
  if (LastRow == NULL) return;
  Strcpy(Filename, OutFilename);
  SetEye();

  VInc = 2.0 / (ImHt - 1);
  UInc = 2.0 / (ImWd - 1);

  for (FrameNum=0; FrameNum<NumFrames; FrameNum++) {

    if (SaveTo) {            // Save the image to a file?
      if (NumObjToAnimate) {
        // If the image is part of an image sequence,
        // append the frame number to the end of the filename.
        AppendFrameNumber(Filename, OutFilename, FrameNum);
      }
      // Open the output file
      if ((OutputFile = fopen(Filename, "wb")) == NULL) {
```

```
      delete LastRow;     // Opening file failed. Quit.
      return;
    }
    // Write a TIFF header to the output file
    if (!WriteRGBTIFFHeader(OutputFile, (long) ImWd, (long) ImHt,
                            12000L)) {
      delete LastRow;     // Writing header failed. Quit.
      return;
    }
  }


RepositionObjects(FrameNum);

// If antialiasing is enabled, precomputes the pixel values
// for the row y-0.5
if (Antialiasing) {
  y = ImHt / 2;
  V = ((float)y-0.5) * VInc;
  x = -ImWd / 2;
  U = ((float)x-0.5) * UInc;
  Dir.x = CenterV.x + U * RightV.x + V * UpV.x;
  Dir.y = CenterV.y + U * RightV.y + V * UpV.y;
  Dir.z = CenterV.z + U * RightV.z + V * UpV.z;
  Intensity(1, From, Dir, &I);

  ClampTo(&I, 1.0);

  LastRow[0].r = I.r * 255;
  LastRow[0].g = I.g * 255;
  LastRow[0].b = I.b * 255;

  for (x=-ImWd/2, sp=1; x<=ImWd/2; x++, sp++) {
    U = ((float)x+0.5) * UInc;
    Dir.x = CenterV.x + U * RightV.x + V * UpV.x;
    Dir.y = CenterV.y + U * RightV.y + V * UpV.y;
    Dir.z = CenterV.z + U * RightV.z + V * UpV.z;
    Intensity(1, From, Dir, &I);

    ClampTo(&I, 1.0);

    LastRow[sp].r = I.r * 255;
    LastRow[sp].g = I.g * 255;
    LastRow[sp].b = I.b * 255;
  }
}

// Compute the colors for the rest of the image
for (y=ImHt/2; y>-ImHt/2; y--) {
  if (Antialiasing) {
```

```
      V = ((float)y+0.5) * VInc;
      x = -ImWd / 2;
      U = ((float)x-0.5) * UInc;

      Dir.x = CenterV.x + U * RightV.x + V * UpV.x;
      Dir.y = CenterV.y + U * RightV.y + V * UpV.y;
      Dir.z = CenterV.z + U * RightV.z + V * UpV.z;
      Intensity(1, From, Dir, &I);

      ClampTo(&I, 1.0);

      PrevColor.r = I.r * 255;
      PrevColor.g = I.g * 255;
      PrevColor.b = I.b * 255;
    }
    else
      V = y * VInc;
    for (x=-ImWd/2, sp=0; x<ImWd/2; x++, sp++) {
      if (kbhit()) break;
      if (Antialiasing)
        U = ((float)x+0.5) * UInc;
      else
        U = x * UInc;
      Dir.x = CenterV.x + U * RightV.x + V * UpV.x;
      Dir.y = CenterV.y + U * RightV.y + V * UpV.y;
      Dir.z = CenterV.z + U * RightV.z + V * UpV.z;
      Intensity(1, From, Dir, &I);

      ClampTo(&I, 1.0);

      Red = I.r * 255;
      Green = I.g * 255;
      Blue = I.b * 255;

      if (Antialiasing) {
        Red = ((int)LastRow[sp].r + (int)LastRow[sp+1].r +
          (int)PrevColor.r + (int)Red) / 4.0;
        Green = ((int)LastRow[sp].g + (int)LastRow[sp+1].g +
          (int)PrevColor.g + (int)Green) / 4.0;
        Blue = ((int)LastRow[sp].b + (int)LastRow[sp+1].b +
          (int)PrevColor.b + (int)Blue) / 4.0;

        if (Red > 255) Red = 255;
        if (Green > 255) Green = 255;
        if (Blue > 255) Blue = 255;

        LastRow[sp].r = PrevColor.r;
        LastRow[sp].g = PrevColor.g;
        LastRow[sp].b = PrevColor.b;
```

```
          PrevColor.r = I.r * 255.0;
          PrevColor.g = I.g * 255.0;
          PrevColor.b = I.b * 255.0;
        }

        PutPixel(hDC, x+ImWd/2, -y+ImHt/2, Red, Green, Blue);

        if (SaveTo) {
          C.r = Red;    C.g = Green;   C.b = Blue;
          fwrite(&C.r, 1, 1, OutputFile);
          fwrite(&C.g, 1, 1, OutputFile);
          fwrite(&C.b, 1, 1, OutputFile);
        }
      }
    }
    if (SaveTo)
      fclose(OutputFile);
  }
  delete LastRow;
}


///////////////////////// AppendFrameNumber \\\\\\\\\\\\\\\\\\\\\\\\
//
// Appends the frame number to the filename. The OutFilename
// string contains the root of the filename and ends in a period.
//
void AppendFrameNumber(char *Filename, char *OutFilename, int Frame)
{
  char Buffer[10];

  itoa(Frame, Buffer, 10);
  strcpy(Filename, OutFilename);
  strcat(Filename, ".");
  strcat(Filename, Buffer);
}


#if !defined(FORWINDOWS)
/////////////////////////// Usage \\\\\\\\\\\\\\\\\\\\\\\\\\\\\
//
// Prints usage statement in DOS if the wrong command-line
// arguments are given
//
void Usage()
{
  printf("\nRAY: Ray tracing program.\n\n");
  printf("Usage:> ray <scene_file>\n");
  printf("\t<scene_file> is a file containing the scene description.\n");
  printf("\n");
```

```
      exit(1);
    }
#endif

/////////////////////// RepositionObjects \\\\\\\\\\\\\\\\\\\\\\\
//
// Updates the positions of all animated objects
//
void RepositionObjects(int FrameNum)
{
  int i;
  float FInc;
  VECTOR V;

  for (i=0; i<NumObjToAnimate; i++) {
    if (Animate[i].CurrStep != NULL &&
        Animate[i].CurrStep->T0 <= FrameNum &&
        Animate[i].CurrStep->T1 >= FrameNum) {
      if (Animate[i].CurrStep->T0 != Animate[i].CurrStep->T1)
        FInc = (float)(FrameNum - Animate[i].CurrStep->T0) /
               (Animate[i].CurrStep->T1-Animate[i].CurrStep->T0);
      else
        FInc = 0;
      V.x = Animate[i].CurrStep->x0 + (Animate[i].CurrStep->x1 -
            Animate[i].CurrStep->x0) * FInc;
      V.y = Animate[i].CurrStep->y0 + (Animate[i].CurrStep->y1 -
            Animate[i].CurrStep->y0) * FInc;
      V.z = Animate[i].CurrStep->z0 + (Animate[i].CurrStep->z1 -
            Animate[i].CurrStep->z0) * FInc;
      switch(Animate[i].Type) {
        case ANIMATEFROM:
          From.x = V.x;  From.y = V.y;  From.z = V.z;
          SetEye();  // Recompute the eye coordinate system
          break;
        case ANIMATEAT:
          At.x = V.x;  At.y = V.y;  At.z = V.z;
          SetEye();  // Recompute the eye coordinate system
          break;
        case ANIMATEOBJLOC:
          Objects[Animate[i].Ndx]->Loc.x = V.x;
          Objects[Animate[i].Ndx]->Loc.y = V.y;
          Objects[Animate[i].Ndx]->Loc.z = V.z;
          break;
      }
    }
    if (NumFrames>1 &&
      Animate[i].CurrStep != NULL &&
      Animate[i].CurrStep->T1 == FrameNum) {
      // Reached the end of the current step. Set the step
```

```
      // pointer to the next step, if there is one.
      Animate[i].CurrStep = Animate[i].CurrStep->Next;
    }
  }
}

///////////////////////// FreeImages \\\\\\\\\\\\\\\\\\\\\\\\\
//
// Free any images that are in memory
//
void FreeImages()
{
  int i;

  for (i=0; i<NumImages; i++)
    farfree(Images[i].Image);
}

///////////////////////// AddImage \\\\\\\\\\\\\\\\\\\\\\\\\
//
//  Adds an image to the list of images
//
int AddImage(char *Filename)
{
  int T, i;

  // See if the image already exists. If it does, return the index
  // of this image.
  for (i=0; i<NumImages; i++)
    if (stricmp(Images[i].Filename,Filename) == 0)
      return i;

  if (NumImages >= MAXIMAGES-1)
    return -1;        // Image list is full

  if (GetImageInfo(Filename, &Images[NumImages].ImWd,
    &Images[NumImages].ImHt, &T) <= 0)
    return -1;        // Failed to read image file's header

  if (T == RGBIMAGE)
    Images[NumImages].Image = (unsigned char huge *)
  farmalloc((long)Images[NumImages].ImWd*(long)Images[NumImages].ImHt*3L);
  else
    Images[NumImages].Image = (unsigned char huge *)
    farmalloc((long)Images[NumImages].ImWd*(long)Images[NumImages].ImHt);

  if (Images[NumImages].Image == NULL) {
    return -1;      // Out of memory
  }
```

```
    Images[NumImages].ImType = T;

    if (!ReadImage(Filename, Images[NumImages].Image))
      return -1;      // Could not open image

    strcpy(Images[NumImages].Filename, Filename);
    NumImages++;
    return NumImages-1;
}


//////////////////// FindClosestIntersection \\\\\\\\\\\\\\\\\\\\
//
// Returns the index of the closest object that the light
// ray intersects. If the ray does not intersect an object, it
// returns -1. The intersection point is also returned in Q.
//
int FindClosestIntersection(Object *Objects[], int I,
  VECTOR *Base, VECTOR *Dir, VECTOR *Q, float *NearestT)
{
  int J, Closest = -1, Tmp;
  float T;

  while (I != -1) {
    // Calculate the intersection with the ray and each object
    if (Objects[I]->Shape == BOUNDINGBOX) {
      if (Objects[I]->ComputeT(Base, Dir) == 1) {
        // Bounding boxes have at least one child
        J = Objects[I]->Group;
        while (J != -1) {
          T = *NearestT;
          Tmp = FindClosestIntersection(Objects, J, Base, Dir, Q, &T);
          if (Tmp != -1) {
            if (T < *NearestT && T > TOL) {
              *NearestT = T;
              Closest = Tmp;
            }
          }
          J = Objects[J]->Group;
        }
      }
    }
    else {
      T = Objects[I]->ComputeT(Base, Dir);
      if (T < *NearestT && T > TOL) {
        *NearestT = T;
        Closest = I;
      }
    }
    I = Objects[I]->Sibling;
```

```
    }
    // Calculate the intersection point in world coordinates
    if (Closest >= 0) {
      Q->x = Base->x + Dir->x * *NearestT;
      Q->y = Base->y + Dir->y * *NearestT;
      Q->z = Base->z + Dir->z * *NearestT;
    }
    return Closest;
}


///////////////////////////// InShadow \\\\\\\\\\\\\\\\\\\\\\\\\
//
//   Returns non-zero if the object is in shadow
//
unsigned char InShadow(Object *Objects[], int Index,
  VECTOR* Q, VECTOR *Ray)
{
  int I=Index, J;
  float T;

  while (I != -1) {
    if (I != Index) {      // Don't check object against itself
      // Note: This precludes objects from casting shadows
      // on themselves.
      if (Objects[I]->Shape == BOUNDINGBOX) {
        // Calculate the intersection point with the ray
        if ((T=Objects[I]->ComputeT(Q, Ray)) > TOL && T < 1) {
          // Bounding spheres have at least one child
          J = Objects[I]->Group;
          while (J != -1) {
            if (InShadow(Objects, J, Q, Ray))
              return TRUE;
            J = Objects[J]->Group;
          }
        }
      }
      else {
        T = Objects[I]->ComputeT(Q, Ray);
        if (T > TOL && T < 1) {
          // Is this point transparent? If so, continue.
          if (Objects[J]->kt < .1)
            return TRUE;
        }
      }
    }
    I = Objects[I]->Sibling;
  }
  return FALSE;
}
```

```c
///////////////////////// ComputeLight \\\\\\\\\\\\\\\\\\\\\\\\\
//
// Given the point (x,y,z) calculates its intensity scale
// between 0 and 1
//
COLOR *ComputeLight(int Index, VECTOR *Q, VECTOR *NormalN,
  VECTOR *From, VECTOR *R, COLOR* I, COLOR *ObjColor, VECTOR *Dir)
{
  VECTOR L;                  // Vector to light source
  VECTOR S;                  // Line of sight vector
  float NDotL;
  float CosAlpha;
  Object *Obj;
  float WValue;
  float Dist;
  float DistScale, Temp;
  int i;

  Obj = Objects[Index];
  S = Subtract(From, Q); // Calculate the sight vector
  Dist = Dot(&S, &S);      // Calculate the distance to the viewer
  Dist = sqrt(Dist);
  Normalize(&S);

  I->r = 0;   I->g = 0;  I->b = 0;       // Initialize the color
  for (i=0; i<NumLights; i++) {
    L = Subtract(&Lights[i]->LFw, Q); // Calculate the light vector
    DistScale = Dot(&L, &L);
    Normalize(&L);

    if (!InShadow(Objects, Index, Q, &L)) {
      // The point Q is not in shadow. Add in the diffuse and
      // specular components of the light.
      DistScale = ScaleLight(sqrt(DistScale)); // Distance to light
      NDotL = Dot(&L, NormalN);
      if (NDotL > 0) {   // Add diffuse light
        Temp = Lights[i]->LightFactor(&L) * Obj->kd *
          NDotL / DistScale;
        I->r += Temp * Lights[i]->Color.r * ObjColor->r;
        I->g += Temp * Lights[i]->Color.g * ObjColor->g;
        I->b += Temp * Lights[i]->Color.b * ObjColor->b;
      }
      // Calculate the reflecting vector
      R->x = -L.x + 2 * NDotL * NormalN->x;
      R->y = -L.y + 2 * NDotL * NormalN->y;
      R->z = -L.z + 2 * NDotL * NormalN->z;
      Normalize(R);
      CosAlpha = -Dot(R, Dir);
```

```
      if (CosAlpha > 0) {  // Add specular light
        WValue = Lights[i]->W(NDotL, Obj->ks);
        if (WValue > 0) {
          Temp = Lights[i]->LightFactor(&L) * WValue *
            pow(CosAlpha, Obj->NO) / DistScale;
          I->r += Temp * Lights[i]->Color.r;
          I->g += Temp * Lights[i]->Color.g;
          I->b += Temp * Lights[i]->Color.b;
        }
      }
    }
  }
  // Add the ambient portion of the light
  I->r += Obj->ka * ObjColor->r;
  I->g += Obj->ka * ObjColor->g;
  I->b += Obj->ka * ObjColor->b;

  AddFog(I, Dist);  // Add fog if desired

  // Make sure the color values don't get too large
  ClampTo(I, 1.0);

  return I;
}


////////////////////////////// AddFog \\\\\\\\\\\\\\\\\\\\\\\\\\\
//
// Adds a portion of the fog's color into the color I based on
// the length of the vector V. Disable the fog by setting FogMax
// to 0.
//
inline void AddFog(COLOR* I, float Dist)
{
  float LightScale = 1.0;

  if (FogMax > 0) {
    if (Dist > FogMin) {
      // Don't apply fog if the distance is too small
      if (Dist < FogMax)
        LightScale = (Dist - FogMin) / (FogMax - FogMin);
      I->r = FogColor.r * LightScale + I->r * (1 - LightScale);
      I->g = FogColor.g * LightScale + I->g * (1 - LightScale);
      I->b = FogColor.b * LightScale + I->b * (1 - LightScale);
    }
  }
}
```

```
//////////////////////// Transparency \\\\\\\\\\\\\\\\\\\\\
//
// Adds in the transmitted color that passes through the
// transparent object
//
void Transparency(int Level, int Index,
  VECTOR *Q, VECTOR *Dir, COLOR *Iq)
{
  COLOR I2;
  float kt;
  VECTOR Dir2, Q2;

  kt = Objects[Index]->kt;
  Q2.x = Q->x;  Q2.y = Q->y;   Q2.z = Q->z;
  Dir2.x = Dir->x;  Dir2.y = Dir->y;   Dir2.z = Dir->z;

  Intensity(Level, Q2, Dir2, &I2);

  Iq->r = (1-kt) * Iq->r + kt * I2.r;
  Iq->g = (1-kt) * Iq->g + kt * I2.g;
  Iq->b = (1-kt) * Iq->b + kt * I2.b;
}

//////////////////////// Intensity \\\\\\\\\\\\\\\\\\\\\\\\\
//
// Performs the ray tracing. Returns the intensity to plot a
// point given a ray.
//
void Intensity(int Level, VECTOR Base, VECTOR Dir, COLOR *I)
{
  int Index;
  COLOR Iq, Ir, ObjColor;
  VECTOR Q, N, R;
  float DotProd;
  float T = 3.4e38;

  if (Level <= MaxLevel) {
    Index = FindClosestIntersection(Objects, 0, &Base, &Dir, &Q, &T);
    if (Index >= 0) {  // An intersection is found
      Objects[Index]->ComputeNormal(&Q, &N);
      if (Dot(&N, &Dir) > 0) {
        N.x = -N.x;    // Swap the sign of the normal if
        N.y = -N.y;    // it pointing away from the light
        N.z = -N.z;    // ray's base
      }
      ObjColor =
        (*Objects[Index]->DeterminePattern)(Objects[Index], &Q);

      ComputeLight(Index, &Q, &N, &Base, &R, &Iq, &ObjColor, &Dir);
```

```c
      if (Objects[Index]->kt > TOL)
        Transparency(Level, Index, &Q, &Dir, &Iq);

      DotProd = -Dot(&Dir, &N);
      R.x = Dir.x + 2 * DotProd * N.x;
      R.y = Dir.y + 2 * DotProd * N.y;
      R.z = Dir.z + 2 * DotProd * N.z;

      // Calculate ray for reflecting vector
      if (Level+1 <= MaxLevel && Objects[Index]->ks > TOL) {
        // See what the reflected ray hits and add its color
        // to the current object's color
        Intensity(Level+1, Q, R, &Ir);
        I->r = Iq.r + Objects[Index]->ks * Ir.r;
        I->g = Iq.g + Objects[Index]->ks * Ir.g;
        I->b = Iq.b + Objects[Index]->ks * Ir.b;
      }
      else {
        I->r = Iq.r;
        I->g = Iq.g;
        I->b = Iq.b;
      }
    }
    else {
      // The ray didn't hit anything. Return the background color.
      // You may want to return the fog color for some outdoor
      // scenes.
      I->r = Background.r;
      I->g = Background.g;
      I->b = Background.b;
    }
  }
}

/////////////////////////////// SetEye \\\\\\\\\\\\\\\\\\\\\\\\\\\\\\\
//
// Calculates the matrix values that are used when calculating
// the locations of the rays in eye coordinates
//
void SetEye()
{
  A3 = Subtract(&At, &From);
  A1 = Cross(&A3, &Up);
  A2 = Cross(&A1, &A3);
  Normalize(&A1);
  Normalize(&A2);
  Normalize(&A3);
  RightV.x = A1.x;  RightV.y = A1.y;  RightV.z = A1.z;
  UpV.x = A2.x;     UpV.y = A2.y;     UpV.z = A2.z;
```

```
   DVal = cos(VuAngle/2.0) / sin(VuAngle/2.0);
   CenterV.x = A3.x * DVal;
   CenterV.y = A3.y * DVal;
   CenterV.z = A3.z * DVal;
   OffsX = -A1.x * From.x - A1.y * From.y - A1.z * From.z;
   OffsY = -A2.x * From.x - A2.y * From.y - A2.z * From.z;
   OffsZ = -A3.x * From.x - A3.y * From.y - A3.z * From.z;
}


/////////////////////// WorldToScreen \\\\\\\\\\\\\\\\\\\\\\\\
//
// Converts the world coordinate in V to a screen coordinate (X,Y)
//
void WorldToScreen(VECTOR& V, float& X, float& Y)
{
   VECTOR NewV;

   NewV.x = (V.x * A1.x + A1.y * V.y + A1.z * V.z + OffsX) * DVal;
   NewV.y = (V.x * A2.x + A2.y * V.y + A2.z * V.z + OffsY) * DVal;
   NewV.z =  V.x * A3.x + A3.y * V.y + A3.z * V.z + OffsZ;

   if (NewV.z != 0.0) {
     X = ImWd/2 * NewV.x/NewV.z;
     Y = ImHt/2 * NewV.y/NewV.z;
   }
   else {
     X = ImWd/2 * NewV.x;
     Y = ImHt/2 * NewV.y;
   }
}
```

• OBJECTS.H

```
// OBJECTS.H: Header file for OBJECTS.CPP.

#ifndef OBJECTSH
#define OBJECTSH

#define SPHERE 1
#define RECTANGLE 2
#define ELLIPSOID 3
#define TRIANGLE 4
#define CYLINDER 5
#define BOUNDINGBOX 98
#define BOUNDINGSPHERE 99

#define CHECKERPATTERN 0x01
#define IMAGEPATTERN 0x02
```

```
#define WATERPATTERN 0x04
#define CLOUDPATTERN 0x08
#define MARBLEPATTERN 0x10
#define BLENDPATTERN 0x20

struct COLOR {
  float r, g, b;
};

// The base class for all the objects
class Object {
public:
  unsigned int Shape;      // The object's type
  int ImageNdx;            // Index of the image mapped to the object
  int Sibling, Group;      // Indexes of sibling and grouped objects
  float MaxTO;
  float ka, kd, ks, kt;    // Lighting model constants
  int NO;                  // Specular reflection constant
  COLOR Ia1, Ia2;          // Object's color
  VECTOR Loc;              // Object's location
  Object();                // Constructor
  virtual float ComputeT(VECTOR* From, VECTOR* Dir) { return 0; }
  virtual void ComputeNormal(VECTOR *Q, VECTOR *N) { }
  virtual void MapToUV(VECTOR* Q, float& U, float& V) { }
  COLOR (*DeterminePattern)(Object *Obj, VECTOR *Q);
};

class RectangleObj : public Object {  // Rectangle object
public:
  VECTOR Normal;
  float D;
  VECTOR V1, V2;
  float Len1, Len2;
  float MinX, MaxX, MinY, MaxY, MinZ, MaxZ;
  float TO, T1;
  RectangleObj(VECTOR *LocV, VECTOR *Vect1, VECTOR *Vect2);
  virtual float ComputeT(VECTOR* From, VECTOR* Dir);
  virtual void ComputeNormal(VECTOR *Q, VECTOR *N);
  virtual void MapToUV(VECTOR* Q, float& U, float& V);
};

class TriangleObj : public RectangleObj {
public:
  TriangleObj(VECTOR* LocV, VECTOR* Vect1, VECTOR* Vect2);
  virtual float ComputeT(VECTOR* From, VECTOR* Dir);
};

// A bounding box object
class BoundingBoxObj : public Object {
```

```
public:
  float MinX, MaxX, MinY, MaxY, MinZ, MaxZ;
  BoundingBoxObj(float XMin, float XMax,
    float YMin, float YMax, float ZMin, float ZMax);
  virtual float ComputeT(VECTOR* From, VECTOR* Dir);
};

class SphereObj : public Object {
public:
  float RSquared;     // Radius squared
  SphereObj(float X, float Y, float Z, float R);
  virtual float ComputeT(VECTOR* From, VECTOR* Dir);
  virtual void ComputeNormal(VECTOR *Q, VECTOR *N);
  virtual void MapToUV(VECTOR* Q, float& U, float& V);
};

class EllipsoidObj : public SphereObj {
public:
  float A, B, C, D;
  VECTOR V1, V2;
  EllipsoidObj(float X, float Y, float Z, float AVal,
    float BVal, float CVal, float DVal);
  virtual float ComputeT(VECTOR* From, VECTOR* Dir);
  virtual void ComputeNormal(VECTOR *Q, VECTOR *N);
};

class CylinderObj : public SphereObj {
public:
  float Radius, Height;
  VECTOR V1;
  CylinderObj(VECTOR LocV, VECTOR Vect1, float R);
  virtual float ComputeT(VECTOR* From, VECTOR* Dir);
  virtual void ComputeNormal(VECTOR *Q, VECTOR *N);
  virtual void MapToUV(VECTOR* Q, float& U, float& V);
};

// Water is a special type of rectangle object
class WaterObj : public RectangleObj {
public:
  float Ht;      // Height of the water's waves
  float Rough;   // Controls the roughness of the water
  WaterObj::WaterObj(VECTOR *LocV, VECTOR *Vect1, VECTOR *Vect2) :
    RectangleObj(LocV, Vect1, Vect2) { }
  virtual void ComputeNormal(VECTOR *Q, VECTOR *N);
};

int AddObject(Object *Obj, int Prev, int Group);
void FreeObjects();
```

```
COLOR PatternOnSurface(Object *Obj, VECTOR *Q);
COLOR Blend(Object* Obj, VECTOR* Q);
COLOR MapImage(Object* Obj, VECTOR* Q);
COLOR ThreeDCloudPattern(Object* ObjPtr, VECTOR* Q);
COLOR TwoDCloudPattern(Object* ObjPtr, VECTOR* Q);
COLOR NoPattern(Object* Obj, VECTOR* Q);
void SetObjectTexture(int ObjId, int PatternType, int Ndx);
float Noise(VECTOR *Q, float TS1, float TS2, float *MaxTO,
  unsigned char TwoD);
float MaxOf(float V1, float V2, float V3, float V4);
float MinOf(float V1, float V2, float V3, float V4);

#endif
```

• OBJECTS.CPP

```
// OBJECTS.CPP: The functions used to render the objects in RAY.

#include <stdio.h>
#include <math.h>
#include <stdlib.h>
#include "ray.h"
#include "objects.h"

//////////////////////////// FreeObjects  \\\\\\\\\\\\\\\\\\\\\\\\\\
//
// Frees all the objects in the objects list
//
void FreeObjects()
{
  int i;

  for (i=0; i<LastObj; i++)
    delete Objects[i];
}


//////////////////////////// AddObject  \\\\\\\\\\\\\\\\\\\\\\\\\\\\
//
// Adds the object, Obj, to the object list. Returns the index
// location where the object is inserted. The function returns
// a -1 if the object list is already full.
//
int AddObject(Object *Obj, int Prev, int Group)
{
  if (LastObj >= MAXOBJECTS) return -1;

  if (Prev != -1)
    Objects[Prev]->Sibling = LastObj;
```

```
  else if (Group != -1)
    Objects[Group]->Group = LastObj;
  Objects[LastObj++] = Obj;

  return LastObj-1;
}

/////////////////////////// Object \\\\\\\\\\\\\\\\\\\\\\\\\\\
//
// Constructor for the Object class
//
Object::Object()
{
  Ia1.r = 1; Ia1.g = 1;  Ia1.b = 1;
  Ia2.r = 0; Ia2.g = 0;  Ia2.b = 0;
  ka = .7;   kd = .6;    ks = .3;    kt = 0;   NO = 4;
  Sibling = -1;
  Group = -1;
  MaxTO = 0;
  DeterminePattern = NoPattern;
}


/////////////////////// BoundingBoxObj \\\\\\\\\\\\\\\\\\\\\\\
//
// Constructor for the bounding box object
//
BoundingBoxObj::BoundingBoxObj(float XMin, float XMax,
  float YMin, float YMax, float ZMin, float ZMax) : Object()
{
  Shape = BOUNDINGBOX;
  MinX = XMin;    MinY = YMin;    MinZ = ZMin;
  MaxX = XMax;    MaxY = YMax;    MaxZ = ZMax;
}


/////////////////////////// SphereObj \\\\\\\\\\\\\\\\\\\\\\\\\\
//
// Constructor for a sphere object
//
SphereObj::SphereObj(float X, float Y, float Z, float R) :
  Object()
{
  Shape = SPHERE;
  RSquared = R * R;
  Loc.x = X;    Loc.y = Y;    Loc.z = Z;
}


/////////////////////////// RectangleObj \\\\\\\\\\\\\\\\\\\\\\\
//
// Constructor for a rectangle object
//
```

```
RectangleObj::RectangleObj(VECTOR *LocV, VECTOR *Vect1,
  VECTOR *Vect2) : Object()
{
  Shape = RECTANGLE;
  V1.x = Vect1->x;
  V2.x = Vect2->x;
  Loc.x = LocV->x;
  V1.y = Vect1->y;
  V2.y = Vect2->y;
  Loc.y = LocV->y;
  V1.z = Vect1->z;
  V2.z = Vect2->z;
  Loc.z = LocV->z;

  Normal = Cross(&V1, &V2);    // The normal is given by V1 x V2
  Normalize(&Normal);
  D = -(Loc.x*Normal.x + Loc.y*Normal.y + Loc.z*Normal.z);
  MinX = MinOf(Loc.x, Loc.x+V1.x, Loc.x+V2.x, Loc.x+V1.x+V2.x);
  MaxX = MaxOf(Loc.x, Loc.x+V1.x, Loc.x+V2.x, Loc.x+V1.x+V2.x);
  MinY = MinOf(Loc.y, Loc.y+V1.y, Loc.y+V2.y, Loc.y+V1.y+V2.y);
  MaxY = MaxOf(Loc.y, Loc.y+V1.y, Loc.y+V2.y, Loc.y+V1.y+V2.y);
  MinZ = MinOf(Loc.z, Loc.z+V1.z, Loc.z+V2.z, Loc.z+V1.z+V2.z);
  MaxZ = MaxOf(Loc.z, Loc.z+V1.z, Loc.z+V2.z, Loc.z+V1.z+V2.z);
  Len1 = Dot(&V1, &V1);   // Precompute these values for
  Len2 = Dot(&V2, &V2);   // the checker/pattern function
}


//////////////////////// EllipsoidObj \\\\\\\\\\\\\\\\\\\\\\\\\
//
// Constructor for an ellipsoid object
//
EllipsoidObj::EllipsoidObj(float X, float Y, float Z, float AVal,
  float BVal, float CVal, float DVal) : SphereObj(X, Y, Z, 0)
{
  Shape = ELLIPSOID;
  A = AVal;    B = BVal;    C = CVal;    D = DVal;
  Loc.x = X;   Loc.y = Y;   Loc.z = Z;
  V2.x = 0;  V2.y = 0;  // Used for cloud texture
}


//////////////////////// CylinderObj \\\\\\\\\\\\\\\\\\\\\\\\\
//
// Constructor for a cylinder object
//
CylinderObj::CylinderObj(VECTOR LocV, VECTOR Vect1, float R) :
  SphereObj(LocV.x, LocV.y, LocV.z, R)
{
  Shape = CYLINDER;
  Radius = R;
```

```
    V1 = Vect1;
    // Precompute dot product of length vector
    Height = Dot(&V1, &V1);  // This is really the cylinder's height
}


////////////////////////// TriangleObj \\\\\\\\\\\\\\\\\\\\\\\\\
//
// Constructor for the triangle object
//
TriangleObj::TriangleObj(VECTOR* LocV, VECTOR* Vect1,
  VECTOR* Vect2) : RectangleObj(LocV, Vect1, Vect2)
{
  Shape = TRIANGLE;
}


////////////////////// BoundingBoxObj::ComputeT \\\\\\\\\\\\\\\\\\\
//
// Returns 1 if the ray (specified by the vectors Base and Dir)
// intersects the bounding box for this object. Otherwise, the
// function returns -1.
//
float BoundingBoxObj::ComputeT(VECTOR *Base, VECTOR *Dir)
{
  float TMinX=-3.4e37, TMaxX=3.4e38;
  float TMinY=-3e37, TMaxY=3e38;
  float TMinZ=-3e37, TMaxZ=3e38;
  float T1, T2;

  if (fabs(Dir->x) < TOL) {
    // The ray is parallel to the planes. Therefore if the base
    // of the ray is outside of the two X planes, it must miss
    // the bounding volume. Return a failure flag.
    if (Base->x < MinX || Base->x > MaxX)
      return 0;
  }
  else {
    T1 = (MinX - Base->x) / Dir->x; // Calculate the intersection
    T2 = (MaxX - Base->x) / Dir->x; // distances with the X planes
    TMinX = (T1 < T2) ? T1 : T2;
    TMaxX = (T1 < T2) ? T2 : T1;
    if (TMaxX < 0) return 0;                 // Box is behind ray
  }
  if (fabs(Dir->y) < TOL) {
    if (Base->y < MinY || Base->y > MaxY)
      return 0;
  }
  else {
    T1 = (MinY - Base->y) / Dir->y; // Calculate the intersection
    T2 = (MaxY - Base->y) / Dir->y; // distances with the Y planes
```

```
    TMinY = (T1 < T2) ? T1 : T2;
    TMaxY = (T1 < T2) ? T2 : T1;
    if (TMaxY < 0) return 0;              // Box is behind ray
  }
  if (fabs(Dir->z) < TOL) {
    if (Base->z < MinZ || Base->z > MaxZ)
      return 0;
  }
  else {
    T1 = (MinZ - Base->z) / Dir->z; // Calculate the intersection
    T2 = (MaxZ - Base->z) / Dir->z; // distances with the Z planes
    TMinZ = (T1 < T2) ? T1 : T2;
    TMaxZ = (T1 < T2) ? T2 : T1;
    if (TMaxZ < 0) return 0;              // Box is behind ray
  }
  if (TMinX > TMinY) {  // Find the largest of TMinX, TMinY,
    if (TMinX > TMinZ)  // and TMinZ
      T1 = TMinX;
    else
      T1 = TMinZ;
  }
  else {
    if (TMinY > TMinZ)
      T1 = TMinY;
    else
      T1 = TMinZ;
  }
  if (TMaxX < TMaxY) {  // Find the smallest of TMaxX, TMaxY,
    if (TMaxX < TMaxZ)  // and TMaxZ
      T2 = TMaxX;
    else
      T2 = TMaxZ;
  }
  else {
    if (TMaxY < TMaxZ)
      T2 = TMaxY;
    else
      T2 = TMaxZ;
  }
  if (T1 > T2)            // If the nearer intersection is farther
    return 0;             // away, the ray misses the box
  return 1;
}


/////////////////// RectangleObj::ComputeT \\\\\\\\\\\\\\\\\\\\
//
// Computes the t value of the intersection between the ray and
// an object. t must be greater than 0. If t is negative, the
// intersection is "behind" the base point. TOL is used to
```

```
// avoid problems with round off errors.
//
float RectangleObj::ComputeT(VECTOR *Base, VECTOR *Dir)
{
  float Denom, t;
  VECTOR Pt;
  float A=Normal.x, B=Normal.y, C=Normal.z;

  // Determine where the ray intersects the plane that contains
  // the rectangle, if the intersection exists
  Denom = A * Dir->x + B * Dir->y + C * Dir->z;
  if (Denom == 0)
    return -1;
  t = -(A * Base->x + B * Base->y + C * Base->z+ D) / Denom;
  if (t < 0) return -1;   // Intersection is behind the viewer

  // Determine if the ray intersects within the bounds of
  // the rectangle. Project the rectangle onto the axis that
  // causes the largest projection--the axis with the largest
  // coefficient. Then test whether the projected intersection
  // point lies within the projected rectangle.
  Pt.x = Base->x + Dir->x * t;
  Pt.y = Base->y + Dir->y * t;
  Pt.z = Base->z + Dir->z * t;

  if (fabs(A) > fabs(B) && fabs(A) > fabs(C)) {
    // X axis plane equation is greatest. Project the rectangle
    // on to the X axis.
    if ((MinZ < Pt.z && Pt.z < MaxZ) &&
        (MinY < Pt.y && Pt.y < MaxY))
      return t;
  }
  else if (fabs(B) > fabs(C)) {
    // Y axis projection is the largest
    if ((MinX < Pt.x && Pt.x < MaxX) &&
      (MinZ < Pt.z && Pt.z < MaxZ))
      return t;
  }
  else {
    if ((MinX < Pt.x && Pt.x < MaxX) &&
      (MinY < Pt.y && Pt.y < MaxY))
      return t;
  }
  return -1;
}


//////////////////////// TriangleObj::ComputeT \\\\\\\\\\\\\\\\\\\\\
//
// Computes the t value of the intersection between the ray and
```

```c
// an object. t must be greater than 0. If t is negative, the
// intersection is "behind" the base point. TOL is used to
// avoid problems with round off errors.
//
float TriangleObj::ComputeT(VECTOR *Base, VECTOR *Dir)
{
  VECTOR Pt, Delta;
  float U[3], V[3];
  int i, j, CrossCount = 0;
  float t, Denom;
  float A=Normal.x, B=Normal.y, C=Normal.z;

  // Determine where the ray intersects the plane that contains
  // the rectangle, if the intersection exists.
  Denom = A * Dir->x + B * Dir->y + C * Dir->z;
  if (Denom == 0)
    return -1;
  t = -(A * Base->x + B * Base->y + C * Base->z + D) / Denom;
  if (t < 0) return -1;   // Possible intersection is behind the viewer

  Pt.x = Base->x + Dir->x * t;
  Pt.y = Base->y + Dir->y * t;
  Pt.z = Base->z + Dir->z * t;

  // Project the triangle onto the axis that causes the largest
  // projection--the axis with the largest coefficient. Then
  // test whether the projected intersection point lies within
  // the projected triangle.
  Delta = Subtract(&Pt, &Loc);
  if (fabs(A) > fabs(B) && fabs(A) > fabs(C)) {
    // Project the triangle onto the x axis, where x = 0
    U[0] = -Delta.y;
    V[0] = -Delta.z;
    U[1] = V1.y - Delta.y;
    V[1] = V1.z - Delta.z;
    U[2] = V2.y - Delta.y;
    V[2] = V2.z - Delta.z;
  }
  else if (fabs(B) > fabs(C)) {
    // Project the triangle onto the y axis
    U[0] = -Delta.x;
    V[0] = -Delta.z;
    U[1] = V1.x - Delta.x;
    V[1] = V1.z - Delta.z;
    U[2] = V2.x - Delta.x;
    V[2] = V2.z - Delta.z;
  }
  else {   // Project the triangle onto the z axis
    U[0] = -Delta.x;
```

```
      V[0] = -Delta.y;
      U[1] = V1.x - Delta.x;
      V[1] = V1.y - Delta.y;
      U[2] = V2.x - Delta.x;
      V[2] = V2.y - Delta.y;
   }

   // Count the number of times that the triangle crosses the
   // positive U axis
   for (i=0, j=1; i<3; i++, j++) {
     if (j == 3) j = 0;
     if ((V[i] < 0 && V[j] >= 0) ||
         (V[i] >= 0 && V[j] < 0)) {
       if (U[i] >= 0 && U[j] >= 0)
         CrossCount++;
       else if (U[i] >= 0 || U[j] >= 0)
         if (U[i] - V[i] * (U[j] - U[i]) /
             (V[j] - V[i]) > 0)
           CrossCount++;
     }
   }
   if (CrossCount%2 == 0)
     return -1;      // No intersection
   return t;
}


/////////////////////  SphereObj::ComputeT  \\\\\\\\\\\\\\\\\\\\\
//
// Determines where the light ray intersects the sphere, if it does.
// The light ray starts at Base and is pointed in the direction Dir.
// Returns -1 if the ray does not intersect the object. Otherwise,
// it returns the parametric t value representing the intersection
// point.
//
float SphereObj::ComputeT(VECTOR *Base, VECTOR *Dir)
{
   float Det, Aq, Bq, Cq, First, Second, Int1, Int2;
   VECTOR Base2;

   Base2 = Subtract(Base, &Loc);
   Aq = Dot(Dir, Dir);
   if (Aq == 0) return -1;
   Bq = 2 * Dot(Dir, &Base2);
   Cq = Dot(&Base2, &Base2) - RSquared;

   Det = Bq * Bq - 4 * Aq * Cq;
   if (Det >= 0) {
     Int1 = sqrt(Det);
     Int2 = 2 * Aq;
```

```
    First = (-Bq + Int1) / Int2;
    if (First > TOL) {
      Second = (-Bq - Int1) / Int2;
      if (First < Second)
        return First;
      if (Second < TOL)
        return First;
      return Second;
    }
    Second = (-Bq - Int1) / Int2;
    if (Second > TOL)
      return Second;
  }
  return -1;
}

/////////////////// EllipsoidObj::ComputeT \\\\\\\\\\\\\\\\\\\
//
// Determines where the light ray (which starts at Base and points
// in the direction Dir) intersects the ellipsoid. Returns -1 if
// the ray does not intersect the object. Otherwise, it returns
// the parametric t value representing the intersection point.
//
float EllipsoidObj::ComputeT(VECTOR *Base, VECTOR *Dir)
{
  float Aq, Bq, Cq, Det, First, Second, Int1, Int2;
  VECTOR Base2;

  // Calculate the ray's base location in the object's
  // coordinate system. The direction is assumed to be
  // the same as the ellipsoid's, that is (0,1,0).
  Base2 = Subtract(Base, &Loc);

  Aq = A * Dir->x * Dir->x + B * Dir->y * Dir->y +
       C * Dir->z * Dir->z;
  Bq = 2 * (A * Base2.x * Dir->x + B * Base2.y * Dir->y +
       C * Base2.z * Dir->z);
  Cq = -D + A * Base2.x * Base2.x +
       B * Base2.y * Base2.y + C * Base2.z * Base2.z;

  Det = Bq * Bq - 4 * Aq * Cq;
  if (Det >= 0) {
    Int1 = sqrt(Det);
    Int2 = 2 * Aq;
    First = (-Bq + Int1) / Int2;
    if (First > TOL) {
      Second = (-Bq - Int1) / Int2;
      if (First < Second)
        return First;
```

```
      if (Second < TOL)
        return First;
      return Second;
    }
    Second = (-Bq - Int1) / Int2;
    if (Second > TOL)
      return Second;
  }
  return -1;
}


///////////////////// CylinderObj::ComputeT \\\\\\\\\\\\\\\\\\\\\
//
// Determines where the light ray (which starts at Base and points
// in the direction Dir) intersects the cylinder. Returns -1 if the
// ray does not intersect the object. Otherwise, it returns the
// parametric t value representing the intersection point.
//
float CylinderObj::ComputeT(VECTOR *Base, VECTOR *Dir)
{
  float Aq, Bq, Cq, Det, FirstT, SecondT, Int1, Int2;
  VECTOR K, D;
  float T1, T2, T3;
  float SmallerT, LargerT;

  // Calculate the ray's base location in the object's
  // coordinate system
  T2 = Dot(Base, &V1) - Dot(&Loc, &V1);
  T1 = T2 / Height;
  K.x = Base->x - Loc.x - T1 * V1.x;
  K.y = Base->y - Loc.y - T1 * V1.y;
  K.z = Base->z - Loc.z - T1 * V1.z;

  T3 = Dot(Dir, &V1);
  T1 = T3 / Height;
  D.x = Dir->x - T1 * V1.x;
  D.y = Dir->y - T1 * V1.y;
  D.z = Dir->z - T1 * V1.z;

  Aq = Dot(&D, &D);
  Bq = 2 * Dot(&D, &K);
  Cq = Dot(&K, &K) - RSquared;

  Det = Bq * Bq - 4 * Aq * Cq;
  if (Det >= 0) {
    Int1 = sqrt(Det);
    Int2 = 2 * Aq;
    FirstT = (-Bq + Int1) / Int2;
    if (FirstT < TOL) {
```

```
      SecondT = (-Bq - Int1) / Int2;
      if (SecondT < TOL)
        return -1;              // Ray missed
      SmallerT = SecondT;
      LargerT = -1;
    }
    else {
      SecondT = (-Bq - Int1) / Int2;
      if (FirstT < SecondT) {
        SmallerT = FirstT;      // First intersection is closer
        LargerT = SecondT;
      }
      else if (SecondT < TOL) {
        SmallerT = FirstT;      // First intersection is closer
        LargerT = -1;
      }
      else {
        SmallerT = SecondT;
        LargerT = FirstT;
      }
    }
    T1 = (T2 + SmallerT * T3) / Height;
    if (T1 >= 0 && T1 <= 1)
      return SmallerT;
    if (LargerT >= 0) {
      T1 = (T2 + LargerT * T3) / Height;
      if (T1 >= 0 && T1 <= 1)
        return LargerT;
    }
  }
  return -1;
}


////////////////  RectangleObj::ComputeNormal  \\\\\\\\\\\\\\\\
//
// Returns the normal of the rectangle
//
void RectangleObj::ComputeNormal(VECTOR*, VECTOR *N)
{
  N->x = Normal.x;    // The normal is normalized in the constructor
  N->y = Normal.y;
  N->z = Normal.z;
}


////////////////  SphereObj::ComputeNormal  \\\\\\\\\\\\\\\\\
//
// Computes the normal of the sphere at point Q
//
void SphereObj::ComputeNormal(VECTOR *Q, VECTOR *N)
```

```
{
  *N = Subtract(Q, &Loc);
  Normalize(N);
}


///////////////////// EllipsoidObj::ComputeNormal \\\\\\\\\\\\\\
//
// Returns the normal of the ellipsoid at the point Q
//
void EllipsoidObj::ComputeNormal(VECTOR *Q, VECTOR *N)
{
  VECTOR Pos = Subtract(Q, &Loc);

  N->x = A * Pos.x;
  N->y = B * Pos.y;
  N->z = C * Pos.z;

  Normalize(N);
}


///////////////////// CylinderObj::ComputeNormal \\\\\\\\\\\\\\\
//
// Returns the normal of the cylinder at the point Q
//
void CylinderObj::ComputeNormal(VECTOR *Q, VECTOR *N)
{
  float t;
  VECTOR C;    // Axis of cylinder
  VECTOR Pt;

  C = V1;
  Normalize(&C);

  // Compute the parametric t value where the center line of
  // the cylinder intersects the plane that contains the point Q
  VECTOR Tmp = Subtract(Q, &Loc);
  t = Dot(&Tmp, &C) / Dot(&C, &V1);

  // Now compute the point along the cylinder's axis using t
  Pt.x = Loc.x + t * V1.x;
  Pt.y = Loc.y + t * V1.y;
  Pt.z = Loc.z + t * V1.z;

  *N = Subtract(Q, &Pt);
  Normalize(N);
}

#define NUMWAVECENTERS 16
```

```
////////////////////  WaterObj::ComputeNormal  \\\\\\\\\\\\\\\\\\\
//
// Computes the normal for water
//
void WaterObj::ComputeNormal(VECTOR *Q, VECTOR *N)
{
  VECTOR Dist;
  VECTOR WaveCenters[NUMWAVECENTERS] =
    {{-4, -4, 0},   {0, 2, -0},   {3, 4, 0},     {-4, 3, 0},
     {10,  2, 0},   {4, 1, -0},   {2, -4, 0},    {-1, 3, 0},
     {-2, -2, 0},   {0, -2, 0},   {3, -1, -0},   {-2, .4, 0},
     {-6, -.4, -0}, {1, 2, 0},    {3, -4, -0},   {2, 1, 0}};
  float fnum[NUMWAVECENTERS] = {10, 44, 18, 24, 36, 35, 54, 22, 19, 22,
  10, 24, 18, 24, 36, 35};
  float M, f, fr, PhaseInc;
  int I;
  Dist = Subtract(&From, Q);
  fr = 0;
  N->x = Normal.x;
  N->y = Normal.y;
  N->z = Normal.z;

  for (I=0; I<NUMWAVECENTERS; I++) {
    f = fnum[I] * Rough + fr;
    PhaseInc = pow(f, 0.25);  // Used in animating the water
    Dist = Subtract(Q, &WaveCenters[I]);
    Dist.x = Dist.x * f;
    Dist.y = Dist.y * f;
    Dist.z = Dist.z * f;
    M = Mag(&Dist);
    Normalize(&Dist);
    N->x += (Ht * sin(M+FrameNum*PhaseInc)) / f;
    N->y += (Ht * sin(M+FrameNum*PhaseInc)) / f;
    N->z += (Ht * cos(M+FrameNum*PhaseInc)) / f;
  }
  Normalize(N);
}


/////////////////////////////  NoPattern  \\\\\\\\\\\\\\\\\\\\\\\\\
//
// Just paints the surface of the object with the color in Ia1
//
COLOR NoPattern(Object* Obj, VECTOR*)
{
  return Obj->Ia1;
}

#define PATTERNWD 2   // Width of the "checker" pattern
#define PATTERNHT 2   // Height of the "checker" pattern
```

```
/////////////////// PatternOnSurface \\\\\\\\\\\\\\\\\\\\\
//
// Paints a checker pattern on the rectangle
//
COLOR PatternOnSurface(Object* Obj, VECTOR* Q)
{
  VECTOR Offset;
  int X, Y;
  float Pos1, Pos2;
  int PatternWd, PatternHt;
  int MultX, MultY;

  // This defines the pattern to apply to the rectangle. A
  // value of 0 returns the color Ia1 and 1 returns Ia2.
  unsigned char Pattern[PATTERNHT][PATTERNWD] = {{0, 1}, {1, 0}};

  PatternWd = PATTERNWD;  PatternHt = PATTERNHT;

  // The MultX and MultY variables specify how many times the
  // pattern is repeated on the rectangle's surface. These
  // multipliers are packed in the ImageNdx variable.
  MultX = Obj->ImageNdx & 0x00FF;
  MultY = (Obj->ImageNdx >> 8) & 0x00FF;

  Obj->MapToUV(Q, Pos1, Pos2);
  X = Pos1 * PatternWd*MultX;
  Y = Pos2 * PatternHt*MultY;

  X %= (PatternWd);
  Y %= (PatternHt);

  if (Pattern[Y][X])  // The Pattern array determines
    return Obj->Ia2;  // which color to display at the
  else                // point Q
    return Obj->Ia1;
}

////////////////////////// Noise \\\\\\\\\\\\\\\\\\\\\\\\\\\
//
// Generates the texture for a cloud. If TwoD is TRUE, the function
// returns a texture value good for rendering two-dimensional, planar
// clouds. Otherwise, Noise returns a texture value that is also varied
// within the Z direction.
//
float Noise(VECTOR *Q, float TS1, float TS2, float *MaxTO,
  unsigned char TwoD)
{
  int i, n;
```

```
float FXi, FYi, Ci, PXi, PYi;
float T0, T1, T2, T;

FYi = 1.0;
FXi = TS1 * FYi;
Ci = 1.0;
n = 4;
// Increase T0 to make clouds thicker. A value of .25 produces
// thick clouds and .1 is good for thinner ones.
T0 = TS2;

T1 = 0.0;
T2 = 0.0;
PXi = 1.5708 * sin(0.5 * FYi * Q->y);
PYi = 1.5708 * sin(0.5 * FXi * Q->x);
if (!TwoD) {
  PXi += sin(FXi * Q->z / 2) * 3.1415927;
  PYi += sin(FXi * Q->z / 2) * 3.1415927;
}

T2 += Ci * sin(FYi * Q->y + PYi) + T0;
PYi = 1.5708 * sin(FXi * Q->x);
PXi = 1.5708 * sin(FYi * Q->y);
if (!TwoD) {
  PXi += sin(FXi * Q->z / 2) * 3.1415927;
  PYi += sin(FXi * Q->z / 2) * 3.1415927;
}
FXi *= 2.0;
FYi *= 2.0;
Ci *= 0.707;
for (i=2; i<=n; i++) {
  T1 += Ci * sin(FXi * Q->x + PXi) + T0;
  T2 += Ci * sin(FYi * Q->y + PYi) + T0;
  PYi = 1.5708 * sin(FXi * Q->x);
  PXi = 1.5708 * sin(FYi * Q->y);
  if (!TwoD) {
    PXi += sin(FXi * Q->z / 2) * 3.1415927;
    PYi += sin(FXi * Q->z / 2) * 3.1415927;
  }
  FXi *= 2.0;
  FYi *= 2.0;
  Ci *= 0.707;
}

if (fabs(T1*T2) > *MaxT0) {
  *MaxT0 = fabs(T1*T2);
  T = fabs(T1 * T2) / *MaxT0 / 0.75;
}
```

```
      else
        T = fabs(T1 * T2) / *MaxT0;

      if (T > 1.0) T = 1.0;
      else if (T < 0) T = 0;

      return T;
    }


//////////////////////// TwoDCloudPattern  \\\\\\\\\\\\\\\\\\\\\\\\
//
// Returns the color to be used for a cloud
//
COLOR TwoDCloudPattern(Object* ObjPtr, VECTOR* Q)
{
    COLOR Color;
    float k, kx, ky, T;

    RectangleObj *Obj = (RectangleObj *)ObjPtr;

    T = Noise(Q, Obj->T0, Obj->T1, &Obj->MaxT0, TRUE);

    Color.r = 1 - T;
    Color.g = 1 - T;
    Color.b = 1 - T;

    Color.r = Obj->Ia1.r + (Obj->Ia2.r - Obj->Ia1.r) * T;
    Color.g = Obj->Ia1.g + (Obj->Ia2.g - Obj->Ia1.g) * T;
    Color.b = Obj->Ia1.b + (Obj->Ia2.b - Obj->Ia1.b) * T;

    return Color;
}


//////////////////////// ThreeDCloudPattern  \\\\\\\\\\\\\\\\\\\\\\\\
//
// Returns the color to be used for a cloud
//
COLOR ThreeDCloudPattern(Object* ObjPtr, VECTOR* Q)
{
    COLOR Color;
    float k, kx, ky, T;

    EllipsoidObj *Obj = (EllipsoidObj *)ObjPtr;

    if (Obj->MaxT0 == 0) {
        // Calculate where the center of the ellipse appears
        // on the sceen. This location is used to fade out
        // the edges of the cloud. This assumes that the object
        // is an ellipse. This calculation is only made the first
```

```
   // time that DetermineCloudPattern is called. Calls after
   // this encounter a nonzero value for MaxT0.
   WorldToScreen(Obj->Loc, Obj->V1.x, Obj->V1.y);
}


T = Noise(Q, Obj->V1.z, Obj->V2.z, &Obj->MaxT0);

kx = (x-Obj->V1.x) * (x-Obj->V1.x);
if (kx > Obj->V2.x)
  Obj->V2.x = kx;

ky = (y-Obj->V1.y) * (y-Obj->V1.y);
if (ky > Obj->V2.y)
  Obj->V2.y = ky * .96;

kx /= Obj->V2.x;
ky /= Obj->V2.y;

k = (kx + ky);

if (k < 0) k = 0;
  else if (k > 1) k = 1;

Obj->kt = k;    // Modulate the transparency
T /= 2;

Color.r = 1 - T;
Color.g = 1 - T;
Color.b = 1 - T;

// If the color is too dark, make the cloud transparent there
if (T < .5 && Obj->kt < T * 2) Obj->kt = T * 2;

  return Color;
}

///////////////////////  Rectangle::MapToUV  \\\\\\\\\\\\\\\\\\\\\\\\\
//
// Maps a point on a rectangle to a parametric space
//
void RectangleObj::MapToUV(VECTOR* Q, float& U, float& V)
{
  VECTOR Offset;

  // Calculate the vector that extends from the location of the
  // object to the intersection point
  Offset = Subtract(Q, &Loc);

  U = Dot(&Offset, &V1);
```

```
  V = Dot(&Offset, &V2);
  U /= Len1;
  V /= Len2;
}


/////////////////////////// Sphere::MapToUV  \\\\\\\\\\\\\\\\\\\\\\\\
//
// Maps a point on a sphere to a parametric space
//
void SphereObj::MapToUV(VECTOR* Q, float& U, float& V)
{
  float Lat, Long, Temp;
  VECTOR N;
  VECTOR PCrossE;
  VECTOR Pole = {0,0,1};
  VECTOR Equator = {1,0,0};

  ComputeNormal(Q, &N);

  Lat = acos(-Dot(&N, &Pole));
  V = Lat * 0.318;            // Latitude divided by pi

  Temp = Dot(&Equator,&N) / sin(Lat);
  if (Temp > 1) Temp = 1; else if (Temp < -1) Temp = -1;
  Long = acos(Temp) * 0.1592;  // Divided by 2 * pi
  PCrossE = Cross(&Pole,&Equator);
  if (Dot(&PCrossE,&N) > 0) U = Long;
    else U = 1 - Long;
}


/////////////////////////// Cylinder::MapToUV  \\\\\\\\\\\\\\\\\\\\\\\\
//
// Maps a point on a cylinder to a parametric space
//
void CylinderObj::MapToUV(VECTOR* Q, float& U, float& V)
{
  VECTOR C, Pt;

  C = V1;
  Normalize(&C);
  VECTOR Tmp = Subtract(Q, &Loc);
  V = Dot(&Tmp, &C) / Dot(&C, &V1);
  U = (Q->x - Loc.x) / Radius;

  // Watch for roundoff error where values are correct but just
  // over the bounds of the arccosine function
  if (U > 1) U = 1; else if (U < -1) U = -1;
  U = acos(U) * 0.15916;    // Divide by 2 * Pi
```

```
  if (U > 1.0) U = 1.0; else if (U < 0.0) U = 0.0;
  if (Q->y - Loc.y < 0)
    U = 1 - U;
  if (V > 1.0) V = 1.0; else if (V < 0.0) V = 0.0;
  V = 1 - V;
}

/////////////////////////// MapImage \\\\\\\\\\\\\\\\\\\\\\\\\\
//
// Maps an image onto an object
//
COLOR MapImage(Object* Obj, VECTOR* Q)
{
  float U, V;
  long X, Y;
  int PatternWd, PatternHt;
  COLOR C;

  Obj->MapToUV(Q, U, V);

  PatternWd = Images[Obj->ImageNdx].ImWd;
  PatternHt = Images[Obj->ImageNdx].ImHt;

  // Calculate the pixel in the image that corresponds to the
  // point (U,V) on the object's surface
  X = U * PatternWd;
  Y = V * PatternHt;
  Y *= PatternWd;
  Y += X;

  if (Images[Obj->ImageNdx].ImType == RGBIMAGE) {
    C.r = Images[Obj->ImageNdx].Image[Y*3L] / 255.0;
    C.g = Images[Obj->ImageNdx].Image[Y*3L+1] / 255.0;
    C.b = Images[Obj->ImageNdx].Image[Y*3L+2] / 255.0;
  }
  else {     // Grayscale image
    C.r = Images[Obj->ImageNdx].Image[Y] / 255.0;
    C.g = Images[Obj->ImageNdx].Image[Y] / 255.0;
    C.b = Images[Obj->ImageNdx].Image[Y] / 255.0;
  }
  return C; // Return the color value
}

/////////////////////////// Blend \\\\\\\\\\\\\\\\\\\\\\\\\\\\\
//
// Gradually blends the two colors Ia1 and Ia2 together.
// This function is good for the sky background.
//
COLOR Blend(Object* Obj, VECTOR* Q)
```

```
{
  VECTOR Offset;
  float U, V;
  COLOR C;

  Obj->MapToUV(Q, U, V);

  // Adjust the blend ratio by the location of the horizon. The
  // horizon occurs where the two colors are blended equally.
  // Set the HorizonOffset to 0 so that the colors blend equally
  // in the rectangle. If HorizonOffset is greater than 0 (but
  // less than or equal to 1), the horizon is in the top
  // portion of the rectangle. If HorizonOffset is negative,
  // the horizon is placed in the lower portion of the rectangle.

  V = V - .5 * HorizonOffset;

  if (V > 1) V = 1;
    else if (V < 0) V = 0;

  C.r = Obj->Ia1.r + (Obj->Ia2.r - Obj->Ia1.r) * V;
  C.g = Obj->Ia1.g + (Obj->Ia2.g - Obj->Ia1.g) * V;
  C.b = Obj->Ia1.b + (Obj->Ia2.b - Obj->Ia1.b) * V;

  return C;
}

////////////////////// SetObjectTexture \\\\\\\\\\\\\\\\\\\\\\\
//
// Sets the object's texture to the settings specified
//
void SetObjectTexture(int ObjId, int PatternType, int Ndx)
{
  Object *Obj;

  Obj = Objects[ObjId];
  Obj->ImageNdx = Ndx;
  switch (PatternType) {
    case IMAGEPATTERN:
      Obj->DeterminePattern = MapImage;
      break;
    case CHECKERPATTERN:
      Obj->DeterminePattern = PatternOnSurface;
      break;
    case CLOUDPATTERN:
      if (Obj->Shape == ELLIPSOID)
        Obj->DeterminePattern = ThreeDCloudPattern;
      else if (Obj->Shape == RECTANGLE)
```

```
      Obj->DeterminePattern = TwoDCloudPattern;
    break;
  case MARBLEPATTERN:
    if (Obj->Shape == RECTANGLE)
      Obj->DeterminePattern = TwoDCloudPattern;
    break;
  case BLENDPATTERN:
    Obj->DeterminePattern = Blend;
    break;
  }
}


/////////////////////////// MaxOf  \\\\\\\\\\\\\\\\\\\\\\\\\\\
//
// Returns the maximum of four floating point values
//
float MaxOf(float V1, float V2, float V3, float V4)
{
  if (V1 > V2) {
    if (V1 > V3) {
      if (V1 > V4)
        return V1;
      else
        return V4;
    }
    else {  // V3 > V1  and V1 > V2
      if (V3 > V4)
        return V3;
      else
        return V4;
    }
  }
  else {    // V2 > V1
    if (V2 > V3) {
      if (V2 > V4)
        return V2;
      else
        return V4;
    }
    else { // V3 > V2  and V2 > V1
      if (V3 > V4)
        return V3;
      else
        return V4;
    }
  }
}
```

```
/////////////////////////// MinOf \\\\\\\\\\\\\\\\\\\\\\\\\\\
//
// Returns the minimum of four floating point values
//
float MinOf(float V1, float V2, float V3, float V4)
{
  if (V1 < V2) {
    if (V1 < V3) {
      if (V1 < V4)
        return V1;
      else
        return V4;
    }
    else {  // V3 < V1  and V1 < V2
      if (V3 < V4)
        return V3;
      else
        return V4;
    }
  }
  else {     // V2 < V1
    if (V2 < V3) {
      if (V2 < V4)
        return V2;
      else
        return V4;
    }
    else {  // V3 < V2  and V2 < V1
      if (V3 < V4)
        return V3;
      else
        return V4;
    }
  }
}
```

• LIGHTS.H

```
// LIGHTS.H: Header file for LIGHTS.CPP.

#ifndef LIGHTSH
#define LIGHTSH

#include "vector.h"
#include "ray.h"

class PointLight {
public:
```

```
  VECTOR LFw;          // Location of light in world coordinates
  COLOR Color;         // r, g, and b intensities of light
  PointLight(VECTOR* Loc, COLOR* I) {
    LFw = *Loc;
    Color = *I;
  }
  float W(float CosTheta, float K);
  virtual float LightFactor(VECTOR*) { return 1.0; }
};

class DirectedLight : public PointLight {
public:
  int DirectPow;
  VECTOR Direction;    // Direction of light source. Not
                       // used by point light sources.
  DirectedLight(VECTOR* Loc, COLOR* I) : PointLight(Loc, I) {
    // The smaller the number (0 or greater), the more widespread
    // a cone or directed light source's light will be
    DirectPow = 10;    // Default to power of 10
    // By default, directed and cone light sources are
    // pointed toward the at point. The at point must already
    // be defined.
    Direction = Subtract(&At, Loc);
    Normalize(&Direction);
  }
  void SetLightDirection(VECTOR *D);
  virtual float LightFactor(VECTOR* L) {
    float CosBeta = -Dot(L, &Direction);
    if (CosBeta > 0)
      return pow(CosBeta, DirectPow);
    return 0.0;
  }
};

class ConeLight : public DirectedLight {
public:
  float CosGamma;      // cosine of half the cone's angle
  ConeLight(VECTOR* Loc, COLOR* I) : DirectedLight(Loc, I) {
    CosGamma = .9397; // Default to 20 degrees
  }
  virtual float LightFactor(VECTOR* L) {
    float CosBeta = -Dot(L, &Direction);
    if (CosBeta > 0 && CosBeta <= CosGamma)
      return pow(CosBeta, DirectPow);
    return 0.0;
  }
  void SetConeLightAngle(float Angle);
};
```

```
extern PointLight* Lights[MAXLIGHTS];
extern int NumLights;

extern float LMin, LMax; // Minimum and maximum dimming scales
extern float DMin;       // Colors closer than this won't be dimmed
extern float DMax;       // Colors will be dimmed past this point

float ScaleLight(float PointToLight);
void InitializeLights(PointLight* Lights[]);
int AddLight(PointLight* L);
void RemoveLights();
#endif
```

• LIGHTS.CPP

```
// LIGHTS.CPP: Provides point, directed, and cone light sources for
// the RAY program.

#include <math.h>
#include "lights.h"

//////////////////////////// ScaleLight \\\\\\\\\\\\\\\\\\\\\\\\\\\
//
// Calculates the distance of the specified point to the eye in
// terms of a lighting constant. At farthest distance (DMax),
// the function returns LMax, which cuts out all light.
//
float ScaleLight(float PointToLight)
{
  float LightScale = (LMax - LMin) * (PointToLight - DMin) /
    (DMax - DMin) + LMin;
  if (LightScale < LMin) return LMin;
  else if (LightScale > LMax) return LMax;
  else return LightScale;
}


//////////////////////////// W \\\\\\\\\\\\\\\\\\\\\\\\\\\\\\\\\\\\
//
// Calculates the w value for the specular light using the
// function:
//                      w = (1 - K) * CosTheta
float PointLight::W(float CosTheta, float K)
{
  return 1- K * CosTheta;
}
```

```
//////////////////////// SetConeLightAngle \\\\\\\\\\\\\\\\\\\\\\
//
// Sets the angle of the specified light to Angle degrees.
// This function only has affect on cone light sources.
//
void ConeLight::SetConeLightAngle(float Angle)
{
  CosGamma = cos(Angle * 0.01745);
}


//////////////////////// SetLightDirection \\\\\\\\\\\\\\\\\\\\\\\
//
// Sets the direction of the specified light to the coordinate
// indicated. This function only affects cone or directed light
// sources.
//
void DirectedLight::SetLightDirection(VECTOR *D)
{
  Direction = Subtract(D, &LFw);
  Normalize(&Direction);
}


//////////////////////////// RemoveLights \\\\\\\\\\\\\\\\\\\\\\\\
//
// Frees all the light sources
//
void RemoveLights()
{
  int i;

  for (i=0; i<NumLights; i++)
    delete Lights[i];
}


//////////////////////////// AddLight \\\\\\\\\\\\\\\\\\\\\\\\\\\\
//
// Adds a light source to the list of light sources
//
int AddLight(PointLight* L)
{
  if (NumLights >= MAXLIGHTS) return -1;

  Lights[NumLights] = L;
  NumLights++;
  return NumLights-1;
}
```

Creating a World

R ay tracing requires a lot of experimentation. It's not uncommon to spend hours tweaking lighting parameters, adjusting the vantage point, relocating objects, and tinkering with the ray tracer's other numerous parameters. An interactive environment that enables you to modify these parameters would be ideal. However, implementing a ray tracer this way would require a tremendous amount of work and force us to restrict ourselves to either DOS or Windows.

Therefore we'll take a different approach. We'll place the ray tracing parameters in text files that you can edit with a text editor and the RAY program can read. The files contain all the information the ray tracer needs to render an image. We'll call these files *scene description files*.

The first part of this chapter introduces the scene description language and presents a parser that reads and processes these files. Then, we'll outline how you can get the RAY program up and running. The last part of this chapter presents several scene files and takes you through the steps of creating your own.

Realize we'll leave some parts of the RAY program to subsequent chapters. Our focus here is on the scene files and getting the RAY program running.

THE SCENE DESCRIPTION LANGUAGE

The scene description files contain a series of commands that list the objects in the scene and how they are viewed. The scene description language does not adhere to any industry standard, but rather was designed to be easy to use and simple to build. Most of the ray tracing parameters have corresponding keywords in the language that enable you to control the ray tracing process. For

Table 4.1 The scene description language.

Keyword	Description
Ambient	Specifies the ambient lighting constant
AntiAliasing	Enables antialiasing
At	Defines the location of the at point
Background	Specifies the color of the background
BeginGroup	Defines the beginning of a group of bounded objects
Blend	Maps two blended colors to an object's surface
Checker	Applies a checker pattern to the current object
Cloud	Maps a cloud texture onto an ellipsoid
Color	Specifies the red, green, and blue components of a color
Color2	Specifies the second color used in a checker pattern
Cone	Creates a cone light source
Cylinder	Creates a cylinder object
Diffuse	Specifies the diffuse lighting constant
Dir	Defines the direction of a cone or directed light source
Directed	Creates a directed light source
DMin	Distance where light intensity is at its maximum
DMax	Distance where light intensity is at its minimum
Ellipsoid	Creates an ellipsoid object
EndGroup	Specifies the end of a group of bounded objects
FogColor	Specifies the color of the fog
FogMax	Distance where fog is at its maximum
FogMin	Distance where fog takes affect
From	Defines the location of the from point
Include	Adds the specified scene description file to the current file
Light	Creates a light source
LMin	Minimum strength of light

instance, the language includes the *From* keyword that sets the from point of the viewer and a *Sphere* keyword that creates a spherical object.

Typically, a scene description file contains two sets of information. The first part defines the viewing parameters, such as the from point, at point, image resolution, and background color. The second part of the file lists the objects in the scene.

Table 4.1 lists the keywords supported in the scene description language. Note that the keywords in the language are not case sensitive, therefore the command "*From*" is equivalent to "*from*" and "*FROM.*"

All of the commands are followed by a set of parentheses, just like functions in C and C++. Parameters are placed inside the parentheses and are separated by commas. For instance, the command that enables antialiasing does not take any parameters, therefore its syntax is:

Table 4.1 The scene description language (*continued*).

Keyword	Description
LMax	Maximum strength of light
Loc	Specifies the location of a light source or object
Map	Maps the specified image to the current object
Marble	Applies a marble pattern to a surface
MaxLevel	Specifies the number of levels that reflected rays are traced
Mode	Sets the video mode in DOS
NumFrames	The number of frames to render in an animation sequence
PathFrom	Defines the starting point of an animation sequence
PathTo	Defines the ending point of an animation sequence
Point	Creates a point light source
Radius	Specifies the radius of a sphere or cylinder
Rectangle	Creates a rectangle object
Resolution	Sets the pixel resolution of the image
SaveTo	Saves the ray traced image to the specified file
SpecSpread	Controls the size of a specular highlight
SpreadAngle	Specifies the angle of a cone light source
SpreadPower	Specifies the power drop-off of a cone light source
Specular	Defines the specular lighting constant
Sphere	Creates a sphere object
Transparency	Sets the transparency constant for an object
Triangle	Creates a triangle object
Up	Sets the direction of the up vector
V1	Specifies one of the dimensions of an object
V2	Specifies one of the dimensions of an object
Water	Applies a water texture to a rectangle

```
AntiAliasing()
```

The *From* command, on the other hand, has three parameters that specify the *x*, *y*, and *z* coordinates of the from point. The following statement, therefore, sets the from point to the world coordinate (10,25,5):

```
From(10,25,5)
```

In some cases, the parameters can include other commands. For instance, the following statement declares a sphere object centered at (4,2,1) with a radius of 3 by using the Sphere, Loc, and Radius commands:

```
Sphere(Loc(4,2,1),Radius(3))
```

The scene description language allows a fairly free format, although generally it's a good idea to place major statements on separate lines. In addition, there are no statement separators, such as periods or semicolons at the end of statements. The scene description language also supports C style comments that begin with the characters /* and end with */.

Finally, as a standard, we'll assume that all scene description files end with an SDF extension. Therefore, we'll often refer to these files as SDF files.

THE PARSER

The source file PARSER.CPP contains all the code for reading and processing scene description files. You'll find these two files listed at the end of this chapter. In the next several sections, we'll go through the details of the parser and explain how it works.

From the parser's standpoint, the basic building blocks of a scene description file are its tokens. The tokens consist of commas, parentheses, numbers, strings, and keywords. Arranged in the proper order, they form statements that the parser can process. The parser, therefore, is designed to read the tokens in an order consistent with the rules of the language.

Reading Tokens

How does PARSER.CPP read tokens? The **GetToken** routine does all the work; it reads a scene file one character at a time until it has completely read a single token. When it returns, **GetToken** returns a code representing the token it has just encountered. The codes for the tokens appear at the top of the PARSER.CPP file. For instance, if the character is a left parenthesis, the **GetToken** function returns with the **LEFTPAREN** token, as shown here:

```
else if (Ch == '(')
  return LEFTPAREN;
```

A left parenthesis, however, is a single character token. What happens if a token contains multiple characters, such as one of the keywords in the language or a string? In these cases, **GetToken** loops until it has fully read the current token. By definition, all keywords and strings begin with a letter or underscore character and are processed in the following **if** statement:

```
if (isalpha(Ch) || Ch == '_') {
  // This is part of a keyword or string
  Buffer[Ndx++] = toupper(Ch);
  while ((Ch=fgetc(fp)) != EOF &&
    (isalpha(Ch) || Ch == '_' || isdigit(Ch) || Ch == '.'))
    Buffer[Ndx++] = toupper(Ch);
  Buffer[Ndx] = '\0';
```

The **while** loop inside the **if** statement reads all characters until a non-keyword character is reached. As the characters are read, they are placed into the global **Buffer** character array. Since keywords and strings may contain only letters, underscores, digits, or periods, anything else signals the end of one. In this case, the last character read is returned to the character stream using **ungetc** and the code attempts to determine which keyword was actually encountered. This is performed by sequencing through the list of keyword strings in the **Keywords** array as shown here:

```
ungetc(Ch, fp);
// Determine which keyword was encountered
for (i=0; i<NUMKEYWORDS; i++) {
  if (stricmp(Keywords[i], Buffer) == 0) {
    return i;  // The index of the string is the token's id
  }
}
return STRING;
```

The position in the **Keywords** array corresponds to that keyword's token value. For instance, the first keyword in the **Keywords** array is *Resolution* and therefore has a token value of 0. You'll find a **#define** statement at the top of PARSER.CPP that sets the constant **RESOLUTION** to 0, as shown here:

```
#define RESOLUTION 0
```

If no keyword is found that matches the characters in **Buffer**, then **GetToken** returns the **STRING** token signaling that the value in **Buffer** contains a string. Other parts of the parser are responsible for determining what the string corresponds to.

Processing comments and numbers is also performed in **GetToken**. They operate in a similar fashion to what we've already covered, so we'll continue on with the rest of the parser.

Parsing a File

The **ReadSceneFile** function is the main entry point to the parser. You pass it the filename of the scene description file to read and process. The function, however, doesn't do much itself; it merely opens the file, calls the function **ProcessFile**, then closes the file.

The **ProcessFile** function, therefore, is the real workhorse. It loops through the file, processing one token at a time, until it reaches the end of the file, as shown here:

```
while ((Token=GetToken(fp)) != EOF) {
  switch(Token) {
```

The **switch** statement within the **while** loop selects the statements that process the token returned by **GetToken**. For instance, when the **FROM** token is encountered, the following **case** statement is executed:

```
case FROM:
  ReadTripple(fp, &From.x, &From.y, &From.z);
  break;
```

The function **ReadTripple**, included in PARSER.CPP, reads the three parameters used in the *From* command into the global **From VECTOR** variable. There is a similar **case** statement for each major keyword in the language.

Processing Parameters

The parser contains a handful of functions that process a command's parameters. The **ReadTripple** function is one example. Specifically, **ReadTripple** reads a left parenthesis, followed by three floating point values separated by commas, then a right parenthesis. **ReadTripple** loads the floating point values that it reads into the parameters passed to it. In the case of the **UP** token, for instance, the components of the **Up** vector, which is globally defined in RAY.CPP, are loaded by this **ReadTripple** routine:

```
case UP:
  ReadTripple(fp, &Up.x, &Up.y, &Up.z);
  break;
```

In addition to **ReadTripple**, the parser includes functions that read a variety of other parameters. The **ReadInt** function, for instance, reads a single integer parameter. Similarly, the **ReadIntPair** function reads a pair of integers.

Handling Nested Commands

Some commands, such as those that create objects and light sources, use other commands as their parameters. These nested commands set the location, size, and color of the figure or light. The **ReadObjectTerms** function reads and processes these nested parameters one parameter at a time, until an outer, right parenthesis is reached.

The order of the nested commands is not important. For instance, when declaring a Rectangle object, you can list the *Color* command before specifying the rectangle's location. In addition, many of the parameters have default settings and, therefore, are not required. You can, for example, leave out the *Color* command for an object. What color would the object use then? The parser will default to the last setting in the file or the parser's default value.

Realize that the parser uses several temporary variables while reading in values from the file. For instance, when a location vector is read, its value is placed in the **Loc** variable. Later, the value in **Loc** is assigned to the proper object in the function **SetObjectParams**. Similarly, lighting parameters that are read from the file are assigned to the proper light object in the function **SetLightParams**. Both of these functions are called after all of the parameters for an object or light are read from the file.

CREATING AN OBJECT

Let's look at how the parser creates an object. When an object token is encountered inside the **ProcessFile** function, the parser calls **ReadObjectTerms** to read the object's parameters. Once the parameters are read, the object is allocated and its pointer is passed to the function **AppendObject**. The following statements, for instance, are executed when a triangle object is to be created:

```
case TRIANGLEOBJ:
  Token = GetToken(fp);
  if (Token == LEFTPAREN) {
    Code = ReadObjectTerms(fp, ANIMATEOBJLOC);
    if ((Obj = new TriangleObj(&Loc, &V1, &V2)) == NULL)
      return -1;
    AppendObject(Obj);
    if (Code == 2)
      Animate[NumObjToAnimate-1].Ndx = ObjId;
  }
  break;
```

The **AppendObject** function does most of the work. It places the new object in the **Objects** array, sets the object's parameters to those read by **ReadObjectTerms**, and updates the grouping arrays.

How is an object defined in a scene description file? The following list illustrates how to declare the dimensions of each type of object:

```
Rectangle(Loc(0,0,0),V1(4,0,0),V2(0,4,0))
Triangle(Loc(0,0,0),V1(4,0,0),V2(0,4,0))
Sphere(Loc(0,0,0),Radius(4))
Ellipsoid(Loc(2,10,35),V1(4,4,8),V2(50,0,0))
Cylinder(Loc(-4,0,-2),V1(0,0,3.75),Radius(1.5))
```

We'll give a more complete example later.

GROUPING OBJECTS

Recall that the ray tracer supports grouping of objects to improve its performance. A group of objects begins whenever the *BeginGroup* keyword is encountered and ends with the *EndGroup* statement. Groupings can be nested, therefore you can have *BeginGroup* statements inside other *BeginGroup-EndGroup* blocks.

Because of this, the parser must keep track of where it is in the current object hierarchy being built. This is the purpose of the **PrevList** and **GroupList** arrays in PARSER.CPP.

The **PrevList** array keeps track of the last object that was added within the current group of objects. It ensures that the correct **Sibling** pointers will be set when a new object is created. Similarly, the **GroupList** array keeps track of which object to assign a new group to. The **GroupNdx** indexes both of the **PrevList** and **GroupList** arrays. The parser increments **GroupNdx** each time a *BeginGroup* statement is encountered and decrements it when an *EndGroup* statement is encountered. This ensures that all objects will be set to the right group.

A part of allocating an object is setting the object's **Sibling** and **Group** fields. Remember, these fields point to the next object in the current group and any subgroups, respectively. Assigning these fields is complicated by the nesting that can occur. That's why the parser uses the **GroupList** and **PrevList** arrays. The fields are assigned to the proper object index when **AddObject** is called (within **AppendObject**) to append the new object to the ray tracer's **Objects** array.

Handling Parser Errors

The parser presented here is not very sophisticated. About the best that can be said for it is that it is functional. For instance, it doesn't handle files with invalid syntax very well. Most of the time, statements with an error will simply be ignored. Therefore, an object command with an improper location vector won't appear at all in a scene.

The parser is kept simple here to save code space. After all, this book is about graphics, not parsers. If you plan on extensively using the ray tracer, you'll probably want to begin by shoring up the parser's code. A simple extension is to keep track of what line the parser is on in the file and write an error to a file if one occurs.

Using the Scene Description Language

Earlier in this chapter, Table 4.1 listed the commands in the scene description language. Now we'll see how to put them to use. A scene description file has two basic components. It begins with the display and viewing settings. These set such things as the resolution of the display, the from point, the light sources, and so on. The second part of the file contains the objects in the scene. The following sections discuss each of these parts of the scene description file.

Setting the Display Parameters

You can use the *Mode* command to select the display's graphics mode and resolution when running under DOS. The *Mode* command does not have any affect in Windows and accepts a single byte parameter that encodes the graphics mode to use. It also specifies whether the image should be rendered in color or with a grayscale palette. The encodings are the same as those that are included in the GRPHICS.H file. For example, to select the 640x480x256 mode, you must set the *Mode* command's parameter to 4, as shown here:

```
Mode(4)
```

By default, the display mode uses a grayscale palette in DOS. To render a color image, you must set the most significant bit of the mode to a 1. This is equivalent to ORing the graphics mode with the value 128. In this case, the Mode command would be:

```
Mode(132)
```

You also must specify the resolution of the image using the *Resolution* command. It takes as its parameters the number of columns in the image followed by its number of rows. For instance, to create an image that is 320x200 in size, you must use the command:

```
Resolution(320,200)
```

Setting the Viewing Parameters

You set the viewing parameters using the *From*, *At*, and *Up* commands. You must place these before any of the lights listed in the file since some of them refer to their values. All three commands take three floating point values as parameters. For instance, if the viewer is at the world coordinate (10,10,10), the up vector is (0,0,1), and the viewer is looking at the origin, then the following commands set up these conditions:

```
From(10,10,10)
At(0,0,0)
Up(0,0,1)
```

In addition to these settings, you'll usually want to place the *Background* command along with these statements. The *Background* command sets the image's background color. For example, the following statement sets the background color to red:

```
Background(1,0,0)
```

You may also want to enable antialiasing in the image. By default, it is disabled. To do this you must use the statement:

```
AntiAliasing()
```

Specifying Lights

The *Light* command adds a single light to the list of light sources in the scene. The number of parameters that it requires depends on the type of light source you specify. Generally, you'll always want to use the *Loc* and *Color* commands to set the location and color of each light source you define. In addition, you must specify the light source's type. For instance, to specify a red, point light source located at (100,10,0), you only need these three parameters:

```
Light(Loc(100,10,0),Point(),Color(1,0,0))
```

You can create a directed light source by replacing the *Point* command with the *Directed* statement. In this case, you must also include the *Dir* command to specify where the light source is aimed toward. The following statement, for example, creates a red directed light source that is aimed at the point (0,0,0):

```
Light(Loc(100,10,0),Directed(),Dir(0,0,0),Color(1,0,0))
```

The *Cone* command adds a cone light source to a scene. A cone light source requires two new parameters. You must also specify the angle of the cone and its power distribution using the commands *SpreadAngle* and *SpreadPower*. The *SpreadAngle* command takes a single floating point parameter that specifies the angle of the cone light source in degrees. The *SpreadPower* command takes a single integer parameter that controls the fall off rate of the light. The larger the value, the faster the light's brightness falls off. The following statement creates a 30-degree-wide cone light source:

```
Light(Loc(100,10,0),Cone(),Dir(0,0,0),SpreadAngle(15),
   SpreadPower(10),Color(1,0,0))
```

SPECIFYING OBJECTS

Objects are listed after the viewing parameters in a scene description file. The five commands supported are: *Cylinder, Ellipsoid, Rectangle, Sphere,* and *Triangle.* Each command uses a variable number of parameters, however, all of them require that you specify the object's location and size. The way that you do this depends on the type of object. For instance, all objects use the *Loc* command to set the object's location. However, the *Sphere* and *Cylinder* commands require a *Radius* parameter and the *Rectangle* and *Triangle* objects use the vector commands, *V1* and *V2*, to specify the dimensions of their figures.

Generally, you'll also want to specify the object's surface properties when you define it. These include such commands as *Color, Ambient, Diffuse, Transparency,* and so on. If you don't provide these parameters, the parser will set their values to the last ones listed in the file. These settings are undefined for the first object, however.

The following statement, for instance, creates a red, opaque triangle:

```
/* Red triangle */
Triangle(Loc(10,1,0),V1(4,0,0),V2(0,4,0),Ambient(.6),
  Diffuse(.3),Specular(.6),Transparency(0),Color(1,0,0))
```

Nesting Files

Sometimes it is useful to split up the objects displayed in a scene between several files. For instance, in a landscape scene you might have one file that contains all the plants, another that contains the contours of the ground, and a third that lists the clouds in the sky. The *Include* statement enables you to keep these files separate. The MAIN.SDF file that follows includes the two files NEST1.SDF and NEST2.SDF. The ray tracer handles these three files as if they were all in one.

```
/* MAIN.SDF: This scene file includes the two files NEST1.SDF
 * and NEST2.SDF.
 */
Include(NEST1.SDF)
Include(NEST2.SDF)

/* NEST1.SDF: Sets the viewing parameters for MAIN.SDF. */
From(10,10,10)
At(0,0,0)
Resolution(100,100)
Light(Loc(10,10,10),Point(),Color(1,1,1))

/* NEST2.SDF: Defines a single triangle. */
Triangle(Loc(10,1,0),V1(4,0,0),V2(0,4,0),Ambient(.6),
  Diffuse(.3),Specular(.6),Transparency(0),Color(1,0,0))
```

Saving an Image

Since ray tracing takes so long, you may want to save your images to disk so that you can later use or display them. To accomplish this, you must place the *SaveTo* command along with the name of the file to write to. The program saves the images to a *TIFF* file. (We'll cover the TIFF format in Chapter 11.) For example, to save the image to the file SAMPLE.TIF, you would use:

```
SaveTo(SAMPLE.TIF)
```

Notice that the name of the file is not enclosed in quotes. When the code encounters the *SaveTo* command, RAY.CPP sets the global **SaveTo** variable and copies the filename to the string **OutFilename**. The **GenImage** function is responsible for opening the file and writing to it using the following statements:

```
if (SaveTo) {
  C.r = Red;   C.g = Green;   C.b = Blue;
  fwrite(&C.r, 1, 1, OutputFile);
  fwrite(&C.g, 1, 1, OutputFile);
  fwrite(&C.b, 1, 1, OutputFile);
}
```

The **GenImage** function also closes the file when the image is complete.

COMPILING AND USING RAY

The RAY program is built from several source files that are located throughout this book. Table 3.1 (shown earlier) lists the files you'll need. Since the program is so large, you'll want to compile it in a large memory model. As with SIMPLRAY, you can compile the program for DOS or Windows. You must follow the same procedure outlined in Chapter 2 for SIMPLRAY if you want to compile RAY for Windows.

To accommodate RAY's large size and still have the ability to render scenes with thousands of objects, you may want to go with Windows. Because of Windows' memory capabilities you'll be able to render far more complex scenes in Windows than you can in DOS. You could add a DOS extender to enhance the DOS version of the program, but with the growing acceptance of Windows, it doesn't seem like the extra work is worthwhile.

How do you run RAY? The RAY program accepts the name of a scene description file as a single command-line argument. The SDF file contains the description of the scene that the program will render. If you wanted to render the file TEST.SDF, for instance with a DOS version of your program, you would enter the following command at the DOS prompt:

```
ray test.sdf
```

What about Windows? Since RAY is expecting a command-line argument, you must supply it with one somehow. If you are trying to launch the program from the Program Manager, you must select the Run menu option in the File menu. In the dialog box that appears, you must type in the name of the scene description file after the program name—much as you would in DOS. Alternatively, if you are using the Borland C++ environment for compiling and running RAY, you can enter the filename of the SDF file in the Arguments menu option in the Run menu.

SAMPLE SCENES

It's time to put the RAY program to use and try out the scene description language. In the next two sections, we'll present several SDF files that illustrate various aspects of the scene description language and the capabilities of the ray tracer. Don't forget, we'll be covering other parts of RAY in subsequent chapters, so we won't be detailing all of its features here.

THINGS ARE SHAPING UP

The SHAPES.SDF file shown here generates the image shown in Figure 4.1. The image contains an instance of each type of object that RAY supports.

```
/* SHAPES.SDF: Displays each of RAY's primary shapes. */

AntiAliasing()
Resolution(200,200)
From(33,0,3)
At(0,0,1)
Up(0.0,0.0,1.0)
Background(0,0,0)

Light(Loc(33,20,3), Point(), Color(1,1,1))
```

Figure 4.1 The image generated by SHAPES.SDF.

```
Rectangle(
  Loc(-10,-10,-5),  V1(0,20,0),  V2(20,0,0),
  Ambient(.6), Diffuse(.8), Specular(.4), SpecSpread(4),
  Transparency(0), Color(.7,.7,.7))
Cylinder(
  Loc(0,-6,0),  V1(0,0,4), Radius(4),
  Ambient(.6), Diffuse(1), Specular(.4), SpecSpread(4),
  Transparency(0), Color(.8,.8,.8))
Ellipsoid(Loc(0,-3,8), V1(4, 4, 8), V2(50, 0, 0),
  Ambient(.6), Diffuse(1), Specular(.4), SpecSpread(4),
  Transparency(0), Color(.9,.9,.9))
Triangle(
  Loc(0,1,5),  V1(0,5,0),  V2(0,5,10),
  Ambient(.8), Diffuse(.6), Specular(.3), SpecSpread(4),
  Transparency(0), Color(.9,.9,.9))
Sphere(
  Loc(0,9,1),  Radius(4),
  Ambient(.6), Diffuse(.5), Specular(.4), SpecSpread(4),
  Transparency(0), Color(.8,.8,.8))
```

GENERATING SWEPT SURFACES

Although the RAY program only supports five basic shapes, there are a great variety of objects you can render using them. All you need to do is combine the shapes to build more complex figures. Of course, creating scenes with lots of objects by hand can be quite tedious.

One painless way of creating complex scene description files is to write a program that generates them for you. In this section, we'll write a program that builds a rather complex-looking vase from only triangles.

In particular, we'll generate the vase using a technique known as *surface of revolution*. As Figure 4.2 illustrates, the idea is to generate a figure by rotating in three dimensions a two-dimensional profile of the object. As the figure's profile is rotated, you can build up a series of patches that represent the surface of the object. Specifically, the program constructs the vase out of a series of triangles. The technique can only generate symmetrical objects, but it's surprising how many objects fit this criteria.

The GENSWEEP.C program, listed at the end of this chapter, creates the GLASS.SDF file that renders the image shown in Figure 4.3. The two-dimensional profile of a glass is placed in the file GLASS.ODF. This file is listed after the GLASS.SDF file. The GENSWEEP program reads the coordinates from the GLASS.ODF file, rotates them about the y axis and outputs a series of triangular patches to GLASS.SDF. These patches make up the surface of the glass.

You can modify GLASS.ODF or create your own file to generate a variety of symmetrical shapes, such as vases, cups, cones, and so on. To run the GENSWEEP program, you must supply two command-line arguments: first the input filename, GLASS.ODF, then the output filename, GLASS.SDF.

Figure 4.2 You can generate a three-dimensional surface from a two-dimensional curve.

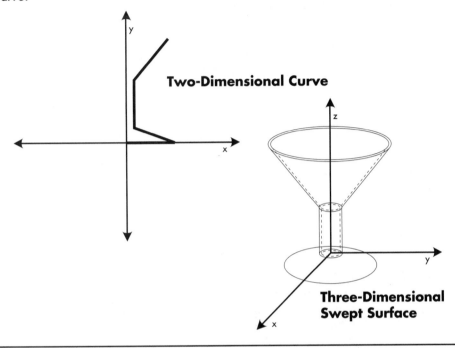

Figure 4.3 The GLASS.SDF file renders this image.

How does the GENSWEEP program work? It reads a text file that specifies the profile of the surface and generates a scene description file from it. The input file also includes a value that controls how many triangles to use to represent the final object. Actually, it specifies the rotational increment between which each triangle is generated. For instance, Figure 4.4 shows a surface swept with only four increments. The smaller the rotational increment the better the final image will appear. Of course, this will lead to many more patches.

The input file has three components. It begins with a number that specifies the number of rotational increments to use. A second integer specifies the number of coordinates in the profile's curve. After this are the x and y coordinates of the profile itself. In the following example, the lines would create the cone shown in Figure 4.5. The profile is defined as a diagonal line that is swept in 18-degree increments:

```
20
2
1 2
0 0
```

The code that generates an SDF file is contained in the **Sweep** function. It writes a series of triangular patches to the file. Currently, the object's surface properties are hard-coded into these **printf** statements. You may want to

---

Figure 4.4 Rotating a profile by 90 degrees generates a swept surface.

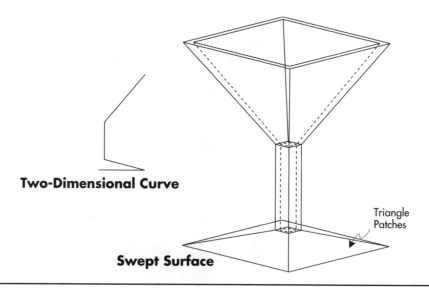

Two-Dimensional Curve

Triangle
Patches

Swept Surface

Figure 4.5 A cone created using a swept curve.

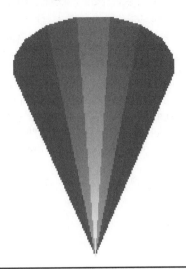

modify GENSWEEP so that the input file specifies the color and properties of the object.

To build GENSWEEP, you must compile and link the program with the vector operations in VECTOR.C. To run the program, you must supply the command line:

```
gensweep glass.odf glass.sdf
```

• GLASS.ODF

```
15
4
1.3   2
.15   1
.125 -.25
1.3  -.3
```

• PARSER.CPP

```
// PARSER.CPP: Parses a scene description file

#include <stdio.h>
#include <math.h>
#include <ctype.h>
#include <string.h>
```

```
#include <stdlib.h>
#include "ray.h"
#include "vector.h"
#include "lights.h"
#include "objects.h"

// To add a new keyword to the language:
//        1. Increment the value for the constant NUMKEYWORDS
//        2. Add the keyword to the Keywords array
//        3. Define a value for the token in the #define section
//        4. Add the code to process the keyword

#define NUMKEYWORDS 51
#define STRING -1
#define RESOLUTION 0
#define VMODE 1
#define FROM 2
#define UP 3
#define AT 4
#define LITE 5
#define RADIUS 6
#define LOC 7
#define AMBIENT 8
#define DIFFUSE 9
#define SPECULAR 10
#define SPECSPREAD 11
#define LEVELS 12
#define TRANSPARENCY 13
#define COLORVAL 14
#define SPHEREOBJ 15
#define TRIANGLEOBJ 16
#define RECTANGLEOBJ 17
#define CYLINDEROBJ 18
#define ELLIPSOIDOBJ 19
#define BLENDCOLORS 20
#define VECTOR1 21
#define VECTOR2 22
#define BACKGROUNDCOLOR 23
#define BEGINGROUPOBJ 24
#define ENDGROUPOBJ 25
#define INCLUDE 26
#define SAVETO 27
#define NUMBEROFFRAMES 28
#define STARTMOVE 29
#define ENDMOVE 30
#define ANTI_ALIASING 31
#define POINTLITE 32
#define DIRECTEDLITE 33
```

```
#define CONELITE 34
#define CONEANGLE 35
#define LIGHTFOCUS 36
#define LIGHTDIR 37
#define MAPIMAGE 38
#define CHECKERTEXTURE 39
#define WATERTEXTURE 40
#define CLOUDTEXTURE 41
#define DMINVAL 42
#define DMAXVAL 43
#define LMINVAL 44
#define LMAXVAL 45
#define CHECKERCOLOR 46
#define MARBLETEXTURE 47
#define FOGMINVAL 48
#define FOGMAXVAL 49
#define FOGCOLORVAL 50
#define LEFTPAREN 100
#define RIGHTPAREN 101
#define COMMA 102
#define NUMBER 103

#define MAXNESTEDGROUPS 10     // Maximum number of nested groups

// The keywords in the language:
char *Keywords[] = {
  "RESOLUTION", "MODE", "FROM", "UP", "AT", "LIGHT", "RADIUS",
  "LOC", "AMBIENT", "DIFFUSE", "SPECULAR", "SPECSPREAD", "MAXLEVEL",
  "TRANSPARENCY", "COLOR", "SPHERE", "TRIANGLE", "RECTANGLE",
  "CYLINDER", "ELLIPSOID", "BLEND", "V1", "V2", "BACKGROUND",
  "BEGINGROUP", "ENDGROUP", "INCLUDE", "SAVETO", "NUMFRAMES",
  "PATHFROM", "PATHTO", "ANTIALIASING", "POINT", "DIRECTED",
  "CONE", "SPREADANGLE", "SPREADPOWER", "DIR", "MAP", "CHECKER",
  "WATER", "CLOUD", "DMIN", "DMAX", "LMIN", "LMAX", "COLOR2",
  "MARBLE", "FOGMIN", "FOGMAX", "FOGCOLOR"
};

#define LITECONEANGLE 0x01
#define LITEDIRECTPOW 0x02
#define LITEDIR 0x04

char Buffer[80];
float ka, kd, ks, kt;    // The following variables are used
float Radius, T0, T1;    // to read in data from the scene
int NO;                  // description file
VECTOR Loc, V1, V2;
COLOR Ia1, Ia2;
char Filename[80];
```

```
      PointLight* Light;
      VECTOR LightDir;
      int Params;
      int CheckerMultX, CheckerMultY;
      int GroupList[MAXNESTEDGROUPS];
      int PrevList[MAXNESTEDGROUPS];
      int GroupNdx;
      unsigned char BeginGroup;
      unsigned char EllipseObj;

      // Function prototypes:
      int ReadString(FILE *fp, char *Str);
      int ReadInt(FILE *fp, int *val);
      int ReadIntPair(FILE *fp, int *val1, int *val2);
      int ReadFloatPair(FILE *fp, float *val1, float *val2);
      int ReadFloat(FILE *fp, float *val);
      int GetTripple(FILE *fp, int Type, float *val1, float *val2, float *val3);
      int ReadTripple(FILE *fp, float *val1, float *val2, float *val3);
      int ReadQuad(FILE *fp, int *t, float *val1, float *val2, float *val3);
      int ReadParenPair(FILE *fp);
      int ReadSceneFile(char *filename);
      int ReadObjectTerms(FILE *fp, int Type);
      int SetObjectParameters(int ObjId);
      int ProcessFile(FILE *fp);
      int GetToken(FILE *fp);
      void SetLightParams(int i);
      int AppendObject(Object *Obj);

      // Call this function to process a scene description file. The
      // filename variable holds the name of the file to process.
      int ReadSceneFile(char *filename)
      {
        FILE *fp;

        GroupNdx = 0;
        PrevList[GroupNdx] = -1;
        GroupList[GroupNdx] = -1;

        fp = fopen(filename, "r");    // Open the scene description file
        if (fp == NULL) {             // Failed to open file
          return 0;
        }
        ProcessFile(fp);              // Process the file
        fclose(fp);
        return 1;
      }

      // Process the scene description file
      int ProcessFile(FILE *fp)
```

```
{
  int Token, ObjId, Code, LiteId;
  Object *Obj;

  while ((Token=GetToken(fp)) != EOF) {
    switch(Token) {
      case AT:
        GetTripple(fp, ANIMATEAT, &At.x, &At.y, &At.z);
        break;
      case COMMA:
        break;
      case FROM:
        GetTripple(fp, ANIMATEFROM, &From.x, &From.y, &From.z);
        break;
      case UP:
        ReadTripple(fp, &Up.x, &Up.y, &Up.z);
        break;
      case LITE:
        Token = GetToken(fp);
        if (Token == LEFTPAREN) {
          ReadObjectTerms(fp, ANIMATELIGHTLOC);
          LiteId = AddLight(Light);
          SetLightParams(LiteId);
        }
        break;
      case LEFTPAREN:
        break;
      case VMODE:
        // Sets the display mode. Only used if the application
        // is compiled as a DOS application.
        ReadInt(fp, &VMode);
        break;
      case NUMBER:
        break;
      case LEVELS:
        ReadInt(fp, &MaxLevel);
        break;
      case RESOLUTION:
        ReadIntPair(fp, &ImWd, &ImHt);
        break;
      case BEGINGROUPOBJ:
        Token = GetToken(fp);
        if (Token == LEFTPAREN) {
          ReadObjectTerms(fp, ANIMATEOBJLOC);

          if ((Obj = new BoundingBoxObj(V1.x, V2.x,
            V1.y, V2.y, V1.z, V2.z)) == NULL)
            return -1;
          if (BeginGroup) {
```

```
        ObjId = AddObject(Obj, -1, GroupList[GroupNdx]);
        PrevList[GroupNdx] = ObjId;
        BeginGroup = 0;
      }
      else {
        ObjId = AddObject(Obj, PrevList[GroupNdx], -1);
        PrevList[GroupNdx] = ObjId;
      }
      GroupNdx++;
      PrevList[GroupNdx] = ObjId;
      GroupList[GroupNdx] = ObjId;
      BeginGroup = 1;   // Start a new group
    }
    break;
  case ENDGROUPOBJ:
    GroupNdx--;
    BeginGroup = 0;
    if (GroupNdx < 0) return -1;  // Too many ENDGROUP statements
    break;
  case SPHEREOBJ:
    Token = GetToken(fp);
    if (Token == LEFTPAREN) {
      Code = ReadObjectTerms(fp, ANIMATEOBJLOC);
      if ((Obj = new SphereObj(Loc.x, Loc.y, Loc.z, Radius)) == NULL)
        return -1;
      ObjId = AppendObject(Obj);
      if (Code == 2)
        Animate[NumObjToAnimate-1].Ndx = ObjId;
    }
    break;
  case TRIANGLEOBJ:
    Token = GetToken(fp);
    if (Token == LEFTPAREN) {
      Code = ReadObjectTerms(fp, ANIMATEOBJLOC);
      if ((Obj = new TriangleObj(&Loc, &V1, &V2)) == NULL)
        return -1;
      ObjId = AppendObject(Obj);
      if (Code == 2)
        Animate[NumObjToAnimate-1].Ndx = ObjId;
    }
    break;
  case RECTANGLEOBJ:
    EllipseObj = 0;
    Token = GetToken(fp);
    if (Token == LEFTPAREN) {
      Code = ReadObjectTerms(fp, ANIMATEOBJLOC);
      if (Params == WATERPATTERN) {
        // Water is a special case of the rectangle object
```

```
        if ((Obj = new WaterObj(&Loc, &V1, &V2)) == NULL)
          return -1;
      }
      else
        if ((Obj = new RectangleObj(&Loc, &V1, &V2)) == NULL)
          return -1;
      ObjId = AppendObject(Obj);
      if (Code == 2)
        Animate[NumObjToAnimate-1].Ndx = ObjId;
    }
    break;
  case CYLINDEROBJ:
    Token = GetToken(fp);
    if (Token == LEFTPAREN) {
      Code = ReadObjectTerms(fp, ANIMATEOBJLOC);
      if ((Obj = new CylinderObj(Loc, V1, Radius)) == NULL)
        return -1;
      ObjId = AppendObject(Obj);
      if (Code == 2)
        Animate[NumObjToAnimate-1].Ndx = ObjId;
    }
    break;
  case ELLIPSOIDOBJ:
    EllipseObj = 1;
    Token = GetToken(fp);
    if (Token == LEFTPAREN) {
      strcpy(Filename, "");
      Code = ReadObjectTerms(fp, ANIMATEOBJLOC);
      if ((Obj = new EllipsoidObj(Loc.x, Loc.y, Loc.z, V1.x,
          V1.y, V1.z, V2.x)) == NULL)
        return -1;
      ObjId = AppendObject(Obj);
      if (Code == 2)
        Animate[NumObjToAnimate-1].Ndx = ObjId;
    }
    break;
  case BACKGROUNDCOLOR:
    ReadTripple(fp, &Background.r, &Background.g, &Background.b);
    break;
  case INCLUDE:
    ReadString(fp, Filename);
    ReadSceneFile(Filename);
    break;
  case SAVETO:
    ReadString(fp, OutFilename);
    SaveTo = 1;
    break;
  case NUMBEROFFRAMES:
```

```
        ReadInt(fp, &NumFrames);
        break;
      case ANTI_ALIASING:
        Antialiasing = 1;
        ReadParenPair(fp);
        break;
      case DMINVAL:
        ReadFloat(fp, &DMin);
        break;
      case DMAXVAL:
        ReadFloat(fp, &DMax);
        break;
      case LMINVAL:
        ReadFloat(fp, &LMin);
        if (LMin < 1) LMin = TOL;   // LMin can't be less than 1
        break;
      case LMAXVAL:
        ReadFloat(fp, &LMax);
        break;
      case FOGMINVAL:
        ReadInt(fp, &FogMin);
        if (FogMin < 0) FogMin = 0;
        break;
      case FOGMAXVAL:
        ReadInt(fp, &FogMax);
        if (FogMax < 1) FogMax = 0;
        break;
      case FOGCOLORVAL:
        ReadTripple(fp, &FogColor.r, &FogColor.g, &FogColor.b);
        break;
    }
  }
  return 1;
}

// Reads a token from the file. It returns an integer code that
// indicates what the token is.
int GetToken(FILE *fp)
{
  char Ch;
  int Ndx, i;

  Ndx = 0;
  while (1) {
    Ch = fgetc(fp);
    if (Ch == '\t' || Ch == ' ' || Ch == '\n') {
      /* Skip whitespace */
      Ch = fgetc(fp);
    }
```

```
    if (Ch == EOF) {
      return EOF;
    }
    if (isalpha(Ch) || Ch == '_') {
      // This is part of a keyword
      Buffer[Ndx++] = toupper(Ch);
      while ((Ch=fgetc(fp)) != EOF &&
        (isalpha(Ch) || Ch == '_' || isdigit(Ch) || Ch == '.'))
        Buffer[Ndx++] = toupper(Ch);
      Buffer[Ndx] = '\0';
      ungetc(Ch, fp);
      // Determines which keyword was encountered
      for (i=0; i<NUMKEYWORDS; i++) {
        if (stricmp(Keywords[i], Buffer) == 0) {
          return i;  // The index of the string is the token's id
        }
      }
      return STRING;
    }
    else if (Ch == '(')
      return LEFTPAREN;
    else if (Ch == ')')
      return RIGHTPAREN;
    else if (Ch == ',')
      return COMMA;
    else if (isdigit(Ch) || Ch == '.' || Ch == '-') {
      Buffer[Ndx++] = Ch;
      while ((Ch=fgetc(fp)) != EOF && (isdigit(Ch) || Ch == '.'))
        Buffer[Ndx++] = Ch;
      Buffer[Ndx] = '\0';
      ungetc(Ch, fp);
      return NUMBER;
    }
    else if (Ch == '/') {
      // Note: Delimiting comments is done with a bit
      // of a trick. The divide sign is used to mark
      // the beginning and end of the comment.
      //
      while ((Ch=fgetc(fp)) != '/' && Ch != EOF) ;
    }
  }
}

// Append an object to the Objects array and set its parameters
int AppendObject(Object *Obj)
{
  int ObjId;
```

```
  if (BeginGroup) {
    ObjId = AddObject(Obj, -1, GroupList[GroupNdx]);
    PrevList[GroupNdx] = ObjId;
    BeginGroup = 0;
  }
  else {
    ObjId = AddObject(Obj, PrevList[GroupNdx], -1);
    PrevList[GroupNdx] = ObjId;
  }
  SetObjectParameters(ObjId);
 return ObjId;
}

// Reads a single string parameter
int ReadString(FILE *fp, char *Str)
{
  int Token;

  Token = GetToken(fp);
  if (Token == LEFTPAREN) {
    Token = GetToken(fp);
    if (Token == STRING) {
      strcpy(Str, Buffer);
      Token = GetToken(fp);
      if (Token == RIGHTPAREN)
        return 1;
    }
  }
  return 0;
}

// Reads a single integer parameter
int ReadInt(FILE *fp, int *val)
{
  int Token;

  Token = GetToken(fp);
  if (Token == LEFTPAREN) {
    Token = GetToken(fp);
    if (Token == NUMBER) {
      *val = atoi(Buffer);
      Token = GetToken(fp);
      if (Token == RIGHTPAREN)
        return 1;
    }
  }
  return 0;
}
```

```
// Reads a single floating point parameter
int ReadFloat(FILE *fp, float *val)
{
  int Token;

  Token = GetToken(fp);
  if (Token == LEFTPAREN) {
    Token = GetToken(fp);
    if (Token == NUMBER) {
      *val = atof(Buffer);
      Token = GetToken(fp);
      if (Token == RIGHTPAREN)
        return 1;
    }
  }
  return 0;
}

// If an animation sequence is read, the first values are returned
// in val1, val2, and val3.
// Returns codes:
//     0  if failure
//     >0 if success
//     2  if read an animation sequence
int GetTripple(FILE *fp, int Type, float *val1, float *val2, float *val3)
{
  int Token;
  STEP *S, *R;

  Token = GetToken(fp);
  if (Token == LEFTPAREN) {
    Token = GetToken(fp);
    if (Token == NUMBER) {
      *val1 = atof(Buffer);
      Token = GetToken(fp);
      if (Token == COMMA) {
        Token = GetToken(fp);
        if (Token == NUMBER) {
          *val2 = atof(Buffer);
          Token = GetToken(fp);
          if (Token == COMMA) {
            Token = GetToken(fp);
            if (Token == NUMBER) {
              *val3 = atof(Buffer);
              Token = GetToken(fp);
              if (Token == RIGHTPAREN)
                return 1;
            }
```

```
          }
        }
      }
    }
    else {
      ReadStep:
      if (Token == STARTMOVE) {
        // Creates a new animation step
        Animate[NumObjToAnimate].Type = Type;
        S = (struct STEP *)malloc(sizeof(struct STEP));
        if (S == NULL) return 0;
        S->Next = NULL;
        if (Animate[NumObjToAnimate].Steps == NULL) {
          // This is the first step for this "object"
          Animate[NumObjToAnimate].Steps = S;
          Animate[NumObjToAnimate].CurrStep = S;
        }
        else {
          R = Animate[NumObjToAnimate].Steps;
          while (R->Next != NULL) R = R->Next;
          R->Next = S;
        }
        ReadQuad(fp, &S->T0, &S->x0, &S->y0, &S->z0);
        // Copies the values read to the parameters
        *val1 = S->x0;
        *val2 = S->y0;
        *val3 = S->z0;
        Token = GetToken(fp);
        if (Token == COMMA) {
          Token = GetToken(fp);
          if (Token == ENDMOVE) {
            ReadQuad(fp, &S->T1, &S->x1, &S->y1, &S->z1);
            Token = GetToken(fp);
            if (Token == RIGHTPAREN) {
              NumObjToAnimate++;
              return 2;    // Return code signaling animation sequence read
            }
            else if (Token == COMMA) {
              Token = GetToken(fp);
              goto ReadStep;    // Reads the next step
            }
            else
              return 0;
          }
        }
      }
    }
  }
}
```

```
    return 0;
}

// Reads three floating point parameters
int ReadTripple(FILE *fp, float *val1, float *val2, float *val3)
{
  int Token;

  Token = GetToken(fp);
  if (Token == LEFTPAREN) {
    Token = GetToken(fp);
    if (Token == NUMBER) {
      *val1 = atof(Buffer);
      Token = GetToken(fp);
      if (Token == COMMA) {
        Token = GetToken(fp);
        if (Token == NUMBER) {
          *val2 = atof(Buffer);
          Token = GetToken(fp);
          if (Token == COMMA) {
            Token = GetToken(fp);
            if (Token == NUMBER) {
              *val3 = atof(Buffer);
              Token = GetToken(fp);
              if (Token == RIGHTPAREN)
                return 1;
            }
          }
        }
      }
    }
  }
  return 0;
}

// Reads a combination of four parameters
int ReadQuad(FILE *fp, int *t, float *val1, float *val2, float *val3)
{
  int Token;

  Token = GetToken(fp);
  if (Token == LEFTPAREN) {
    Token = GetToken(fp);
    if (Token == NUMBER) {
      *t = atoi(Buffer);
      Token = GetToken(fp);
      if (Token == COMMA) {
        Token = GetToken(fp);
```

```
            if (Token == NUMBER) {
              *val1 = atof(Buffer);
              Token = GetToken(fp);
              if (Token == COMMA) {
                Token = GetToken(fp);
                if (Token == NUMBER) {
                  *val2 = atof(Buffer);
                  Token = GetToken(fp);
                  if (Token == COMMA) {
                    Token = GetToken(fp);
                    if (Token == NUMBER) {
                      *val3 = atof(Buffer);
                      Token = GetToken(fp);
                      if (Token == RIGHTPAREN)
                        return 1;
                    }
                  }
                }
              }
            }
          }
        }
      }
    }
  }
  return 0;
}

// Reads two integer parameters
int ReadIntPair(FILE *fp, int *val1, int *val2)
{
  int Token;

  Token = GetToken(fp);
  if (Token == LEFTPAREN) {
    Token = GetToken(fp);
    if (Token == NUMBER) {
      *val1 = atoi(Buffer);
      Token = GetToken(fp);
      if (Token == COMMA) {
        Token = GetToken(fp);
        if (Token == NUMBER) {
          *val2 = atoi(Buffer);
          Token = GetToken(fp);
          if (Token == RIGHTPAREN)
            return 1;
        }
      }
    }
  }
}
```

```
    return 0;
}

// Reads two floating point parameters
int ReadFloatPair(FILE *fp, float *val1, float *val2)
{
  int Token;

  Token = GetToken(fp);
  if (Token == LEFTPAREN) {
    Token = GetToken(fp);
    if (Token == NUMBER) {
      *val1 = atof(Buffer);
      Token = GetToken(fp);
      if (Token == COMMA) {
        Token = GetToken(fp);
        if (Token == NUMBER) {
          *val2 = atof(Buffer);
          Token = GetToken(fp);
          if (Token == RIGHTPAREN)
            return 1;
        }
      }
    }
  }
  return 0;
}

// Reads two parentheses with no parameters
int ReadParenPair(FILE *fp)
{
  int Token;

  Token = GetToken(fp);
  if (Token == LEFTPAREN) {
    Token = GetToken(fp);
    if (Token == RIGHTPAREN) {
      return 1;
    }
  }
  return 0;
}

// Reads the terms that are in an object's parameter list
int ReadObjectTerms(FILE *fp, int Type)
{
  int Token, Code=1;
```

```
Params = 0;
strcpy(Filename, "");

while ((Token=GetToken(fp)) != EOF) {
  switch(Token) {
    case RIGHTPAREN:
      return Code;     // Done. Return the success code
    case COMMA:
      break;
    case LOC:
      Code = GetTripple(fp, Type, &Loc.x, &Loc.y, &Loc.z);
      break;
    case RADIUS:
      ReadFloat(fp, &Radius);
      break;
    case AMBIENT:
      ReadFloat(fp, &ka);
      break;
    case DIFFUSE:
      ReadFloat(fp, &kd);
      break;
    case SPECULAR:
      ReadFloat(fp, &ks);
      break;
    case SPECSPREAD:
      ReadInt(fp, &NO);
      break;
    case TRANSPARENCY:
      ReadFloat(fp, &kt);
      break;
    case COLORVAL:
      ReadTripple(fp, &Ia1.r, &Ia1.g, &Ia1.b);
      break;
    case CHECKERCOLOR:
      ReadTripple(fp, &Ia2.r, &Ia2.g, &Ia2.b);
      break;
    case VECTOR1:
      ReadTripple(fp, &V1.x, &V1.y, &V1.z);
      break;
    case VECTOR2:
      ReadTripple(fp, &V2.x, &V2.y, &V2.z);
      break;
    case POINTLITE:
      ReadParenPair(fp);
      Light = new PointLight(&Loc, &Ia1);
      break;
    case DIRECTEDLITE:
      ReadParenPair(fp);
      Light = new DirectedLight(&Loc, &Ia1);
```

```
          break;
      case CONELITE:
        ReadParenPair(fp);
        Light = new ConeLight(&Loc, &Ia1);
        break;
      case CONEANGLE:
        ReadFloat(fp, &((ConeLight *)Light)->CosGamma);
        Params |= LITECONEANGLE;
        break;
      case LIGHTDIR:
        ReadTripple(fp, &LightDir.x, &LightDir.y, &LightDir.z);
        Params |= LITEDIR;
        break;
      case LIGHTFOCUS:
        ReadInt(fp, &((DirectedLight *)Light)->DirectPow);
        Params |= LITEDIRECTPOW;
        break;
      case BLENDCOLORS:
        ReadFloat(fp, &HorizonOffset);
        Params |= BLENDPATTERN;
        break;
      case MAPIMAGE:
        ReadString(fp, Filename);
        Params |= IMAGEPATTERN;
        break;
      case CHECKERTEXTURE:
        ReadIntPair(fp, &CheckerMultX, &CheckerMultY);
        Params |= CHECKERPATTERN;
        break;
      case WATERTEXTURE:
        ReadFloatPair(fp, &T0, T1);
        Params |= WATERPATTERN;
        break;
      case CLOUDTEXTURE:
        ReadFloatPair(fp, &T0, &T1);
        Params |= CLOUDPATTERN;
        break;
      case MARBLETEXTURE:
        ReadParenPair(fp);
        Params |= MARBLEPATTERN;
        break;
    }
  }
  return Code;
}


// Sets the parameters for a new object
int SetObjectParameters(int ObjId)
```

```
{
  int Id;

  Objects[ObjId]->ka = ka;
  Objects[ObjId]->kd = kd;
  Objects[ObjId]->ks = ks;
  Objects[ObjId]->NO = NO;
  Objects[ObjId]->kt = kt;
  Objects[ObjId]->Ia1.r = Ia1.r;
  Objects[ObjId]->Ia1.g = Ia1.g;
  Objects[ObjId]->Ia1.b = Ia1.b;
  Objects[ObjId]->Ia2.r = Ia2.r;
  Objects[ObjId]->Ia2.g = Ia2.g;
  Objects[ObjId]->Ia2.b = Ia2.b;

  if (Params & IMAGEPATTERN) {
    Id = AddImage(Filename);
    if (Id >= 0) {
      SetObjectTexture(ObjId, IMAGEPATTERN, Id);
      return 1;
    }
    else
      return -1;
  }
  else if (Params & CHECKERPATTERN) {
    CheckerMultX |= (CheckerMultY << 8);
    SetObjectTexture(ObjId, CHECKERPATTERN, CheckerMultX);
  }
  else if (Params & WATERPATTERN) {
    ((WaterObj *)Objects[ObjId])->Ht = T0;
    ((WaterObj *)Objects[ObjId])->Rough = T1;
  }
  else if (Params & CLOUDPATTERN) {
    SetObjectTexture(ObjId, CLOUDPATTERN, Id);
    if (EllipseObj) {
      ((EllipsoidObj *)Objects[ObjId])->V1.z = T0;
      ((EllipsoidObj *)Objects[ObjId])->V2.z = T1;
    }
    else {
      ((RectangleObj *)Objects[ObjId])->T0 = T0;
      ((RectangleObj *)Objects[ObjId])->T1 = T1;
    }
  }
  else if (Params & MARBLEPATTERN) {
    SetObjectTexture(ObjId, MARBLEPATTERN, Id);
    ((RectangleObj *)Objects[ObjId])->T1 = .2;
    ((RectangleObj *)Objects[ObjId])->T0 = .1;
  }
```

```
    else if (Params & BLENDPATTERN) {
      SetObjectTexture(ObjId, BLENDPATTERN, Id);
    }
    return 1;
}

// Sets the parameters for a new light object
void SetLightParams(int i)
{
  if (Params & LITEDIRECTPOW) {
    ((DirectedLight *)Lights[i])->DirectPow =
      ((DirectedLight *)Light)->DirectPow;
  }
  if (Params & LITECONEANGLE) {
    ((ConeLight *)Lights[i])->SetConeLightAngle(
      ((ConeLight *)Light)->CosGamma);
  }
  if (Params & LITEDIR)
    ((DirectedLight *)Lights[i])->SetLightDirection(&LightDir);
}
```

• GENSWEEP.C

```
// GENSWEEP.C: Creates a three-dimensional surface of revolution
// from a two-dimensional curve. To run the program, enter at the
// DOS prompt:
//        gensweep <infile.odf> <outfile.sdf>
// where:
//        infile.odf is the filename of the object description file
//        outfile.sdf is the filename of the scene description file

#include <stdio.h>
#include <stdlib.h>
#include <string.h>
#include <math.h>
#include "vector.h"

#define MAXNAME 80
#define MAXPOINTS 20

struct POINT {
  float x, y;
};

char Outfile[MAXNAME];
char Infile[MAXNAME];
int NumPoints, NumRotInc;
struct POINT Points[MAXPOINTS];
FILE *Infp, *Outfp;
```

```c
void Usage();
void Sweep(FILE *Outfp, int np, struct POINT p[], int nrot);
int ReadPoints(FILE *fp, int *NumPoints, int *NumRotInc,
               struct POINT Points[]);

int main(int argc, char *argv[])
{
  if (argc != 3)    // Did the user enter enough arguments?
    Usage();
  else {
    strcpy(Infile, argv[1]);    // Copies the filenames to the
    strcpy(Outfile, argv[2]);   // correct variables
  }

  printf("argv[0]=%s argv[1]=%s  argv[2]=%s\n",
    argv[0],  argv[1],  argv[2]);
  Infp = fopen(Infile, "r");    // Opens the object description file
  if (Infp == NULL) {
    printf("Could not open the input file: %s.\n", Infile);
    exit(1);
  }
  Outfp = fopen(Outfile, "w"); // Opens the scene description file
  if (Outfp == NULL) {
    printf("Could not open the output file: %s.\n", Outfile);
    exit(1);
  }

  fprintf(Outfp, "/* %s: Sweep generated from %s. */\n\n",
    Outfile, Infile);
  fprintf(Outfp, "Resolution(128,128)\n");
  fprintf(Outfp, "From(3,3,1)\n");
  fprintf(Outfp, "At(0,0,1)\n");
  fprintf(Outfp, "Up(0.0,0.0,1.0)\n");
  fprintf(Outfp, "Background(.2,.2,.2)\n");
  fprintf(Outfp, "Light(Loc(10,7,4), Point(), Color(1,1,1))\n");

  ReadPoints(Infp, &NumPoints, &NumRotInc, Points);

  Sweep(Outfp, NumPoints, Points, NumRotInc);

  fclose(Outfp);
  fclose(Infp);
  return 0;
}


// When the user has entered the wrong number of command-line
// arguments, this function is called to print the correct
// usage and exit the program.
void Usage()
```

```
{
  printf("Usage: gensweep <infile.odf> <outfile.sdf>\n");
  printf("where:\n");
  printf("\tinfile.odf is the filename of the object description file\n");
  printf("\toutfile.sdf is the filename of the scene description file\n");
  exit(1);
}

// Reads the points for the curve
int ReadPoints(FILE *fp, int *NumPoints, int *NumRotInc,
               struct POINT Points[])
{
  int i;

  fscanf(fp, "%d", NumRotInc);
  fscanf(fp, "%d", NumPoints);
  for (i=0; i<*NumPoints; i++)
    fscanf(fp, "%f %f", &Points[i].x, &Points[i].y);
  return 1;
}


// Generates a surface of revolution for the points p about.
// the y axis
void Sweep(FILE *Outfp, int np, struct POINT p[], int nrot)
{
  int i, last, start, rot;
  float radinc;
  VECTOR Loc, P1, P2, P3;
  VECTOR V1, V2;

  p[np].x = p[0].x;  p[np].y = p[0].y;
  if (p[0].x == 0)
    start = 1;
  else start = 0;
  if (p[np-1].x == 0)  // If last point is zero, don't calculate it yet
    last = np - 2;
  else
    last = np - 1;
  radinc = 2 * 3.1416 / nrot;
  for (rot=0; rot<nrot; rot++) {    // Calculate all inner vertices
    for (i=start; i<last; i++) {
      Loc.x = p[i].x * cos(rot*radinc);
      Loc.y = -p[i].x * sin(rot*radinc);
      Loc.z = p[i].y;

      P1.x = p[i+1].x * cos(rot*radinc);
      P1.y = -p[i+1].x * sin(rot*radinc);
      P1.z = p[i+1].y;
```

```
        P2.x = p[i+1].x * cos((rot+1)*radinc);
        P2.y = -p[i+1].x * sin((rot+1)*radinc);
        P2.z = p[i+1].y;

        P3.x = p[i].x * cos((rot+1)*radinc);
        P3.y = -p[i].x * sin((rot+1)*radinc);
        P3.z = p[i].y;

        V1 = Subtract(&P1, &Loc);
        V2 = Subtract(&P2, &Loc);

        fprintf(Outfp,
"TRIANGLE(Loc(%3.5f,%3.5f,%3.5f),V1(%3.5f,%3.5f,%3.5f),\
V2(%3.5f,%3.5f,%3.5f),\n", Loc.x, Loc.y, Loc.z,
        V1.x, V1.y, V1.z, V2.x, V2.y, V2.z);
        fprintf(Outfp,"Ambient(.45), Diffuse(.9), Specular(.6),
                SpecSpread(4),\n");
        fprintf(Outfp,"Transparency(0), Color(.047,.38,.84))\n");

        V1 = Subtract(&P3, &Loc);
        fprintf(Outfp,
"TRIANGLE(Loc(%3.5f,%3.5f,%3.5f),V1(%3.5f,%3.5f,%3.5f),\
V2(%3.5f,%3.5f,%3.5f),\n", Loc.x, Loc.y, Loc.z,
        V2.x, V2.y, V2.z, V1.x, V1.y, V1.z);
        fprintf(Outfp,"Ambient(.45), Diffuse(.9), Specular(.6),
                SpecSpread(4),\n");
        fprintf(Outfp,"Transparency(0), Color(.047,.38,.84))\n");
      }
    }

  if (p[0].x == 0) {     // Test to see if top is pointed
    for (i=0; i<nrot; i++) {
      Loc.x = p[1].x * cos(i*radinc);
      Loc.y = -p[1].x * sin(i*radinc);
      Loc.z = p[1].y;
      V1.x = -Loc.x;     // Add offset if not sweeping around z axis
      V1.y = -Loc.y;
      V1.z = p[0].y - Loc.z;
      V2.x = p[1].x * cos((i+1)*radinc);
      V2.y = -p[1].x * sin((i+1)*radinc);
      V2.z = p[1].y;
      V2 = Subtract(&V2, &Loc);
fprintf(Outfp,
"TRIANGLE(Loc(%3.5f,%3.5f,%3.5f),V1(%3.5f,%3.5f,%3.5f),\
V2(%3.5f,%3.5f,%3.5f),\n", Loc.x, Loc.y, Loc.z,
        V1.x, V1.y, V1.z, V2.x, V2.y, V2.z);
        fprintf(Outfp,"Ambient(.45), Diffuse(.9), Specular(.6),
                SpecSpread(4),\n");
```

```
        fprintf(Outfp,"Transparency(0), Color(.047,.38,.84))\n");
      }
    }
    if (p[np-1].x == 0) {
      for (i=0; i<nrot; i++) {
        Loc.x = p[np-2].x * cos(i*radinc);
        Loc.y = -p[np-2].x * sin(i*radinc);
        Loc.z = p[np-2].y;
        V1.x = p[np-2].x * cos((i+1)*radinc);
        V1.y = -p[np-2].x * sin((i+1)*radinc);
        V1.z = p[np-2].y;
        V1 = Subtract(&V1, &Loc);
        V2.x = -Loc.x;     // Add offset if not sweeping around z axis
        V2.y = -Loc.y;
        V2.z = p[np-1].y - Loc.z;
fprintf(Outfp,
"TRIANGLE(Loc(%3.5f,%3.5f,%3.5f),V1(%3.5f,%3.5f,%3.5f),\
V2(%3.5f,%3.5f,%3.5f),\n", Loc.x, Loc.y, Loc.z,
        V1.x, V1.y, V1.z, V2.x, V2.y, V2.z);
        fprintf(Outfp,"Ambient(.45), Diffuse(.9), Specular(.6),
                SpecSpread(4),\n");
        fprintf(Outfp,"Transparency(0), Color(.047,.38,.84))\n");
      }
    }
}
```

5

Textures and Patterns

You now have all the basic components to build a wide variety of complex shapes. However, it takes more than just the right shape to make an object appear realistic. In fact, it's often the subtleties that can really make the difference. The right lighting parameters, for instance, can have a major impact on the quality of a rendering. One other way to enhance the appearance of objects is to add a texture or pattern to them. This makes sense, since almost all objects have some type of texture. In this chapter, you'll learn the secrets of some of the most commonly used texturing and patterning techniques.

We'll begin by exploring how RAY is able to render objects with a simple checker pattern. Then we'll discuss a more general technique that can map a complete image onto the surface of an object. The last pattern mapping technique we'll discuss paints a gradual blending of colors onto an object's surface.

In all, we have three important goals. First, we'll reveal how RAY implements its texturing features. Second, we'll discuss how to add a pattern to an object using RAY's scene description language. And third, we'll put these techniques to work and develop an impressive ray traced scene complete with patterned and textured objects.

RENDERING A PATTERN

We could build textured objects out of stacks of smaller objects. However, the ray tracer would then have an explosion of objects to manage. And since a ray tracer's performance decreases with additional objects, this is not the best way to go.

A better technique—and the one we'll discuss in this chapter—is to paint the texture right onto the surface of the object. Although this technique might seem limiting, you'll be surprised at the wide variety of textures you can simulate with it.

In general, we'll take a two-dimensional pattern, such as that shown in Figure 5.1, and map it to the surface of an object. Therefore, if the two-dimensional pattern is a checker pattern, the object will have a checker pattern on it. A variation of this technique is to base the object's color on a mathematical formula. This latter technique is sometimes referred to as a *procedural texture*, since a function defines how the texture is applied. This is in fact what we'll use to render objects with gradual shading.

Setting the Texture

The texture that an object displays depends on the function that the **DeterminePattern** field in the **Object** class is pointing to. Recall that **DeterminePattern** is a function pointer.

When the object is being rendered, the routine pointed to by **DeterminePattern** is invoked from within RAY's **Intensity** function to determine what basic color to use for each point on the object's surface. Here's the somewhat complicated looking call that performs this step:

```
ObjColor =
  (*Objects[Index]->DeterminePattern)(Objects[Index], &Q);
```

The color returned by **DeterminePattern** and saved in **ObjColor** is passed to **ComputeLight** and used in the lighting model to render the point **Q** on the object.

Figure 5.1 Mapping a pattern onto an object.

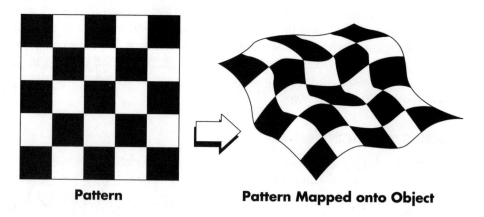

Pattern   **Pattern Mapped onto Object**

By default, **DeterminePattern** points to a function that always returns the same color value for all points on the object's surface. As a result, the object is painted with one color. In this chapter, you'll learn how to use other types of **DeterminePattern** functions that are able to paint object's with various patterns.

Mapping onto Three-Dimensional Objects

Wrapping a two-dimensional pattern around a three-dimensional surface requires a bit of finesse. To solve the problem, we'll introduce a coordinate system that blankets each object, as illustrated in Figure 5.2. We'll call this the (U,V) coordinate system. The (U,V) coordinate system is useful because each of its coordinates correspond to coordinates of the two-dimensional pattern.

The mapping process begins by determining what (U,V) coordinate a surface point falls on. This effectively gives us a two-dimensional coordinate for the surface point. The next step is to determine what point in the pattern corresponds to the (U,V) coordinate. The color for this location in the pattern is returned and used in the lighting model.

Of course, the (U,V) coordinate system is different for each object. Therefore, each object defines its own function to convert a three-dimensional surface point into the (U,V) coordinate space. This is the purpose of the **MapToUV** virtual function in the **Object** class. Generally, it's overridden for each type of object to provide its own coordinate mapping. We'll get back to the **MapToUV** functions in a bit.

Figure 5.2 The (U,V) coordinate system is used to map patterns to a three-dimensional surface.

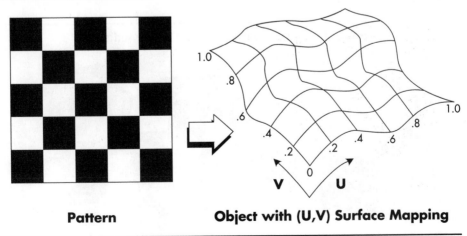

Pattern　　　　**Object with (U,V) Surface Mapping**

RENDERING A CHECKER PATTERN

The **PatternOnSurface** function in OBJECTS.CPP generates a checker pattern. Therefore, when you assign it to an object's **DeterminePattern** pointer, the object will appear with a checker pattern.

Internally, **PatternOnSurface** defines a two-dimensional checker pattern that is mapped to the surface of the object. The pattern is defined in the **Pattern** array as

```
unsigned char Pattern[PATTERNHT][PATTERNWD] = {{0, 1}, {1, 0}};
```

A value of 0 indicates that the object's **Ia1** color should be used on the object and a value of 1 tells the ray tracer to use the object's **Ia2** color. Since the 1s and 0s alternate in **Pattern**, the checker design is created. Of course, the checkering only appears if the colors in **Ia1** and **Ia2** are different.

If the **Pattern** array were applied directly to an object, the object would only have a 2-by-2 pattern on it. To make the checker pattern more flexible, the **PatternOnSurface** function can repeat the **Pattern** array any number of times in the U and V directions, as illustrated in Figure 5.3.

The number of times the checker sequence is repeated depends on the value packed into the **ImageNdx** field of the **Object** class. The lower byte of **ImageNdx** specifies how many times to repeat the checker pattern in the U direction. The upper byte specifies how many times to repeat the pattern in the V direction. (The **ImageNdx** name doesn't make much sense here because it's also used in another texturing function.) The code places these two multipliers in the variables **MultX** and **MultY**, as shown here:

```
MultX = Obj->ImageNdx & 0x00FF;
MultY = (Obj->ImageNdx >> 8) & 0x00FF;
```

Figure 5.3 A small checker pattern is repeated over a surface.

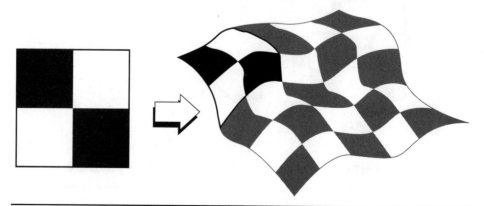

The **ImageNdx** variable is set in the parser when it encounters a command that selects a checker pattern.

Mapping the Checker Pattern

The goal of **PatternOnSurface** is to determine what point in the **Pattern** array corresponds to the point **Q** passed into the function. The point **Q** is the three-dimensional point on the object's surface being rendered. The first step, therefore, is to convert the three-dimensional point **Q** to the object's (U,V) coordinate system. This is accomplished by calling the object's **MapToUV** routine. The U and V coordinates, which range between 0 and 1, are returned in the parameters **Pos1** and **Pos2**, as shown here:

```
Obj->MapToUV(Q, Pos1, Pos2);
```

The next step is to convert the two coordinates to **X** and **Y** indexes in the **Pattern** array:

```
X = Pos1 * PatternWd*MultX;
Y = Pos2 * PatternHt*MultY;

X %= PatternWd;
Y %= PatternHt;
```

The last step in **PatternOnSurface** is to return the proper color for the checker pattern:

```
if (Pattern[Y][X])   // The Pattern array determines
  return Obj->Ia2;   // which color to display at the
else                 // point Q
  return Obj->Ia1;
```

Realize that the size of the blocks in the checker pattern depends on the size of the object and the multipliers used. A 2-by-2 checker pattern, for instance, will appear smaller on a smaller object.

RENDERING NON-CHECKER PATTERNS

The **PatternOnSurface** function is currently designed to map a checker pattern onto a surface. However, you can easily modify it to render other types of patterns. To do so, you must modify the **Pattern** array and its dimensions specified by **PATTERNHT** and **PATTERNWD**. This **Pattern** array, for example, defines the pattern shown in Figure 5.4:

```
#define PATTERNWD 6
#define PATTERNHT 6
```

```
unsigned char Pattern[PATTERNHT][PATTERNWD] = {
  {0, 0, 0, 0, 0, 0}, {0, 1, 0, 1, 0, 1}, {0, 1, 0, 1, 0, 0},
  {0, 1, 1, 1, 0, 1}, {0, 1, 0, 1, 0, 1}, {0, 1, 0, 1, 0, 1}};
```

Mapping to Planar Objects

The **MapToUV** function in the **Object** class is an important part of mapping a pattern to an object. It's responsible for converting a three-dimensional point on an object to an object-based, two-dimensional coordinate system. The next several sections describe specific implementations of **MapToUV** for each object type in RAY.

Mapping to a Rectangle

Converting a three-dimensional point on a rectangle into a (U,V) parametric space is fairly straightforward. Specifically, the **MapToUV** function in the **RectangleObj** class converts the point **Q** to parameters **U** and **V** that range between 0 and 1.

The first step is to determine the position of the point **Q** relative to the rectangle's origin, which is located at **Loc**, as shown here:

```
Offset = Subtract(Q, &Loc);
```

Next, the code determines in relative terms where the **Offset** vector points to within the object. This process is illustrated in Figure 5.5 and is calculated by the statements

```
U = Dot(&Offset, &V1) / Len1;
V = Dot(&Offset, &V2) / Len2;
```

The **Len1** and **Len2** variables ensure that the **U** and **V** values will fall between 0 and 1. The values of **Len1** and **Len2** are precomputed in **RectangleObj**'s constructor.

Figure 5.4 A non-checker pattern rendered by the PatternOnSurface function.

Figure 5.5 Converting a point Q to the parametric (U,V) space on a rectangle.

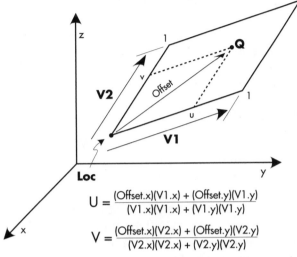

$$U = \frac{(Offset.x)(V1.x) + (Offset.y)(V1.y)}{(V1.x)(V1.x) + (V1.y)(V1.y)}$$

$$V = \frac{(Offset.x)(V2.x) + (Offset.y)(V2.y)}{(V2.x)(V2.x) + (V2.y)(V2.y)}$$

Technically, mapping a pattern to a triangle requires a different process. However, to keep things simple, a triangle object inherits a rectangle object's **MapToUV** function. As a result, only half of the pattern will appear on the triangle, as shown in Figure 5.6. In most cases, though, this is not a problem.

Figure 5.6 The (U,V) mapping of a triangle.

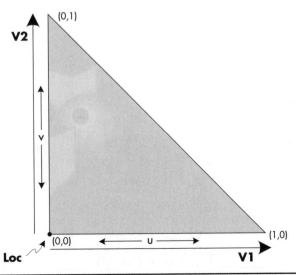

Mapping to a Sphere and Ellipse

At first, the thought of mapping a rectangular pattern onto a sphere seems like an unsolvable brain teaser. However, it is possible. The parametric mapping is shown in Figure 5.7. The orientation of the mapping depends on the directions of the **Pole** and **Equator** vectors, which are defined in **MapToUV** as the two unit vectors

```
VECTOR Pole = {0,0,1};
VECTOR Equator = {1,0,0};
```

In other words, these two vectors mean that the V axis will be aligned with the z axis and that the origin of the equator is located at the x axis. You can modify these two vectors to orient the pattern differently. This could be useful, for instance, if you want to spin the pattern around the sphere.

The **V** coordinate is calculated first in **MapToUV**. The idea is to compare the angle between the normal at **Q** and the **Pole** vector, as Figure 5.8 illustrates.

Mathematically, this comes down to computing the angle in radians between the normal at point **Q** and the pole of the sphere, then dividing it by pi. Here are the statements that make these calculations:

```
ComputeNormal(Q, &N);

Lat = acos(-Dot(&N,&Pole));
V = Lat * 0.318;          // Latitude divided by pi
```

Figure 5.7 Parametric mapping of a sphere.

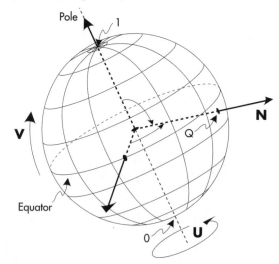

Figure 5.8 The value of V depends on the angle between the normal and pole.

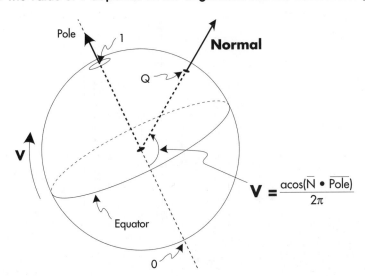

Computing the value of **U** is a little more complicated, but the idea is similar. The code determines where the point **Q** lies with respect to the equator's origin. This value is then scaled by 2 times and its sign is set so that **U** always ranges between 0 and 1, as shown here:

```
Temp = Dot(&Equator,&N) / sin(Lat);
if (Temp > 1) Temp = 1; else if (Temp < -1) Temp = -1;
Long = acos(Temp) * 0.1592;  // Divided by 2 * pi
PCrossE = Cross(&Pole,&Equator);
if (Dot(&PCrossE,&N) > 0) U = Long;
   else U = 1 - Long;
```

Mapping to a Cylinder

The parametric (U,V) mapping for cylinders is shown in Figure 5.9. The **V** coordinate is simply the relative angle between the vectors stretching from **Loc** to the points **Q** and **V1**, as shown here:

```
C = V1;
Normalize(&C);
VECTOR Tmp = Subtract(Q,&Loc);
V = Dot(&Tmp,&C) / Dot(&C,&V1);
```

Figure 5.9 Parametric mapping for a cylinder.

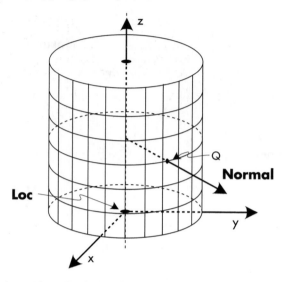

The **U** variable is based on the angle between the location of point **Q** and the x axis. As with spheres, the angle is also divided by 2 times   so that its magnitude is between 0 and 1:

```
U = (Q->x - Loc.x) / Radius;

// Watch for roundoff error where values are correct but just
// over the bounds of the arccosine function
if (U > 1) U = 1; else if (U < -1) U = -1;
U = acos(U) * 0.15916;    // Divide by 2 * pi
```

Realize that this code only handles the case of a vertical cylinder. You must modify the calculations for **U** if you want to support cylinders of any angle.

DEFINING A CHECKER PATTERN

The ray tracer paints a checker pattern on an object when the *Checker* command is listed along with the object's other commands. The *Checker* command has two parameters. The first specifies how many times to repeat the basic 2-by-2 checker pattern in the object's U direction. The second parameter specifies the repetition factor in the V direction. Therefore, to add a 4-by-4 checker pattern to an object, you'd add *Checker(2,2)* to the object's list of parameters.

Figure 5.10 Two rectangles with a checker pattern.

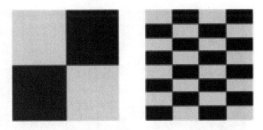

The *Color* and *Color2* commands define the two colors in the checker pattern. To create a red and white checker pattern, for instance, you could use the statements *Color(1,0,0)* and *Color2(1,1,1)*.

Here's a more complete example. The following statements create the two rectangles shown in Figure 5.10. The first statement renders the rectangle on the left with a 2-by-2 checker pattern. The second statement creates the rectangle on the right. Notice that its *Checker* statement sets the multipliers to 2 and 4, creating a 4-by-8 pattern.

```
Rectangle(Loc(0,-6,0),V1(4,0,0),V2(0,4,0),
  Checker(1,1),Color(0,0,0),Color2(1,1,1),
  Ambient(.8),Diffuse(.2),Specular(.1))
Rectangle(Loc(0,6,0),V1(4,0,0),V2(0,4,0),
  Checker(2,4),Color(0,0,0),Color2(1,1,1),
  Ambient(.8),Diffuse(.2),Specular(.1))
```

MAPPING IMAGES

Now let's extend the idea of mapping a pattern to that of mapping a complete image. This technique can be quite powerful because you can map a picture of any texture you want right onto an object's surface. You can create a wooden floor, for instance, by simply mapping an image of a wooden floor onto a rectangle. This can be a lot easier than trying to represent the wood grain mathematically.

The RAY program enables you to map an image onto any of its objects. Of course, the image may appear different on different shapes, as shown in Figure 5.11.

The **MapImage** function supports the image mapping feature. When assigned to the **DeterminePattern** function pointer in an object, the object will appear with an image mapped to its surface.

Figure 5.11 The same image mapped to different objects.

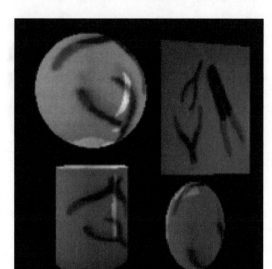

As with all the texturing functions, the **MapImage** routine takes two parameters. The first specifies the object being rendered and the second a point on the object. The function returns the color to plot for the point passed to **MapImage**.

Managing Images

Before we get any further into the details of **MapImage**, we have a few loose ends to cover. We need some way of managing the images that the **MapImage** function is going to use. We could place all the information about the image to map within the **Object** class. However, a slightly better approach is to introduce a second structure that holds this information. This will also make it easier to share an image between multiple objects.

The RAY.H file defines the **IMAGE** structure in order to hold the necessary information to process an image. It contains the name of the image file, its width and height, a flag that specifies whether it's a grayscale or RGB image, and a pointer to the image itself, as shown here:

```
struct IMAGE {
    char Filename[13];         // Image's filename
    int ImWd, ImHt;            // Pixel width and height of image
    unsigned char ImType;      // Type of image: RGB or grayscale
    unsigned char huge *Image; // Pointer to image data
};
```

The ray tracer defines an array of these **IMAGE** structures to hold the information about the images in the scene:

```
IMAGE Images[MAXIMAGES];
int NumImages;
```

The **NumImages** variable keeps track of the number of images in the **Images** array.

The parser is responsible for adding image information to the **Images** array. If an object is supposed to have an image associated with it, the parser adds the information about the image to **Images** and increments the **NumImages** variable. In addition, the object's **ImageNdx** field in the **Object** class is assigned to the index location in **Images** where the information is placed. This arrangement is shown in Figure 5.12 for a set of three objects. The first two objects have images associated with them and the third one does not. As you'll see in the next section, the **MapImage** function extracts this information as the image is mapped to the object.

From Point to Pixel

The first step in **MapImage** is to call the object's **MapToUV** function to convert the three-dimensional surface point that is passed to it to the two-dimensional (U,V) parametric space:

```
Obj->MapToUV(Q, U, V);
```

Figure 5.12 The Images array keeps track of images mapped to objects.

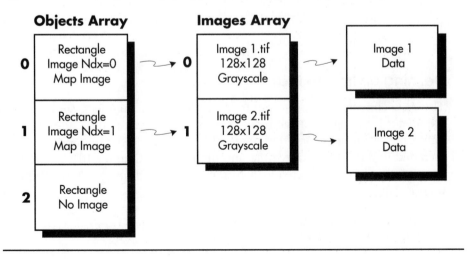

In preparation for rendering the image, the code also retrieves the image's width and height from the **Images** array:

```
PatternWd = Images[Obj->ImageNdx].ImWd;
PatternHt = Images[Obj->ImageNdx].ImHt;
```

Next, the function determines which image pixel corresponds to the (U,V) coordinates calculated earlier:

```
X = U * PatternWd;
Y = V * PatternHt;
```

Remember, the **U** and **V** values range between 0 and 1. Therefore, this calculation places **X** and **Y** somewhere between 0 and **PatternWd** and **PatternHt**, respectively.

The last step is to return the image's color at pixel (X,Y). Although images are always stored in single dimension arrays, the code handles grayscale and RGB images differently because of their different organization. Grayscale images have only one byte per pixel. Color images, however, have three bytes per pixel arranged in red, green, and blue order. In both cases, the byte values are divided by 255 so that the colors are scaled between 0 and 1, as shown here:

```
if (Images[Obj->ImageNdx].ImType == RGBIMAGE) {
  C.r = Images[Obj->ImageNdx].Image[Y*3L] / 255.0;
  C.g = Images[Obj->ImageNdx].Image[Y*3L+1] / 255.0;
  C.b = Images[Obj->ImageNdx].Image[Y*3L+2] / 255.0;
}
else {     // Grayscale image
  C.r = Images[Obj->ImageNdx].Image[Y] / 255.0;
  C.g = Images[Obj->ImageNdx].Image[Y] / 255.0;
  C.b = Images[Obj->ImageNdx].Image[Y] / 255.0;
}
return C; // Return the color value
```

Defining an Image Map

The *Map* command tells the ray tracer to map an image to a surface. Its sole parameter is the name of the image file to use. Currently, the code only allows grayscale or 24-bit color TIFF image files. (The code for reading TIFF files is included in the TIFF.C source file and discussed in Chapter 10.) The following statement, for instance, creates a rectangle with the image TEST.TIF mapped onto its surface:

```
Rectangle(Loc(0,0,0), V1(1,0,0), V2(0,1,0), Ambient(1),
  Diffuse(.1), Specular(.1), Map(TEST.TIF))
```

Notice that the *Color* command is not necessary, since the object's color comes from the image.

Blended Colors

The **Blend** function is a variation on the mapping functions we've discussed earlier. It gradually blends two colors together as shown in Figure 5.13. This pattern is particularly good for rendering the sky behind a landscape scene, although there are other uses, too.

The **Blend** function does not use a pattern array to define the blending. Instead, **Blend** interpolates between two colors, based on their position on the object's surface. You can control the mixing of the colors using the **HorizonOffset** variable. By default, **HorizonOffset** is set to 0, which has the effect of placing a horizon (where the two colors blend equally) at the middle of the object. You can control the location of the horizon by changing **HorizonOffset**, as illustrated in Figure 5.14.

The object's **Ia1** and **Ia2** fields contain the colors that are blended together. The combination of these two colors depends on the parametric **V** coordinate of the point being rendered, as shown here:

```
C.r = Obj->Ia1.r + (Obj->Ia2.r - Obj->Ia1.r) * V;
C.g = Obj->Ia1.g + (Obj->Ia2.g - Obj->Ia1.g) * V;
C.b = Obj->Ia1.b + (Obj->Ia2.b - Obj->Ia1.b) * V;
```

Figure 5.13 A rectangle with two blended colors.

Figure 5.14 HorizonOffset sets the location of the horizon.

-1 < HorizonOffset < 0
Places Horizon in the
Upper Portion of the Object

HorizonOffset = 0
Places Horizon at the
Center of the Object

0 < HorizonOffset < 1
Places Horizon in the
Lower Portion of the Object

HorizonOffset = 1

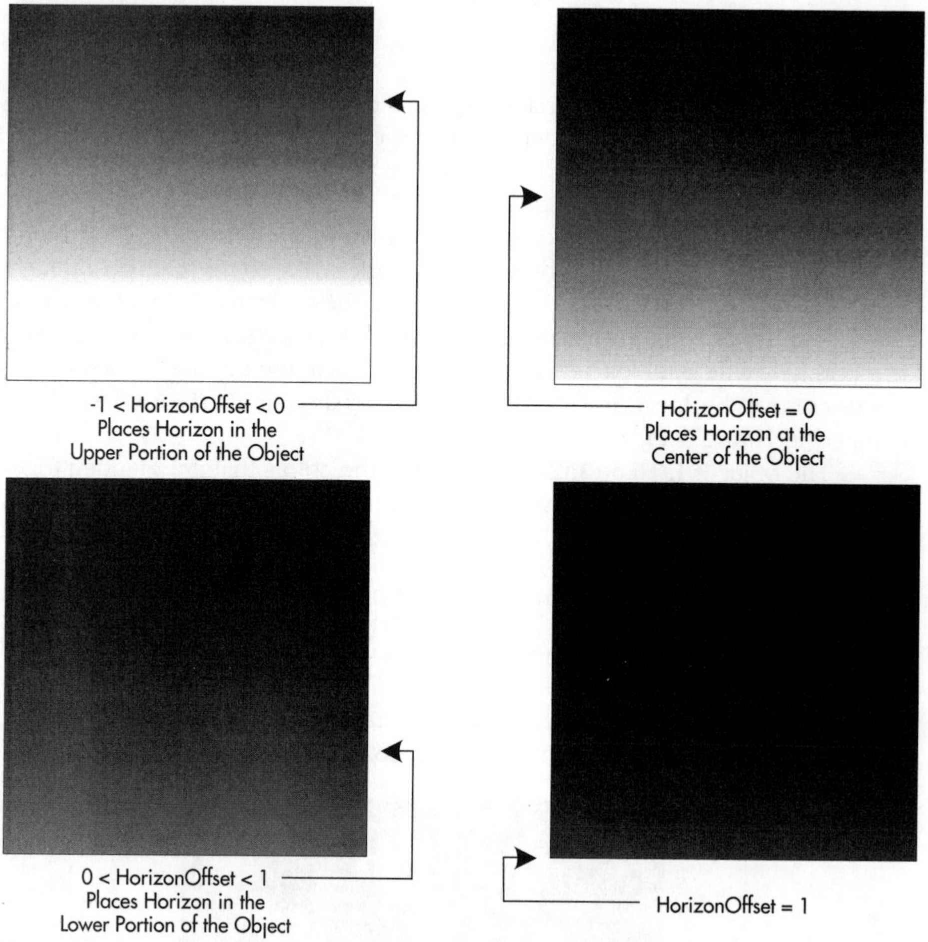

As these statements dictate, the color returned by **Blend** is completely **Ia1** when **V** equals 0 and is completely **Ia2** when **V** equals 1. The color falls somewhere in between when **V** is between 0 and 1.

The scene description language includes the *Blend* command to enable the blending function. The colors that it uses are set by the *Color* and *Color2* commands. The location of the horizon is passed as a parameter to the *Blend* command, as outlined earlier. The following statements, for example, created the three rectangular patches shown in Figure 5.14:

```
Rectangle(
   Loc(0,-21,21),  V1(0,20,0),  V2(0,0,-20),
   Ambient(1), Diffuse(.3), Specular(.3), SpecSpread(4),
   Transparency(0), Color(0,0,0), Color2(0,0,1), Blend(-.5))
Rectangle(
   Loc(0,1,21),  V1(0,20,0),  V2(0,0,-20),
   Ambient(.7), Diffuse(.3), Specular(.3), SpecSpread(4),
   Transparency(0), Color(0,0,0), Color2(0,0,1), Blend(0))
Rectangle(
   Loc(0,-21,-1),  V1(0,20,0),  V2(0,0,-20),
   Ambient(.7), Diffuse(.3), Specular(.3), SpecSpread(4),
   Transparency(0), Color(0,0,0), Color2(0,0,1),  Blend(.5))
Rectangle(
   Loc(0,1,-1),  V1(0,20,0),  V2(0,0,-20),
   Ambient(.7), Diffuse(.3), Specular(.3), SpecSpread(4),
   Transparency(0), Color(0,0,0), Color2(0,0,1),  Blend(1))
```

A Textured Scene

It's time to put these texturing techniques to work. In this section, we'll develop a kitchen scene that contains a variety of objects and patterns. The image we'll create is shown in Color Plate 1. The scene description file that renders the picture is listed at the end of this chapter.

As you can see, the image contains a rich set of textures. The floor has a red and white checker pattern, the cabinets are built from wood-like strips, and there is even a soup can with a realistic label painted on its surface.

Figure 5.15 displays the coordinates of the principle objects in the scene. You may want to refer to this as you go over the following sections and begin to experiment with the scene description file.

Constructing the Room

Like many of the objects in the scene, the room is built from a sparse set of rectangles. In particular, the room consists of a checker floor and two walls. The lighting comes from two overhead, directed light sources. The floor is a polished, black-and-white-checkered rectangle created with the following statement:

```
Rectangle(            /* Floor */
  Loc(-14,-28,0),  V1(54,0,0),  V2(0,58,0),
  Ambient(.8), Diffuse(.3), Specular(.1), SpecSpread(4),
  Transparency(0), Color(1,1,1), Color2(0,0,0), Checker(8, 8))
```

Recall that the *Color* and *Color2* keywords in the statement specify the colors of the checker pattern. In this case, *Color* represents the white squares (1,1,1) and *Color2* represents the black squares (0,0,0).

Figure 5.15 The coordinates of the kitchen's world model.

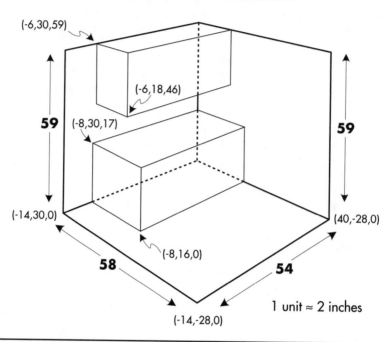

The walls in the room are white, matte surfaces built from two rectangles, as shown here:

```
Rectangle(              /* Left wall */
  Loc(-14,30,0),  V1(54,0,0),  V2(0,0,59),
  Ambient(.35), Diffuse(1), Specular(0), SpecSpread(4),
  Transparency(0), Color(.98,1,.9))
Rectangle(              /* Right wall */
  Loc(40,-28,0),  V1(0,58,0),  V2(0,0,59),
  Ambient(.35), Diffuse(1), Specular(0), SpecSpread(4),
  Transparency(0), Color(.98,1,.9))
```

Constructing the Cabinets

The cabinets are also built from a series of rectangles. For simplicity, they only have rectangles for the three sides that are visible in the image. For instance, here are the three rectangles that make the upper cabinets:

```
Rectangle(              /* Front of cupboards */
  Loc(-6,18,46),  V1(44,0,0),  V2(0,0,-16),
  Ambient(.8), Diffuse(.5), Specular(0), SpecSpread(4),
```

```
       Transparency(0), Color(0.55,0.38,0.17), Map(WOOD.TIF))
Rectangle(              /* Left side of cupboards */
  Loc(-6,18,46),  V1(0,0,-16),  V2(0,14,0),
  Ambient(.8), Diffuse(.5), Specular(0), SpecSpread(4),
  Transparency(0), Color(0.55,0.38,0.17), Map(WOOD.TIF))
Rectangle(              /* Bottom of cupboards */
  Loc(-6,18,30),  V1(44,0,0),  V2(0,14,0),
  Ambient(.8), Diffuse(.5), Specular(0), SpecSpread(4),
  Transparency(0), Color(0.55,0.38,0.17), Map(WOOD.TIF))
```

Where does the wood texture come from? As these three statements indicate, we're mapping a picture of wood onto the rectangles. In fact, the same wood image, shown in Figure 5.16, is used in all parts of the cabinets. Fortunately, since the cabinet's components are different sizes, the image doesn't appear the same on each rectangle.

Where can you get an image like WOOD.TIF? If you have access to a video camera and frame grabber, you can create your own. However, the source code disk contains the WOOD.TIF image. If you don't want to order the source code disk, the WOOD.TIF image is also available on the bulletin board listed on the disk order page at the back of the book.

Figure 5.16 The WOOD.TIF image is used to create a wood grain texture.

The cabinet doors are formed from rectangles that are slightly offset from the face of the cabinets. A typical door has the settings

```
Rectangle(              /* Left cupboard door */
  Loc(-3.5,17.75,44),  V1(11,0,0),  V2(0,0,-12),
  Ambient(.6), Diffuse(.8), Specular(0), SpecSpread(4),
  Transparency(0), Color(0.55,0.38,0.17), Map(WOOD.TIF))
Rectangle(              /* Left side of cupboard door */
  Loc(-3.5,17.75,44),  V1(0,0,-12),  V2(0,0.25,0),
  Ambient(.6), Diffuse(.8), Specular(0), SpecSpread(4),
  Transparency(0), Color(0.55,0.38,0.17), Map(WOOD.TIF))
Rectangle(              /* Bottom of cupboard door */
  Loc(-3.5,17.75,32),  V1(11,0,0),  V2(0,0.25,0),
  Ambient(.6), Diffuse(.8), Specular(0), SpecSpread(4),
  Transparency(0), Color(0.55,0.38,0.17), Map(WOOD.TIF))
```

Again, only the three visible portions of the doors are defined here.

Making the Soup Can

One of the objects in the kitchen image that probably catches your attention right away is the Campbell's soup can. How is it created? The trick is to map an image of an actual soup can label onto the surface of a cylinder. The label was cut from a Campbell's tomato soup can and digitized using a video camera and frame grabber. A color scanner could also have been used. The image was saved as a 24-bit RGB TIFF file under the name SOUP.TIF. A grayscale version of the image is shown in Figure 5.17. The image is mapped onto the soup can by including the *Map* command in the can's *Cylinder* definition, as shown here:

```
Cylinder(      /* Soup can */
  Loc(-4,22,17),  V1(0,0,4), Radius(1.5),
  Ambient(1), Diffuse(.5), Specular(.05), SpecSpread(4),
  Transparency(0), Color(1,0,0), Map(soup2.tif))
```

Making a Pot

Like the soup can, the pot is made from a cylinder. Actually, it consists of two cylinders that are created by the statements

```
Cylinder(      /* Bottom of pot */
  Loc(2,22,17),  V1(0,0,.5), Radius(3),
  Ambient(1), Diffuse(0), Specular(.2), SpecSpread(4),
  Transparency(0), Color(.58,.36,.14))
Cylinder(      /* Top of pot */
  Loc(2,22,17.5),  V1(0,0,3), Radius(3),
  Ambient(.8), Diffuse(0), Specular(.5), SpecSpread(4),
  Transparency(0), Color(.63,.63,.63))
```

Figure 5.17 This image is mapped to a cylinder to create a soup can.

The first statement renders the top portion of the pot; the second statement renders the copper portion of the pot. Both parts of the pot have a shiny, metallic surface.

The pot's handle is made from a black cylinder using the statement

```
Cylinder(              /* Handle */
   Loc(4.1,19.1,19.75),  V1(3.1,-3.1,.5), Radius(.275),
   Ambient(1), Diffuse(0), Specular(.2), SpecSpread(4),
   Transparency(0), Color(0,0,0))
```

Using Bounding Boxes

The KITCHEN.SDF file contains a large enough number of objects to make the ray tracing annoyingly slow. To speed it up, the file includes three bounding boxes. The first encompasses the top cabinets, the second contains the bottom cabinets, and a third groups all the objects in between. By using these three bounding objects, you'll be able to cut the ray tracing time in at least half. For example, without them it took almost one hour to render a 500 by 500 version of the image on a 33MHz 80486. However, with the three bounding boxes, the ray tracing time was cut to just under 30 minutes. This illustrates how powerful bounding boxes can be.

NOTHING'S PERFECT

There's a lot more we could do to make the kitchen scene look more realistic. We could add additional walls, cabinets, power outlets, cups, and so on. You might want to try adding these objects to see how realistic you can make the kitchen scene.

In addition, realize that several of the cylinders don't have ends on them. For instance, there's no top to the soup can and the pot doesn't have a bottom. You can remedy this situation by placing very thin ellipsoids at their ends. In a similar manner, you may also want to add the remaining sides to the other objects in the scene.

Here's the scene description file that renders the kitchen image:

```
/* KITCHEN.SDF: Renders a kitchen scene. */

AntiAliasing()
Resolution(500,500)
From(-10,-20,26)
At(0,0,21.5)
Up(0.0,0.0,1.0)
Background(.7,.7,.7)
MaxLevel(2)
DMin(50)
DMax(150)

Light(Loc(0,13,59), Color(1,1,1), Directed(), SpreadPower(2),
      LightDir(0,10,0))
Light(Loc(15,13,59), Color(1,1,1), Directed(), SpreadPower(2),
      LightDir(15,10,0))

SaveTo(KITCHEN.TIF)

Rectangle(              /* Floor */
   Loc(-14,-28,0),  V1(54,0,0),  V2(0,58,0),
   Ambient(.8), Diffuse(.3), Specular(.1), SpecSpread(4),
   Transparency(0), Color(1,1,1), Color2(0,0,0), Checker(8, 8))

Rectangle(              /* Left wall */
   Loc(-14,30,0),  V1(54,0,0),  V2(0,0,59),
   Ambient(.35), Diffuse(1), Specular(0), SpecSpread(4),
   Transparency(0), Color(.98,1,.9))
Rectangle(              /* Right wall */
   Loc(40,-28,0),  V1(0,58,0),  V2(0,0,59),
   Ambient(.35), Diffuse(1), Specular(0), SpecSpread(4),
   Transparency(0), Color(.98,1,.9))

/* The cupboards above the counter form a group */
BeginGroup(V1(-6,17.75,30),V2(38,32,46))
Rectangle(              /* Front of cupboards */
   Loc(-6,18,46),  V1(44,0,0),  V2(0,0,-16),
   Ambient(.8), Diffuse(.5), Specular(0), SpecSpread(4),
   Transparency(0), Color(0.55,0.38,0.17), Map(WOOD.TIF))
Rectangle(              /* Left side of cupboards */
   Loc(-6,18,46),  V1(0,0,-16),  V2(0,14,0),
```

```
       Ambient(.8), Diffuse(.5), Specular(0), SpecSpread(4),
       Transparency(0), Color(0.55,0.38,0.17), Map(WOOD.TIF))
   Rectangle(              /* Bottom of cupboards */
     Loc(-6,18,30),  V1(44,0,0),  V2(0,14,0),
     Ambient(.8), Diffuse(.5), Specular(0), SpecSpread(4),
     Transparency(0), Color(0.55,0.38,0.17), Map(WOOD.TIF))

   Rectangle(              /* Left cupboard door */
     Loc(-3.5,17.75,44),  V1(11,0,0),  V2(0,0,-12),
     Ambient(.6), Diffuse(.8), Specular(0), SpecSpread(4),
     Transparency(0), Color(0.55,0.38,0.17), Map(WOOD.TIF))
   Rectangle(              /* Left side of cupboard door */
     Loc(-3.5,17.75,44),  V1(0,0,-12),  V2(0,0.25,0),
     Ambient(.6), Diffuse(.8), Specular(0), SpecSpread(4),
     Transparency(0), Color(0.55,0.38,0.17), Map(WOOD.TIF))
   Rectangle(              /* Bottom of cupboard door */
     Loc(-3.5,17.75,32),  V1(11,0,0),  V2(0,0.25,0),
     Ambient(.6), Diffuse(.8), Specular(0), SpecSpread(4),
     Transparency(0), Color(0.55,0.38,0.17), Map(WOOD.TIF))

   Rectangle(              /* Middle cupboard door */
     Loc(10.5,17.75,44),  V1(11,0,0),  V2(0,0,-12),
     Ambient(.6), Diffuse(.8), Specular(0), SpecSpread(4),
     Transparency(0), Color(0.55,0.38,0.17), Map(WOOD.TIF))
   Rectangle(              /* Left side of cupboard door */
     Loc(10.5,17.75,44),  V1(0,0,-12),  V2(0,0.25,0),
     Ambient(.6), Diffuse(.8), Specular(0), SpecSpread(4),
     Transparency(0), Color(0.55,0.38,0.17), Map(WOOD.TIF))
   Rectangle(              /* Bottom of cupboard door */
     Loc(10.5,17.75,32),  V1(11,0,0),  V2(0,0.25,0),
     Ambient(.6), Diffuse(.8), Specular(0), SpecSpread(4),
     Transparency(0), Color(0.55,0.38,0.17), Map(WOOD.TIF))

   Rectangle(              /* Right cupboard door */
     Loc(24.5,17.75,44),  V1(11,0,0),  V2(0,0,-12),
     Ambient(.6), Diffuse(.8), Specular(0), SpecSpread(4),
     Transparency(0), Color(0.55,0.38,0.17), Map(WOOD.TIF))
   Rectangle(              /* Left side of cupboard door */
     Loc(24.5,17.75,44),  V1(0,0,-12),  V2(0,0.25,0),
     Ambient(.6), Diffuse(.8), Specular(0), SpecSpread(4),
     Transparency(0), Color(0.55,0.38,0.17), Map(WOOD.TIF))
   Rectangle(              /* Bottom of cupboard door */
     Loc(24.5,17.75,32),  V1(11,0,0),  V2(0,0.25,0),
     Ambient(.6), Diffuse(.8), Specular(0), SpecSpread(4),
     Transparency(0), Color(0.55,0.38,0.17), Map(WOOD.TIF))
   EndGroup()

   /* The cupboards below the counter form a group */
   BeginGroup(V1(-8,14,0),V2(40,30,17))
```

```
Rectangle(              /* Countertop */
  Loc(-8,14,17),  V1(48,0,0),  V2(0,16,0),
  Ambient(.7), Diffuse(.3), Specular(.3), SpecSpread(4),
  Transparency(0), Color(0.8,0.8,0.8), Color2(.3,.3,.3), Marble())
Rectangle(              /* Right edge of countertop */
  Loc(-8,14,17),  V1(48,0,0),  V2(0,0,-1),
  Ambient(.8), Diffuse(.6), Specular(.1), SpecSpread(4),
  Transparency(0), Color(0.8,0.8,0.8))
Rectangle(              /* Left edge of countertop */
  Loc(-8,15,17),  V1(0,0,-1),  V2(0,15,0),
  Ambient(.8), Diffuse(.6), Specular(.1), SpecSpread(4),
  Transparency(0), Color(0.8,0.8,0.8))

Rectangle(              /* Front of counter's base */
  Loc(-6,18,16),  V1(44,0,0),  V2(0,0,-16),
  Ambient(.6), Diffuse(.6), Specular(0), SpecSpread(4),
  Transparency(0), Color(0.55,0.38,0.17), Map(WOOD.TIF))
Rectangle(              /* Left side of counter's base */
  Loc(-6,18,16),  V1(0,0,-16),  V2(0,12,0),
  Ambient(.6), Diffuse(.6), Specular(0), SpecSpread(4),
  Transparency(0), Color(0.55,0.38,0.17), Map(WOOD.TIF))

Rectangle(              /* Left cupboard door */
  Loc(-3.5,17.75,14),  V1(11,0,0),  V2(0,0,-12),
  Ambient(.6), Diffuse(.8), Specular(0), SpecSpread(4),
  Transparency(0), Color(0.55,0.38,0.17), Map(WOOD.TIF))
Rectangle(              /* Left side of cupboard door */
  Loc(-3.5,17.75,14),  V1(0,0,-12),  V2(0,0.25,0),
  Ambient(.6), Diffuse(.8), Specular(0), SpecSpread(4),
  Transparency(0), Color(0.55,0.38,0.17), Map(WOOD.TIF))
Rectangle(              /* Top of cupboard door */
  Loc(-3.5,17.75,14),  V1(11,0,0),  V2(0,0.25,0),
  Ambient(.6), Diffuse(.8), Specular(0), SpecSpread(4),
  Transparency(0), Color(0.55,0.38,0.17), Map(WOOD.TIF))

Rectangle(              /* Middle cupboard door */
  Loc(10.5,17.75,14),  V1(11,0,0),  V2(0,0,-12),
  Ambient(.6), Diffuse(.8), Specular(0), SpecSpread(4),
  Transparency(0), Color(0.55,0.38,0.17), Map(WOOD.TIF))
Rectangle(              /* Left side of cupboard door */
  Loc(10.5,17.75,14),  V1(0,0,-12),  V2(0,0.25,0),
  Ambient(.6), Diffuse(.8), Specular(0), SpecSpread(4),
  Transparency(0), Color(0.55,0.38,0.17), Map(WOOD.TIF))
Rectangle(              /* Top of cupboard door */
  Loc(10.5,17.75,14),  V1(11,0,0),  V2(0,0.25,0),
  Ambient(.6), Diffuse(.8), Specular(0), SpecSpread(4),
  Transparency(0), Color(0.55,0.38,0.17), Map(WOOD.TIF))
```

```
Rectangle(              /* Right cupboard door */
  Loc(24.5,17.75,14),  V1(11,0,0),  V2(0,0,-12),
  Ambient(.6), Diffuse(.8), Specular(0), SpecSpread(4),
  Transparency(0), Color(0.55,0.38,0.17), Map(WOOD.TIF))
Rectangle(              /* Left side of cupboard door */
  Loc(24.5,17.75,14),  V1(0,0,-12),  V2(0,0.25,0),
  Ambient(.6), Diffuse(.8), Specular(0), SpecSpread(4),
  Transparency(0), Color(0.55,0.38,0.17), Map(WOOD.TIF))
Rectangle(              /* Top of cupboard door */
  Loc(24.5,17.75,14),  V1(11,0,0),  V2(0,0.25,0),
  Ambient(.6), Diffuse(.8), Specular(0), SpecSpread(4),
  Transparency(0), Color(0.55,0.38,0.17), Map(WOOD.TIF))
EndGroup()

/* The objects on the countertop form a group */
BeginGroup(V1(-6,14,16),V2(40,30,30))
Cylinder(      /* Soup can */
  Loc(-4,22,17),  V1(0,0,4), Radius(1.5),
  Ambient(1), Diffuse(.5), Specular(.05), SpecSpread(4),
  Transparency(0), Color(1,0,0), Map(SOUP.TIF))

Cylinder(      /* Bottom of pot */
  Loc(2,22,17),  V1(0,0,.5), Radius(3),
  Ambient(1), Diffuse(0), Specular(.2), SpecSpread(4),
  Transparency(0), Color(.58,.36,.14))
Cylinder(      /* Top of pot */
  Loc(2,22,17.5),  V1(0,0,3), Radius(3),
  Ambient(.8), Diffuse(0), Specular(.5), SpecSpread(4),
  Transparency(0), Color(.63,.63,.63))
Cylinder(              /* Handle */
  Loc(4.1,19.1,19.75),  V1(3.1,-3.1,.5), Radius(.275),
  Ambient(1), Diffuse(0), Specular(.2), SpecSpread(4),
  Transparency(0), Color(0,0,0))

Rectangle(             /* Top of microwave */
  Loc(20,19,24),  V1(12,0,0),  V2(0,9,0),
  Ambient(.7), Diffuse(.3), Specular(0), SpecSpread(4),
  Transparency(0), Color(0.4,0.27,0.01), Map(WOOD.TIF))
Rectangle(             /* Front of microwave */
  Loc(20,19,17),  V1(12,0,0),  V2(0,0,7),
  Ambient(.7), Diffuse(.3), Specular(0), SpecSpread(4),
  Transparency(0), Color(0.4,0.27,0.01), Map(WOOD.TIF))
Rectangle(             /* Front of microwave */
  Loc(21,18.9,18),  V1(9,0,0),  V2(0,0,5),
  Ambient(1), Diffuse(0), Specular(0), SpecSpread(4),
  Transparency(0), Color(0,0,0))
Rectangle(             /* Left of microwave */
  Loc(20,19,17),  V1(0,0,7),  V2(0,9,0),
```

```
   Ambient(.7), Diffuse(.3), Specular(0), SpecSpread(4),
   Transparency(0), Color(0.4,0.27,0.01), Map(WOOD.TIF))

 Cylinder(              /* Paper towels */
   Loc(24,22,27.5),  V1(6,0,0), Radius(2),
   Ambient(.83), Diffuse(.35), Specular(0), SpecSpread(4),
   Transparency(0), Color(.85,.85,.85))
 /* An ellipsoid makes the left edge of the paper towels */
 Ellipsoid(Loc(25,22,27.5), V1(.04, .01, .01), V2(.04, 0, 0),
   Ambient(.83), Diffuse(.35), Specular(0), SpecSpread(4),
   Transparency(0), Color(0.85,0.85,0.85))
 Rectangle(             /* Paper towel holder */
   Loc(24,23,30),  V1(0,-1,0),  V2(0,0,-3),
   Ambient(.6), Diffuse(.6), Specular(0), SpecSpread(4),
   Transparency(0), Color(0.55,0.38,0.17))
 Rectangle(             /* Paper towel holder */
   Loc(30,23,30),  V1(0,-1,0),  V2(0,0,-3),
   Ambient(.6), Diffuse(.6), Specular(0), SpecSpread(4),
   Transparency(0), Color(0.55,0.38,0.17))

 Cylinder(      /* Cookie jar 1 */
   Loc(17.5,27,17),  V1(0,0,6), Radius(2),
   Ambient(.8), Diffuse(.2), Specular(.1), SpecSpread(4),
   Transparency(0), Color(1,1,1), Color2(0,0,.4), Blend(-.25))
 Cylinder(      /* Cookie jar 2 */
   Loc(13.25,27.25,17),  V1(0,0,5), Radius(1.75),
   Ambient(.8), Diffuse(.2), Specular(.1), SpecSpread(4),
   Transparency(0), Color(1,1,1), Color2(0,0,.4), Blend(-.25))
 Cylinder(      /* Cookie jar 3 */
   Loc(9.5,27.5,17),  V1(0,0,4), Radius(1.5),
   Ambient(.8), Diffuse(.2), Specular(.1), SpecSpread(4),
   Transparency(0), Color(1,1,1), Color2(0,0,.4), Blend(-.25))
 EndGroup()

 Rectangle(             /* Front side of garbage can */
   Loc(-12,19,0),  V1(5,0,0),  V2(0,0,12),
   Ambient(.5), Diffuse(1), Specular(0),
   Transparency(0), Color(.6,.6,.9))
 Rectangle(             /* Left side of garbage can */
   Loc(-12,19,0),  V1(0,0,12),  V2(0,10,0),
   Ambient(.5), Diffuse(1), Specular(0),
   Transparency(0), Color(.6,.6,.9))
 Rectangle(             /* Back of garbage can */
   Loc(-7,29,0),  V1(-5,0,0),  V2(0,0,12),
   Ambient(.5), Diffuse(1), Specular(0),
   Transparency(0), Color(.6,.6,.9))
 Rectangle(             /* Far right side of garbage can */
   Loc(-7,29,0),  V1(0,-10,0),  V2(0,0,12),
   Ambient(.5), Diffuse(1), Specular(0),
   Transparency(0), Color(.6,.6,.9))
```

6

Adding Animation

O
ne of the more intriguing aspects of the RAY program is its animation capabilities. Currently, the program enables you to animate
the position of objects, as well as the from and at positions of the
viewer. Although this list may seem limiting, it's quite flexible.
You'll be able to generate movies complete with moving objects and unencum-
bered fly-bys through your synthetic worlds. This chapter will show you how.

ANIMATION OVERVIEW

Ray tracing is too slow to display animated images as they are generated.
Instead, RAY precomputes each frame in an animated sequence and saves them
to files so that later they can be played back. In the next several sections, we'll
"pop the hood" and take an up-close look at RAY's animation capabilities.

You'll find most of the code that supports animation in the file RAY.CPP. It's
centered primarily around the **GenImage** function, which as you might recall,
generates a single ray traced image. To support image sequences, therefore,
GenImage now includes a **for** loop that wraps around the image generator so
that it renders multiple frames. Of course, the program repositions the necessary objects between these images.

To animate a scene, we must supply the locations of objects in each image.
Actually, we'll specify the initial and final positions of the moving objects and
viewer, as outlined in Figure 6.1. The ray tracer will interpolate straight-line
paths between these positions to fill in the gaps and make the animation
smooth.

The locations of objects are listed as a series of positions that coincide with
specific frames. For instance, assume RAY is going to render a rectangle that

---

Figure 6.1 The ray tracer calculates intermediate positions while moving objects.

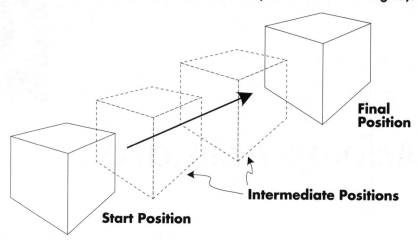

Final Position

Intermediate Positions

Start Position

---

moves from (10,10,1) to (18,18,1) during its first four frames. The ray tracer will calculate that it must move the rectangle 2 units in the x and y directions between each frame. Essentially, RAY determines the intermediate locations by solving the equation

$$NewPosition = StartPosition + \frac{EndPosition - StartPosition}{EndFrame - StartFrame} \star FrameNumber$$

SUPPORTING ANIMATION

To support animation, the ray tracer maintains a list of the objects that it is to animate. This list contains the locations of the objects at specific frames in the sequence. Each animation step is stored in a separate **STEP** structure, which is defined as

```
struct STEP {          // Describes a move to make
  int T0, T1;          // Start and stop frame numbers
  float x0, y0, z0;    // Beginning value or location
  float x1, y1, z1;    // Ending value or location
  STEP *Next;          // Next step in the animation sequence
};
```

The **STEP** structure contains the start and stop locations of a moving object. Specifically, the coordinate (x0,y0,z0) supplies the initial location of the object and the coordinate (x1,y1,z1) provides the object's final position. The fields **T0** and **T1** specify the frame numbers when the object is at its starting and final positions, respectively. The **Next** field points to any additional movements that the object should take. Quite often it'll be set to **NULL**, indicating that there aren't any more moves to make.

The Animating Structure

To keep each object's animation steps organized, the RAY.H header file also defines the **ANIMATE** structure, shown here:

```
struct ANIMATE {
    unsigned char Type;      // Type of "object" to animate
    int Ndx;                 // The object's index in array
    STEP *Steps;             // List of steps in animation
    STEP *CurrStep;          // Current step in animation
};
```

The program uses one **ANIMATE** structure for each animated object. The **Ndx** field in the **ANIMATE** structure tells the ray tracer which object in the **Objects** array that the structure corresponds to.

The **Type** field specifies what type of object or viewer position is being animated. Currently, the ray tracer can animate either the from point, at point, or an object. Therefore, the ray tracer defines the following three constants to represent each category of animation:

```
#define ANIMATEOBJLOC 1    // Animate an object's location
#define ANIMATEFROM 2      // Animate the from point
#define ANIMATEAT 3        // Animate the at point
```

For instance, if the from point is being animated, **ANIMATEFROM** is assigned to the **Type** field.

The actual positions of the object's motion are placed in a **STEP** structure that is pointed to by the **Steps** field. Since an object can have multiple steps, the **Steps** pointer may point to a linked list, as shown in Figure 6.2. And finally, the last field in **ANIMATE**, **CurrStep**, is used while ray tracing the image frames to point to the current **STEP** structure being executed.

The ray tracer defines the **Animate** array to hold a list of animated objects, as shown here:

```
#define MAXANIMATEOBJ 10   // Can't animate more than 10 objects
ANIMATE Animate[MAXANIMATEOBJ];
int NumObjToAnimate;       // Number of "objects" to animate
```

Currently, **Animate** is designed only to hold up to 10 animated objects. Therefore, you must increase the value of **MAXANIMATEOBJ** if you want to animate

Figure 6.2 The ANIMATE structure keeps track of the animated objects.

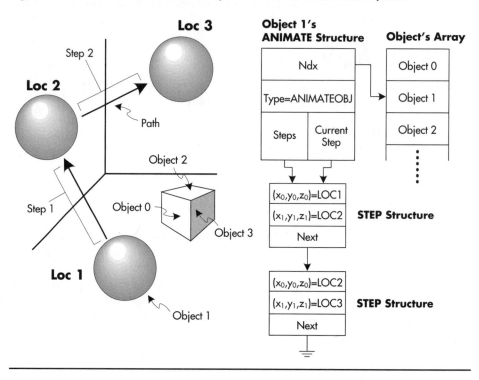

a larger number of figures. The **NumObjToAnimate** variable holds the number of entries in the **Animate** array. It's incremented each time the parser encounters a new animated object. The parser is also responsible for allocating the **STEP** structures and setting up the **Animate** array.

Animating Objects

How does the ray tracer process the animation information? As mentioned earlier, the **GenImage** function contains the biggest clue. The **for** loop within the routine generates an image each time through the loop. In all, it creates **NumFrames** images. The value of **NumFrames** is set in the scene description file. By default, it is only 1, meaning that only a single frame is created. Here's the top of the **for** loop:

```
for (FrameNum=0; FrameNum<NumFrames; FrameNum++) {
```

As the code illustrates, the current frame is specified by the **FrameNum** variable that gets incremented each time through the **for** loop. In a sense, the

FrameNum variable keeps track of time. The ray tracer calculates the positions of objects based on the current value of **FrameNum**.

Another key part of the **GenImage** loop is its call to the **RepositionObjects** function, shown here:

```
RepositionObjects(FrameNum);
```

The **RepositionObjects** function loops through each of the objects in the **Animate** array and updates their positions if necessary. (Remember, each element in **Animate** represents a single object or entity to be animated.) Specifically, an object's position is updated if its **CurrStep** pointer is not **NULL** and the current frame number is between that step's **T0** and **T1** index:

```
for (i=0; i<NumObjToAnimate; i++) {
  if (Animate[i].CurrStep != NULL &&
      Animate[i].CurrStep->T0 <= FrameNum &&
      Animate[i].CurrStep->T1 >= FrameNum) {
```

If these conditions are met, the code calculates how much the object should be incremented in each frame. This value is placed in the variable **FInc**:

```
if (Animate[i].CurrStep->T0 != Animate[i].CurrStep->T1)
  FInc = (float)(FrameNum - Animate[i].CurrStep->T0) /
      (Animate[i].CurrStep->T1-Animate[i].CurrStep->T0);
else
  FInc = 0;
```

Next, the function computes the new location of the animated object. This coordinate is temporarily placed in the **VECTOR V**:

```
V.x = Animate[i].CurrStep->x0 + (Animate[i].CurrStep->x1 -
      Animate[i].CurrStep->x0) * FInc;
V.y = Animate[i].CurrStep->y0 + (Animate[i].CurrStep->y1 -
      Animate[i].CurrStep->y0) * FInc;
V.z = Animate[i].CurrStep->z0 + (Animate[i].CurrStep->z1 -
      Animate[i].CurrStep->z0) * FInc;
```

The next step is to assign the **V** vector to the proper object or variable. The **Type** field in the **ANIMATE** structure tells the code which variable to update. For instance, if **Type** is equal to the value for **ANIMATEFROM**, the **From** variable is updated, as shown here:

```
switch(Animate[i].Type) {
  case ANIMATEFROM:
    From.x = V.x;  From.y = V.y;  From.z = V.z;
    SetEye();  // Recompute the eye coordinate system
    break;
```

Notice that the code must also recalculate the eye coordinate settings, since the location of the viewer has changed. A similar set of statements updates the at vector if **Type** is equal to **ANIMATEAT**. Here's the portion of the **switch** statement that updates the at point:

```
case ANIMATEAT:
  At.x = V.x;  At.y = V.y;  At.z = V.z;
  SetEye();  // Recompute the eye coordinate system
  break;
```

On the other hand, if the ray tracer is supposed to update an object, the code processes these statements:

```
case ANIMATEOBJLOC:
  Objects[Animate[i].Ndx]->Loc.x = V.x;
  Objects[Animate[i].Ndx]->Loc.y = V.y;
  Objects[Animate[i].Ndx]->Loc.z = V.z;
  break;
```

Notice that the object to update is specified by the **Ndx** field in the **ANIMATE** structure. In addition, **GenImage** only updates the location vector of the object. It doesn't have to modify the other vectors in the object since they are always relative to **Loc**.

Going the Next Step

After an object's position is updated, **RepositionObjects** determines whether the object has reached its destination:

```
if (NumFrames>1 &&
  Animate[i].CurrStep != NULL &&
  Animate[i].CurrStep->T1 == FrameNum) {
  // Reached the end of the current step. Set the step
  // pointer to the next step, if there is one.
  Animate[i].CurrStep = Animate[i].CurrStep->Next;
}
```

If the object has reached its destination, the inner part of the **if** statement is executed and the **CurrStep** pointer is set to the next **STEP** structure. Realize that the next step might be **NULL**, but at this point it doesn't matter.

THE ANIMATION LANGUAGE

Surprisingly, the scene description language only introduces three keywords to support animation: *NumFrames*, *PathFrom*, and *PathTo*. The next several sections describe each of these.

Specifying the Number of Frames

The *NumFrames* keyword tells the ray tracer how many frames to render for an animation sequence. It takes a single integer parameter that specifies the number of frames to use. Therefore, if the statement *NumFrames(10)* is included in a scene description file, the ray tracer will generate 10 frames. If *NumFrames* is not included, however, RAY only renders a single image.

Specifying a Motion Path

The *PathFrom* and *PathTo* commands specify the initial and final positions of an animated object. Each of these commands takes four parameters. The first is a frame number; the remaining three define a three-dimensional coordinate. For example, the following statements would specify a moving sphere that travels from (1,1,1) to (10,5,15) in four frames:

```
NumFrames(4)
Sphere(Loc(PathFrom(0,1,1,1),PathTo(3,10,5,15)),Radius(2))
```

Notice that the frame times listed in the *PathFrom* and *PathTo* commands start at 0 and go up to the number of frames minus one.

As mentioned earlier, objects can have sequences of steps that they are to travel. This is particularly useful in specifying curved paths as short line segments. All you need to do is place additional *PathFrom* and *PathTo* commands in the **Loc** statement. Each one should be separated by a comma. For example, the following statement moves a sphere from (1,1,1) to (10,5,15) and back again in eight frames:

```
NumFrames(8)
Sphere(Loc(PathFrom(0,1,1,1),PathTo(3,10,5,15),
  PathFrom(4,10,5,15),PathTo(7,1,1,1)),Radius(2))
```

There's no limit on the number of steps you can have, except that there must be enough memory to allocate **STEP** structures for them.

Moving the Viewer

You can move the viewer's from and at points using the *PathFrom* and *PathTo* commands. You simply must place these two commands within the appropriate viewer setting. For instance, to move the at point from the point (2,2,2) to (4,20,4), you could use

```
At(PathFrom(0,2,2,2),PathTo(2,4,20,4))
```

Similarly, to move the from point along the same path, you could use

```
From(PathFrom(0,2,2,2),PathTo(2,4,20,4))
```

Saving the Image Sequence

The *SaveTo* command instructs the ray tracer to save the images that it renders to files. However, the ray tracer generates several images for an animation sequence, so where are these images stored? Rather than save them all to one file, RAY places each frame in a different image file. Of course, now the problem becomes what filename should be used for these files?

This problem is solved by having the ray tracer generate a unique filename for each image. RAY uses the filename from the *SaveTo* command as the root of the filename and the current frame number as the image file's extension. For instance, if MYMOVIE is the filename supplied in the *SaveTo* statement

```
SaveTo(MYMOVIE)
```

then the filenames used to store the first three frames will be MYMOVIE.0, MYMOVIE.1, and MYMOVIE.2.

The modified filename is created by the **AppendFrameNumber** function, which you'll find in RAY.CPP. Notice that the function supplies the period that separates the filename's root and extension:

```
void AppendFrameNumber(char *Filename, char *OutFilename, int Frame)
{
  char Buffer[10];

  itoa(Frame, Buffer, 10);
  strcpy(Filename, OutFilename);
  strcat(Filename, ".");
  strcat(Filename, Buffer);
}
```

Once the filename is created, the output file is opened and the TIFF header is written to the file as usual:

```
if (SaveTo) {          // Save the image to a file?
  if (NumObjToAnimate) {
    // If the image is part of an image sequence,
    // append the frame number to the end of the filename.
    AppendFrameNumber(Filename, OutFilename, FrameNum);
  }
  // Open the output file
  if ((OutputFile = fopen(Filename, "wb")) == NULL) {
    delete LastRow;    // Opening file failed. Quit.
    return;
  }
  // Write a TIFF header to the output file
  if (!WriteRGBTIFFFileHeader(OutputFile)) {
    delete LastRow;    // Writing header failed. Quit.
```

```
    return;
  }
}
```

PLAYING BACK AN IMAGE SEQUENCE

The RAY program can generate a sequence of images, but you need a second program to play back the images. Listed at the end of this chapter is one such program that you can use. The program, PLAYBACK.C, runs under MS Windows. Because it's a Windows application, you'll be able to have far more images in the sequence than you would otherwise.

The program reads each of the images in the sequence into a separate bitmap. Once all the images are read, the program continually displays the bitmaps in a loop. You can stop the program at any time by closing the display window as you would any window. The rate at which the images are displayed on the screen is set by the timer. Currently, it is set so that PLAYBACK displays a new bitmap every 100 milliseconds. The timer isn't enabled until after all of the bitmaps have been read into memory.

There are three things to keep in mind with the PLAYBACK program. First, the number of images you'll be able to load into memory and create bitmaps for depends on the memory available in your system. Second, the update rate of the images is primarily set by the timer. You'll want reasonably fast times for smooth looking animation. Third, larger images will take longer to display and will, therefore, slow down the animation.

Building the PLAYBACK program requires that you compile it with a Windows-capable compiler and link it with the TIFF.C tools discussed in Chapter 10. To run the program, you must supply two command-line arguments. The first is the base name of the image sequence; the second is the number of images to read. For instance, to read the three images BALLS.0, BALLS.1, and BALLS.2, you would use

```
playback balls 3
```

AN ANIMATION EXAMPLE

The scene description file (BALLS.SDF) that follows this section creates a sequence of nine, mirrored balls spinning over a checkered plane. The three frames are shown in Figure 6.3. As you can see, the balls are in a different position in each frame. Therefore, when they are played back they create the sensation of smooth, circular motion.

The scene file saves the images to the files BALLS.0, BALLS.1, and BALLS.2. Currently, the images are saved in 24-bit TIFF format. This makes it easy to display them on a Super VGA or 24-bit mode using the PLAYBACK program.

Figure 6.3 The three frames generated with BALLS.SDF.

• **BALLS.SDF**

```
/* BALLS.SDF: Displays mirrored, moving balls over a
 * checker pattern.
 */

AntiAliasing()
Resolution(200,200)
From(65,58,20)
At(20,20,1)
Up(0.0,0.0,1.0)
Background(0,0,0)
Light(Loc(65,58,20), Color(1,1,1), Dir(20,20,0), Directed())

NumFrames(4)
SaveTo(BALLS)

Rectangle(
  Loc(0,0,0),  V1(40,0,0),  V2(0,40,0),
  Ambient(.3), Diffuse(1), Specular(1), SpecSpread(4),
  Transparency(0), Color(1,0,0), Color2(1,1,1), Checker(1,1))
Rectangle(
  Loc(40,0,0),  V1(0,0,-7),  V2(0,40,0),
  Ambient(.3), Diffuse(1), Specular(1), SpecSpread(4),
  Transparency(0), Color(1,0,0), Color2(1,1,1), Checker(0,1))
Rectangle(
  Loc(40,40,0),  V1(0,0,-7),  V2(-20,0,0),
  Ambient(.3), Diffuse(1), Specular(1), SpecSpread(4),
  Transparency(0), Color(1,1,1))
Rectangle(
  Loc(20,40,0),  V1(0,0,-7),  V2(-20,0,0),
  Ambient(.3), Diffuse(1), Specular(1), SpecSpread(4),
  Transparency(0), Color(1,0,0))
```

```
Sphere(
  Loc(PathFrom(0,3,20,3.5),PathTo(3,7.981,7.981,3.5)), Radius(2.75),
  Ambient(.3), Diffuse(0), Specular(1), SpecSpread(10),
  Transparency(0), Color(.8,.8,.8))
Sphere(
  Loc(PathFrom(0,7.981,7.981,3.5),PathTo(3,20,3,3.5)), Radius(2.75),
  Ambient(.3), Diffuse(0), Specular(1), SpecSpread(10),
  Transparency(0), Color(.8,.8,.8))
Sphere(
  Loc(PathFrom(0,20,3,3.5),PathTo(3,32.019,7.981,3.5)), Radius(2.75),
  Ambient(.3), Diffuse(0), Specular(1), SpecSpread(10),
  Transparency(0), Color(.8,.8,.8))
Sphere(
  Loc(PathFrom(0,32.019,7.981,3.5),PathTo(3,37,20,3.5)), Radius(2.75),
  Ambient(.3), Diffuse(0), Specular(1), SpecSpread(10),
  Transparency(0), Color(.8,.8,.8))
Sphere(
  Loc(PathFrom(0,37,20,3.5),PathTo(3,32.019,32.019,3.5)), Radius(2.75),
  Ambient(.3), Diffuse(0), Specular(1), SpecSpread(10),
  Transparency(0), Color(.8,.8,.8))
Sphere(
  Loc(PathFrom(0,32.019,32.019,3.5),PathTo(3,20,37,3.5)), Radius(2.75),
  Ambient(.3), Diffuse(0), Specular(1), SpecSpread(10),
  Transparency(0), Color(.8,.8,.8))
Sphere(
  Loc(PathFrom(0,20,37,3.5),PathTo(3,7.981,32.019,3.5)), Radius(2.75),
  Ambient(.3), Diffuse(0), Specular(1), SpecSpread(10),
  Transparency(0), Color(.8,.8,.8))
Sphere(
  Loc(PathFrom(0,7.981,32.019,3.5),PathTo(3,3,20,3.5)), Radius(2.75),
  Ambient(.3), Diffuse(0), Specular(1), SpecSpread(10),
  Transparency(0), Color(.8,.8,.8))
```

• PLAYBACK.C

```
/* PLAYBACK.C: Loops through a series of images.
 * Compile with the large memory model.
 */

#include <windows.h>
#include <stdlib.h>
#include <stdio.h>
#include <string.h>
#define  FORWINDOWS
#include "grphics.h"
#include "tiff.h"

#define TIMER_ID 1
#define NUMFRAMES 20
```

```
#define LASTFRAME (NUMFRAMES-1)
#define UPDATE_RATE 100   // 100 millisecond screen update

//#define PAL 1

int ImWd, ImHt;
char Filename[80];
int LastFrame;

int readimage(char *Filename, HDC MemDC);
long FAR PASCAL PlaybackWndProc(HWND, UINT, WPARAM, LPARAM);

int PASCAL WinMain(HANDLE hInstance, HANDLE hPrevInstance,
  LPSTR lpszCmdLine, int cmdShow)
{
  HWND hWnd;
  MSG Msg;
  WNDCLASS WndClass;
  int i;

  if (!hPrevInstance) {
    WndClass.lpszClassName = "PLAY:MAIN";
    WndClass.hInstance = hInstance;
    WndClass.lpfnWndProc = PlaybackWndProc;
    WndClass.hIcon = LoadIcon(NULL, IDI_APPLICATION);
    WndClass.hCursor = LoadCursor(NULL, IDC_ARROW);
    WndClass.hbrBackground = GetStockObject(BLACK_BRUSH);
    WndClass.lpszMenuName = NULL;
    WndClass.style = CS_HREDRAW | CS_VREDRAW;
    WndClass.cbClsExtra = 0;
    WndClass.cbWndExtra = 0;

    RegisterClass(&WndClass);
  }

  hWnd = CreateWindow("PLAY:MAIN",
                      "",
                      WS_OVERLAPPEDWINDOW,
                      CW_USEDEFAULT,
                      0,
                      CW_USEDEFAULT,
                      0,
                      NULL,
                      NULL,
                      hInstance,
                      NULL);

  // Read the commandline arguments
  i = 0;
```

```
    while (*lpszCmdLine != '\0' && *lpszCmdLine != ' ') {
      Filename[i] = *lpszCmdLine;
      lpszCmdLine++;
      i++;
    }
    Filename[i] = '\0';
    LastFrame = 0;
    while (*lpszCmdLine != '\0' && *lpszCmdLine != ' ')
      lpszCmdLine++;
    LastFrame = atoi(lpszCmdLine);

    ShowWindow(hWnd, cmdShow);
    while (GetMessage(&Msg, 0, 0, 0)) {
      TranslateMessage(&Msg);
      DispatchMessage(&Msg);
    }
    return 0;
}

long FAR PASCAL PlaybackWndProc(HWND hWnd, UINT Msg,
  WPARAM wParam, LPARAM lParam)
{
    int NumColors, i;
    static LPLOGPALETTE LogPal;      /* The logical palette */
    static HPALETTE hLogPal;         /* A handle to the logical palette */
    static HPALETTE hLogPal2;
    PAINTSTRUCT ps;
    RECT rect;
    HDC hDC;
    static HDC MemDC;
    static HBITMAP hBitmap[NUMFRAMES];
    static BOOL First = TRUE;
    static int Frame = 0;
    HBITMAP hTmpBmp;
    char CurrentFile[80], Buffer[80];

    switch(Msg) {
      case WM_CREATE:
        /* Creates a logical palette for the program that contains
         * 64 shades of blue. Since the VGA and Super VGA have only
         * 6 bits of resolution per red, green, or blue this is the
         * maximum number of shades we can get. This is true even on
         * a 32,768-color card.
         */
#ifdef PAL
        NumColors = 64;
        LogPal = (LPLOGPALETTE)farmalloc(sizeof(LOGPALETTE) +
          sizeof(PALETTEENTRY) * (NumColors-1));
        LogPal->palVersion = 0x300;
```

```
        LogPal->palNumEntries = NumColors;
        for (i=0; i<64; i++) {
          /* A Super VGA supports 64 simultaneous shades of a color */
          LogPal->palPalEntry[i].peRed = i * 4;
          LogPal->palPalEntry[i].peGreen = i * 4;
          LogPal->palPalEntry[i].peBlue = i * 4;
          LogPal->palPalEntry[i].peFlags = 0;
        }
        hLogPal = CreatePalette(LogPal);
        hLogPal2 = CreatePalette(LogPal);
#endif
        Frame = LastFrame;
        break;

    case WM_DESTROY:
#ifdef PAL
        farfree(LogPal);
        DeleteObject(hLogPal);
#endif
        KillTimer(hWnd, TIMER_ID);
        for (i=0; i<=LastFrame; i++)
          DeleteObject(hBitmap[i]);
        PostQuitMessage(0);
        break;

    case WM_TIMER:
        if (Frame > 1)
          Frame--;
        else
          Frame = LastFrame;
        InvalidateRect(hWnd, NULL, FALSE);
        break;

    case WM_PAINT:
        hDC = BeginPaint(hWnd, &ps);
        GetClientRect(hWnd, &rect);
#ifdef PAL
        SelectPalette(hDC, hLogPal, 0);
        RealizePalette(hDC);
#endif
        /* The first time through, calculate the ray traced image.
         * Place the image in a bitmap. Later, update the screen
         * with the bitmap rather than recalculating the image.
         */
        MemDC = CreateCompatibleDC(hDC);
        if (First) {
          /* The first time through the paint function, create
           * and read in the four images
           */
```

```
            for (i=0; i<LastFrame; i++) {
                hBitmap[i] = CreateCompatibleBitmap(hDC, ImWd, ImHt);
                hTmpBmp = SelectObject(MemDC, hBitmap[i]);
#ifdef PAL
                SelectPalette(MemDC, hLogPal2, 0);
                RealizePalette(MemDC);
#endif
                itoa(i, Buffer, 10);  /* Build the filename to read */
                strcpy(CurrentFile, Filename);
                strcat(CurrentFile, ".");
                strcat(CurrentFile, Buffer);

#ifdef PAL
                readimage(CurrentFile, MemDC);
#else
                if (ReadImage(CurrentFile, hDC) < 0) {
                   MessageBox(NULL, "Failed opening image file", "Error", MB_OK);
                }

                BitBlt(MemDC, 0, 0, ImWd, ImHt, hDC, 0, 0, SRCCOPY);
                SelectObject(MemDC, hTmpBmp);
#endif
            }
            First = FALSE;

            /* Starts a timer that will signal when to display the next
             * frame of an animated sequence.
             */
            SetTimer(hWnd, TIMER_ID, UPDATE_RATE, NULL);
        }

        SelectObject(MemDC, hBitmap[Frame]);

#ifdef PAL
        SelectPalette(MemDC, hLogPal2, 0);
        RealizePalette(MemDC);
#endif
        /* Displays the bitmap in the window */
        BitBlt(hDC, 0, 0, ImWd, ImHt, MemDC, 0, 0, SRCCOPY);

        DeleteDC(MemDC);
        EndPaint(hWnd, &ps);
        break;

      default:
        return DefWindowProc(hWnd, Msg, wParam, lParam);
    }
    return 0L;
}
```

```c
int readimage(char *Filename, HDC MemDC)
{
  int T;
  long x, y;
  BYTE Red, Green, Blue;
  unsigned char huge *Image;

  if (GetImageInfo(Filename, &ImWd, &ImHt, &T) <= 0)
    return -1;

  if (T == 2)
    Image = (unsigned char huge *)farmalloc((long)ImWd*(long)ImHt*3L);
  else
    Image = (unsigned char huge *)farmalloc((long)ImWd*(long)ImHt);

  if (Image == NULL) {
    return -1;     // Out of memory
  }

  if (!ReadImage(Filename, Image)) {
    return -1;     // Could not open image
  }

  for (y=0; y<ImHt; y++)
    for (x=0; x<ImWd; x++) {
      if (T == 2) {   // 24-bit image
        Red = Image[(y*(long)ImWd + x)*3L];
        Green = Image[(y*(long)ImWd + x)*3L+1];
        Blue = Image[(y*(long)ImWd + x)*3L+2];
      }
      else {
        Red = Image[y*ImWd + x];
        Green = Red;
        Blue = Red;
      }
#ifdef PAL
      SetPixel(MemDC, x, y, PALETTERGB(Red,Red,Red));
#else
      SetPixel(MemDC, x, y, RGB(Red,Green,Blue));
#endif
    }
  }
  farfree(Image);
  return 1;
}
```

Rendering Water and Clouds

S o far, we've been ray tracing surfaces that can be modeled with simple equations. But what about natural objects, such as water, clouds, and mountains, that aren't so regular? Sometimes you can apply a texture to one of RAY's basic object types to create the desired effect. In the first part of this chapter, for instance, you'll learn how to render rippling water using this approach. At other times, the objects are too complex for a single texture to work well. In these cases, you can often divide the object into smaller component objects and render each one separately. The second half of this chapter, for example, will show you how to use this strategy to render a variety of clouds. In Chapter 8, we'll take these ideas further and generate scenes complete with mountains, lakes, and clouds.

DESIGNING A MODEL OF WATER

There isn't a single, "correct" way to add water to a ray traced image. The reason is that water has many different appearances. A mirror-smooth lake, for instance, is much different than a ten-foot ocean wave crashing onto a rocky beach.

We could try to develop a model for water that would enable us to render water scenes of all types. However, this would be extremely difficult to do. Besides, we're more concerned with making the water appear realistic in an image than modeling water accurately. Our model does not have to be realistic; whatever works is good enough.

The disadvantage with this ad hoc approach is that we'll be forced to develop a custom water algorithm for every form of water we want to render. The code to generate a lake will be different than that to render a waterfall, Hawaiian-sized wave, or thrashing sea.

In the following sections, we'll focus on rendering water like you'd see in a lake, pond, or puddle. We'll simulate small waves that emanate from various points in the water. The code will also enable us to run sequences of images together to create the illusion of flowing water.

THE ESSENCE OF WATER

Water is somewhat difficult to model because of its free form. In general, water is colorless and transparent. Its appearance depends heavily upon the surroundings reflecting on its surface, the depth of the water, and what the water is in. These are only general rules, however. We can do whatever it takes to render a realistic-looking scene.

In practice, there are two keys to rendering realistic water. First, the water's surface must be highly reflective. Second, the surface must have at least a rippling texture across it. This second step is important for rendering outdoor water because it is rarely completely smooth and motionless. You probably have an idea of what lighting parameters to select to make the water reflective, but how are the small, rippling waves added?

The first thing to realize is that we'll be dealing with *small* waves. Large waves, like those crashing into the coastline, are more challenging to model and are not our focus here.

The key to rendering small waves is using a special *cycloid* function. As the name implies, a cycloid function generates a repetitive pattern. In our case, we want cycles of waves. A good function to use is the sine function. Indeed, as Figure 7.1 illustrates, a two-dimensional sine wave looks much like a string of rolling waves.

To create a wavy surface, all we need to do is add the value of a sine function to each point on a rectangle's surface. What value should we plug into the sine function? A good strategy is to base the value on the distance from one or more three-dimensional points, as Figure 7.2 illustrates. If Q is a point on an

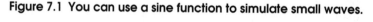

Figure 7.1 You can use a sine function to simulate small waves.

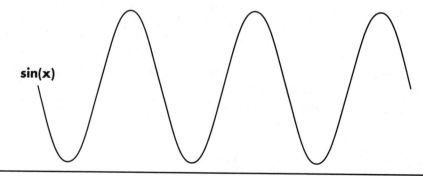

sin(x)

Figure 7.2 Basing the sine function on the distance to a center point creates concentric waves of circles.

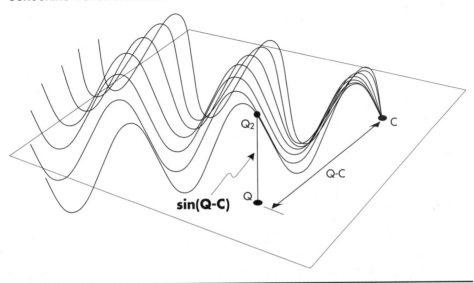

object's surface and C is the center of the wave, then the new surface point Q_2 can be calculated with the equation

$$Q_2 = Q + \sin(Q-C)$$

Each point C, in a sense, acts as a wave generator. In three dimensions, the waves appear as concentric spheres centered about the wave generators. On a plane, they appear as concentric circles. If you use several dispersed points, you get a realistic-looking water effect. Generally, the more points you use the rougher the water appears.

ANIMATING WAVES

In the real world, waves don't sit still. So how can we extend the wave model to enable them to move? All we need to do is add a phase shift to the sine function, as Figure 7.3 illustrates. Each successive image frame will slightly increase the phase shift, causing the wave to move along the object's surface. The amount that the phase shift is altered coincides with the speed of the wave front. For instance, to move the wave 10 degrees between each frame, we could multiply the current frame number by 10 and add this value to the wave's frequency value:

```
Q2 = Q + sin(f + (10)Frame_number)
```

Figure 7.3 Adding a phase shift to the sine function makes the wave appear to move.

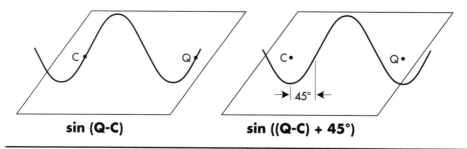

$$\sin (Q-C) \qquad\qquad \sin ((Q-C) + 45°)$$

Using Normals to Make Waves

Although we can add a sine wave to the surface of an object to create a wave effect, we'll enlist a slightly faster, ray tracing technique. We'll apply the sine values only to the surface's normal. For small waves, the viewer won't be able to tell that we're only modifying the surface normal. When the lighting model uses the perturbed normal, it will give the object its textured shape. This makes sense, since the shading of an object is based on the object's normal. This form of texturing is called *bump mapping*.

Realize that the shading gives the illusion that the surface has waves, but the surface is really flat. If you look at the waves from the side you won't see any bumps or depressions. This won't cause a problem as long as the viewer is not too close to the surface.

A WATER OBJECT

Although RAY renders water as a special texture, it uses a different texturing technique than you've seen earlier. Recall that all the textures we explored in Chapter 5 mapped their textures through the **DeterminePattern** function pointer in the **Object** class. The water effect, in contrast, defines a special-purpose water object, **WaterObj**. Here's its definition as it appears in RAY.H:

```
class WaterObj : public RectangleObj {
public:
  float Ht;     // Height of water's waves
  float Rough;  // Controls roughness of water
  int NumWaveCenters; // Number of wave centers
  WaterObj::WaterObj(VECTOR *LocV, VECTOR *Vect1, VECTOR *Vect2) :
    RectangleObj(LocV, Vect1, Vect2) { }
  virtual void ComputeNormal(VECTOR *Q, VECTOR *N);
};
```

Notice that RAY.H derives **WaterObj** from the **RectangleObj** class. In other words, **RectangleObj** gives the water its basic shape and **WaterObj** applies a rippling texture to it.

WaterObj overrides the object's **ComputeNormal** function to supply the textured normals, thereby giving the rectangle its rippled effect. The class also defines a few variables that it uses to control the frequency and magnitude of the waves. These values are set by the parser.

Creating Waves

The key to rendering waves is **WaterObj's ComputeNormal** function. It offsets the orientation of the surface's normal by adding in a series of sine values. The sine values correspond to waves that emanate from a series of points, which are defined in the **WaveCenters** array:

```
VECTOR WaveCenters[NUMWAVECENTERS] =
  {{-4, -4, 0},   {0, 2, -0},   {3, 4, 0},   {-4, 3, 0},
   {10,  2, 0},   {4, 1, -0},   {2, -4, 0},   {-1, 3, 0},
   {-2, -2, 0},   {0, -2, 0},   {3, -1, -0},  {-2, .4, 0},
   {-6, -.4, -0}, {1, 2, 0},    {3, -4, -0},  {2, 1, 0}}};
```

The **NUMWAVECENTERS** constant defines 16 wave generators. Realize that the center points of the waves can be anywhere. They don't have to be on the surface of the object.

ComputeNormal also defines the **fnum** array to specify a frequency for each wave generator:

```
float fnum[NUMWAVECENTERS] = {10, 44, 18, 24, 36, 35, 54, 22, 19, 22,
   10, 24, 18, 24, 36, 35};
```

The **fnum** values control how widely spaced the waves are from the wave center. Larger values represent bigger frequencies. Figure 7.4 shows two waves: one with a frequency of 5 and the other with a frequency of 10.

The first step **ComputeNormal** takes is to compute the normal of the water's plane. This effectively retrieves the normal of the rectangle:

```
N = ComputeNormal(Q);
```

Next, the code steps through a **for** loop that adds a sine value for each wave generator:

```
for (I=0; I<NumWaveCenters; I++) {
  f = fnum[I] * Rough + fr;
  PhaseInc = pow(f, 0.25);  // Used in animating the water
  Dist = Subtract(Q, &WaveCenters[I]);
```

Figure 7.4 A frequency setting controls the separation between the waves.

```
Dist.x = Dist.x * f;
Dist.y = Dist.y * f;
Dist.z = Dist.z * f;
M = Mag(&Dist);
N->x += (Ht * sin(M+FrameNum*PhaseInc));
N->y += (Ht * sin(M+FrameNum*PhaseInc));
N->z += (Ht * cos(M+FrameNum*PhaseInc));
}
```

Let's walk through each of these statements.

The top two statements in the **for** loop determine the frequency and incremental phase shift of each wave. The calculations that follow these statements multiply the wave's frequency times the distance from the surface coordinate **Q** to a wave's center point. This result is used in the sine calculation. Here's the code that adds in the current wave's contribution to the normal:

```
N->x += (Ht * sin(M+FrameNum*PhaseInc));
N->y += (Ht * sin(M+FrameNum*PhaseInc));
N->z += (Ht * cos(M+FrameNum*PhaseInc));
```

The value of **Ht** scales the height of the wave. The value of **f** is different for each wave generator and therefore adds variety to the waves.

Once the **for** loop is finished, the normal, **N**, is normalized and returned. Its value is used in the lighting model calculations to determine the diffuse lighting of the water and its specular highlights.

ADDING WATER TO A SCENE

You can use the scene description language's *Water* command to add a water effect to a rectangle object. The *Water* command requires three parameters. The first two scale the height and frequency of the waves, respectively. Usually, you'll want to set these two values to 1. The last parameter is an integer that specifies the number of wave centers to use. This value must range between 1 and the value of **NUMWAVECENTERS**, defined in OBJECTS.CPP. For example, the following statement creates a rectangular patch of blue, reflective water:

```
Rectangle(Loc(0,0,0),V1(100,0,0),V2(0,100,0),Color(0,0,.8),
   Ambient(.85),Diffuse(0),Specular(.9),SpecSpread(4),
   Transparency(0),Water(1,1,16))
```

These settings will work fine in many cases. Notice that the water is highly reflective. Therefore, its final color depends a great deal on its surroundings and the background color. If the background color is light blue, for instance, the water will appear light blue. If it's black, the water will be deep blue. The reflective nature of the water may give you some problems.

How can you use *Water*'s three parameters to control the appearance of the water? For most scenes, you'll want to use the settings given here. However, when you want smooth water, you'll want to scale down the waves and use fewer wave centers. A good set of numbers to use is *Water(.1,1,4)*.

Sample Water Scene

The following scene description file, WATER1.SDF, illustrates how to use RAY's water feature. The file generates the scene shown in Color Plate 2.

```
/* WATER1.SDF
 */

AntiAliasing()
Resolution(500,500)
From(90,0,5)
At(-100,0,7)
Up(0.0,0.0,1.0)
Background(0,0,0)
MaxLevel(2)

DMin(50)
DMax(200)
Light(Loc(140,20,60), Color(1,1,1), Point())

/* The water */
Rectangle(Loc(-100,-100,0),V1(200,0,0),V2(0,200,0),Color(0,0,.5),
   Ambient(1), Diffuse(0), Specular(.9), SpecSpread(0), Water(.1,1,16))
```

```
Sphere(Loc(28,20,0),Radius(6),Color(1,0,0),Ambient(1),Diffuse(0),
   Specular(1), SpecSpread(1), Transparency(0))
Sphere(Loc(30,0,0),Radius(6),Color(.84,.66,.04),Ambient(1),Diffuse(0),
   Specular(1), SpecSpread(1), Transparency(0))
Sphere(Loc(43,-15,0),Radius(6),Color(0,.8,.1),Ambient(1),Diffuse(0),
   Specular(1), SpecSpread(1), Transparency(0))

Cylinder(Loc(10,-20,20),V1(-20,-40,0),Radius(5),
   Color(0,0,1),Ambient(.6),Diffuse(1),Specular(.2),SpecSpread(1))
Cylinder(Loc(10,-20,0),V1(0,0,30),Radius(5),
   Color(0,0,1),Ambient(.6),Diffuse(1),Specular(.2),SpecSpread(1))
Cylinder(Loc(10,-20,20),V1(-20,40,0),Radius(5),Color(0,0,1),
   Ambient(.6),Diffuse(1),Specular(.2),SpecSpread(1))
Cylinder(Loc(-10,20,0),V1(0,0,30),Radius(5),
   Color(0,0,1),Ambient(.6),Diffuse(1),Specular(.2),SpecSpread(1))
Cylinder(Loc(-10,20,20),V1(20,40,0),Radius(5),
   Color(0,0,1),Ambient(.6),Diffuse(1),Specular(.2),SpecSpread(1))
```

You can generate animated water by adding the *NumFrames* keyword with a value greater than 1. The frames in Color Plate 3, for instance, were generated using the statement:

```
NumFrames(4)
```

You can use the PLAYBACK program in Chapter 6 to display the image sequence.

Realize that the water's scale does not change with the size of the object. If you want larger appearing waves, you'll need to get closer to the object's surface. Similarly, when the viewer is far away, the water's surface may appear too rough. You may want to use the *Water* command's parameters to tone the waves down.

A WATERY GLASS

It's time for another trick. We can use the **WaterObj** class to render non-water objects too. One particularly pleasing result comes from applying the water function to glass surfaces. The wave pattern gives the glass a realistic wavy texture. BLOCKS.SDF, shown here, renders the stack of glass blocks shown in Color Plate 3.

```
/* BLOCKS.SDF */

AntiAliasing()
Resolution(200,200)
From(10,3,5)
At(0,3,5)
Up(0.0,0.0,1.0)
```

```
Background(.66,.88,1)
MaxLevel(2)

DMin(50)
DMax(200)
Light(Loc(60,-10,60), Color(1,1,1), Point())

Rectangle(Loc(-50,-200,200),V1(0,400,0),V2(0,0,400),Color(1,0,0),
  Transparency(0),Ambient(.8), Diffuse(.8), Specular(0), SpecSpread(0))

/* Top row of blocks */
Rectangle(Loc(-10,-10,10),V1(0,4.5,0),V2(0,0,-4.5),Color(0,0,1),
  Transparency(.3),Ambient(.3), Diffuse(0), Specular(.7), SpecSpread(2),
  Water(1,1,14))
Rectangle(Loc(-10,-5,10),V1(0,4.5,0),V2(0,0,-4.5),Color(0,0,1),
  Ambient(.3), Diffuse(0), Specular(.7), SpecSpread(2), Water(1,1,16))
Rectangle(Loc(-10,0,10),V1(0,4.5,0),V2(0,0,-4.5),Color(0,0,1),
  Ambient(.3), Diffuse(0), Specular(.7), SpecSpread(2), Water(.2,.4,13))
Rectangle(Loc(-10,5,10),V1(0,4.5,0),V2(0,0,-4.5),Color(0,0,1),
  Ambient(.3), Diffuse(0), Specular(.7), SpecSpread(2), Water(.2,.4,15))
Rectangle(Loc(-10,10,10),V1(0,4.5,0),V2(0,0,-4.5),Color(0,0,1),
  Ambient(.3), Diffuse(0), Specular(.7), SpecSpread(2), Water(1,1,16))

Rectangle(Loc(-10,-10,5),V1(0,4.5,0),V2(0,0,-4.5),Color(0,0,1),
  Ambient(.3), Diffuse(0), Specular(.7), SpecSpread(2), Water(.6,.4,14))
Rectangle(Loc(-10,-5,5),V1(0,4.5,0),V2(0,0,-4.5),Color(0,0,1),
  Ambient(.3), Diffuse(0), Specular(.7), SpecSpread(2), Water(.4,.6,16))
Rectangle(Loc(-10,0,5),V1(0,4.5,0),V2(0,0,-4.5),Color(0,0,1),
  Ambient(.3), Diffuse(0), Specular(.7), SpecSpread(2), Water(1.1.15))
Rectangle(Loc(-10,5,5),V1(0,4.5,0),V2(0,0,-4.5),Color(0,0,1),
  Ambient(.3), Diffuse(0), Specular(.7), SpecSpread(2), Water(1,1,14))
Rectangle(Loc(-10,10,5),V1(0,4.5,0),V2(0,0,-4.5),Color(0,0,1),
  Ambient(.3), Diffuse(0), Specular(.7), SpecSpread(2), Water(1,1,16))

Rectangle(Loc(-10,-10,0),V1(0,4.5,0),V2(0,0,-4.5),Color(0,0,1),
  Ambient(.3), Diffuse(0), Specular(.7), SpecSpread(2), Water(1,2,16))
Rectangle(Loc(-10,-5,0),V1(0,4.5,0),V2(0,0,-4.5),Color(0,0,1),
  Ambient(.3), Diffuse(0), Specular(.7), SpecSpread(2), Water(.2,.4,15))
Rectangle(Loc(-10,0,0),V1(0,4.5,0),V2(0,0,-4.5),Color(0,0,1),
  Ambient(.3), Diffuse(0), Specular(.7), SpecSpread(2), Water(1,2,13))
Rectangle(Loc(-10,5,0),V1(0,4.5,0),V2(0,0,-4.5),Color(0,0,1),
  Ambient(.3), Diffuse(0), Specular(.7), SpecSpread(2), Water(.4,.6,14))
Rectangle(Loc(-10,10,0),V1(0,4.5,0),V2(0,0,-4.5),Color(0,0,1),
  Ambient(.3), Diffuse(0), Specular(.7), SpecSpread(2), Water(1,1,16))

/* Horizontal strips between blocks */
Rectangle(Loc(-10,-10.5,10.5),V1(0,25,0),V2(0,0,-.5),Color(0,0,0),
  Ambient(.8), Diffuse(.3), Specular(0), SpecSpread(0), Transparency(0))
```

```
Rectangle(Loc(-10,-10.5,5.5),V1(0,25,0),V2(0,0,-.5),Color(0,0,0),
   Ambient(.8), Diffuse(.3), Specular(0), SpecSpread(0))
Rectangle(Loc(-10,-10.5,.5),V1(0,25,0),V2(0,0,-.5),Color(0,0,0),
   Ambient(.8), Diffuse(.3), Specular(0), SpecSpread(0))

/* Vertical strips between blocks */
Rectangle(Loc(-10,-10.5,10.5),V1(0,.5,0),V2(0,0,-15),Color(0,0,0),
   Ambient(.8), Diffuse(.3), Specular(0), SpecSpread(0))
Rectangle(Loc(-10,-5.5,10.5),V1(0,.5,0),V2(0,0,-15),Color(0,0,0),
   Ambient(.8), Diffuse(.3), Specular(0), SpecSpread(0))
Rectangle(Loc(-10,-.5,10.5),V1(0,.5,0),V2(0,0,-15),Color(0,0,0),
   Ambient(.8), Diffuse(.3), Specular(0), SpecSpread(0))
Rectangle(Loc(-10,4.5,10.5),V1(0,.5,0),V2(0,0,-15),Color(0,0,0),
   Ambient(.8), Diffuse(.3), Specular(0), SpecSpread(0))
Rectangle(Loc(-10,9.5,10.5),V1(0,.5,0),V2(0,0,-15),Color(0,0,0),
   Ambient(.8), Diffuse(.3), Specular(0), SpecSpread(0))
Rectangle(Loc(-10,14.5,10.5),V1(0,.5,0),V2(0,0,-15),Color(0,0,0),
   Ambient(.8), Diffuse(.3), Specular(0), SpecSpread(0))
```

Extending the Water Model

You may want to try experimenting with a few variations on the water model. For instance, you might try adding a decay function so that the waves get smaller as their distance from the wave generator increases. In addition, you can make the waves decrease over time. Once you have added these, you can simulate rain drops falling on a puddle.

In the real world, water is noticeably refractive. For instance, when you place a straw in a glass of water, the straw bends at the water's surface. To render a truly realistic water scene, we should adjust for this refraction. However, it turns out that in many cases the refraction can be left out without anyone noticing. If you want complete realism, you must add it in to the ray tracer's lighting model. You can do this by bending light rays as they pierce through the surface of a transparent object. The amount that the light is redirected depends on the object's index of refraction. For simplicity, refraction is left out of our ray tracer.

RENDERING CLOUDS

Of all the ray traced objects discussed in this book, clouds are the most challenging to render. It's easy to understand why. Clouds come in so many different forms, shapes, densities, and sizes that it's too difficult to come up with a single cloud model that works well. Actually, it's a challenge to come up with one that works at all.

There are three basic types of clouds: cirrus, stratus, and cumulus. Cirrus clouds are high, wispy clouds. Stratus clouds are typically relatively low layers

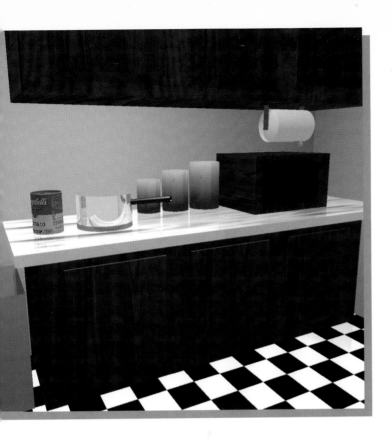

You can construct interesting ray traced scenes by applying textures to simple geometric shapes. The textures in this scene include a checker floor pattern, marble countertop, and frosted glasses. The woodgrain effect was created by mapping an image of wood onto a series of rectangles. Similarly, the soup can was rendered by mapping an image of a soup can label onto a cylinder.

The ray tracing program presented in Chapters 3 and 4 can animate the locations of objects or the position and orientation of the viewer. In this example, nine balls spin above the surface of a collection of checkered rectangles. You can use the PLAYBACK program in Chapter 6 to preview animation sequences that the ray tracing program produces.

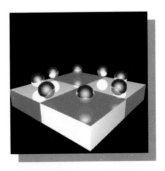

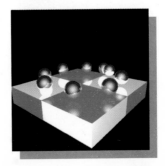

The water in the image at le[ft] was created by mapping a special water texture to a rectangle. The surface of the rectangle actually isn't changed though. Instead, on[ly] the normal of the rectangle i[s] modified giving the illusion [of] wavy water.

The four frames at right are part of an animated sequence in which the viewer "flies" through the scene shown above. When an animated scene includes a water object, such as this one, the water is automatically animated. The water's waves appear to spread out from several dispersed points, like ripples in a pond.

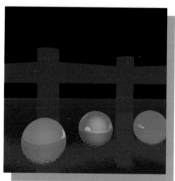
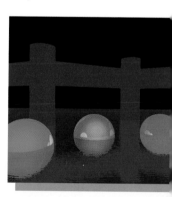

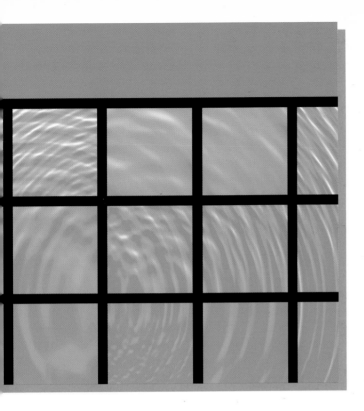

Sometimes textures can be used in non-standard ways. In this image a water texture is applied to an array of transparent rectangles giving the illusion of glass blocks. Each rectangle defines a different set of constants for the water to give each block a unique appearance.

The mountains at right and bottom were constructed from a series of fractalized triangles. The two images use different fractal parameters and levels of recursion to produce different effects. The clouds are drawn using three textured ellipsoids. Again, the two scenes use distinct sets of texturing parameters, yielding slightly different clouds.

Simple geometric shapes ofte[n] can be used to produce strik[ing] ray traced images. In this scene, the ground, road, and stripes are all built from rectangles. The sky is also a plane, however, it has a blen[d] pattern painted on it. The mountains, in constrast, are built from fractalized triangle[s] and the clouds are constructe[d] from a series of textured ellipsoids.

The frames above are part of a movie generated using the morphing program discussed in Chapter 12. The top-left and bottom-right frames are the original images. The frames in between were synthesized with the morphing program.

of clouds that don't have much texture. Cumulus clouds are also at lower altitudes and form in highly textured heaps.

The cloud model we'll present here enables you to render each of these types of clouds. We'll experiment with two different techniques. The first models the sky as a plane with streaks of clouds painted on them. This approach is good for rendering high cirrus and stratus clouds, but not much more. The second technique paints the cloud texture onto ellipsoids. By grouping ellipsoids together you can generate a wide variety of cloud shapes, particularly cumulus clouds.

A TWO-DIMENSIONAL SKY

The simplest way to create a cloudless sky is to set the background color for the image to a bluish color. A variation on this technique is to encompass the scene with a sky-blue sphere or a set of planes. Of course, this doesn't account for any clouds in the sky.

One common way to add clouds is to map an image of an actual photograph of the sky onto a plane. In many cases, this looks quite realistic. However, this doesn't give us much control over the clouds in the scene.

A slightly better approach is to map a cloud texture to the sky surface. What formula can we use? One technique that works reasonably well is to map a collection of sine waves to the surface. In a sense, it's like mapping a special kind of water to the sky. This makes sense when you consider the fluid nature of clouds. The formula we'll use is an approximation to what is called the *Fourier series*. It calculates a texture value, T, using the equation

$$T(x,y,z) = k \ [C_1 \sin(FX_1 X + PX_1) + T_0] \ [C_1 \sin(FY_1 Y + PY_1) + T_0]$$

Essentially, the function sums up a series of ever-decreasing sine waves that are based on the coordinates of the point being rendered. Specifically, the frequencies are calculated by the subexpressions

$$FX_{i+1} = 2 \ FX_i$$
$$FY_{i+1} = 2 \ FY_i$$
$$C_{i+1} = .707 \ C_i$$

The values of C_i control the amplitudes of the texture at various frequencies. Notice that each subsequent value of C is smaller than its predecessor. The values FX_i and FY_i are frequencies based on the coordinate of the point being rendered. The PX_i and PY_i variables add in phase shifts so that the function does not generate a highly repetitive pattern. These ratios generate fairly natural appearing, ever-smaller textures.

The phase shifts PX_i and PY_i add randomness to the texture based on the equations:

$$PX_1 = (\pi/2)\sin(FY_1 \ Y/2)$$
$$PY_1 = (\pi/2)\sin(FX_1 \ X/2)$$

Notice that the phase shift added in the x direction is partially based on the y coordinate and similarly the y phase shift is partially based on values of x. A z term can also be added in to ensure that the patterns are not too repetitive for different orientations of the sky plane.

Implementing A Sky Plane

Let's see how RAY implements the cloud texturing function. As you might expect, RAY defines a texture function to generate the sky pattern. The function, **TwoDCloudPattern**, is located in OBJECTS.CPP. When it is assigned to a rectangle object's **DeterminePattern** function, it returns varying shades of colors between the objects **Ia1** and **Ia2** colors.

TwoDCloudPattern is deceptively simple. The reason is that most of the work is performed in the **Noise** function. The **Noise** routine returns the texture value to apply to the sky-plane. The value of **T**, which ranges between 0 and 1, is used to partially determine the color to paint the sky. Specifically, the function returns a value that falls between the two colors **Ia1** and **Ia2**. Recall that these are **COLOR** fields in the **Object** class. If one is set to sky blue and the other to white, you'll get a variety of clouds in the sky. Here's the complete **TwoDCloudPattern** function:

```
COLOR TwoDCloudPattern(Object* ObjPtr, VECTOR* Q)
{
  COLOR Color;
  float k, kx, ky, T;

  RectangleObj *Obj = (RectangleObj *)ObjPtr;

  T = Noise(Q, Obj->V1.z, Obj->V2.z, &Obj->MaxTO);

  Color.r = 1 - T;
  Color.g = 1 - T;
  Color.b = 1 - T;

  Color.r = Obj->Ia1.r + (Obj->Ia2.r - Obj->Ia1.r) * T;
  Color.g = Obj->Ia1.g + (Obj->Ia2.g - Obj->Ia1.g) * T;
  Color.b = Obj->Ia1.b + (Obj->Ia2.b - Obj->Ia1.b) * T;

  return Color;
}
```

Calculating the Texture

The **Noise** function hides the details of calculating the texture value for a specific point. **Noise** implements the texturing equations we outlined earlier. Its parameters set the strength of the resulting texture. These settings are assigned to various fields in the **Object** class by the parser.

Defining Two-Dimensional Clouds

You can use the *Cloud* command in conjunction with a *Rectangle* command to create a two-dimensional sky plane. The *Cloud* command takes two parameters. The first sets the amount of texture and the second the transparency threshold. The first parameter typically ranges between .1 and 3. Larger values create clouds with greater variety. The second parameter usually falls between 0 and 5. It controls how much of the clouds will be visible. Larger values produce thicker clouds.

Figure 7.5 presents four images with different cloud settings. They can be created using the following scene description file:

```
/* CLOUDS.SDF */

AntiAliasing()
Resolution(200,200)
From(80,0,0)
At(5,0,50)
Up(0.0,0.0,1.0)
Background(.6,.8,1)
MaxLevel(1)

Light(Loc(0,0,1), Color(1,1,1), Point())
Light(Loc(0,0,1), Color(1,1,1), Point())

/* Top-left cloud */
Rectangle(Loc(-200,-200,40),V1(400,0,0),V2(0,400,0),Color(1,1,1),
        Color2(0,0,1), Ambient(1), Diffuse(0), Specular(0),
        SpecSpread(0), Cloud(.2,1.5))
/* Top-right cloud */
Rectangle(Loc(-200,-200,40),V1(400,0,0),V2(0,400,0),Color(1,1,1),
        Color2(0,0,1), Ambient(1), Diffuse(0), Specular(0),
        SpecSpread(0), Cloud(1,1.5))
/* Bottom-left cloud */
Rectangle(Loc(-200,-200,40),V1(400,0,0),V2(0,400,0),Color(1,1,1),
        Color2(0,0,1), Ambient(1), Diffuse(0), Specular(0),
        SpecSpread(0), Cloud(.2,3))
/* Bottom-right cloud */
Rectangle(Loc(-200,-200,40),V1(400,0,0),V2(0,400,0),Color(1,1,1),
        Color2(0,0,1), Ambient(1), Diffuse(0), Specular(0),
        SpecSpread(0), Cloud(.2,.7))
```

Figure 7.5 Four images with different cloud settings.

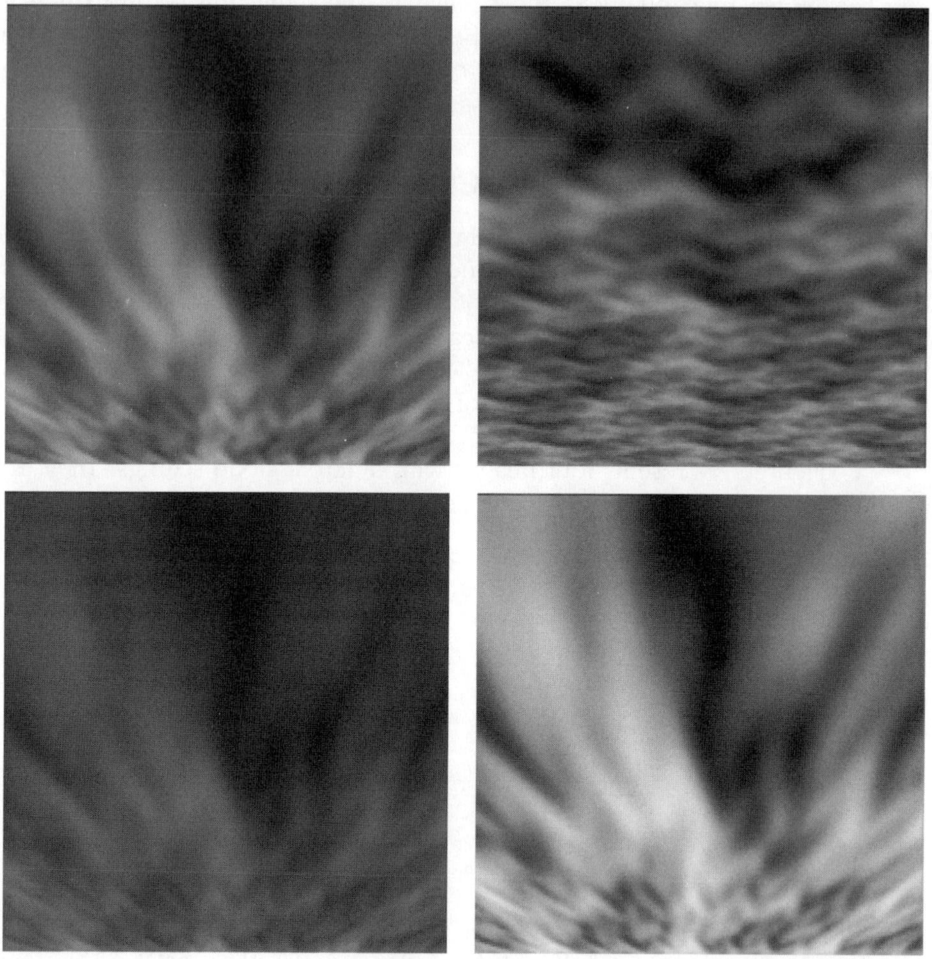

A drawback to the sky-plane approach to rendering clouds is that the cloud function applies to the whole sky. It doesn't allow you to limit the clouds to just above the horizon, for instance. We'll introduce three-dimensional clouds later in this chapter to help you get around this problem.

Cloudy Marble

You may be wondering if we can use the cloud texture in other ways. Yes, we can. With the right settings, we can create a rather realistic marble effect. In fact, we did exactly this in Chapter 6 for the kitchen scene to render the marble

Figure 7.6 A sample marble pattern.

pattern on the countertop. RAY's parser defines the *Marble* command for this purpose. It maps the two-dimensional cloud texture to a planar object. The function uses two colors specified by the *Color* and *Color2* commands in the marble. The fluid nature of a marble pattern is very similar to high, fair weather clouds. The following statement, for instance, renders the marble pattern shown in Figure 7.6:

```
Rectangle(Loc(-100,-50,0),V1(150,0,0),V2(0,100,0),Color(1,1,1),
         Color2(0,0,1), Ambient(1), Diffuse(0), Specular(0),
         SpecSpread(0), Marble())
```

THREE-DIMENSIONAL CLOUDS

A two-dimensional cloud texture is fine for rendering high, distant clouds. But sometimes, you'll want clouds to appear in front of objects or placed at different heights in a scene. Or you may want to have greater control over how the clouds appear. In order to render clouds like these, we must expand our cloud generation technique. The rest of this chapter describes how RAY is able to ray trace three-dimensional clouds.

Creating Three-Dimensional Clouds

RAY uses textured ellipsoids to render three-dimensional clouds. The ellipsoids produce the basic shape of the cloud and the texture makes them appear more cloud-like. The texturing algorithm is similar to that which we used to render two-dimensional clouds. We must make a few changes, however.

Figure 7.7 An ellipsoid with the cloud texture mapped to it.

If we were to simply map the earlier technique to an ellipsoid, we'd get a cloud like that shown in Figure 7.7. RAY improves upon this technique by taking two additional steps. First, it modulates the transparency of the ellipsoid by making the ellipsoid transparent wherever its texture is too dark. Figure 7.8 illustrates what affect this change has on the ellipsoid shown in Figure 7.7. The second modification is to make the edges of the ellipsoid more transparent than its middle. This softens the edges, as Figure 7.9 shows.

Figure 7.8 A textured ellipsoid with transparency modulation.

Figure 7.9 A textured ellipsoid with transparency modulation in the image plane.

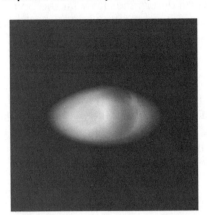

The Three-Dimensional Cloud Function

The **ThreeDCloudPattern** function is the texturing routine that applies a cloud texture to an ellipsoid. When it is assigned to the **DeterminePattern** function pointer in an **EllipsoidObj** object, the ellipsoid will appear as a cloud. The function is similar to the **TwoDCloudPattern** routine that generates two-dimensional clouds.

Like its two-dimensional counterpart, **ThreeDCloudPattern** calls the **Noise** function to retrieve a texture value that partially determines the color of the cloud at the point being rendered. However, in **ThreeDCloudPattern**, if the texture value is below a specified threshold, then the cloud's transparency parameter, **kt**, is set high so that the spot on the cloud will be transparent.

The code also gradually fades the edges of the clouds by making the edges of the cloud transparent. The rationale behind this step is that clouds are less dense and more transparent around their perimeters. Realize, that we're referring to the cloud's edges in the image and not to the ellipsoid's three-dimensional surface. How is this gradual fading implemented? The code increases the clouds transparency by increasing the object's **kt** value at the points that are farthest from the cloud's center.

The coordinate of the current image pixel being rendered is available through the **x** and **y** variables. They are globally defined in RAY.CPP. The center of the cloud is calculated by the **WorldToScreen** function. It's called when **MaxT0** is 0, which is only true the first time **ThreeDCloudPattern** is executed.

```
if (Obj->MaxT0 == 0) {
  WorldToScreen(Obj->Loc, Obj->V1.x, Obj->V1.y);
}
```

The center coordinates are placed in the otherwise unused fields **V1.x** and **V1.y**. Next, the function determines how far the point (**x,y**) is from (**V1.x,V1.y**). The square of the distance in the x direction is placed in the **kx** variable using the equation

```
kx = (x-Obj->V1.x) * (x-Obj->V1.x);
```

A similar calculation is made for the y direction, and the result is stored in **ky**. In addition, **ThreeDCloudPattern** keeps track of the largest distances in **kx** and **ky** and places them in the object's fields **V2.x** and **V2.y**, respectively. Here's the test that updates the **V2.x** field:

```
if (kx > Obj->V2.x)
  Obj->V2.x = kx;
```

After the values of **kx** and **ky** are computed, they are scaled against their largest values stored in **V2.x** and **V2.y**:

```
kx /= Obj->V2.x;
ky /= Obj->V2.y;
```

This ensures that **kx** and **ky** will be less than 1. These two values are then added together and the result is placed in the variable **k**:

```
k = (kx + ky);

if (k < 0) k = 0;
  else if (k > 1) k = 1;
```

The value of **k** is clipped so that it falls between 0 and 1 and the result is assigned to the transparency field, **kt**:

```
Obj->kt = k;   // Modulate the transparency
```

Recall that **kt** is used in RAY.CPP to specify how transparent the object is. Normally, **kt** is constant for a whole object. For a cloud, however, it varies. At the edges of the ellipse, **kt** will be its largest, forcing the cloud to gradually fade away. Near the cloud's center, **k** will be its smallest and the ellipse will be the least transparent.

ThreeDCloudPattern also increases the transparency of the ellipsoid if the texture value in **T** is too large. This ensures that the ellipse won't have highly contrasting dark spots. This adjustment is made by the statement

```
if (Obj->kt < T && Obj->kt < T * 2) Obj->kt = T * 2;
```

The last step is to compute the color to return for the cloud. This is simply a portion of the texture computed in **Noise**:

```
T /= 2;
Color.r = 1 - T;
Color.g = 1 - T;
Color.b = 1 - T;
```

The value of **Color** is returned so that it can be used in the lighting model to render the cloud at the point **Q**.

DEFINING CLOUDS

When you use the *Cloud* command in conjunction with *Ellipsoid*, RAY generates a single three-dimensional cloud. The *Cloud* command takes the same two parameters discussed for two-dimensional clouds. The first sets the texturing contrast and the second the transparency threshold. The first parameter typically ranges between .1 and 3. Larger values create clouds with greater contrast. The second parameter usually falls between 0 and 5. It controls how much of the cloud will be transparent. Smaller values make the cloud more solid.

Sample Clouds

The CLOUDS1.SDF file that follows creates the three-dimensional cloud shown in Figure 7.10. There really isn't anything sacred about the parameters in the file, but you may want to try experimenting with them to get a feel for how they work. Chapter 8 provides a few more examples of clouds.

Figure 7.10 CLOUDS1.SDF generates this image.

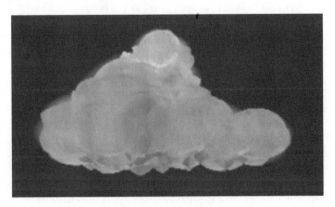

```
/* CLOUDS1.SDF */

AntiAliasing()
Resolution(400,400)
From(50,0,20)
At(1,2,24)
Up(0.0,0.0,1.0)
Background(.047,.38,.84)     /* Deep blue sky */
Light(Loc(3,-8,60), Color(1,1,1), Point())
DMin(0) DMax(3)


Ellipsoid(Loc(2,-10,35), V1(4, 4, 8), V2(50, 0, 0),
   Ambient(.9), Diffuse(1), Specular(0), Cloud(.4, 2))
Ellipsoid(Loc(3,-6,35), V1(4, 4, 8), V2(50, 0, 0),
   Ambient(.9), Diffuse(1), Specular(0), Cloud(.1, 2))
Ellipsoid(Loc(3,-2,35.5), V1(4, 4, 5), V2(50, 0, 0),
   Ambient(.8), Diffuse(1), Specular(0), Cloud(.2, 2))
Ellipsoid(Loc(3,1.5,35.5), V1(4, 4, 5), V2(50, 0, 0),
   Ambient(.9), Diffuse(1), Specular(0), Cloud(.4, 2))
Ellipsoid(Loc(3,6,35), V1(4, 4, 6), V2(50, 0, 0),
   Ambient(.9), Diffuse(1), Specular(0), Cloud(.8, 2))
Ellipsoid(Loc(2,10,35), V1(4, 4, 8), V2(50, 0, 0),
   Ambient(.9), Diffuse(1), Specular(0), Cloud(1.1, 2))


Ellipsoid(Loc(-1,-10,35), V1(4, 4, 8), V2(50, 0, 0),
   Ambient(.9), Diffuse(1), Specular(0), Cloud(.5, 2))
Ellipsoid(Loc(-2,-6,35), V1(4, 4, 8), V2(50, 0, 0),
   Ambient(.85), Diffuse(1), Specular(0), Cloud(.2, 2))
Ellipsoid(Loc(-2,-1.5,35.5), V1(4, 4, 5), V2(50, 0, 0),
   Ambient(.75), Diffuse(1), Specular(0), Cloud(.3, 2))
Ellipsoid(Loc(-2,2,35.5), V1(4, 4, 5), V2(50, 0, 0),
   Ambient(.85), Diffuse(1), Specular(0), Cloud(.5, 2))
Ellipsoid(Loc(-2,6.5,35), V1(4, 4, 6), V2(50, 0, 0),
   Ambient(.85), Diffuse(1), Specular(0), Cloud(.7, 2))
Ellipsoid(Loc(-1,10.5,35), V1(4, 4, 8), V2(50, 0, 0),
   Ambient(.85), Diffuse(1), Specular(0), Cloud(1.1, 2))


Ellipsoid(Loc(-4,-10,35), V1(4, 4, 8), V2(50, 0, 0),
   Ambient(.77), Diffuse(1), Specular(0), Cloud(.6, 2))
Ellipsoid(Loc(-5,-7,35), V1(4, 4, 8), V2(50, 0, 0),
   Ambient(.85), Diffuse(1), Specular(0), Cloud(.3, 2))
Ellipsoid(Loc(-5,-2,35.3), V1(4, 4, 5), V2(50, 0, 0),
   Ambient(.77), Diffuse(1), Specular(0), Cloud(.2, 2))
Ellipsoid(Loc(-5,1,35.5), V1(4, 4, 5), V2(50, 0, 0),
   Ambient(.85), Diffuse(1), Specular(0), Cloud(.5, 2))
Ellipsoid(Loc(-5,5,35), V1(4, 4, 6), V2(50, 0, 0),
   Ambient(.77), Diffuse(1), Specular(0), Cloud(.8, 2))
Ellipsoid(Loc(-4,9,35), V1(4, 4, 8), V2(50, 0, 0),
   Ambient(.82), Diffuse(1), Specular(0), Cloud(1, 2))
```

```
/* Second row of clouds */
Ellipsoid(Loc(-1,-10,37.7), V1(4, 4, 8), V2(50, 0, 0),
  Ambient(.9), Diffuse(1), Specular(0), Cloud(.8, 2))
Ellipsoid(Loc(-1,-5,37), V1(2, 2, 2), V2(50, 0, 0),
  Ambient(.9), Diffuse(1), Specular(0), Cloud(.5, 2))
Ellipsoid(Loc(0,-5,37), V1(4, 4, 8), V2(50, 0, 0),
  Ambient(.9), Diffuse(1), Specular(0), Cloud(.3, 2))
Ellipsoid(Loc(0,-5,39), V1(2, 2, 2), V2(50, 0, 0),
  Ambient(.9), Diffuse(1), Specular(0), Cloud(.3, 2))
Ellipsoid(Loc(0,-2,38), V1(4, 4, 8), V2(50, 0, 0),
  Ambient(.9), Diffuse(1), Specular(0), Cloud(.4, 2))
Ellipsoid(Loc(1,1,36), V1(4, 4, 8), V2(50, 0, 0),
  Ambient(.9), Diffuse(1), Specular(0), Cloud(.5, 2))
Ellipsoid(Loc(0,4,37), V1(4, 4, 8), V2(50, 0, 0),
  Ambient(.9), Diffuse(1), Specular(0), Cloud(.75, 2))
Ellipsoid(Loc(-1,10,36), V1(4, 4, 8), V2(50, 0, 0),
  Ambient(.9), Diffuse(1), Specular(0), Cloud(1, 2))

Ellipsoid(Loc(-4,-10,37.7), V1(4, 4, 8), V2(50, 0, 0),
  Ambient(.9), Diffuse(1), Specular(0), Cloud(.8, 2))
Ellipsoid(Loc(-6,-5,37), V1(2, 2, 2), V2(50, 0, 0),
  Ambient(.9), Diffuse(1), Specular(0), Cloud(.5, 2))
Ellipsoid(Loc(-5,-5,37), V1(4, 4, 8), V2(50, 0, 0),
  Ambient(.9), Diffuse(1), Specular(0), Cloud(.3, 2))
Ellipsoid(Loc(-5,-5,39), V1(2, 2, 2), V2(50, 0, 0),
  Ambient(.9), Diffuse(1), Specular(0), Cloud(.3, 2))
Ellipsoid(Loc(-5,-2,38), V1(4, 4, 8), V2(50, 0, 0),
  Ambient(.9), Diffuse(1), Specular(0), Cloud(.4, 2))
Ellipsoid(Loc(-4,1,36), V1(4, 4, 8), V2(50, 0, 0),
  Ambient(.9), Diffuse(1), Specular(0), Cloud(.5, 2))
Ellipsoid(Loc(-3,4,37), V1(4, 4, 8), V2(50, 0, 0),
  Ambient(.9), Diffuse(1), Specular(0), Cloud(.75, 2))
Ellipsoid(Loc(-4,10,36), V1(4, 4, 8), V2(50, 0, 0),
  Ambient(.9), Diffuse(1), Specular(0), Cloud(1, 2))

/* Third row of clouds */
Ellipsoid(Loc(-3,-8,41), V1(4, 4, 8), V2(20, 0, 0),
  Ambient(.9), Diffuse(1), Specular(0), Cloud(1, 2))
Ellipsoid(Loc(-4,-3,42.5), V1(4, 4, 8), V2(40, 0, 0),
  Ambient(.9), Diffuse(1), Specular(0), Cloud(1, 2))
Ellipsoid(Loc(-6,0,43), V1(4, 8, 8), V2(50, 0, 0),
  Ambient(.9), Diffuse(1), Specular(0), Cloud(.9, 2))

Ellipsoid(Loc(-2.5,0,40), V1(4, 4, 8), V2(40, 0, 0),
  Ambient(.9), Diffuse(1), Specular(0), Cloud(.6, 2))
Ellipsoid(Loc(-4,2,41), V1(4, 4, 8), V2(50, 0, 0),
  Ambient(.9), Diffuse(1), Specular(0), Cloud(1, 2))
Ellipsoid(Loc(-4,2.5,39), V1(4, 4, 8), V2(80, 0, 0),
  Ambient(.9), Diffuse(1), Specular(0), Cloud(1, 2))
```

```
Ellipsoid(Loc(-8,0,45), V1(4, 4, 8), V2(50, 0, 0),
   Ambient(1), Diffuse(1), Specular(0), Cloud(1, 2))
Ellipsoid(Loc(-7,-4,43), V1(4, 4, 8), V2(100, 0, 0),
   Ambient(1), Diffuse(1), Specular(0), Cloud(1, 2))

Ellipsoid(Loc(-12,0,47), V1(4, 4, 8), V2(100, 0, 0),
   Ambient(1), Diffuse(1), Specular(0), Cloud(.7, 2))
Ellipsoid(Loc(-2,-1,46), V1(4, 4, 8), V2(30, 0, 0),
   Ambient(1), Diffuse(1), Specular(0), Cloud(.4, 2))
Ellipsoid(Loc(-10,2,48.5), V1(4, 8, 16), V2(30, 0, 0),
   Ambient(.9), Diffuse(1), Specular(0), Cloud(.7, 2))
Ellipsoid(Loc(-10,-3,47.5), V1(4, 4, 8), V2(40, 0, 0),
   Ambient(1), Diffuse(1), Specular(0), Cloud(.7, 2))

Ellipsoid(Loc(-10,0,49.5), V1(6, 4, 8), V2(50, 0, 0),
   Ambient(1), Diffuse(1), Specular(0), Cloud(1.25, 2))
```

Tips on Constructing Clouds

Creating realistic clouds can be a time-consuming task. Not only does it take a relatively long time to render the clouds, but it also takes a lot of trial-and-error work. The best way to build a cloud is to use many small ellipsoids. Place them one or two at a time in the scene description file and try rendering them to see what they look like. By slowly adding in ellipsoids, you'll find it much easier to make adjustments to the clouds.

One problem with clouds built from several ellipsoids is that scenes can take an hour or more to render. For this reason, while you're working with your clouds keep the scene simple. In addition, liberally placing bounding boxes around the ellipsoids can dramatically speed up the rendering.

Large cumulus clouds can be the most challenging to create. You'll want to use ellipsoids with different sizes and cloud textures. To save time, you may want to write a program that generates cloud formations for you. You can use a technique similar to that discussed in Chapter 8 to create mountains.

Realize that the three-dimensional clouds may appear quite different with different perspectives. This is caused by the operation that gradually fades the ellipsoids. Since it's done in image coordinates, it may significantly distort the ellipsoid. Therefore, design your clouds for the view that they will be seen from. Sometimes a cloud will look fine from one angle, but unacceptable from another.

Rendering Fractal Mountains

Often, natural objects are the most challenging to model since their shapes are usually quite random and varied. Sometimes, a good texture is the key to rendering a natural object realistically. The clouds in Chapter 7, for instance, were designed around a special purpose texture function. However, many times there isn't a convenient texture function to use or the texture is too large in relation to the object's size. In these situations, you can usually construct the object from a collection of smaller objects. In this chapter, you'll learn how to model extremely complex mountain landscapes using triangular patches. To generate these patches, we'll use a fractal technique known as the *midpoint displacement method*. With this technique, you'll be able to generate a surprising spectrum of surfaces that range from smooth, rolling hills to jagged mountains.

RENDERING NATURAL OBJECTS

Constructing a mountain scene from small shapes requires a large number of objects. Furthermore, the more detail you want, the more objects you'll need. Manually creating a scene description file with hundreds, if not thousands, of objects would demand an extensive amount of work.

How can we automate the process? One way is to use fractals. With fractals, you only need to provide a crude representation of the scene, such as a single plane. The fractal algorithm then breaks this representation up into smaller and smaller pieces, varying the height of each piece in order to create the desired surface contour.

The amount that the components are perturbed is based on a scale factor and random number. The random number gives the figure its natural, random appearance and the scale factor guides its overall shape. A decay factor is also used to decrease the scale factor with each successively smaller region. Therefore, initially the perturbations are their largest and at each smaller region the perturbations become smaller and smaller. You can think of this as if the algorithm first generates the general contour of a mountain's peaks and then adds in finer levels of texture, such as rocks and mounds of dirt. You can control the resulting contour by selecting specific combinations of the scale and decay factors.

How Fractals Work

Let's take a more detailed look at how fractals work. Consider a two-dimensional line segment that only lies in the x and y dimensions. How do you apply the fractal algorithm to it? The process begins by determining the midpoint of the line segment. It then bends the line at the midpoint, as shown in Figure 8.1. The amount that the line is deformed depends on the value of a scaled, random number. Fractalizing the line then continues by taking both sides of the original line segment and bending them in half, too. You can repeat the process for as many times as you like. At each successive level, the line segments get smaller and the amount that each line is perturbed is decreased. Since the algorithm perturbs the midpoint of the shape, it is known as the midpoint displacement method.

Using Triangles

We won't be using line segments to represent our mountains, of course. Instead, we'll construct the landscapes from triangular patches. The generation process begins with one or more triangles that define the general layout of the

Figure 8.1 Fractalizing a line segment is a recursive process.

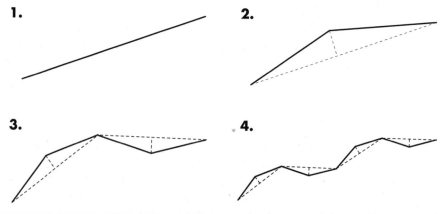

Figure 8.2 An example of fractalizing a three-dimensional triangle.

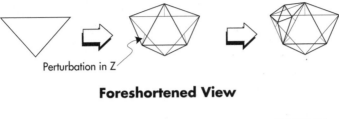

Perturbation in Z

Foreshortened View

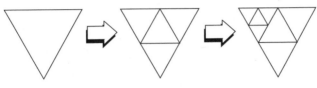

Top View

landscape. For now, assume that only one triangle is being used. The fractalization sequence begins by determining the midpoint of each of the triangle's sides. Next, the initial triangle is divided into four smaller triangles, as illustrated in Figure 8.2. The new triangles are built by connecting the existing vertices of the original triangle and the midpoints calculated.

To create a new contour, each new midpoint is perturbed up or down by some randomly scaled value. This results in four connected triangles that vary in height. But the process doesn't have to end there. The four new triangles can each be subdivided into four more triangles and perturbed in height. This process can be repeated for each successive level of smaller triangles.

Realize that only the height (z component) of the midpoints are perturbed. The x and y components do not change. Although this may seem like a severe restriction, you can still generate a wide variety of impressive surfaces with it.

Why use triangles to represent the mountains? Triangles are a good choice because they guarantee that we'll always be working with planar objects. No matter how we perturb one of their vertices, we'll get a planar surface that we can easily calculate the normal for. Recall, the normal is important for the lighting model calculations.

GENERATING MOUNTAINS

The GENMTN.C program listed near the end of this chapter uses the midpoint displacement technique to generate mountain landscapes. The program begins with one or more initial triangles that it fractalizes according to scale factors you specify. The final mountain surface is made up of many smaller triangles that you can embellish and include in a scene description file.

Reading the Initial Triangles

The initial triangles and the parameters used to control the fractalization process are read from a text file that we'll call an *object description file*. The syntax of the object description file is similar to what we've been using for RAY's scene description files. In fact, you may want to integrate the two once you've customized them to your liking.

To read the object description files, we'll build a miniature parser, similar to the one that RAY uses. The parser is included in the source file PARSERA.C. It's listed at the end of this chapter along with its header file, PARSERA.H.

The new parser supports the keywords listed in Table 8.1. The function **ReadObjectTerms** in GENMTN reads and processes each of these commands. The **ReadObjectTerms** function is much like its counterpart in RAY's PARSER.CPP file.

What about the keywords that RAY supports that are not included in Table 8.1? The GENMTN program does not use them so they aren't explicitly supported by PARSERA.C. However, you can include them in an object description file so that they are copied to the scene description file. All you need to do is enclose the desired command or group of commands with the curly bracket characters { and }. For instance, the following command copies the **Background** statement to the output file:

```
{Background(0,0,.8)}
```

Table 8.1 Keywords supported in PARSERA.C.

Keyword	Meaning
Ambient	Ambient color to use for a triangle
Diffuse	Diffuse lighting for a triangle
Color	Color of the triangle
H	Decay factor used in fractalization
Loc	The location of a triangle
NumLevels	Number of recursive levels in fractalization
RockGradient	Triangles that slope more than this amount are set to the rock color
Scale	Scale factor used in fractalization
SnowLine	The height where snow begins
Specular	Specular setting for a triangle
SpecSpread	Specular highlight constant
Transparency	Transparency constant for a triangle
V1	One side of a triangle
V2	One side of a triangle

The **GetToken** and **ReadObjectTerms** functions in PARSERA.C join forces to handle this new syntax. Specifically, when **GetToken** encounters a { character, it returns the new **OPENCURLYBRACKET** token:

```
else if (Ch == '{')     // This is a new primary character
  return OPENCURLYBRACKET;
```

The **ReadObjectTerms** function in GENMTN is then responsible for reading all of the characters that follow the opening bracket until it reaches a closing bracket. Each of the characters read are copied to the scene description file using the following statements:

```
case OPENCURLYBRACKET:
  // Copy everything between two curly brackets to the
  // output file
  Ch = fgetc(fp);
  while (!feof(fp)) {
    if ((Ch=fgetc(fp)) == '}') {
      fprintf(Outfp, "\n");
      break;        // End the copy process
    }
    else
      fprintf(Outfp, "%c", Ch);
  }
  break;
```

Setting the Fractal Parameters

An object description file typically has four components: a scale factor, decay factor, number of levels to iterate, and one or more triangles. We'll use a *Triangle* command that is identical to RAY's to specify the triangles. The *Scale* and *H* keywords specify the scale and decay factors, respectively. The value of the *H* command is used in the following equation to determine the value of the global variable **Ratio**:

```
Ratio = 1.0 / pow(2.0,H);
```

Ratio is used to decrease the fractal's scale value with each successive level. Similarly, the value of *Scale* is assigned to the global variable **Std**. It's used to scale the amount that the triangles are perturbed.

You'll also want to specify the number of subdivisions that the program performs. Using the *NumLevels* keyword, you can set the iteration level desired. For instance, to subdivide a triangle two levels, you would use

```
NumLevels(2)
```

Subdividing Triangles

When GENMTN reaches a triangle object in an object description file, it immediately fractalizes it. This involves subdividing the triangle, perturbing the new triangles, and writing them to an output file.

The **Fractal** routine in GENMTN is where most of the work is done. You'll find the call to **Fractal** in **ReadObjectTerms**:

```
case TRIANGLEOBJ:
  Token = GetToken(fp);
  if (Token == LEFTPAREN) {
    if (ReadObjectTerms(fp)) {
      Fractal(&Loc, &V1, &V2, MaxLevel, Std, Ratio);
    }
  }
  break;
```

At first glance, you might think that **Fractal** itself is a complicated function; however, taken in pieces it's not that bad. The function accepts four sets of parameters. The first three are the location and dimensions of the triangle to subdivide. The **Level** parameter is the current level of the subdivision. **Fractal** is a recursive routine and the **Level** parameter is used to terminate the recursion when it reaches 0. (**Level** is decremented with each successive call to **Fractal**.) The **Std** variable is the current scale factor that is used to perturb each new vertex. And finally, the **Ratio** variable, which ranges between 0 and 1, is multiplied with **Std** to decrease it with each recursive call to **Fractal**.

The first statements in **Fractal** determine the midpoints of each side of the triangle passed into it. These coordinates are stored in the variables **Mid01**, **Mid02**, and **Mid12**, as shown in Figure 8.3.

Next, the **z** coordinate of each midpoint is adjusted by adding a scaled, random value. For instance, the **z** coordinate of the midpoint along the triangle's **V1** vector is given by the statement

```
Mid01.z += Gauss(Seed) * Std;
```

The **Gauss** function returns a random number that ranges between -6 and 6, and **Std** magnifies this value based on the current scale setting. In the next section, we'll discuss how the random number is generated. (Notice that the **x** and **y** coordinates are not modified.)

Once the midpoints are perturbed, the **V1** and **V2** vectors for the four new triangles are calculated and stored in the array **Triangles**:

```
Triangles[Tri0].V1 = Subtract(&Mid01, &Triangles[Tri0].Loc);
Triangles[Tri0].V2 = Subtract(&Mid02, &Triangles[Tri0].Loc);
```

Figure 8.3 Mid01, Mid02, and Mid12 hold the midpoints of each side of a triangle.

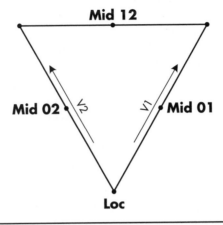

```
Triangles[Tri1].V1 = Subtract(&Mid12, &Triangles[Tri1].Loc);
Triangles[Tri1].V2 = Subtract(&Mid01, &Triangles[Tri1].Loc);

Triangles[Tri2].V1 = Subtract(&Mid02, &Triangles[Tri2].Loc);
Triangles[Tri2].V2 = Subtract(&Mid12, &Triangles[Tri2].Loc);

Triangles[Tri3].Loc = Mid01;
Triangles[Tri3].V1 = Subtract(&Mid12, &Mid01);
Triangles[Tri3].V2 = Subtract(&Mid02, &Mid01);
```

In case you're wondering, the **Loc** fields for the first three triangles in the **Triangles** array are calculated at the beginning of **Fractal**:

```
Triangles[Tri0].Loc = *Loc;
Triangles[Tri1].Loc = Add(Loc, V1);
Triangles[Tri2].Loc = Add(Loc, V2);
```

Writing the Triangles

The **for** loop located at the end of the **Fractal** function writes the fractalized triangles to the output file. Actually, the **for** loop only prints the triangles if **Fractal** has reached the maximum recursion level. This occurs when the **Level** parameter is 0. This also signals the end of the recursion.

Using a series of **fprintf** statements, **Fractal** outputs a separate *Triangle* command for each triangle to the scene description file. Each statement includes the position of the triangle, its color, and the current lighting parameters.

Setting the Color

If you look closely at the statements that print the triangle information to the scene description file, you'll notice that they may write out one of three different colors. The program either writes a whitish snow color, a reddish rock color, or the color the user has specified in the object description file.

All triangles above a user-specified snow level are set white. The snow level is specified by the **SnowLine** variable using the *SnowLine* command in the object description file. Specifically, **Fractal** outputs a white triangle if its **Loc.z** field is greater than the value in **SnowLine**:

```
if (Obj->Loc.z > SnowLine)
  fprintf(Outfp,"Color(.8,.8,.8))\n");
```

By default, **SnowLine** is set to the rather large 3.4e38 value. Therefore, for all practical purposes, the snow effect is disabled. However, you can redefine the snow level using the *SnowLine* command in the input file.

The triangles below the *SnowLine* altitude are either set to the color in **Ia1**, which is read by the parser, or the color of a rock. GENMTN defines the rock color in the **Rock** variable.

GENMTN paints the triangle a rock color when the triangle is at a steep angle. What constitutes a steep triangle? The **GetMaxGradient** function determines how much the triangle's **z** component changes for each of its sides. The largest of these three values is returned as the steepness of the triangle. The larger the value, the steeper the triangle. Here's the complete **GetMaxGradient** function:

```
float GetMaxGradient(VECTOR *V1, VECTOR *V2)
{
  float DeltaZ1, DeltaZ2, DeltaZ3;

  DeltaZ1 = fabs(V1->z);        // Determine how much the z
  DeltaZ2 = fabs(V2->z);        // coordinate changes for each
  DeltaZ3 = fabs(V1->z - V2->z); // side of the triangle

  // Return the largest change in z as the triangle's slope
  return MaxOf(DeltaZ1, DeltaZ2, DeltaZ3);
}
```

The value returned by **GetMaxGradient** is then compared with that stored in the global variable **RockGradient**. If the triangle's gradient is larger than the value in **RockGradient**, then the triangle is painted a rock color:

```
else if (GetMaxGradient(&Obj->V1, &Obj->V2) > RockGradient)
  fprintf(Outfp,"Color(%3.2f,%3.2f,%3.2f))\n",
    Rock.r, Rock.g, Rock.b);
```

```
else
  fprintf(Outfp,"Color(%3.2f,%3.2f,%3.2f))\n",
    Ia1.r, Ia1.g, Ia1.b);
```

By default, **RockGradient** is set to a large value so that no triangles will be set to the rock color. You can redefine the value of **RockGradient** by including the *RockGradient* command in your object description file.

Generating a Random Number

The random number used in the fractal process is very important since it gives the mountain scene its random, natural appearance. However, we can't simply use any random number function, mainly because we must use the same random number to perturb connecting vertices from different triangles. Otherwise, there will be gaps between triangles, as shown in Figure 8.4.

The only way to prevent the gaps is to apply the same random number to each of the connecting vertices. We could store the random numbers as we go, however, a better technique is to design the random function so that it always returns the same value for each vertex. How is this done? The trick is to use the (x,y,z) coordinate of the vertex as a seed to the random function. A seed value primes the randomizing process. The **rand** function, for instance, in C/C++ will always return the same random number immediately after the same seed value is passed to it.

In **Fractal**, the seed is based on the coordinates of the midpoints being perturbed. Here, for example, is how the seed for the point **Mid01** is computed:

```
Seed = (unsigned int)(Mid01.x * 10000 + Mid01.y * 100 + Mid01.z);
```

Figure 8.4 Random numbers must be repeatable or there will be gaps in the triangles.

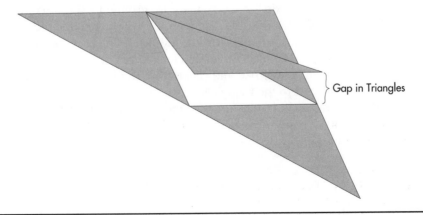

Gap in Triangles

The **Seed** value is then passed to the **Gauss** function to retrieve a random number. The **Gauss** routine is an extension of the **rand** function built into C. It returns a random number that is distributed around the value of 0. **Gauss** accomplishes this by adding a sequence of 12 random numbers. Each random number is scaled so that it falls between 0 and 1. Therefore, the running sum falls between 0 and 12. The final step is to recenter the number so that it is between -6 and 6. The resulting value is returned to be used in the **Fractal** routine. Here's the complete **Gauss** routine:

```
float Gauss(unsigned int Seed)
{
  float Sum = 0;
  int i;

  srand(Seed);
  // Add twelve numbers that will range between 0 and 1
  for (i=0; i<GAUSSADD; i++)
    Sum += rand() / (float)RAND_MAX;
  return Sum - GAUSSSHIFT;    // Center random numbers around 0
}
```

Using Bounding Boxes

Since a fractal mountain scene will have hundreds of objects, we must use bounding boxes to keep the ray tracing time reasonable. We could place a single bounding box around the whole mountain scene, however, this would only partially help. A better approach is to use numerous nested bounding boxes.

GENMTN places bounding boxes around triangles generated at even levels of the recursion. The **MakeBoundingBox** function takes care of the details. **MakeBoundingBox** determines the minimum box that will fit around the triangle passed to the routine, as shown in Figure 8.5. Remember, the sides of bounding boxes are always parallel to the major axes.

The bounding planes for the box are determined using a combination of **MinOf** and **MaxOf** function calls that determine the extents of the triangle. This takes care of the x and y dimensions of the bounding box, but what about its height? Since the triangle hasn't been fractalized yet, we really don't know how tall the inner triangles will become. Therefore, the function adds a multiple of the scale value in **Std** to the triangle's z extents. This gives enough room for the inner triangles that will be perturbed. Once the bounds of the box are determined, they are written to the output file:

```
fprintf(Outfp, "BEGINGROUP(V1(%3.2f,%3.2f,%3.2f), ",
  MinX, MinY, MinZ);
fprintf(Outfp, "V2(%3.2f,%3.2f,%3.2f))\n", MaxX, MaxY, MaxZ);
```

Realize that there will be many nested levels of bounding boxes.

Figure 8.5 A bounding box encloses the fractalized triangles.

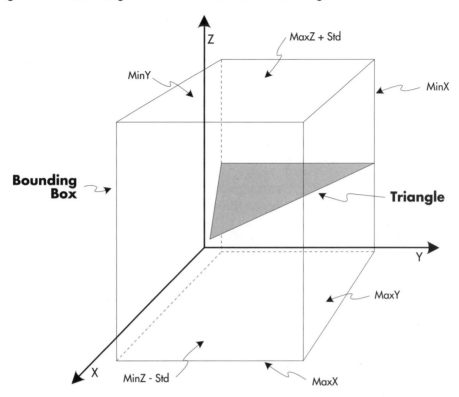

COMPILING AND RUNNING GENMTN

You can build GENMTN.C with either a C or C++ compiler by compiling and linking it with the files PARSERA.C and VECTOR.C. Therefore, if you are using Borland's compiler, you must create a project file with these three files.

To run GENMTN, you must supply two command-line arguments. The first parameter should specify the input object description file. The second parameter should be the name of the output scene description file containing the scene to render.

The following object description file, MTN1.ODF, defines a single, flat triangle that is to be subdivided into four levels:

```
/* MTN1.ODF */
{
AntiAliasing()
Resolution(200,200)
From(75,0,20)
```

```
At(0,0,3)
Up(0,0,1)
Background(1,1,1)
MaxLevel(1)
DMin(50)
DMax(200)

Light(Loc(40,0,100), Color(1,1,1), Point())
Light(Loc(40,0,100), Color(1,1,1), Point())
}

H(.8)
Scale(10)
NumLevels(4)
Triangle(Loc(-30,0,0),V1(60,-30,0),V2(60,30,0),
  Ambient(.6),Diffuse(1),Specular(0),Transparency(0),Color(.7,.7,.7))
```

To generate a mountain from this file, you must use the following command line:

```
genmtn mtn1.odf mtn1.sdf
```

Figure 8.6 shows the four phases of the fractal generation process used in MTN1.SDF. The top-left picture is the initial triangle; the bottom-right image contains the final image. Notice that the triangle only expands in the vertical direction.

The images in Figure 8.6 are not very smooth. The problem is that the triangle patches are relatively large. In order to render less patchy looking mountains, you must increase the number of iterations specified in the object description file. The drawback, of course, is that you'll increase the number of triangle patches generated. For instance, at 10 levels GENMTN generates over a million triangles.

Most interesting scenes, unfortunately, will require thousands of objects and a lot of computation time. Bounding boxes help, but don't solve the problem. You can expect some of the scenes shown in the next section to take an hour or more to render. In addition, the large number of triangle objects also places a burden on your system's memory resources. The object list will be quite large, so you may be forced to run highly detailed scenes under Windows to take advantage of its extensive memory capabilities. Either way, make sure that **MAXOBJECTS** in RAY.H is large enough to hold the number of objects that GENMTN generates. Remember, the bounding boxes are counted as objects too.

Because the mountain scenes can take a long time to compute, you may want to work with only a few fractal iterations and low-resolution images, until you have worked out the scene's basic design. Once you have these details completed, you can increase the number of iterations used. Another timesaver is to minimize the number of reflected rays that are traced because the distant

Figure 8.6 The four phases of fractalizing the triangle in MTN1.ODF.

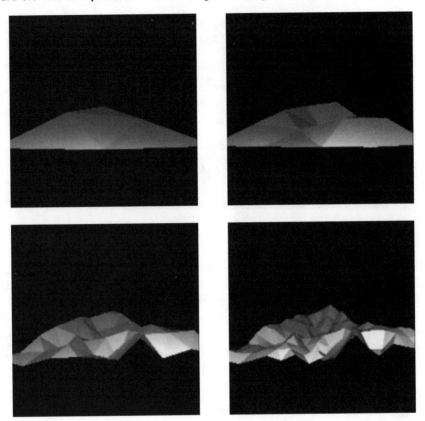

mountain scenes won't be affected by them. The only exception to this is if you have other objects in the scene that are reflective.

DESIGNING YOUR MOUNTAINS

You can control the appearance of the mountains using the *Scale* and *H* keywords in the object description file. The *Scale* command tells GENMTN how far to offset the first level of fractalized triangles. The value you specify with the *Scale* command depends on the size of the triangle you are working with and how big you want the mountain to appear. A scale value of 10 will look small on a triangle that has a length of 150, but extremely large for a triangle with a length of 1. Of course, the bigger the *Scale* value is, the larger the mountain will appear.

Figure 8.7 The H value controls the roughness of the surface.

The *H* factor, which can range between 0 and 1, controls the roughness of the mountain. The closer the value is to 1, the smoother the mountain will appear. Smaller values generate more rugged mountains. Figure 8.7, for instance, shows the same triangle fractalized with two different *H* settings. Both are fractalized with *four* levels of recursion, but the image on the left uses an *H* value of .2; the image on the right uses an *H* value of .9. Notice that the smoother surface on the right is generated with a larger *H* value.

MAKING MORE INTERESTING IMAGES

The GENMTN program generates mountain landscapes, but how can we enhance the scenes to make them more interesting? The first step is to add a sky. Setting the scene's background color to light blue is one possibility. The following statement, for instance, creates a light blue sky:

```
Background(.66,.88,1)
```

We can make the sky appear a little more realistic by placing distant vertical rectangles with blend textures behind and above the mountains:

```
Rectangle(Loc(-100,-100,10),V1(0,200,0),V2(0,0,100),
    Color(.66,.88,1),Color2(.17,.13,.39),Blend(0), Ambient(1))
```

If you place a lighter color at the bottom of the rectangle you'll get a very realistic sky effect. In this example, the *Blend* function gradually fades the sky from light to dark blue.

An even better approach is to enclose the scene and viewer in a sphere that uses the *Blend* command:

```
Sphere(Loc(0,0,0),Radius(200),
  Color(.66,.88,1),Color2(.17,.13,.39),Blend(0),Ambient(1))
```

What about clouds in the sky? You can use a variety of clouds to enhance the sense of depth in the scene or add drama. Use the *Cloud* keyword in the scene description file, as outlined in Chapter 7. Because the mountain scenes may take a long time to render, you'll probably want to perfect your clouds separately.

The following object description file and its scene description file generate the desert scene shown in Color Plate 5. Here's the object description file DSRT1.ODF:

```
/* DSRT1.ODF */

H(0.65)
Scale(13)
NumLevels(5)

/* Redish mountain with snowlevel at z greater than 45 */
SnowLine(45)
Triangle(Loc(0,-30,0),V1(0,30,50),V2(30,30,0),
  Ambient(.55),Color(.61,.08,.12))
Triangle(Loc(30,0,0),V1(-30,0,50),V2(-30,30,0))
Triangle(Loc(0,30,0),V1(0,0,50),V2(30,-30,50))

H(0.80)
Scale(12)
Triangle(Loc(-70,-70,-5),V1(0,0,40),V2(-20,30,0))
Triangle(Loc(-70,-70,-5),V1(0,0,40),V2(-20,-30,0))

/* Gently rolling ground */
Scale(15)
Numlevels(4)
Triangle(Loc(-100,-100,10),V1(200,0,0),V2(0,200,0),
  Ambient(.55))
Triangle(Loc(100,100,10),V1(-200,0,0),V2(0,-200,0))
```

Here's the scene description file, DSRTMTN.SDF, that generates the desert image:

```
/* DSRTMTN.SDF: Renders the desert scene in Color Plate 5. */

AntiAliasing()
Resolution(700,700)
From(50,-15,45)
```

```
At(0,-15,40)
Up(0.0,0.0,1.0)
Background(.66,.88,1)
MaxLevel(1)

DMin(50)
DMax(200)
Light(Loc(40,0,100), Color(1,1,1), Point())
Light(Loc(40,0,100), Color(1,1,1), Point())

/* Include the output of DSRT.ODF */
include(dsrt.sdf)

Rectangle(Loc(-100,-100,10),V1(0,200,0),V2(0,0,100),
   Color(.66,.88,1),Color2(.17,.13,.39),Blend(0), Ambient(1))

/* Long thin clouds */
Ellipsoid(Loc(-70,0,47), V1(80, 3, 75), V2(500, 0, 0),
   Ambient(.8), Diffuse(1), Specular(0), Cloud(.1, 2))
Ellipsoid(Loc(-70,-30,47), V1(80, 1, 75), V2(500, 0, 0),
   Ambient(.8), Diffuse(1), Specular(0), Cloud(.1, 2))
Ellipsoid(Loc(-75,-55,52), V1(80, .2, 75), V2(500, 0, 0),
   Ambient(.8), Diffuse(1), Specular(0), Cloud(.1, 2))
```

There are other simple techniques you can use to enhance your landscapes. For instance, you can place a blue, water-textured plane in the scene to simulate a lake. At low vantage points, you can take advantage of reflections in the water to render impressive scenes. It's probably best here to reduce the intensity of the water's ripples as much as you can.

Color Plate 6 presents another technique. This image is of a distant mountain range. In the foreground is a large green rectangle that forms the ground and a road that cuts through the center of it. The road and stripes are built using a series of rectangles. The image also contains a set of Cumulus clouds that hover over the ground. The clouds are constructed from a series of ellipsoids with a cloud texture mapped to them. Here's the object description file that generates the mountains in Color Plate 6:

```
/* ROADMTN.ODF: Generates a mountain range */
SnowLine(30)
H(0.45)
Scale(25)
NumLevels(4)
Triangle(Loc(-100,-150,0),V1(0,300,0),V2(-40,0,20),Ambient(.6),
   Diffuse(1),Color(.31,.34,.46))
Triangle(Loc(-100,-150,0),V1(40,300,-20),V2(0,300,0),Ambient(.6),
   Diffuse(1),Color(.31,.34,.46))
```

You'll need to run the ROADMTN.ODF file through GENMTN and include its output in the following scene description file (ROAD.SDF) to render the image in Color Plate 6:

```
/* ROAD.SDF: Renders the mountain road scene in Color Plate 6. */

AntiAliasing()
Resolution(500,500)
From(100,0,5)
At(-100,0,13)
Up(0.0,0.0,1.0)
Background(.66,.88,1)
MaxLevel(1)

DMin(50)
DMax(200)
Light(Loc(40,0,100), Color(1,1,1), Point())
Light(Loc(40,0,100), Color(1,1,1), Point())

include(roadmtn.sdf)

/* Sky: */
Rectangle(Loc(-150,-200,10),V1(0,400,0),V2(0,0,150),
  Color(.66,.88,1),Color2(.11,.09,.47),Blend(0), Ambient(1))

/* Main ground plane */
Rectangle(Loc(-100,-100,0),V1(200,0,0),V2(0,200,0),Color(0,.8,0),
  Ambient(.6), Diffuse(.40), Specular(0), SpecSpread(0))
/* Road */
Rectangle(Loc(100,-7,.001),V1(0,14,0),V2(-200,0,0),Color(.1,.1,.1),
  Ambient(.6), Diffuse(.40), Specular(0), SpecSpread(0))

/* Road stripes */
BeginGroup(V1(-98,-0.4,.13),V2(100,.4,.16))
Rectangle(Loc(100,-0.3,.15),V1(0,.6,0),V2(-3.5,0,0),Color(1,1,0),
  Ambient(1), Diffuse(0), Specular(0), SpecSpread(0))
Rectangle(Loc(94,-0.3,.15),V1(0,.6,0),V2(-3.5,0,0),Color(1,1,0),
  Ambient(1), Diffuse(0), Specular(0), SpecSpread(0))
Rectangle(Loc(88,-0.3,.15),V1(0,.6,0),V2(-3.5,0,0),Color(1,1,0),
  Ambient(1), Diffuse(0), Specular(0), SpecSpread(0))
Rectangle(Loc(82,-0.3,.15),V1(0,.6,0),V2(-3.5,0,0),Color(1,1,0),
  Ambient(1), Diffuse(0), Specular(0), SpecSpread(0))
Rectangle(Loc(76,-0.3,.15),V1(0,.6,0),V2(-3.5,0,0),Color(1,1,0),
  Ambient(1), Diffuse(0), Specular(0), SpecSpread(0))
Rectangle(Loc(70,-0.3,.15),V1(0,.6,0),V2(-3.5,0,0),Color(1,1,0),
  Ambient(1), Diffuse(0), Specular(0), SpecSpread(0))
Rectangle(Loc(64,-0.3,.15),V1(0,.6,0),V2(-3.5,0,0),Color(1,1,0),
  Ambient(1), Diffuse(0), Specular(0), SpecSpread(0))
```

```
Rectangle(Loc(58,-0.3,.15),V1(0,.6,0),V2(-3.5,0,0),Color(1,1,0),
  Ambient(1), Diffuse(0), Specular(0), SpecSpread(0))
Rectangle(Loc(52,-0.3,.15),V1(0,.6,0),V2(-3.5,0,0),Color(1,1,0),
  Ambient(1), Diffuse(0), Specular(0), SpecSpread(0))
Rectangle(Loc(46,-0.3,.15),V1(0,.6,0),V2(-3.5,0,0),Color(1,1,0),
  Ambient(1), Diffuse(0), Specular(0), SpecSpread(0))
Rectangle(Loc(40,-0.3,.15),V1(0,.6,0),V2(-3.5,0,0),Color(1,1,0),
  Ambient(1), Diffuse(0), Specular(0), SpecSpread(0))
Rectangle(Loc(34,-0.3,.15),V1(0,.6,0),V2(-3.5,0,0),Color(1,1,0),
  Ambient(1), Diffuse(0), Specular(0), SpecSpread(0))
Rectangle(Loc(28,-0.3,.15),V1(0,.6,0),V2(-3.5,0,0),Color(1,1,0),
  Ambient(1), Diffuse(0), Specular(0), SpecSpread(0))
Rectangle(Loc(22,-0.3,.15),V1(0,.6,0),V2(-3.5,0,0),Color(1,1,0),
  Ambient(1), Diffuse(0), Specular(0), SpecSpread(0))
Rectangle(Loc(16,-0.3,.15),V1(0,.6,0),V2(-3.5,0,0),Color(1,1,0),
  Ambient(1), Diffuse(0), Specular(0), SpecSpread(0))
Rectangle(Loc(10,-0.3,.15),V1(0,.6,0),V2(-3.5,0,0),Color(1,1,0),
  Ambient(1), Diffuse(0), Specular(0), SpecSpread(0))
Rectangle(Loc(4,-0.3,.15),V1(0,.6,0),V2(-3.5,0,0),Color(1,1,0),
  Ambient(1), Diffuse(0), Specular(0), SpecSpread(0))
Rectangle(Loc(-2,-0.3,.15),V1(0,.6,0),V2(-3.5,0,0),Color(1,1,0),
  Ambient(1), Diffuse(0), Specular(0), SpecSpread(0))
Rectangle(Loc(-8,-0.3,.15),V1(0,.6,0),V2(-3.5,0,0),Color(1,1,0),
  Ambient(1), Diffuse(0), Specular(0), SpecSpread(0))
Rectangle(Loc(-14,-0.3,.15),V1(0,.6,0),V2(-3.5,0,0),Color(1,1,0),
  Ambient(1), Diffuse(0), Specular(0), SpecSpread(0))
Rectangle(Loc(-20,-0.3,.15),V1(0,.6,0),V2(-3.5,0,0),Color(1,1,0),
  Ambient(1), Diffuse(0), Specular(0), SpecSpread(0))
Rectangle(Loc(-26,-0.3,.15),V1(0,.6,0),V2(-3.5,0,0),Color(1,1,0),
  Ambient(1), Diffuse(0), Specular(0), SpecSpread(0))
Rectangle(Loc(-32,-0.3,.15),V1(0,.6,0),V2(-3.5,0,0),Color(1,1,0),
  Ambient(1), Diffuse(0), Specular(0), SpecSpread(0))
Rectangle(Loc(-38,-0.3,.15),V1(0,.6,0),V2(-3.5,0,0),Color(1,1,0),
  Ambient(1), Diffuse(0), Specular(0), SpecSpread(0))
Rectangle(Loc(-44,-0.3,.15),V1(0,.6,0),V2(-3.5,0,0),Color(1,1,0),
  Ambient(1), Diffuse(0), Specular(0), SpecSpread(0))
Rectangle(Loc(-50,-0.3,.15),V1(0,.6,0),V2(-3.5,0,0),Color(1,1,0),
  Ambient(1), Diffuse(0), Specular(0), SpecSpread(0))
Rectangle(Loc(-56,-0.3,.15),V1(0,.6,0),V2(-3.5,0,0),Color(1,1,0),
  Ambient(1), Diffuse(0), Specular(0), SpecSpread(0))
Rectangle(Loc(-62,-0.3,.15),V1(0,.6,0),V2(-3.5,0,0),Color(1,1,0),
  Ambient(1), Diffuse(0), Specular(0), SpecSpread(0))
Rectangle(Loc(-68,-0.3,.15),V1(0,.6,0),V2(-3.5,0,0),Color(1,1,0),
  Ambient(1), Diffuse(0), Specular(0), SpecSpread(0))
Rectangle(Loc(-74,-0.3,.15),V1(0,.6,0),V2(-3.5,0,0),Color(1,1,0),
  Ambient(1), Diffuse(0), Specular(0), SpecSpread(0))
Rectangle(Loc(-80,-0.3,.15),V1(0,.6,0),V2(-3.5,0,0),Color(1,1,0),
  Ambient(1), Diffuse(0), Specular(0), SpecSpread(0))
```

```
Rectangle(Loc(-86,-0.3,.15),V1(0,.6,0),V2(-3.5,0,0),Color(1,1,0),
   Ambient(1), Diffuse(0), Specular(0), SpecSpread(0))
Rectangle(Loc(-92,-0.3,.15),V1(0,.6,0),V2(-3.5,0,0),Color(1,1,0),
   Ambient(1), Diffuse(0), Specular(0), SpecSpread(0))
Rectangle(Loc(-98,-0.3,.15),V1(0,.6,0),V2(-3.5,0,0),Color(1,1,0),
   Ambient(1), Diffuse(0), Specular(0), SpecSpread(0))
EndGroup()

/* Relatively large cloud on the left that extends to the
 * left of the image */
BeginGroup(V1(-95,-99,45),V2(-76,-52,60))
Ellipsoid(Loc(-90,-60,50), V1(8, 3, 35), V2(300, 0, 0),
   Ambient(.8), Diffuse(1), Specular(0), Cloud(.2, .5))
Ellipsoid(Loc(-90,-70,52), V1(8, 3, 7), V2(300, 0, 0),
   Ambient(.8), Diffuse(1), Specular(0), Cloud(.2, .5))
Ellipsoid(Loc(-90,-80,52), V1(8, 3, 6), V2(300, 0, 0),
   Ambient(.8), Diffuse(1), Specular(0), Cloud(.2, .5))
Ellipsoid(Loc(-90,-90,52), V1(8, 3, 60), V2(300, 0, 0),
   Ambient(.8), Diffuse(1), Specular(0), Cloud(.2, .5))
Ellipsoid(Loc(-90,-92,54), V1(8, 3, 60), V2(300, 0, 0),
   Ambient(.8), Diffuse(1), Specular(0), Cloud(.2, .5))

Ellipsoid(Loc(-85,-60,50), V1(8, 3, 35), V2(300, 0, 0),
   Ambient(.8), Diffuse(1), Specular(0), Cloud(.2, .5))
Ellipsoid(Loc(-85,-65,52), V1(8, 10, 8), V2(300, 0, 0),
   Ambient(.8), Diffuse(1), Specular(0), Cloud(.2, .5))
Ellipsoid(Loc(-85,-70,52), V1(8, 3, 7), V2(300, 0, 0),
   Ambient(.8), Diffuse(1), Specular(0), Cloud(.2, .5))
Ellipsoid(Loc(-85,-80,52), V1(8, 3, 6), V2(300, 0, 0),
   Ambient(.8), Diffuse(1), Specular(0), Cloud(.2, .5))
Ellipsoid(Loc(-85,-90,52), V1(8, 3, 6), V2(300, 0, 0),
   Ambient(.8), Diffuse(1), Specular(0), Cloud(.2, .5))

Ellipsoid(Loc(-80,-80,52), V1(8, 3, 6), V2(300, 0, 0),
   Ambient(.8), Diffuse(1), Specular(0), Cloud(.2, .5))
Ellipsoid(Loc(-80,-90,52), V1(8, 3, 6), V2(300, 0, 0),
   Ambient(.8), Diffuse(1), Specular(0), Cloud(.2, .5))

Ellipsoid(Loc(-85,-80,56), V1(8, 3, 6), V2(300, 0, 0),
   Ambient(.8), Diffuse(1), Specular(0), Cloud(.2, .5))
Ellipsoid(Loc(-85,-90,56), V1(8, 3, 6), V2(300, 0, 0),
   Ambient(.8), Diffuse(1), Specular(0), Cloud(.2, .5))

Ellipsoid(Loc(-82,-85,53), V1(8, 3, 4), V2(300, 0, 0),
   Ambient(.8), Diffuse(1), Specular(0), Cloud(.2, .5))
EndGroup()
```

```
/* Cloud on the right in the forefront */
Ellipsoid(Loc(-25,20,50), V1(8, 3, 20), V2(300, 0, 0),
  Ambient(.8), Diffuse(1), Specular(.1), Cloud(.2, .5))
Ellipsoid(Loc(-24,30,52), V1(8, 3, 7), V2(300, 0, 0),
  Ambient(.8), Diffuse(1), Specular(.1), Cloud(.2, .5))
Ellipsoid(Loc(-24,40,52.5), V1(8, 3, 6), V2(300, 0, 0),
  Ambient(.8), Diffuse(1), Specular(.1), Cloud(.2, .5))
Ellipsoid(Loc(-25,50,50), V1(8, 3, 60), V2(300, 0, 0),
  Ambient(.8), Diffuse(1), Specular(.1), Cloud(.2, .5))
Ellipsoid(Loc(-25,52,53), V1(8, 3, 6), V2(300, 0, 0),
  Ambient(.8), Diffuse(1), Specular(.1), Cloud(.2, .5))

Ellipsoid(Loc(-35,20,50), V1(8, 3, 20), V2(300, 0, 0),
  Ambient(.8), Diffuse(1), Specular(.1), Cloud(.2, .5))
Ellipsoid(Loc(-34,30,52), V1(8, 3, 7), V2(300, 0, 0),
  Ambient(.8), Diffuse(1), Specular(.1), Cloud(.2, .5))
Ellipsoid(Loc(-34,40,52.5), V1(8, 3, 6), V2(300, 0, 0),
  Ambient(.8), Diffuse(1), Specular(.1), Cloud(.2, .5))
Ellipsoid(Loc(-35,50,50), V1(8, 3, 60), V2(300, 0, 0),
  Ambient(.8), Diffuse(1), Specular(.1), Cloud(.2, .5))
Ellipsoid(Loc(-35,55,53), V1(8, 3, 6), V2(300, 0, 0),
  Ambient(.8), Diffuse(1), Specular(.1), Cloud(.2, .5))

Ellipsoid(Loc(-30,30,58), V1(8, 3, 7), V2(300, 0, 0),
  Ambient(.8), Diffuse(1), Specular(.1), Cloud(.2, .5))
Ellipsoid(Loc(-30,40,58), V1(8, 3, 6), V2(300, 0, 0),
  Ambient(.8), Diffuse(1), Specular(.1), Cloud(.2, .5))
Ellipsoid(Loc(-30,50,57), V1(8, 3, 60), V2(300, 0, 0),
  Ambient(.8), Diffuse(1), Specular(.1), Cloud(.2, .5))
Ellipsoid(Loc(-30,52,57), V1(8, 3, 6), V2(300, 0, 0),
  Ambient(.8), Diffuse(1), Specular(.1), Cloud(.2, .5))

Ellipsoid(Loc(-32,50,62), V1(8, 3, 10), V2(300, 0, 0),
  Ambient(.8), Diffuse(1), Specular(.1), Cloud(.2, .5))
Ellipsoid(Loc(-32,52,63), V1(8, 3, 10), V2(300, 0, 0),
  Ambient(.8), Diffuse(1), Specular(.1), Cloud(.2, .5))
Ellipsoid(Loc(-34,42,66), V1(8, 3, 6), V2(300, 0, 0),
  Ambient(.8), Diffuse(1), Specular(.1), Cloud(.2, .5))

/* Distant cloud on the right */
Ellipsoid(Loc(-90,20,49), V1(8, 3, 40), V2(300, 0, 0),
  Ambient(.8), Diffuse(1), Specular(.1), Cloud(.2, .5))
Ellipsoid(Loc(-90,25,50), V1(8, 3, 27), V2(300, 0, 0),
  Ambient(.8), Diffuse(1), Specular(.1), Cloud(.2, .5))
Ellipsoid(Loc(-90,30,50), V1(8, 3, 26), V2(300, 0, 0),
  Ambient(.8), Diffuse(1), Specular(.1), Cloud(.2, .5))
Ellipsoid(Loc(-90,35,52), V1(8, 3, 9), V2(300, 0, 0),
  Ambient(.8), Diffuse(1), Specular(.1), Cloud(.2, .5))
```

```
Ellipsoid(Loc(-90,40,48), V1(8, 3, 90), V2(300, 0, 0),
  Ambient(.8), Diffuse(1), Specular(.1), Cloud(.2, .5))
```

The following section contains the listings for the files GENMTN.C, PARSERA.H, and PARSERA.C.

• GENMTN.C

```c
// GENMTN.C: Generates a fractal mountain. The program reads
// the specifications of the mountain from an object description
// file (.ODF), creates the mountain using the midpoint-
// displacement method of fractalization, and outputs the
// mountain's components to a scene description file (.SDF).
//
// To use the program, enter at the DOS prompt:
//        genmtn <infile.odf> <outfile.sdf>
// where:
//        infile.odf is the filename of the object description file
//        outfile.sdf is the filename of the scene description file

#include <stdio.h>
#include <stdlib.h>
#include <time.h>
#include <string.h>
#include <math.h>
#include "vector.h"
#include "parsera.h"

#define MAXNAME 80              // Maximum length of filenames

char Outfile[MAXNAME];         // Scene description filename
char Infile[MAXNAME];          // Object description filename
int MaxLevel = 2;              // Number of fractal levels
float Std, Ratio;              // Used to control fractalization
float H = 0.3;                 // Roughness control
float Scale = 50;              // Perturbation scale
float SnowLine=3.4e38;         // Altitude of snow level
float RockGradient=3.4e38;     // Gradients larger than this are rock
FILE *Infp, *Outfp;            // File pointers for the two text files
COLOR Rock = {.7,.6,.6};       // Color of rocks is gray
unsigned int NumObjects=0;

struct ATRIANGLE {             // Single structure used to hold
  VECTOR Loc, V1, V2;          // a triangle
};

// Function prototypes
void Usage(void);
```

```
void Fractal(VECTOR *Loc, VECTOR *V1,
  VECTOR *V2, int Iteration, float Std, float Ratio);
float Gauss(unsigned int Seed);
void MakeBoundingBox(FILE *Outfp,
  VECTOR *Loc, VECTOR *V1, VECTOR *V2, float Std);
float GetMaxGradient(VECTOR *V1, VECTOR *V2);
int ReadObjectTerms(FILE *fp);
float MinOf(float A, float B, float C);
float MaxOf(float A, float B, float C);

/////////////////////////////// main \\\\\\\\\\\\\\\\\\\\\\\\\\\\
//
// Main entry point of the program
//
int main(int argc, char *argv[])
{
  randomize();

  if (argc != 3)            // Did the user enter the correct
    Usage();                // number of arguments?
  else {
    strcpy(Infile, argv[1]);   // Copy the filenames to the
    strcpy(Outfile, argv[2]);  // correct variables
  }

  Infp = fopen(Infile, "r");   // Open the object description file
  if (Infp == NULL) {
    printf("Could not open the input file: %s.\n", Infile);
    exit(1);
  }
  Outfp = fopen(Outfile, "w"); // Open the scene description file
  if (Outfp == NULL) {
    printf("Could not open the output file: %s.\n", Outfile);
    exit(1);
  }

  Ratio = 1.0 / pow(2.0,H);
  Std = Scale * Ratio;
  Ia1.r = 0.0; Ia1.g = 1.0; Ia1.b = 0.0;  // Default mountain color
  ka = 0.6; kd = 1.0; ks = 0; kt = 0; NO = 4;

  do {
    ReadObjectTerms(Infp); // Get the mountain's specifications
  } while (!feof(Infp));
  printf("Created %u objects.\n", NumObjects);
  fclose(Outfp);
  fclose(Infp);
  return 0;
}
```

```
/////////////////////////// Usage \\\\\\\\\\\\\\\\\\\\\\\\\\\
//
// Displays the command-line arguments for the program if the
// user has entered them incorrectly. The program exits if
// the wrong number of command-line arguments are entered.
//
void Usage(void)
{
  printf("Usage: genmtn <infile.odf> <outfile.sdf>\n");
  printf("where:\n");
  printf("\tinfile.odf: Filename of the object description file\n");
  printf("\toutfile.sdf: Filename of the scene description file\n");
  exit(1);
}


/////////////////////////// Fractal \\\\\\\\\\\\\\\\\\\\\\\\\\\
//
// Fractalizes a triangle specified by Loc, V1, and V2 into four
// smaller triangles. The variable Level is the current
// recursion level. It's decremented with each recursive call.
// Std and Ratio control the amount the new triangles are
// perturbed in the z direction. The function only writes the
// triangle information to a file when Level equals 0.
//
void Fractal(VECTOR *Loc, VECTOR *V1, VECTOR *V2,
  int Level, float Std, float Ratio)
{
  struct ATRIANGLE Triangles[4];
  int Tri0=0, Tri1=1, Tri2=2, Tri3=3, Tri;
  VECTOR Mid01, Mid12, Mid02, Temp;
  unsigned int Seed;
  struct ATRIANGLE *Obj;

  if (!Level) return;

  Triangles[Tri0].Loc = *Loc;
  Triangles[Tri1].Loc = Add(Loc, V1);
  Triangles[Tri2].Loc = Add(Loc, V2);
  Mid01.x = Loc->x + V1->x / 2.0;
  Mid01.y = Loc->y + V1->y / 2.0;
  Mid01.z = Loc->z + V1->z / 2.0;

  Mid02.x = Loc->x + V2->x / 2.0;
  Mid02.y = Loc->y + V2->y / 2.0;
  Mid02.z = Loc->z + V2->z / 2.0;

  Mid12.x = Triangles[Tri1].Loc.x + (V2->x - V1->x) / 2.0;
  Mid12.y = Triangles[Tri1].Loc.y + (V2->y - V1->y) / 2.0;
  Mid12.z = Triangles[Tri1].Loc.z + (V2->z - V1->z) / 2.0;
```

```
// Computes a seed that is unique and repeatable for the midpoint
Seed = (unsigned int)(Mid12.x * 10000 + Mid12.y * 100 + Mid12.z);
// Perturbs the midpoint between vertex 1 and 2
Mid12.z += Gauss(Seed) * Std;

// Perturbs the midpoint of the other two sides
Seed = (unsigned int)(Mid01.x * 10000 + Mid01.y * 100 + Mid01.z);
Mid01.z += Gauss(Seed) * Std;

Seed = (unsigned int)(Mid02.x * 10000 + Mid02.y * 100 + Mid02.z);
Mid02.z += Gauss(Seed) * Std;

Triangles[Tri0].V1 = Subtract(&Mid01, &Triangles[Tri0].Loc);
Triangles[Tri0].V2 = Subtract(&Mid02, &Triangles[Tri0].Loc);

Triangles[Tri1].V1 = Subtract(&Mid12, &Triangles[Tri1].Loc);
Triangles[Tri1].V2 = Subtract(&Mid01, &Triangles[Tri1].Loc);

Triangles[Tri2].V1 = Subtract(&Mid02, &Triangles[Tri2].Loc);
Triangles[Tri2].V2 = Subtract(&Mid12, &Triangles[Tri2].Loc);

Triangles[Tri3].Loc = Mid01;
Triangles[Tri3].V1 = Subtract(&Mid12, &Mid01);
Triangles[Tri3].V2 = Subtract(&Mid02, &Mid01);

Level--;

printf("\nLevel=%d\n",Level);
// Puts a bounding box around every four triangles
if (Level % 2 == 0) {
  MakeBoundingBox(Outfp, Loc, V1, V2, Std * 3);
}
for (Tri=Tri0; Tri<=Tri3; Tri++) {
  Obj = &Triangles[Tri];
  Temp = Subtract(&Obj->V2, &Obj->V1);

  // Output the new triangles to the scene description file if
  // the program has reached the maximum fractalization level
  if (!Level) {
    fprintf(Outfp,"Triangle(Loc(%3.5f,%3.5f,%3.5f),",
      Obj->Loc.x, Obj->Loc.y, Obj->Loc.z);
    fprintf(Outfp,"V1(%3.5f,%3.5f,%3.5f),\n",
      Obj->V1.x, Obj->V1.y, Obj->V1.z);
    fprintf(Outfp,"   V2(%3.5f,%3.5f,%3.5f),",
      Obj->V2.x, Obj->V2.y, Obj->V2.z);
    fprintf(Outfp,"Ambient(%3.2f),Diffuse(%3.2f),Specular(%3.2f),\n",
      ka, kd, ks);
    fprintf(Outfp,"   SpecSpread(%d),Transparency(%3.2f),", NO, kt);
```

```c
    // If the z coordinate is above the snowline, set the
    // triangle's color to white
    if (Obj->Loc.z > SnowLine)
      fprintf(Outfp,"Color(.8,.8,.8))\n");
    else if (GetMaxGradient(&Obj->V1, &Obj->V2) > RockGradient)
      fprintf(Outfp,"Color(%3.2f,%3.2f,%3.2f))\n",
        Rock.r, Rock.g, Rock.b);
    else
      fprintf(Outfp,"Color(%3.2f,%3.2f,%3.2f))\n",
        Ia1.r, Ia1.g, Ia1.b);
    NumObjects++;
  }
  if (Level)
    Fractal(&Obj->Loc, &Obj->V1, &Obj->V2, Level, Std*Ratio, Ratio);
  }
  if (Level%2 == 0)
    fprintf(Outfp, "ENDGROUP()\n");
}


#define GAUSSADD 12     // Add this many terms together
#define GAUSSSHIFT 6    // Shift gauss sum so it's centered around 0

///////////////////////////// Gauss  \\\\\\\\\\\\\\\\\\\\\\\\\\\
//
// Returns a random number between -GAUSSSHIFT and GAUSSSHIFT
// that is based on the value of Seed
//
float Gauss(unsigned int Seed)
{
  float Sum = 0;
  int i;

  srand(Seed);
  // Add twelve numbers that will range between 0 and 1
  for (i=0; i<GAUSSADD; i++)
    Sum += rand() / (float)RAND_MAX;
  return Sum - GAUSSSHIFT;    // Center random numbers around 0
}


//////////////////////// MakeBoundingBox  \\\\\\\\\\\\\\\\\\\\\
//
// Writes a bounding box object to the file Outfp that contains
// the triangle specified by Loc, V1, and V2. The Std field
// is used to determine how "tall" to make the box. Since the
// triangle's fractalized interior will be randomly perturbed,
// we really don't know how big it will be. But we can use Std
// to determine a worst case.
//
```

```
void MakeBoundingBox(FILE *Outfp,
  VECTOR *Loc, VECTOR *V1, VECTOR *V2, float Std)
{
  float MinX, MaxX, MinY, MaxY, MinZ, MaxZ;
  VECTOR LV1, LV2;

  LV1 = Add(Loc, V1);
  LV2 = Add(Loc, V2);

  MinX = MinOf(Loc->x, LV1.x, LV2.x);
  MaxX = MaxOf(Loc->x, LV1.x, LV2.x);
  MinY = MinOf(Loc->y, LV1.y, LV2.y);
  MaxY = MaxOf(Loc->y, LV1.y, LV2.y);
  MinZ = MinOf(Loc->z, LV1.z, LV2.z);
  MaxZ = MaxOf(Loc->z, LV1.z, LV2.z);
  MinZ -= Std;
  MaxZ += Std;

  fprintf(Outfp, "BEGINGROUP(V1(%3.2f,%3.2f,%3.2f), ",
    MinX, MinY, MinZ);
  fprintf(Outfp, "V2(%3.2f,%3.2f,%3.2f))\n", MaxX, MaxY, MaxZ);
  NumObjects++;
}


//////////////////////// GetMaxGradient \\\\\\\\\\\\\\\\\\\\\\\
//
// Determines the maximum vertical gradient for the triangle
// specified
//
float GetMaxGradient(VECTOR *V1, VECTOR *V2)
{
  float DeltaZ1, DeltaZ2, DeltaZ3;

  DeltaZ1 = fabs(V1->z);        // Determine how much the z
  DeltaZ2 = fabs(V2->z);        // coordinate changes for each
  DeltaZ3 = fabs(V1->z - V2->z); // side of the triangle

  // Return the largest change in z as the triangle's slope
  return MaxOf(DeltaZ1, DeltaZ2, DeltaZ3);
}


//////////////////////// ReadObjectTerms \\\\\\\\\\\\\\\\\\\\\\\
//
// Reads and processes the keywords in the object description
// file. The keywords are defined in PARSERA.C.
//
int ReadObjectTerms(FILE *fp)
{
```

```
int Token;
char Ch;

while ((Token=GetToken(fp)) != EOF) {
  switch(Token) {
    case RIGHTPAREN:
      return 1;
    case COMMA:
      break;
    case LOC:
      ReadTripple(fp, &Loc.x, &Loc.y, &Loc.z);
      break;
    case AMBIENT:
      ReadFloat(fp, &ka);
      break;
    case DIFFUSE:
      ReadFloat(fp, &kd);
      break;
    case SPECULAR:
      ReadFloat(fp, &ks);
      break;
    case SPECSPREAD:
      ReadInt(fp, &NO);
      break;
    case TRANSPARENCY:
      ReadFloat(fp, &kt);
      break;
    case COLORVAL:
      ReadTripple(fp, &Ia1.r, &Ia1.g, &Ia1.b);
      break;
    case VECTOR1:
      ReadTripple(fp, &V1.x, &V1.y, &V1.z);
      break;
    case VECTOR2:
      ReadTripple(fp, &V2.x, &V2.y, &V2.z);
      break;
    case FRCTLH:
      ReadFloat(fp, &H);
      Ratio = 1.0 / pow(2.0,H);
      Std = Scale * Ratio;
      break;
    case FRCTLSCALE:
      ReadFloat(fp, &Scale);
      Std = Scale * Ratio;
      break;
    case NUMBEROFLEVELS:
      ReadInt(fp, &MaxLevel);
      break;
```

```
          case TRIANGLEOBJ:
            Token = GetToken(fp);
            if (Token == LEFTPAREN) {
              if (ReadObjectTerms(fp)) {
                Fractal(&Loc, &V1, &V2, MaxLevel, Std, Ratio);
              }
            }
            break;
          case OPENCURLYBRACKET:
            // Copy everything between two curly brackets to the
            // output file
            Ch = fgetc(fp);
            while (!feof(fp)) {
              if ((Ch=fgetc(fp)) == '}') {
                fprintf(Outfp, "\n");
                break;          // End the copy process
              }
              else
                fprintf(Outfp, "%c", Ch);
            }
            break;
          case SNOWLINE:
            ReadFloat(fp, &SnowLine);
            break;
          case ROCKGRADIENT:
            ReadFloat(fp, &RockGradient);
            break;
          default: return 0;
      }
    }
  return 0;
}


///////////////////////////// MaxOf \\\\\\\\\\\\\\\\\\\\\\\\\\\\\
//
// Returns the maximum of three values
//
float MaxOf(float A, float B, float C)
{
  A = (B > A) ? B : A;
  return (C > A) ? C : A;
}


///////////////////////////// MinOf \\\\\\\\\\\\\\\\\\\\\\\\\\\\\
//
// Returns the minimum of three values
//
float MinOf(float A, float B, float C)
```

```
{
  A = (B < A) ? B : A;
  return (C < A) ? C : A;
}
```

• PARSERA.H

```
// PARSERA.H: Header file for PARSERA.C.

#ifndef PARSERAH
#define PARSERAH

#include "vector.h"

#define NUMKEYWORDS 15
#define UNKNOWN -1
#define LOC 0
#define AMBIENT 1
#define DIFFUSE 2
#define SPECULAR 3
#define SPECSPREAD 4
#define TRANSPARENCY 5
#define COLORVAL 6
#define TRIANGLEOBJ 7
#define VECTOR1 8
#define VECTOR2 9
#define NUMBEROFLEVELS 10
#define FRCTLH 11
#define FRCTLSCALE 12
#define SNOWLINE 13
#define ROCKGRADIENT 14
#define LEFTPAREN 100
#define RIGHTPAREN 101
#define COMMA 102
#define NUMBER 103
#define OPENCURLYBRACKET 104
#define CLOSECURLYBRACKET 105

typedef struct CLR {
  float r, g, b;
} COLOR;

extern char *Keywords[];
extern float ka, kd, ks, kr, kt;
extern float Radius;
extern int NO;
extern VECTOR Loc, V1, V2;
extern COLOR Ia1;
```

```
int GetToken(FILE *fp);
int ReadTripple(FILE *fp, float *val1, float *val2, float *val3);
int ReadInt(FILE *fp, int *val);
int ReadFloat(FILE *fp, float *val);

#endif
```

• PARSERA.C

```
// PARSERA.C: Parser support for GENMTN.C.

#include <stdio.h>
#include <string.h>
#include <stdlib.h>
#include <ctype.h>
#include "parsera.h"
#include "vector.h"

// Keywords supported for GENMTN.C
char *Keywords[] = {
  "LOC", "AMBIENT", "DIFFUSE", "SPECULAR", "SPECSPREAD",
  "TRANSPARENCY", "COLOR", "TRIANGLE", "V1", "V2", "NUMLEVELS",
  "H", "SCALE", "SNOWLINE", "ROCKGRADIENT"
};

char Buffer[256];
float ka, kd, ks, kr, kt;
float Radius;
int NO;
VECTOR Loc, V1, V2;
COLOR Ia1;


/////////////////////////// GetToken \\\\\\\\\\\\\\\\\\\\\\\\\\
//
// Retrieves a token from the file fp. This routine is similar
// to the one in PARSER.C. The difference is that it now
// supports curly brackets. If it encounters a left curly
// bracket, it returns the constant OPENCURLYBRACKET.
//
int GetToken(FILE *fp)
{
  char Ch;
  int Ndx, i;

  Ndx = 0;
  while (1) {
    Ch = fgetc(fp);
    if (Ch == '\t' || Ch == ' ' || Ch == '\n') {
```

```
        // Skip whitespace
        Ch = fgetc(fp);
      }
      if (Ch == EOF) {
        return EOF;
      }
      if (isalpha(Ch) || Ch == '_') {
        // This is part of a keyword
        Buffer[Ndx++] = toupper(Ch);
        while ((Ch=fgetc(fp)) != EOF &&
          (isalpha(Ch) || Ch == '_' || isdigit(Ch)))
          Buffer[Ndx++] = toupper(Ch);
        Buffer[Ndx] = '\0';
        ungetc(Ch, fp);
        // Determine which keyword was encountered
        for (i=0; i<NUMKEYWORDS; i++) {
          if (stricmp(Keywords[i], Buffer) == 0) {
              return i;  // The index of the string is the token's id
          }
        }
        return UNKNOWN;
      }
      else if (Ch == '(')
        return LEFTPAREN;
      else if (Ch == ')')
        return RIGHTPAREN;
      else if (Ch == ',')
        return COMMA;
      else if (isdigit(Ch) || Ch == '.' || Ch == '-') {
        Buffer[Ndx++] = Ch;
        while ((Ch=fgetc(fp)) != EOF && (isdigit(Ch) || Ch == '.'))
          Buffer[Ndx++] = Ch;
        Buffer[Ndx] = '\0';
        ungetc(Ch, fp);
        return NUMBER;
      }
      else if (Ch == '{')      // This is a new primary character
        return OPENCURLYBRACKET;
      else if (Ch == '/') {
        // Note: Delimiting comments is done with a bit
        // of a trick. The divide sign is used to mark
        // the beginning and end of the comment.
        //
        while ((Ch=fgetc(fp)) != '/' && Ch != EOF) ;
      }
    }
  }
}
```

```
////////////////////////// ReadInt \\\\\\\\\\\\\\\\\\\\\\\\
//
// Reads an integer from the input file
//
int ReadInt(FILE *fp, int *val)
{
  int Token;

  Token = GetToken(fp);
  if (Token == LEFTPAREN) {
    Token = GetToken(fp);
    if (Token == NUMBER) {
      *val = atoi(Buffer);
      Token = GetToken(fp);
      if (Token == RIGHTPAREN)
        return 1;
    }
  }
  return 0;
}


////////////////////////// ReadFloat \\\\\\\\\\\\\\\\\\\\\\\\
//
// Reads a floating point number from the input file
//
int ReadFloat(FILE *fp, float *val)
{
  int Token;

  Token = GetToken(fp);
  if (Token == LEFTPAREN) {
    Token = GetToken(fp);
    if (Token == NUMBER) {
      *val = atof(Buffer);
      Token = GetToken(fp);
      if (Token == RIGHTPAREN)
        return 1;
    }
  }
  return 0;
}


////////////////////////// ReadTripple \\\\\\\\\\\\\\\\\\\\\\\\
//
// Reads three floating point numbers from the input file
//
int ReadTripple(FILE *fp, float *val1, float *val2, float *val3)
{
  int Token;
```

```
    Token = GetToken(fp);
    if (Token == LEFTPAREN) {
      Token = GetToken(fp);
      if (Token == NUMBER) {
        *val1 = atof(Buffer);
        Token = GetToken(fp);
        if (Token == COMMA) {
          Token = GetToken(fp);
          if (Token == NUMBER) {
            *val2 = atof(Buffer);
            Token = GetToken(fp);
            if (Token == COMMA) {
              Token = GetToken(fp);
              if (Token == NUMBER) {
                *val3 = atof(Buffer);
                Token = GetToken(fp);
                if (Token == RIGHTPAREN)
                  return 1;
              }
            }
          }
        }
      }
    }
    return 0;
}
```

A PCX Toolkit

Saving your graphics images to disk is almost as important as rendering them in the first place. Fortunately, there are several widely used graphics file formats from which we can choose to support. We'll focus on two of the most popular file formats: PCX and TIFF. In this chapter, we'll construct a PCX toolkit. Then, in Chapter 10, we'll discuss the TIFF standard.

OVERVIEW OF PCX FILES

The PCX file format was developed by ZSoft Corporation for its PC Paintbrush program and related products. The goal at ZSoft was to provide a simple file format that encodes the screen images their products used. The result was a file format that essentially copies the graphics adapter's video memory to disk. To save disk space, however, they added a twist: The images are compressed using a run-length encoding technique. The idea behind run-length encoding is to save sequences of unchanging pixels as a length and pixel value combination rather than as individual pixels. As a result, the PCX format can be an excellent technique for storing and compressing graphics screens that don't vary much, like those on a 16-color display.

The PCX format supports all the common graphics adapters. However, since the file format is tightly coupled with the organization of the original display's graphics mode, the same image saved from a monochrome screen, 16-color EGA/VGA display, and 256-color Super VGA graphics adapter creates vastly different PCX files. The reason is that each graphics adapter organizes its video memory differently. Rather than support all the PCX variants, we'll focus on those that support 256-color and 24-bit RGB images. This won't be a severe restriction since we're primarily interested in photo-quality images, for which the other modes are inadequate.

The PCX File Format

As Figure 9.1 illustrates, a PCX file usually consists of two parts: a header and its image data. Every PCX file begins with a fixed-length, 128-byte header that contains information about the image, such as its size and the colors it uses. The image data follows the header and is usually stored in a compressed, binary form. Actually, there can be a third element in a PCX file, or more precisely an extension of the header section. All 256-color images store a list of the image's colors (called a *color palette*) at the end of the file. A 16-color image also has a palette, but it is smaller and is stored in the header itself. In contrast, 24-bit images don't have palettes at all. (Further information on using the VGA's palette is included in Appendix B.)

The PCX File Header

Table 9.1 lists the components of a PCX header. The first byte is always the hexadecimal value 0x0A (decimal 10). This marker helps to identify the file as a PCX file. The next byte in the header specifies which version of PC Paintbrush the PCX file is compatible with. For our purposes, we'll always use a value of 5, though earlier PCX versions have numbers less than this.

The third byte in the header specifies the image compression that the file uses. Here again, we'll only use a value of 1, signaling that we're using run-length encoding. The fourth header byte specifies the number of bits in the file

Figure 9.1 The three components of a PCX file.

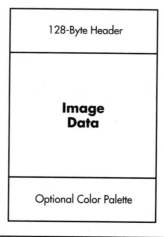

Table 9.1 The format of a PCX header.

Item	Number of bytes	Description
PCX id	1	Identifies the file as a PCX file. It is always 0x0A.
Version	1	Specifies what version of PC Paintbrush the PCX file is created for. We'll only support files with a value of 5.
Encoding	1	Image compression type. 0 means none. A value of 1 uses run-length encoding.
Bits per pixel	1	Number of bits per pixel used in each video adapter's plane
Left	2	Left column where image is displayed
Top	2	Top row where image is displayed
Right	2	Right column where image is displayed
Bottom	2	Bottom row where image is displayed
Horizontal resolution	2	Horizontal resolution of the device that displays the image
Vertical resolution	2	Vertical resolution of the device that displays the image
Color map	48	Color palette used by 16-color or similar images
Reserved	1	Not used
Number of planes	1	Number of color planes used in each image's display device
Bytes per line	2	Number of bytes per scan line per color plane. It is always even.
Palette type	2	If 0, no palette exists. If 1, a palette is included. If 2, the image is a grayscale image.
Filler	58	Blanks that fill out header

that represent a pixel value. This will be set to 8 since all of our images will consist of byte values—even 24-bit images have byte-sized red, green, and blue color components.

The next four integer values specify the location where the image is to appear on the screen. They also indirectly specify the dimensions of the image, as shown in Figure 9.2. The next two integers represent the screen resolution to use when displaying the image, followed by a 48-byte color map. It's used by 16-color images to store their palette of colors. Since we're not supporting this mode, we'll ignore these entries.

The byte that stores the number of color planes will either be set to a value of 1 for 256-color images or 3 for 24-bit images. As you'll see later in this chapter, the color components of 24-bit images are stored as three separate rows of colors.

Figure 9.2 The dimensions of a PCX image.

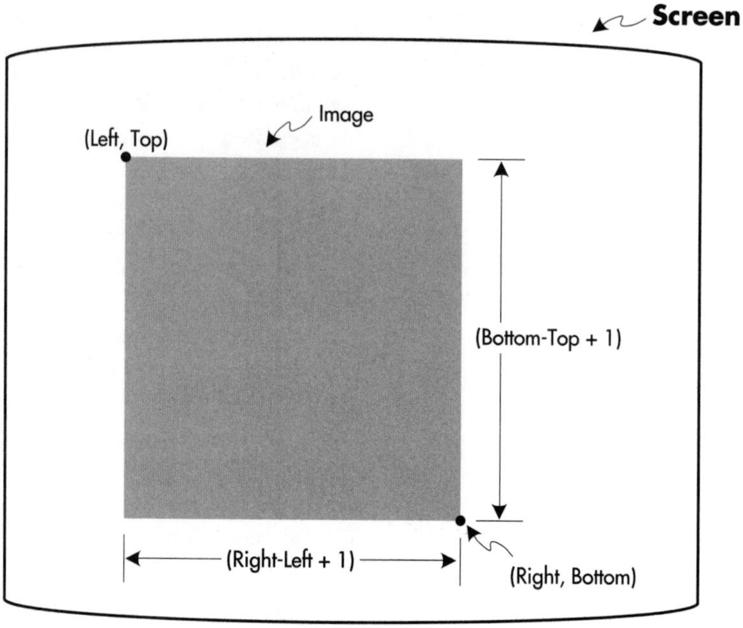

Run-Length Encoding

PCX files employ a simple image compression technique called run-length encoding. The compression process is fairly straightforward. The idea is to store the number of times a color repeats on a row rather than the individual color values. Run-length encoding saves these pixels as a length count followed by the actual value. For instance, if an image row consists of 10 consecutive values of 36:

36 36 36 36 36 36 36 36 36 36

by using run-length encoding, they can be stored as:

10 36

Thus, this image sequence can be stored in two bytes rather than ten.

If a value doesn't repeat, it is simply stored by itself, without a preceding run-length count. How does the decoder know which values are actual pixel colors and which are run-length counts? The PCX format sets the most significant two bits to one if the value represents a repeat count. The six remaining bits give the actual repeat count. Since a PCX file stores its data as bytes, this means that a repeat count can't be larger than 63. What if the run is longer than 63 pixels? You simply break up the run into a chain of separate runs.

Let's look at an example. Suppose an image contains 120 consecutive pixels of value 13. The first 63 can be encoded as a run of 13 and the remaining as a run of 57. Here's how the resulting encoded data would appear in the PCX file:

63 13 57 13

There's one more special case to handle with PCX files. Since the upper two bits have special meaning, we can't directly store image values greater than or equal to 192 because they have the upper two bits set. To get around this, PCX files store values equal to or greater than 192 using a repeat count followed by the actual value. Therefore, a pixel value of 194 is stored using the two bytes:

1 194

Realize that if there are numerous high intensity pixels in an image, the PCX file may not have good compression because the higher values always require a repeat count, even when there is only a one-pixel run.

Decoding a PCX File

Decoding the image data in a PCX file is the inverse of the encoding process discussed in the last section. The header tells the decoder the size of the image to expect and its color resolution. Using this information, the image data is read one byte at a time using the following algorithm:

```
while not end of file
   Read Byte
   if upper two bits of byte are set
     then set repeat count to the lower six bits of the byte
     Read next byte
     Store the value read to the image buffer
        repeat count number of times
   else
     Store value in image array
```

THE PCX TOOLKIT

The source files PCXTOOL.C and PCXTOOL.H, listed at the end of this chapter, provide routines to read and write PCX images. As mentioned earlier, our toolkit only supports 256-color, palette-based images and 24-bit, RGB images.

PCXTOOL assumes that the image is organized in one of the two ways shown in Figure 9.3. If the image uses a palette, then every pixel is one byte in

Figure 9.3 The two types of images that PCXTOOL supports.

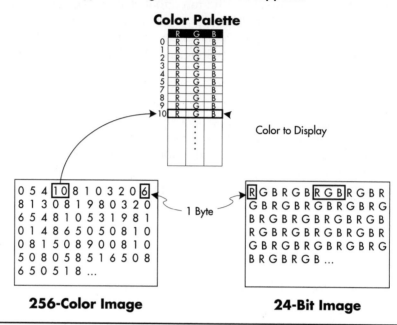

size. The value acts as an index into a palette of red, green, and blue values that specify the actual color to paint the pixel. Alternately, 24-bit images are organized as consecutive red, green, and blue values. This is the same format used by RAY programs presented in earlier chapters.

Table 9.2 lists the functions included in PCXTOOL.C. The first six are used to write a PCX image, the remaining ones are used to read one.

Processing the Header

The PCXTOOL.H file defines the following **PCXHEADER** structure to represent a PCX file's 128-byte header:

```
typedef struct PCXHDR {
  unsigned char PCXId;                        // 0x0A for PCX files
  unsigned char Version;                      // PCX file format version
  unsigned char Encoding;                     // 1 for run-length compression
  unsigned char BitsPerPixel;                 // Number of bits per pixel
  unsigned int  LeftX, LeftY;                 // Upper-left corner
  unsigned int  RightX, RightY;               // Bottom-right corner
  unsigned int  DisplayXRes, DisplayYRes;     // Resolution of display
  unsigned char Palette[48];                  // Palette data
  unsigned char Reserved;
```

Table 9.2 The functions in PCXTOOL.C.

Function	Description
WritePCXHeader	Writes a PCX header to a file
SetPCXHeader	Sets most of the fields in a PCX header
EncodePut	Encodes an image value and writes it to a file
WritePCXImage	High-level routine to write an image to a PCX file
WritePCXRow	Writes one row of an image to a PCX file
WritePCXPalette	Writes a 256-color palette to a file
ReadPCXHeader	Reads a PCX header from a file
GetPCXInfo	Retrieves the dimensions of an image from a PCX header
IsValidPCX	Determines whether a PCX file contains an image type supported by PCXTOOL.C
GetPCXRow	Reads and decodes a single row of image data from a PCX file
ReadPCXImage	High-level routine that reads an image from a PCX file

```
   unsigned char NPlanes;          // Number of bit planes of data
   unsigned int  BytesPerRow;      // Number of bytes in
                                   // an uncompressed line

   unsigned int  PaletteInfo;
   unsigned char Reserved2[58];
} PCXHEADER;
```

Each field in **PCXHEADER** corresponds to one of the components in a PCX header. Notice that the fields are the same size as those listed for the fields in Table 9.1. For instance, the first field, **PCXId**, is a single byte value that holds the file's special marker.

Because of the way we've declared **PCXHeader**, we can read and write a header using a single file operation. For instance, to read a header, we can use:

```
fread(&PCXHeader, sizeof(PCXHeader), 1, Inputfp);
```

Initializing a Header

When creating a PCX file, you can use the **SetPCXHeader** function to initialize most of the fields in a PCX header structure. The routine accepts four arguments: the header structure to update, the expected image's width and height, and the number of bytes used to represent each pixel's color. Here's the complete **SetPCXHeader** function:

```
void SetPCXHeader(PCXHEADER *PCXHdr, int ImWd, int ImHt,
  int BytesPerPixel)
{
  PCXHdr->PCXId = 0x0A;
```

```
PCXHdr->Version = 5;
PCXHdr->Encoding = 1;              // Use run-length encoding
PCXHdr->BitsPerPixel = 8;         // 8 bits per pixel
PCXHdr->LeftX = 0;                // Display image at (0,0)
PCXHdr->LeftY = 0;
PCXHdr->RightX = ImWd-1;
PCXHdr->RightY = ImHt-1;
PCXHdr->DisplayXRes = 640;        // Screen resolution
PCXHdr->DisplayYRes = 480;
// The number of planes equals the number of bytes per pixel
PCXHdr->NPlanes = BytesPerPixel;
// The number of bytes per row should be even
PCXHdr->BytesPerRow = (ImWd % 2 == 0) ? ImWd : ImWd + 1;
// RGB images don't have a palette, but 256-color images do
PCXHdr->PaletteInfo = (BytesPerPixel == 1) ? 1 : 0;
}
```

Notice that the display resolution fields, **DisplayXRes** and **DisplayYRes**, are set to 640 and 480, respectively. They represent the screen resolution that a program should use to display the image. We'll be ignoring these fields ourselves, but we'll set them to these values so they aren't left undefined for other applications. Also, notice that the header is set so that the image will be displayed at the top left of the screen. This is accomplished by setting **LeftX** and **LeftY** to 0.

Writing the Header

The **WritePCXHeader** function writes a PCX header to the top of an output file. The header should be initialized either by manually setting its fields or calling **SetPCXHeader** before calling this routine. For example, to prepare for a 256-color image that is 128 by 128 pixels, you could make the call:

```
SetPCXHeader(&PCXHeader, 128, 128, 1);
```

To write the header, you would use:

```
WritePCXHeader(Output_filepointer, &PCXHeader);
```

Writing an Image

The PCXTOOL.C source file packs six routines to assist in writing an image to a PCX file. All of the functions return 1 if they are successful and 0 if they are not.

The function **WritePCXRow** writes one row of image data to a file. With 24-bit images, the routine first stores the red color components for a row, then the green, and finally the blue. **WritePCXRow** takes four parameters. The first,

Outfp, is the file to write to. The second is a pointer to the file buffer. The third parameter is the pixel width of the row. The last, **BytesPerPixel** is the number of bytes that represent each pixel: one for 256-color images and three for 24-bit images.

The **WritePCXImage** function is an all-in-one function for writing an image to a PCX file. However, use this routine with care. The function requires that the image be less than 64k—even if you compile the code in large memory model. You can get around this by setting the image pointer to huge, but this may not be the best technique. A better approach is simply to write your own version of **WritePCXImage** that calls **WritePCXRow** for each row of the image.

Processing the Palette

If an image has an extended palette, it'll be organized as shown earlier in Figure 9.3. You can define a palette as an array of bytes. You'll need 256 sets of bytes that hold red, green, and blue colors. Here's one way to do this:

```
unsigned char Palette[256*3];
```

The **ReadPCXPalette** and **WritePCXPalette** functions read and write a 256-color palette. Remember, they are not used with 24-bit, RGB images. Both routines take two parameters. The first is the PCX file to use, the second is a pointer to a 768-byte buffer. This is large enough to hold the 256 red, green, and blue color palette entries.

In the case of **ReadPCXPalette**, the function moves the file pointer 769 bytes before the end of the file, tests for the special marker byte—a value of 12—and then transfers the remaining 768 bytes to the palette buffer. Here are the statements that perform these operations:

```
if (fseek(Infp, 256L*-3-1, SEEK_END)) return 0;
if (fread(&Code, 1, 1, Infp) != 1) return 0;
if (Code == 12)   // If the marker exists, read the palette
  if (fread(Palette, 256*3, 1, Infp) != 1) return 0;
return 1;
```

READING A PCX FILE

Reading a PCX image is only slightly more complicated than writing one. You'll want to process a PCX file in three chunks. First, you must read the file header and make sure that it represents a valid PCX file. At this time, you'll also need to allocate memory to hold the image to be read, or at least one row of it. Next, you should call **GetPCXRow** to read each row of the image. Once you've made it this far you can read the palette, if the file contains one.

Reading a Header

ReadPCXHeader retrieves the first 128 bytes in a file and returns them in a **PCXHEADER** structure. With this structure, you can determine the dimensions of the image and whether it is a 256-color or 24-bit image. The **ReadPCXHeader** routine, however, makes no attempt to determine if the header contains a valid PCX file. For this, you should call **IsValidPCX**. The **IsValidPCX** routine returns non-zero if the header passed to it contains the settings that are consistent with those supported by PCXTOOL.C. Namely, it checks whether the file is a 256-color or 24-bit color image. If the image is neither of these, **IsValidPCX** returns 0. Here's the complete **IsValidPCX** function:

```
int IsValidPCX(PCXHEADER *PCXHdr)
{
  if (PCXHdr->PCXId == 0x0A &&
      PCXHdr->Version == 5) {
    // Correct format but is the image type one supported?
    if (PCXHdr->Encoding == 1 &&    // Uses run-length encoding
        PCXHdr->BitsPerPixel == 8) { // 8 bits per pixel
      if (PCXHdr->NPlanes == 3)
        return 1;   // 24-bit RGB image
      else if (PCXHdr->NPlanes == 1)
        return 1;   // 256-color image
    }
  }
  return 0;          // Image type not supported by PCXTOOL.C
}
```

PCXTOOL.C also defines the **GetPCXInfo** function that enables you to extract the image width, height, and number of bytes per pixel from a **PCXHEADER** structure. The following statement, for instance, returns these three values:

```
GetPCXInfo(&PCXHeader, &ImageWidth, &ImageHeight, &BytesPerPixel);
```

Reading the Image

You're now prepared to read the image data. You can call **GetPCXRow** to read a single row of image data from the file. It uses **getc** to read the file one byte at a time. If the value read is greater than 0xC0, the code must be processing a repeat count, in which case the count is stripped from the byte and the actual value is read by another call to **getc**. If, on the other hand, the value is not a repeat count, the run-length variable, **RunLen**, is set to 1. These statements are shown next:

```
for (p=0; p<BytesPerPixel; p++) {   // Get each color component
  x = 0;
  while (x<BytesPerRow) {            // Get the whole image row
    if (EOF == (b=getc(Infp)))
      return 0;
    if (b > 0xC0) {                  // This is a repeat count
      RunLen = b & 0x3F;
      if (EOF == (b=getc(Infp)))     // Get the pixel value
        return 0;
    }
    else
      RunLen = 1;                    // A single pixel value
```

In either case, the following **for** loop is executed to unpack the image data into the buffer passed to **GetPCXRow**.

```
for (i=0; i<RunLen; i++) {          // Copy the value to the image
  Image[x*BytesPerPixel+p] = b;
  x++;
}
```

The outer **for** loop is only used for 24-bit images. It reads each of the red, green, and blue rows of compressed data. Remember, for 24-bit images the three color components are stored on separate rows.

A Sample Read Function

The **ReadPCXImage** function is a high-level routine that demonstrates how to read PCX files. You simply pass the function a file pointer to the PCX file and a pointer to the image buffer. **ReadPCXImage** does the rest of the work. Realize, however, that you must allocate the image array so that it is large enough to hold the whole image.

Of course, you don't know the size of the image until after **ReadPCXImage** returns. Therefore, a better idea is to use **ReadPCXImage** as a guideline, and do the work yourself. Instead of calling **ReadPCXImage**, take the following five steps:

1. Call **ReadPCXHeader** to retrieve the header from the file.
2. Use **IsValidPCX** to determine whether the header represents a valid PCX that PCXTOOL supports.
3. Allocate memory for the whole image or one row of it.
4. Invoke **GetPCXRow** to read the image one row at a time.
5. Call **ReadPCXPalette** to read the image palette, if one exists.

Testing PCXTOOL.C

The TESTPCX.C program that follows this section exercises the routines in PCXTOOL.C. The program generates a grayscale image, writes it to a palette-based PCX file, reads it back in, and displays the resulting image. The intermediate image is placed in the file TEST.PCX. Figure 9.4 shows what the image should look like. You may want to try reading this file into one of your applications, such as PC Paintbrush, to verify that the file is readable by other programs.

A few points are worth noting regarding the TEST.PCX program. First, the image is less than 64k in size. The image is created with the following nested **for** loops:

```
for (j=0; j<IMHT; j++) {
  for (i=0; i<IMWD; i++) {
    Im[j*IMWD+i] = i;
  }
}
```

In addition, a grayscale palette is created by setting a 256-byte palette to equal red, green, and blue components:

```
for (i=0; i<256; i++) {
  Palette[i*3] = i;
  Palette[i*3+1] = i;
  Palette[i*3+2] = i;
}
```

Creating the PCX file is then a simple matter of opening the output file and writing the image to the PCX file:

```
fp = fopen("TEST.PCX", "wb");
if (fp == NULL) {
  printf("Could not open output file: TEST.PCX.\n");
  exit(1);
}

if (!WritePCXImage(fp, Im, IMWD, IMHT, BYTESPERPIXEL, Palette)) {
  printf("Write operation not successful.\n");
```

Figure 9.4 The PCX image generated by TESTPCX.C.

```
    exit(1);
}
```

After the image has been successfully written, the output file is closed and read back into memory using **ReadPCXImage**. The image's dimensions are also checked to see if they are consistent with those that TESTPCX.C expects:

```
if (!ReadPCXImage(fp, Im, &ImWd, &ImHt, &b, Palette)) {
  printf("Failed to read TEST.PCX.\n");
  exit(1);
}
// Make sure the image is the same as was written
if (ImWd != IMWD || ImHt != IMHT || b != BYTESPERPIXEL) {
  printf("Unexpected image dimensions in TEST.PCX.\n");
  exit(1);
}
```

If everything is still working correctly, the image is displayed by the following statements:

```
// Switch to graphics mode and display the image
if (SetupDisplay(M320x200x256 | COLORPALETTE)) {
  for (j=0; j<ImHt; j++) {
    for (i=0; i<ImWd; i++) {
      PutPixel(0, i, j, Im[j*ImWd+i], Im[j*ImWd+i],
        Im[j*ImWd+i]);
    }
  }
  getch();        // Wait for a keypress
}
EndDisplay();     // Exit graphics mode
```

To build the TESTPCX program, you must compile and link TESTPCX.C with PCXTOOL.C and GRPHICS.C. Running the program is as simple as typing TESTPCX at the DOS prompt. When the program runs, you'll see it switch to graphics mode and eventually display the TEST.PCX image. Once the image is fully displayed, you'll need to press a key to exit the program.

Here's the complete listing for the TESTPCX program:

```
// TESTPCX.C: Tests the PCXTOOL.C toolkit. It creates a 256-color,
// grayscale image, writes it to a PCX file, reads it back into
// memory, and displays it. Compile and link with GRPHICS.C and
// PCXTOOL.C.

#include <stdio.h>
#include <stdlib.h>
#include "pcxtool.h"
```

```c
#include "grphics.h"

#define IMWD 200              // Image width and height
#define IMHT 200
#define BYTESPERPIXEL 1       // One byte per pixel

FILE *fp;
unsigned char Im[IMWD*IMHT];   // The image array
unsigned char Palette[768];    // The palette array

/////////////////////////// main \\\\\\\\\\\\\\\\\\\\\\\\\\\\\
//
// The main function
//
main()
{
  unsigned int i, j, ImWd, ImHt, b;

  // Create the image
  for (j=0; j<IMHT; j++) {
    for (i=0; i<IMWD; i++) {
      Im[j*IMWD+i] = i;
    }
  }
  // Make a grayscale palette
  for (i=0; i<256; i++) {
    Palette[i*3] = i;
    Palette[i*3+1] = i;
    Palette[i*3+2] = i;
  }

  fp = fopen("TEST.PCX", "wb");
  if (fp == NULL) {
    printf("Could not open output file: TEST.PCX.\n");
    exit(1);
  }

  if (!WritePCXImage(fp, Im, IMWD, IMHT, BYTESPERPIXEL, Palette)) {
    printf("Write operation not successful.\n");
    exit(1);
  }
  fclose(fp);

  // Open the PCX file again--this time for reading
  fp = fopen("TEST.PCX", "rb");
  if (fp == NULL) {
    printf("Could not open input file: TEST.PCX.\n");
    exit(1);
  }
```

```
    // Read the image from the PCX file
    if (!ReadPCXImage(fp, Im, &ImWd, &ImHt, &b, Palette)) {
      printf("Failed to read TEST.PCX.\n");
      exit(1);
    }
    // Make sure the image is the same as was written
    if (ImWd != IMWD || ImHt != IMHT || b != BYTESPERPIXEL) {
      printf("Unexpected image dimensions in TEST.PCX.\n");
      exit(1);
    }

    // Switch to graphics mode and display the image
    if (SetupDisplay(M320x200x256 | COLORPALETTE)) {
      for (j=0; j<ImHt; j++) {
        for (i=0; i<ImWd; i++) {
          PutPixel(0, i, j, Im[j*ImWd+i], Im[j*ImWd+i],
            Im[j*ImWd+i]);
        }
      }
      getch();        // Wait for a keypress
    }
    EndDisplay();    // Exit graphics mode
    printf("Done\n");
    fclose(fp);
    return 0;
}
```

• PCXTOOL.H

```
// PCXTOOL.H: Header file for PCXTOOL.C.

#ifndef PCXTOOLH
#define PCXTOOLH

// A PCX file has a header with the following format:
typedef struct PCXHDR {
  unsigned char PCXId;                      // 0x0A for PCX files
  unsigned char Version;                    // PCX file format version
  unsigned char Encoding;                   // 1 for run-length compression
  unsigned char BitsPerPixel;               // Number of bits per pixel
  unsigned int  LeftX, LeftY;               // Upper-left corner
  unsigned int  RightX, RightY;             // Bottom-right corner
  unsigned int  DisplayXRes, DisplayYRes;   // Resolution of display
  unsigned char Palette[48];                // Palette data
  unsigned char Reserved;
  unsigned char NPlanes;                    // Number of bit planes of data
  unsigned int  BytesPerRow;                // Number of bytes in
                                            // an uncompressed line
```

```
  unsigned int  PaletteInfo;
  unsigned char Reserved2[58];
} PCXHEADER;

// Function prototypes
int WritePCXHeader(FILE *Outfp, PCXHEADER *PCXHdr);
void SetPCXHeader(PCXHEADER *PCXHdr, int ImWd, int ImHt,
  int BytesPerPixel);
int EncodePut(FILE *Outfp, unsigned char Val,
  unsigned char Count);
int WritePCXImage(FILE *Outfp, unsigned char *Image, int ImWd,
  int ImHt, int BytesPerPixel, unsigned char *Palette);
int WritePCXRow(FILE *Outfp, unsigned char *Image,
  int ImWd, int BytesPerPixel);
int WritePCXPalette(FILE *Outfp, unsigned char *Palette);
int ReadPCXHeader(FILE *Outfp, PCXHEADER *PCXHdr);
void GetPCXInfo(PCXHEADER *PCXHdr, int *ImWd, int *ImHt,
  int *BytesPerPixel);
int IsValidPCX(PCXHEADER *PCXHdr);
int GetPCXRow(FILE *Infp, unsigned char *Image, int BytesPerPixel,
  int BytesPerScan, int ImWd);
int ReadPCXImage(FILE *Infp, unsigned char *Image, int *ImWd,
  int *ImHt, int *BytesPerPixel, unsigned char *Palette);
int ReadPCXPalette(FILE *Infp, unsigned char *Palette);

#endif
```

• PCXTOOL.C

```
// PCXTOOL.C: PCX toolkit that supports 256-color and 24-bit
// color images.

#include <stdio.h>
#include "pcxtool.h"

/////////////////////////  WritePCXHeader  \\\\\\\\\\\\\\\\\\\\\\\
//
// Writes a PCX header to a file. The header is written before
// the image is placed in the file. Returns 0 if the write
// operation fails. Otherwise, it returns 1. The header should
// be initialized to its proper settings before calling this
// routine.
//
int WritePCXHeader(FILE *Outfp, PCXHEADER *PCXHdr)
{
  if (fseek(Outfp, 0L, SEEK_SET)) return 0;
  // Write header to file
  if (!fwrite(PCXHdr, sizeof(PCXHEADER), 1, Outfp))
```

```
      return 0;
    return 1;
  }


  //////////////////////////// SetPCXHeader \\\\\\\\\\\\\\\\\\\\\\\\\\\\
  //
  // Sets the default values in a PCX header. ImWd and ImHt are
  // the image's pixel width and height. Set BytesPerPixel to 1
  // for 256-color images and 3 for RGB images.
  //
  void SetPCXHeader(PCXHEADER *PCXHdr, int ImWd, int ImHt,
    int BytesPerPixel)
  {
    PCXHdr->PCXId = 0x0A;
    PCXHdr->Version = 5;
    PCXHdr->Encoding = 1;              // Use run-length encoding
    PCXHdr->BitsPerPixel = 8;         // 8 bits per pixel
    PCXHdr->LeftX = 0;                // Display image at (0,0)
    PCXHdr->LeftY = 0;
    PCXHdr->RightX = ImWd-1;
    PCXHdr->RightY = ImHt-1;
    PCXHdr->DisplayXRes = 640;        // Screen resolution
    PCXHdr->DisplayYRes = 480;
    PCXHdr->NPlanes = BytesPerPixel;  // Number of planes equals the
    PCXHdr->BytesPerRow = ImWd;       // number of bytes per pixel
    // RGB images don't have a palette, but 256-color images do
    PCXHdr->PaletteInfo = (BytesPerPixel == 1) ? 1 : 0;
  }


  //////////////////////////// EncodePut \\\\\\\\\\\\\\\\\\\\\\\\\\\\\\\
  //
  // Encodes and writes the value in Val to the PCX file. Count
  // is the repeat count for the value.
  //
  int EncodePut(FILE *Outfp, unsigned char Val, unsigned char Count)
  {
    if (Count == 1 && 0xC0 != (0xC0 & Val)) {
      // Write the value because it only has a length of one
      if (EOF == putc((int)Val, Outfp))
        return 0; // Disk write error
    }
    else {
      // The value is greater than 0xC0 or it represents a
      // repeat count. Write them as two bytes in the file.
      // First write the run-length and then the value.
      if (EOF == putc((int)(0xC0 | Count), Outfp))
        return 0; // Disk write error
      if (EOF == putc((int)Val, Outfp))
```

```
      return 0; // Disk write error
  }
  return 1;
}


/////////////////////////  WritePCXImage  \\\\\\\\\\\\\\\\\\\\\\\\
//
// Writes the image data to a PCX file. This code handles
// 256-color and 24-bit color images. Returns 1 if successful;
// 0 otherwise. Set Palette to NULL and BytesPerPixel to 3 for
// 24-bit images. Note: This function only handles images less
// than 64k.
//
int WritePCXImage(FILE *Outfp, unsigned char *Image, int ImWd,
  int ImHt, int BytesPerPixel, unsigned char *Palette)
{
  int y;
  PCXHEADER PCXHeader;

  SetPCXHeader(&PCXHeader, ImWd, ImHt, BytesPerPixel);
  if (!WritePCXHeader(Outfp, &PCXHeader))
    return 0;

  for (y=0; y<ImHt; y++)
    if (!WritePCXRow(Outfp, &Image[y*ImWd*BytesPerPixel],
      ImWd, BytesPerPixel))
      return 0;
  // If there is a palette and the image is a 256-color
  // image, write the palette to the file
  if (Palette != NULL && BytesPerPixel == 1)
    if (!WritePCXPalette(Outfp, Palette))
      return 0;
  return 1;     // Success
}


/////////////////////////  WritePCXRow  \\\\\\\\\\\\\\\\\\\\\\\\\
//
// Writes a single line of an image to a PCX file. This routine
// only supports 256-color and 24-bit RGB images. The 256-color
// images are written one byte (pixel) at a time to the file.
// The RGB images are written as a red row, then green row, the
// blue row. Set BytesPerPixel to 1 for 256-color images and 3
// for RGB images.
//
int WritePCXRow(FILE *Outfp, unsigned char *Image,
  int ImWd, int BytesPerPixel)
{
  unsigned char PrevVal, Val, Rep;
  int x, i, p, EndOfRow;
```

```
  for (p=0; p<BytesPerPixel; p++) {
    x = p;              // First pixel on image row to write
    PrevVal = Image[x]; // First image pixel
    x += BytesPerPixel; // Go to the next pixel in the row
    EndOfRow = ImWd * BytesPerPixel + p;  // Last pixel to write
    Rep = 1;            // You begin with only one pixel
    do {
      Val = Image[x];   // The next image pixel to write
      x += BytesPerPixel;
      if (Val == PrevVal) {
        // If the next is the same as the current, increment
        // the repetition counter
        Rep++;
        // Maximum run count reached. Write out current data.
        if (Rep == 63) {
          if (!(i=EncodePut(Outfp, PrevVal, Rep)))
            return 0;   // Write operation failed
          Rep = 0;      // Reset the repetition counter
        }
      }
      else {            // PrevVal != Val, so write PrevVal if
        if (Rep) {      // the repetition count is not zero
          if (!(i=EncodePut(Outfp, PrevVal, Rep)))
            return 0;
        }
        PrevVal = Val;  // Set the previous pixel to the current
        Rep = 1;        // one and reset the run-length counter
      }
    } while (x < EndOfRow);   // Reached end of the image row?

    if (Rep) {          // Write out unwritten pixels on line
      if (!(i=EncodePut(Outfp, PrevVal, Rep)))
        return 0;
    }
    // If there are an odd number of bytes in the image row,
    // write another pixel to the row
    if (ImWd % 2 == 1)
      EncodePut(Outfp, 0, 1);
  }
  return 1;
}


/////////////////////////  WritePCXPalette  \\\\\\\\\\\\\\\\\\\\\\\
//
// Writes a 256-color palette to the end of the PCX file. The
// palette should be 256*3 (768) bytes long. It should have
// 256 RGB triples. The palette is written to the end of the
// file and is preceded by a value of 12.
//
```

```
int WritePCXPalette(FILE *Outfp, unsigned char *Palette)
{
  unsigned char Code=12;

  if (fseek(Outfp, 0L, SEEK_END)) return 0;
  if (!fwrite(&Code, 1, 1, Outfp)) return 0;
  if (!fwrite(Palette, 256*3, 1, Outfp)) return 0;
  return 1;
}


//////////////////////// ReadPCXHeader \\\\\\\\\\\\\\\\\\\\\\\\
//
// Reads a PCX file's header. Returns 0 if the read operation
// fails. Otherwise, it returns 1.
//
int ReadPCXHeader(FILE *Infp, PCXHEADER *PCXHdr)
{
  if (fseek(Infp, 0L, SEEK_SET)) return 0;
  if (fread(PCXHdr, sizeof(PCXHEADER), 1, Infp) != 1)
    return 0;    // Could not read header
  return 1;
}


//////////////////////// GetPCXInfo \\\\\\\\\\\\\\\\\\\\\\\\\\\
//
// Retrieves the image width, height, and the number of bytes
// per color from the header PCXHdr
//
void GetPCXInfo(PCXHEADER *PCXHdr, int *ImWd, int *ImHt,
  int *BytesPerPixel)
{
  *ImWd = PCXHdr->RightX - PCXHdr->LeftX + 1;
  *ImHt = PCXHdr->RightY - PCXHdr->LeftY + 1;
  *BytesPerPixel = PCXHdr->NPlanes;
}


//////////////////////// IsValidPCX \\\\\\\\\\\\\\\\\\\\\\\\\\\
//
// Returns a value of 1 if the header passed to the routine
// represents either a 256-color or 24-bit image for which
// PCXTOOL.C is designed
//
int IsValidPCX(PCXHEADER *PCXHdr)
{
  if (PCXHdr->PCXId == 0x0A &&
      PCXHdr->Version == 5) {
    // Correct format but is the image type one supported?
    if (PCXHdr->Encoding == 1 &&    // Uses run-length encoding
      PCXHdr->BitsPerPixel == 8) { // 8 bits per pixel
```

```
      if (PCXHdr->NPlanes == 3)
        return 1;    // 24-bit RGB image
      else if (PCXHdr->NPlanes == 1)
        return 1;    // 256-color image
    }
  }
  return 0;          // Image type not supported by PCXTOOL.C
}

///////////////////////// GetPCXRow  \\\\\\\\\\\\\\\\\\\\\\\\
//
// Reads and decodes a single pixel row. The image row is
// returned in the Image array. There must be enough room in
// Image to hold BytesPerRow*BytesPerPixel pixels.
//
int GetPCXRow(FILE *Infp, unsigned char *Image, int BytesPerPixel,
  int BytesPerRow, int ImWd)
{
  int i, b, x, p, RunLen;

  for (p=0; p<BytesPerPixel; p++) {  // Get each color component
    x = 0;
    while (x<BytesPerRow) {          // Get the whole image row
      if (EOF == (b=getc(Infp)))
        return 0;
      if (b > 0xC0) {                // This is a repeat count
        RunLen = b & 0x3F;
        if (EOF == (b=getc(Infp)))   // Get the pixel value
          return 0;
      }
      else
        RunLen = 1;                  // A single pixel value
      if (x >= ImWd) break;          // Only copy the image's pixels
      for (i=0; i<RunLen; i++) {     // Copy the value to the image
        Image[x*BytesPerPixel+p] = b;
        x++;
      }
    }
  }
  return 1;
}

///////////////////////// ReadPCXImage  \\\\\\\\\\\\\\\\\\\\\\\\
//
// Sample routine that reads the image data to a PCX file. This
// code handles 256-color and 24-bit color images. Returns 1 if
// successful; 0 otherwise. Set Palette to NULL for 24-bit
// images. The image must be less than 64k in size and the Image
// array must be large enough to hold the whole uncompressed image.
//
```

```
int ReadPCXImage(FILE *Infp, unsigned char *Image, int *ImWd,
  int *ImHt, int *BytesPerPixel, unsigned char *Palette)
{
  int y;
  PCXHEADER PCXHdr;

  if (!ReadPCXHeader(Infp, &PCXHdr))  // Read the headers
    return 0;
  if (!IsValidPCX(&PCXHdr)) // Does the header say the image is
    return 0;               // the right type?
  // Extract the image dimensions from the header
  GetPCXInfo(&PCXHdr, ImWd, ImHt, BytesPerPixel);

  for (y=0; y<*ImHt; y++)    // Read each image row
    if (!GetPCXRow(Infp, &Image[y*(*ImWd)*(*BytesPerPixel)],
      PCXHdr.NPlanes, PCXHdr.BytesPerRow, *ImWd))
      return 0;
  // Read the image palette if there is one
  if (*BytesPerPixel == 1 && PCXHdr.PaletteInfo == 1)
    ReadPCXPalette(Infp, Palette);
  return 1;
}


///////////////////////// ReadPCXPalette \\\\\\\\\\\\\\\\\\\\\\\\\
//
// Reads the 256-color palette from the end of the file. The
// palette should be 256*3 bytes in size. The Palette array
// should be 768 bytes in size.
//
int ReadPCXPalette(FILE *Infp, unsigned char *Palette)
{
  unsigned char Code;

  // Seek to the file location where the palette marker is. It
  // should be the value 12.
  if (fseek(Infp, 256L*-3-1, SEEK_END)) return 0;
  if (fread(&Code, 1, 1, Infp) != 1) return 0;
  if (Code == 12)   // If the marker exists, read the palette
    if (fread(Palette, 256*3, 1, Infp) != 1) return 0;
  return 1;
}
```

TIFF: A Flexible Image File Format

The PCX tools we developed in Chapter 9 enable you to read and write images from a variety of commercial applications. However, since the PCX format was originally designed to capture and display screen images, it does have limitations. For instance, it doesn't account for the aspect ratio of the image or the size that the image should be printed or displayed. As a result, many image manipulation programs favor another file standard: the Tagged Image File Format (TIFF). The TIFF format is designed to work with a wide range of images from a wide range of devices.

In this chapter, we'll explore the TIFF standard and develop a toolkit that can read and write TIFF files. We'll begin by discussing the general format of TIFF files, then we'll cover the specifics of a custom TIFF toolkit. (Recall that the RAY program stores its images as TIFF files.)

TIFF Overview

The TIFF file format was developed by Aldus and Microsoft primarily for the desktop publishing industry. Their goal was to make an image file format that could endure the endless evolutionary advancements of computer equipment. In addition, they designed TIFF so that it could work on a variety of computer platforms, thereby making it a true standard.

The key to TIFF's success is its flexible and extensible nature. The TIFF standard details a variety of information that can be included in a TIFF file. An application only needs to use what information is required to adequately store the images that it works with. Further, the application can choose to organize the information in a variety of ways, rather than having to adhere to a fixed format.

The information is organized into small blocks. Each block begins with a unique code, or *tag*, that specifies what information is contained in the block. A collection of tags is referred to as an *Image File Directory* (IFD). The TIFF standard defines what each tag means and how to read that block's data. For example, each TIFF file has a tag entry that specifies the image's width and one that specifies its height. In all, images typically contain a dozen or more tags that specify information specific to its needs. For instance, only images that have a color palette have a palette tag. In addition, there are many optional tags that a file may contain. Consequently, different applications may store the same image differently.

Working with Classes

The flexibility built into TIFF makes it a bit of a challenge to program for. However, we can conform to a modest yet powerful subset of the TIFF standard that is able to process a variety of TIFF images.

Specifically, we'll support eight-bit grayscale images, such as those captured from a digital camera or frame grabber, and 24-bit RGB images, such as those that the ray tracer in this book generates. The TIFF standard refers to these two categories of images as class G and R images.

The Pieces of a TIFF File

Although the contents of TIFF files vary, they always have the following three basic components:

- A header that identifies the file as a TIFF file
- One or more subheads containing a sequence of tags that describes the image(s) included in the TIFF file
- The data for the image(s)

Figure 10.1 presents the overall format of a TIFF file. As the figure illustrates, a TIFF file always begins with an eight-byte header. The first two bytes are the capital letters II or MM. They signal whether the file was written for an Intel- or Motorola-based computer. As you'll see in Figure 10.2, these two competing types of computers store their multibyte integers in different orders. Therefore, a TIFF reader needs to know how the bytes are arranged to read them correctly.

The next two bytes in the header hold the integer value 42. It, at least in part, signals that the file is a TIFF file. Although this value is considered a version number, it probably will never change unless the TIFF format is significantly revised.

Figure 10.1 The format of a TIFF file.

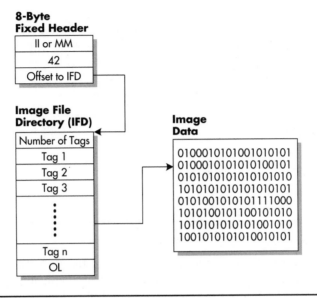

Figure 10.2 Intel- and Motorola-based computers store their multibyte integers differently.

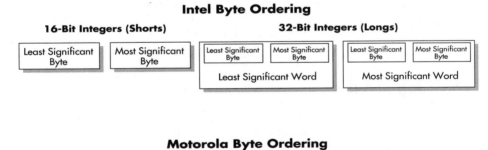

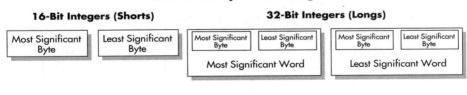

Figure 10.3 The typical structure of an IFD.

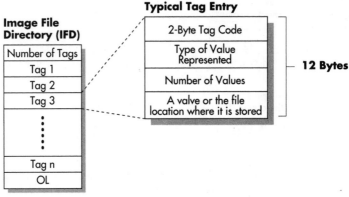

The last four bytes in the header hold the file location of an IFD. The file offset is always relative to the top of the file. For simplicity, we'll be placing the IFD immediately after the fixed header, though this does not need to be the case.

An IFD contains all the information your program needs to determine how to read the image in the file and display it. Actually, a TIFF file can have more than one IFD describing more than one image, however, we'll assume that there is only one image per file.

Figure 10.3 shows the structure of a typical IFD. Its first entry is a two-byte integer that specifies how many tags are to follow. The tag entries are always 12 bytes in size, although the way that its bytes are interpreted varies. At the end of each IFD is a four-byte file pointer to the next IFD, if there is one. The last IFD ends in four zeroes. A final rule is that all the tags are sorted in ascending order.

Working with Tags

The key to decoding a TIFF image is in deciphering the tag entries in an IFD. Although tag entries can specify many different things, they always have the organization listed in Table 10.1.

The two topmost bytes in a tag entry hold the tag's integer code. Table 10.2 lists the tags we'll be using. Realize that while the TIFF standard defines over forty tags, we only need a subset of them to process G and R class images.

Table 10.3 lists the values we'll be using in conjunction with the tags in Table 10.2.

Since tag entries can specify different information, they may also hold different data types. Specifically, the data in a tag entry can have one of five different basic data types. These are encoded in the second and third bytes of the tag entry using the integer values listed in Table 10.4.

Where is the data for a tag placed? If it's small enough, it is located in bytes 8 through 11. If it can't fit there, the last four bytes specify the file location where the data is stored. The preceding four bytes tell the TIFF reader how many pieces of data to expect.

Table 10.1 The fields in a tag.

Bytes	Description
0-1	Contains an integer code that identifies the tag
2-3	Specifies the type of data to follow, such as whether it is a short or long integer
4-7	Length of the tag's information
8-11	Contains a value for the tag field or an offset to a location in the file that lists the value

Table 10.2 A minimal set of tags.

Name	Value	Type	Description
NewSubfileType	254	Long	Specifies whether the image is a bit-mask, low-resolution image, and so on
ImageWidth	256	Short or Long	Pixel width of the image
ImageLength	257	Short or Long	Number of rows in the image
BitsPerSample	258	Short	Number of bits per pixel
Compression	259	Short	Image compression used
Photometric-Interpretation	262	Short	Specifies how to interpret the image, such as whether it is monochrome, has a palette, or is RGB
StripOffsets	273	Short or Long	Offsets of each strip
SamplesPerPixel	277	Short	Samples per pixel
RowsPerStrip	278	Short or Long	Rows per strip
StripByteCounts	279	Short or Long	Length of each strip
XResolution	282	Rational	Horizontal resolution
YResolution	283	Rational	Vertical resolution
PlanarConfiguration	284	Short	Whether the pixels are organized in planes
ResolutionUnit	296	Short	Units of resolution

Table 10.3 The values associated with the tags in Table 10.2.

Tag	Value
BitsPerSample	Set to 8 for byte-sized grayscale images and 8,8,8 for 24-bit images. Three 8s are required for 24-bit images since there are three byte-sized values.
Compression	A value of 1 indicates no compression
ImageLength	The pixel height of the image
ImageWidth	The pixel width of the image
NewSubFile	A normal image has a value of 0 for this tag
Photometric-Interpretation	1 for grayscale images and 2 for RGB images
PlanarConfiguration	A value of 1 specifies that the pixels are stored contiguously rather than in planes
ResolutionUnit	The units of measure for the output device. Set to 2 to select inches.
RowsPerStrip	The number of image rows in each strip. This value cannot be zero.
SamplesPerPixel	1 for grayscale images and 3 for RGB images
StripByteCounts	The length of each image strip
StripOffsets	The file locations of each strip
XResolution	The number of pixels per resolution unit in the x direction. This defaults to 75.
YResolution	The number of pixels per resolution unit in the y direction. This defaults to 75.

Table 10.4 Data types used in tag entry fields.

Value	Data type	Description
1	Byte	Eight-bit unsigned value
2	ASCII	NULL-terminated string
3	Short	16-bit (two bytes) unsigned integer
4	Long	32-bit (four bytes) unsigned integer
5	Rational	Fractional value listed as two 32-bit numbers. The first value is a numerator, the second is the denominator.

The Image Format

An image is usually stored in a TIFF file as a series of strips. Strips are used so that the TIFF reader can read and process images in small pieces. The *StripOffsets* tag entry specifies where these strips are located and the *StripByteCounts* tag specifies how long each strip is. Actually, the use of the strips is a little misleading, because you can arrange the strips so that they form a contiguous image. This is, in fact, what most TIFF writers do.

The image data in each strip is written sequentially. For eight-bit images, the image is simply written to the file from the top-left pixel to the bottom-right. Figure 10.4 shows a TIFF file that stores a single 128x128 grayscale image (16K in size) in two 8K strips. We'll save RGB images as red, green, and blue triples stored in sequential order. Realize, however, that the TIFF format also allows us to save the color components as separate planes.

TIFF supports a couple different image compression techniques, such as Lempel-Ziv & Welch (LZW) compression. However, our TIFF toolkit won't provide any. If you plan on working with large 24-bit color images, you'll probably want the convenience of LZW compression or you'll need a lot of disk space.

THE TIFF.C TOOLKIT

The rest of this chapter discusses a toolkit that provides a reasonably powerful collection of TIFF routines. The toolkit consists of the file TIFF.C and its header file TIFF.H, both of which are listed at the end of this chapter.

Figure 10.4 TIFF images are usually stored in strips.

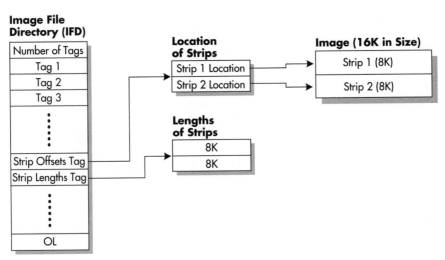

Currently, TIFF.C only supports grayscale and 24-bit color images. While it has been successfully tested with a variety of images created by various applications, there's no guarantee that it will be able to read all TIFF images, since the TIFF reader does not attempt to support the full TIFF standard.

Table 10.5 lists the functions included in TIFF.C. The next several sections highlight how these functions work and how to use them.

Reading a TIFF File

Before we explain how to use the TIFF toolkit, let's explore how it reads a typical TIFF file. The process always begins at a TIFF file's eight-byte header. For convenience, TIFF.H defines the **TIFFHEADER** structure to hold these bytes. It's defined as:

```
typedef struct {              // Fixed header
  unsigned int ByteOrder;     // Intel or Motorola byte ordering
  unsigned int Version;       // TIFF version identifier
  unsigned long Offset;       // Offset to first IFD
} TIFFHEADER;
```

Table 10.5 The functions included in TIFF.C.

Function	Description
GetImageInfo	High-level routine to get an image's dimensions
GetTIFFImageInfo	Retrieves the dimensions of a TIFF image
ReadFxdHdr	Reads the fixed header in a TIFF file
ReadGrayTIFFImage	Reads a grayscale TIFF image
ReadImage	High-level routine to read a TIFF file
ReadRGBTIFFImage	Reads a 24-bit color TIFF image
ReadStrips	Reads an image as a series of strips
ReadTag	Reads a single tag from a TIFF file
ReadTags	Reads all the tags from a TIFF file
ReadULong	Reads a long integer from a file
ReadWord	Reads a single integer from a TIFF file
SwapLongOrder	Swaps the order of bytes in a long integer
SwapWordOrder	Swaps the order of an integer's bytes
WriteFxdHdr	Writes a TIFF file's fixed header
WriteGrayTIFFHeader	Writes the tags for a grayscale image
WriteRGBTIFFHeader	Writes the tags for a 24-bit image
WriteTag	Writes a single tag to a TIFF file

The following statements in the **ReadFxdHdr** function read the header into the **TIFFHdr** variable:

```
TIFFHEADER TIFFHdr;  // Structure to hold the header

fseek(fp, 0L, SEEK_SET);                      // Go to top of file
fread(&TIFFHdr, sizeof(TIFFHEADER), 1, fp);   // Read header
```

Next, **ReadFxdHdr** determines whether the file uses Intel- or Motorola-style byte ordering. This is an important step; without it the reader may not process the file correctly. If the first two bytes of the header are II, the global flag **IntelOrdr** is set to 1. Otherwise, the flag is set to 0.

If **IntelOrdr** is set to 0, the **SwapWordOrder** function is called to rearrange the bytes in each integer. A similar function, **SwapLongOrder**, reorganizes the bytes in a four-byte integer. Both of these functions are located in TIFF.C.

The following statements, therefore, test whether the third and fourth bytes contain the integer 42. As these statements show, the integer's byte order is swapped if Intel byte ordering is not present:

```
// Set global decoding flag to use correct byte ordering
IntelOrdr = (TIFFHdr.ByteOrder == INTELBYTES) ? 1 : 0;

if (!IntelOrdr)                 // If not Intel byte ordering,
  SwapWordOrder(&TIFFHdr.Version);        // swap byte order

if (TIFFHdr.Version != TIFFVERSION)     // Check TIFF version
  return TIFFFORMATNOTSUPPORTED;
```

If the value 42 is not found, specified here by the constant **TIFFVERSION**, then **ReadFxdHdr** returns with the error flag **TIFFFORMATNOTSUPPORTED**. This is a negative value defined in TIFF.H.

The last step in **ReadFxdHdr** is to move the file pointer to the location of the first IFD, specified in the **Offset** field of the **TIFFHEADER** structure. As with the version number, its value must be reordered if the file is a Motorola format:

```
if (!IntelOrdr) SwapLongOrder(FileOffs);
*FileOffs = TIFFHdr.Offset;
fseek(fp, *FileOffs, SEEK_SET);
```

The toolkit is now ready to process the tag entries.

Processing the Tags

The **ReadTags** function processes the tag entries in a file. It's designed to be called immediately after **ReadFxdHdr**, when the file pointer is positioned at the two-byte integer that specifies the number of tags in the IFD. **ReadTags** reads and stores this value into the variable **NumTags**.

A **for** loop then steps through **NumTags** of tag entries and copies their information to the **IMAGEINFO** structure defined in TIFF.H as:

```
typedef struct {                    // Values read from the tag entries
  int BitsPerSample;                // 8 for grayscale; 8,8,8 for RGB
  int Compression;                  // Compression flag
  int SamplesPerPixel;              // 1 for grayscale; 3 for RGB
  int NumStrips;                    // Number of strips in file
  unsigned long *StripLengths;      // Array of strip lengths
  unsigned long *StripOffsets;      // Array of strip file offsets
} IMAGEINFO;
```

Each of **IMAGEINFO**'s fields corresponds to one of the tags in the IFD. Actually, the **IMAGEINFO** structure contains only the information required to read grayscale and 24-bit color images. The other tags in a TIFF file are ignored.

The TIFF.H header file defines the **TAGENTRY** structure to read each tag entry. It's defined as:

```
typedef struct {                    // A tag entry
  unsigned int Tag;                 // Tag identifier
  unsigned int DataType;            // Data type of value stored in entry
  unsigned long Length;             // Number of values in tag entry
  unsigned long Offset;             // Offset or value of tag
} TAGENTRY;
```

A **switch** statement, within the **for** loop mentioned earlier, selects the code that decodes each tag entry. Extracting the information from a tag entry can involve a variety of steps; however, the code almost always begins by checking whether **TAGENTRY**'s **DataType** field specifies the correct data type and that the **Length** field is reasonable. Where there is only one expected piece of information, for instance, the code verifies that **Length** equals 1. If this is the case, the tag entries' information is located in the **Offset** field and the code copies its data to the proper field in the **IMAGEINFO** structure. The following code, for example, processes the **TGSAMPLESPERPIXEL** tag entry:

```
case TGSAMPLESPERPIXEL:      // Samples per pixel
  if (Entry.DataType != TIFFSHORT || Entry.Length != 1)
    return TIFFFORMATNOTSUPPORTED;
    ImInfo->SamplesPerPixel = (int)Entry.Offset;
  break;
```

This tag entry essentially specifies how many bytes represent each image pixel. It is set to 1 for grayscale images and 3 for 24-bit images. The other tags are processed in a similar manner.

Determining an Image's Size

When reading an image from a TIFF file, you'll need to know how big of an image array to allocate. How can you determine the size of the image? All you need to do is call the function **GetImageInfo**. It's a smaller version of **ReadTags** that only checks for the pixel width and height of the image and the photometric interpretation tag, which indicates whether the image is grayscale or 24-bit color. If the flag is set to 1, the file contains a grayscale image. If it's set to 2, the image is a 24-bit color image. It's important to know whether the images are grayscale or 24-bit color since we'll assume that grayscale images always have one byte per pixel and 24-bit images have three.

Reading the Image

TIFF images are typically stored as a series of strips that can be placed almost anywhere in the file. Fortunately, the **TGSTRIPOFFSETS** and **TGSTRIPBYTECOUNTS** tags, defined in TIFF.H, tell us where the strips are located and how long each strip is. The **ReadTags** function looks for these two tags and copies their information to the **IMAGEINFO** structure.

When the **TGSTRIPOFFSETS** tag is encountered, for instance, the **Length** field in the **TAGENTRY** structure specifies how many strips the image is stored as. It also dictates how many strip offsets we should expect. We'll copy the file's strip positions to the **StripOffsets** field of the **IMAGEINFO** structure. In preparation for this, the code allocates an array of long integers to store the offsets. The **Length** field, which is copied to **NumStrips**, specifies how many long integers to allocate.

```
ImInfo->NumStrips = (int)Entry.Length; // Number of strips
// Allocate memory to hold the file pointers that point
// to where each strip begins in the file
ImInfo->StripOffsets = (unsigned long *)malloc
  (sizeof(unsigned long)*ImInfo->NumStrips);
```

If the image is stored as only one strip, the single file offset is stored in the **Offset** field of the **TAGENTRY** structure.

```
if (ImInfo->NumStrips == 1) {
  // Only one strip length, so the value is in the
  //  Offset field
  ImInfo->StripOffsets[0] = Entry.Offset;
}
```

Otherwise, the strip offsets are located elsewhere in the file and the **Offset** field points to the beginning of this list. The file pointer is then moved to this location and the current position of the file is saved in **FilePos**. The strip offsets are read one at a time using a **for** loop and copied to the **StripOffsets** array. Actually, the code is a bit more complicated than this because the offsets may be stored as two- or four-byte integers. As a result, the code provides two **for** loops: the top one reads a series of long integers and the bottom one reads a series of two-byte integers. The **DataType** field in the **TAGENTRY** structure selects between these two **for** loops. If **DataType** equals the constant **TIFFLONG**, the top **for** loop is executed; otherwise, the lower one is used. Here's the code that reads the full list of strip offsets:

```
else {  // The strip offsets are stored later in the file
  FilePos = ftell(fp);  // Remember where the file is now
  // Skip ahead to the list of strip offsets
  fseek(fp, Entry.Offset, SEEK_SET);
  // Read the strip offset. It may be stored as either a
  // long or short.
  if (Entry.DataType == TIFFLONG)
    for (j=0; j<ImInfo->NumStrips; j++)
      ReadULong(fp, &ImInfo->StripOffsets[j]);
  else {
    for (j=0; j<ImInfo->NumStrips; j++) {
      ReadWord(fp, &Val);
      ImInfo->StripOffsets[j] = Val;
    }
  }
}
```

The **ReadWord** and **ReadULong** functions used in the previous code retrieve the strip offsets from the file and reorder the bytes if necessary.

The **TGSTRIPBYTECOUNTS** tag retrieves the lengths of these strips and operates in a similar fashion. Each strip length is placed in the **IMAGEINFO** field's **StripLengths** array. Memory for the strip lengths is allocated in **ReadTags** and freed after the image is completely read from the file.

A High-Level Read Function

Now that we have a behind the scenes look at the TIFF toolkit, let's outline how you can use it to read a TIFF file. Basically, there are two steps involved. First, call **GetImageInfo** to determine the size of the image so that you can allocate memory to hold it. **GetImageInfo**'s first parameter is the file to read and the next two return the pixel width and height of the image. Its rightmost parameter specifies the type of image in the file. If it returns as 1, the image is a grayscale image. If it's 2, the image is a 24-bit color image.

Once you've allocated memory to hold the image, you can call either **ReadRGBTIFFImage** or **ReadGrayTIFFImage** to read the image. In both cases, the image array is declared as a huge pointer so that these functions can read images up to 1Mb in size. Here's a sample block of code that shows how you might call these two routines to read an image in a TIFF file:

```
// Retrieve the dimensions of the image and its type
if (GetTIFFImageInfo(fp, &ImWd, &ImHt, &ImType) <= 0) {
  fclose(fp);
  printf("Failed to read TIFF header.\n");
  return;
}
// Read the image
if (ImType == 2) {            // 24-bit color image
  if ((ErrCode=ReadRGBTIFFImage(fp, Im)) <= 0) {
    printf("Failed to read %s. Error code=%d\n", Filename, ErrCode);
    return;
  }
}
else {                        // Grayscale image
  if ((ErrCode=ReadGrayTIFFImage(fp, Im)) <= 0) {
    printf("Failed to read %s. Error code=%d\n", Filename, ErrCode);
    return;
  }
}
```

Writing a TIFF File

There are three steps in writing an image to a TIFF file:

1. Open the file as a binary file.
2. Write the header and tags to the file.
3. Append the image data to the file.

TIFF.C includes two high-level functions that perform all the chores of setting up a TIFF file. The **WriteGrayTIFFHeader** function prepares a TIFF file to store a grayscale image. The function **WriteRGBTIFFHeader** is its 24-bit image counterpart. Both functions take four parameters. The first is the file to write to, the second and third are the dimensions of the image, and the fourth is the length of the strips to use. In addition, both functions return a value of 1 if they succeed and 0 otherwise. The following statements, for instance, prepare a TIFF file to hold a grayscale image that is **ImWd** by **ImHt** in size:

```
if (!WriteGrayTIFFHeader(fp, ImWd, ImHt, ImWd)) {
  printf("Could not write TIFF header.\n");
```

```
    return;
}
```

In this case, each row is stored as a separate strip, since the strip length is set to **ImWd**.

Most of the code in **WriteGrayTIFFHeader** and **WriteRGBTIFFHeader** is hard coded. This may cause some problems. For instance, they both assume that the image is larger than a single strip. In addition, they fix the display resolution to 75 dots per inch (dpi). This is accomplished through the three tags **TGXRESOLUTION**, **TGYRESOLUTION**, and **TGRESOLUTIONUNIT**. The **TGRESOLUTIONUNIT** tag is set to 2, which selects inches as the unit of measure. The two other tags specify how many dots appear in each unit.

In TIFF.C, the display resolution is set to 75 dpi, which is the resolution of a typical display. Multiply the pixel width and height of the image by these values to determine the size in inches that the image will display. For example, a 75-by 75-pixel image will be one inch square. You may want to increase the resolution if you plan on printing your images on a high-resolution printer. The color plates in this book, for instance, were generated at 400 dpi. Of course, this means the image will have to be much larger to appear the same size.

Writing the Image Data

After the TIFF file's header is written, the file pointer is positioned where the image should begin. However, TIFF.C does not include any functions to write the image data; you must do this yourself. Fortunately, the process is straightforward since TIFF.C organizes the file so that the image strips form a contiguous image. As a result, all you need to do is write the pixel one byte at a time. The following statements, for instance, append the values in the **Image** array to a TIFF file:

```
for (j=0; j<ImHt; j++) {
  for (i=0; i<ImWd; i++) {
    fwrite(Image[j*ImWd+i], 1, 1, fp);
  }
}
```

To save a 24-bit color image, you'll want to write the red, green, and blue color components for each pixel.

Testing the TIFF Tools

The TESTTIFF.C file listed after the next section tests the TIFF.C toolkit. By default, TESTTIFF creates a 24-bit, RGB image, writes it to a TIFF file, reads the image into memory, and displays the resulting picture. However, the program also doubles as a TIFF viewer. You'll be able to view a wide variety of TIFF images, written on a PC or Macintosh.

You can locate the TIFF-related code in the **Setup** function. It creates an RGB TIFF file that is **IMWD** and **IMHT** pixels in size, both of which are set to a value of 128. The TIFF file is prepared by writing the TIFF header using the following statements:

```
if (!WriteRGBTIFFHeader(fp, ImWd, ImHt, IMWD)) {
  printf("Could not write TIFF header.\n");
  return;
}

// Create and write the image directly to the TIFF file
for (j=0; j<ImHt; j++) {
  for (i=0; i<ImWd; i++) {
    Red = i % 256;   Green = i % 256;  Blue = i % 256;
    fwrite(&Red, 1, 1, fp);
    fwrite(&Green, 1, 1, fp);
    fwrite(&Blue, 1, 1, fp);
  }
}
```

Recall, that the rightmost parameter of **WriteRGBTIFFHeader** specifies the size of the image strips.

The image is then written one byte at a time as red, green, and blue triples. It's not too complicated to write the image because TIFF.C places the image strips back to back.

Reading the image is only slightly more complicated. First, the program determines the filename to use. If a command-line argument is provided, it is passed to the **Setup** function and used as the input filename. Otherwise, the test image written earlier is read.

The process of reading the image begins by calling **GetTIFFImageInfo** to determine the image's size and type so that the memory for the image can be properly allocated:

```
if (GetTIFFImageInfo(fp, &ImWd, &ImHt, &ImType) <= 0) {
  fclose(fp);
  printf("Failed to read TIFF header.\n");
  return;
}
printf("ImWd=%d ImHt=%d ImType=%d\n", ImWd, ImHt, ImType);

if (ImType == 2)
  BytesPerPixel = 3;
```

```
ImSize = (long)ImWd * (long)ImHt * (long)BytesPerPixel;

Im = (unsigned char huge *)farmalloc(ImSize);
```

Then, based on the type of image in the file, the proper function is called to read the image into the **Im** array:

```
// Read the image
if (ImType == 2) {              // 24-bit color image
  if ((ErrCode=ReadRGBTIFFImage(fp, Im)) <= 0) {
    printf("Failed to read %s. Error code=%d\n", Filename, ErrCode);
    return;
  }
}
else {                          // Grayscale image
  if ((ErrCode=ReadGrayTIFFImage(fp, Im)) <= 0) {
    printf("Failed to read %s. Error code=%d\n", Filename, ErrCode);
    return;
  }
}
DisplayIm = 1;    // The file was successfully read
```

If everything goes well, the **DisplayIm** flag is set to 1, signaling that the read operation was successful. Later, the **GenImage** function in TESTTIFF.C will only display the image if the **DisplayIm** flag is not zero.

COMPILING AND RUNNING **TESTTIFF**

You can compile TESTTIFF as a DOS or Windows application. To build it as a DOS application, you must compile and link TESTTIFF.C with the files GRPHICS.C and TIFF.C using a large memory model. You'll need to include these three files in your project or make file. If you decide to go with Windows, you must also link the program with WINSHELL.C and define the compiler constant **FORWINDOWS**. This is the same procedure outlined in Appendix C and used in the ray tracing programs.

You can run TESTTIFF in one of two ways. If you don't supply a command-line argument when you invoke the program, it will create a 24-bit image of various shades of red. The image is placed in the file TEST.TIF. After TESTTIFF creates the image, it will read it back into memory and display it.

Alternatively, you can use TESTTIFF.C as a TIFF viewer. The program will display the image you specify on the command-line. For instance, to display the image CLOUDS.TIF, type the following command at the DOS prompt:

```
testtiff clouds.tif
```

The TESTTIFF program reads the whole image into memory, and may run out of memory if it tries to read one that is too large. This may be a particularly troubling problem in DOS. However, if you compile the program for Windows, you'll be able to use its memory management capabilities and read much larger images.

Here's the complete listing for TESTTIFF.C:

```c
// TESTTIFF.C: Tests the TIFF.C toolkit. By default, this program
// creates a 24-bit RGB image, writes it to a TIFF file, reads
// it back into memory, and displays it. Alternatively, you can
// specify a TIFF filename on the command line and the program
// will display that image. You can compile TESTTIFF under DOS
// or Windows. To build it as a DOS application, compile and
// link TESTTIFF.C with GRPHICS.C and TIFF.C using a large
// memory model. For Windows, you must also define the constant
// FORWINDOWS and link TESTTIFF.C with WINSHELL.C.

#include <stdio.h>
#include <stdlib.h>
#include <string.h>
#include "tiff.h"
#include "grphics.h"

#define IMWD 128                // Image width and height
#define IMHT 128
#define BYTESPERPIXEL 1         // One byte per pixel

FILE *fp;
unsigned char huge *Im;         // The image array
char far Filename[13];          // File to read
int ImWd, ImHt;                 // Image width and height
int ImType;                     // Image type
int VMode;                      // DOS video mode
unsigned char DisplayIm;        // Display image if not zero

void Usage(void);


/////////////////////////////  main  \\\\\\\\\\\\\\\\\\\\\\\\\\\\

#if !defined(FORWINDOWS)
int main(int argc, char *argv[])
{
  if (argc != 2)
    Usage();
```

```
    // Set the default video mode to 320x200x256 so that
    // it uses a color palette. This field only affects the
    // program if it is compiled as a DOS application.
    VMode = M320x200x256 | COLORPALETTE;

    Setup(argv[1]);

    if (SetupDisplay(VMode)) {
      GenImage(0);
      EndDisplay();
      Cleanup();
    }
    return 0;
  }
#endif

void Usage(void)
{
}

/////////////////////////////// Setup \\\\\\\\\\\\\\\\\\\\\\\\\\\\\
//
// Sets up default values for variables
//
void Setup(char far *Str)
{
  unsigned char Red, Green, Blue;
  unsigned long i, j, ImSize;
  int ErrCode, BytesPerPixel=1;

  DisplayIm = FALSE;
  ImWd = IMWD;
  ImHt = IMHT;
  if (strcmp(Str,"") == 0) {
    // No command-line argument given. Create a TIFF file and
    // then read it back in. TEST.TIF is the intermediate file.
    strcpy(Filename, "TEST.TIF");   // Default filename

    // Write the test image to TEST.TIF
    fp = fopen(Filename, "wb");
    if (fp == NULL) {
      printf("Could not open output file: %s.\n", Filename);
      return;
    }
    // Write the file's header
    if (!WriteRGBTIFFHeader(fp, ImWd, ImHt, IMWD)) {
      printf("Could not write TIFF header.\n");
      return;
    }
```

```
  // Create and write the image directly to the TIFF file
  for (j=0; j<ImHt; j++) {
    for (i=0; i<ImWd; i++) {
      Red = i % 256;   Green = i % 256;   Blue = i % 256;
      fwrite(&Red, 1, 1, fp);
      fwrite(&Green, 1, 1, fp);
      fwrite(&Blue, 1, 1, fp);
    }
  }
  fclose(fp);
}
else {
  // Get the command-line argument specified
  strncpy(Filename, Str, 12);
  Filename[12] = '\0';   // NULL terminate just in case
}

// Open the TIFF file just created or the file specified on
// the command line
fp = fopen(Filename, "rb");
if (fp == NULL) {
  printf("Could not open input file: %s.\n", Filename);
  return;
}

if (GetTIFFImageInfo(fp, &ImWd, &ImHt, &ImType) <= 0) {
  fclose(fp);
  printf("Failed to read TIFF header.\n");
  return;
}
printf("ImWd=%d ImHt=%d ImType=%d\n", ImWd, ImHt, ImType);

if (ImType == 2)
  BytesPerPixel = 3;

ImSize = (long)ImWd * (long)ImHt * (long)BytesPerPixel;

Im = (unsigned char huge *)farmalloc(ImSize);
if (Im == NULL) {
  printf("Failed to allocate image array.\n");
  return;
}

// Read the image
if (ImType == 2) {                 // 24-bit color image
  if ((ErrCode=ReadRGBTIFFImage(fp, Im)) <= 0) {
    printf("Failed to read %s. Error code=%d\n", Filename, ErrCode);
    return;
  }
```

```
    }
    else {                           // Grayscale image
      if ((ErrCode=ReadGrayTIFFImage(fp, Im)) <= 0) {
        printf("Failed to read %s. Error code=%d\n", Filename, ErrCode);
        return;
      }
    }
    DisplayIm = 1;    // The file was successfully read. Set the
    fclose(fp);       // display flag to true.
  }


///////////////////////////// Cleanup  \\\\\\\\\\\\\\\\\\\\\\\\\
//
// Performs any clean actions
//
void Cleanup()
{
  farfree(Im);
}


///////////////////////////// GenImage  \\\\\\\\\\\\\\\\\\\\\\\\\
//
// This is the main entry point for the image display code. If
// compiled as a DOS application, the hDC parameter is not used.
// In Windows, hDC is a handle to the device context to draw on.
//
void GenImage(int hDC)
{
  unsigned long i, j, Offs;

  if (DisplayIm) {                  // The image was successfully
    for (j=0; j<ImHt; j++) {        // read from the file. Now
      Offs = j * ImWd;              // display it.
      for (i=0; i<ImWd; i++) {
        if (ImType == 2)            // RGB image
          PutPixel(hDC, (unsigned int)i, (unsigned int)j,
            Im[(Offs+i)*3], Im[(Offs+i)*3+1], Im[(Offs+i)*3+2]);
        else                        // Grayscale image
          PutPixel(hDC, (unsigned int)i, (unsigned int)j,
            Im[Offs+i], Im[Offs+i], Im[Offs+i]);
      }
    }
  }
  return;
}
```

- **TIFF.H**

```
// TIFF.H: Header for the TIFF tools in TIFF.C.

#ifndef TIFFH
#define TIFFH

// TIFF's primary data types
#define TIFFBYTE        1       // An eight-bit unsigned integer
#define TIFFASCII       2       // An eight-bit byte that stores ASCII codes
#define TIFFSHORT       3       // A 16-bit (two-byte) unsigned integer
#define TIFFLONG        4       // A 32-bit (four-byte) unsigned integer
#define TIFFRATIONAL    5       // Two longs: the first is the numerator
                                // and the second is the denominator

// TIFF tag constants
#define TGNEWSUBFILETYPE            254
#define TGOLDSUBFILETYPE           255
#define TGIMAGEWIDTH               256
#define TGIMAGELENGTH              257
#define TGBITSPERSAMPLE           258
#define TGCOMPRESSION             259

#define TGPHOTOMETRICINTERPRETATION 262
#define TGTHRESHHOLDING           263
#define TGCELLWIDTH               264
#define TGCELLLENGTH              265
#define TGFILLORDER               266

#define TGDOCUMENTNAME            269
#define TGIMAGEDESCRIPTION        270
#define TGMAKE                    271
#define TGMODEL                   272
#define TGSTRIPOFFSETS            273
#define TGORIENTATION             274

#define TGSAMPLESPERPIXEL         277
#define TGROWSPERSTRIP            278
#define TGSTRIPBYTECOUNTS         279
#define TGMINSAMPLEVALUE          280
#define TGMAXSAMPLEVALUE          281
#define TGXRESOLUTION             282
#define TGYRESOLUTION             283
#define TGPLANARCONFIGURATION     284
#define TGPAGENAME                285
#define TGXPOSITION               286
#define TGYPOSITION               287
#define TGFREEOFFSETS             288
#define TGFREEBYTECOUNTS          289
#define TGGRAYUNIT                290
#define TGGRAYCURVE               291
```

```
#define TGRESOLUTIONUNIT              296
#define TGPAGENUMBER                  297

#define TGCOLORRESPONSECURVES         301

#define TGSOFTWARE                    305
#define TGDATETIME                    306

#define TGARTIST                      315
#define TGHOSTCOMPUTER                316

#define TGPREDICTOR                   317
#define TGWHITEPOINT                  318
#define TGPRIMARYCHROMATICITIES       319
#define TGCOLORMAP                    320

#define INTELBYTES 0x4949             // Intel byte ordering
#define TIFFVERSION 0x002A            // TIFF file version
#define NOCOMPRESSION 1               // Compression not used

// Error flags
#define TIFFFORMATNOTSUPPORTED -2     // TIFF format now supported
#define IMAGEFILETOOBIG -3            // Image is too big
#define OUTOFMEMORY -4                // Out of memory

#define STRIPSIZE 8192                // Size of image strips

typedef struct {                     // Fixed header
  unsigned int ByteOrder;            // Intel or Motorola byte ordering
  unsigned int Version;              // TIFF version identifier
  unsigned long Offset;              // Offset to first IFD
} TIFFHEADER;

typedef struct {                     // A tag entry
  unsigned int Tag;                  // Tag identifier
  unsigned int DataType;             // Data type of value stored in entry
  unsigned long Length;              // Number of values in tag entry
  unsigned long Offset;              // Offset or value of tag
} TAGENTRY;

typedef struct {                     // Values read from the tag entries
  int BitsPerSample;                 // 8 for grayscale; 8,8,8 for RGB
  int Compression;                   // Compression flag
  int SamplesPerPixel;               // 1 for grayscale; 3 for RGB
  int NumStrips;                     // Number of strips in file
  unsigned long *StripLengths;       // Array of strip lengths
  unsigned long *StripOffsets;       // Array of strip file offsets
} IMAGEINFO;
```

```
// Functions in TIFF.C:
int ReadStrips(FILE *fp, IMAGEINFO *ImInfo,
  unsigned char huge *Im);
int ReadGrayTIFFImage(FILE *fp, unsigned char huge *Im);
int ReadRGBTIFFImage(FILE *fp, unsigned char huge *Im);
int GetTIFFImageInfo(FILE *fp, int *ImWd, int *ImHt, int *ImType);
int GetImageInfo(char *Path, int *ImWd, int *ImHt, int *ImType);
int ReadImage(char *Path, unsigned char huge *Im);
int WriteTag(FILE *fp, unsigned int Tag, unsigned int DataType,
  unsigned long Len, unsigned long Offs);
int WriteRGBTIFFHeader(FILE *fp, unsigned long ImWd,
  unsigned long ImHt, unsigned long StripSize);
int WriteGrayTIFFHeader(FILE *fp, unsigned long ImWd,
  unsigned long ImHt, unsigned long StripSize);
int WriteFxdHdr(FILE *fp);
void SwapWordOrder(unsigned int *Word);
void SwapLongOrder(unsigned long *Long);
int ReadTag(FILE *fp, TAGENTRY *Entry);
int ReadWord(FILE *fp, unsigned int *Val);
int ReadULong(FILE *fp, unsigned long *Val);
int ReadTags(FILE *fp, IMAGEINFO *ImInfo);
int ReadFxdHdr(FILE *fp, unsigned long *FileOffs);

#endif
```

• TIFF.C

```
// TIFF.C: Reads grayscale and 24-bit uncompressed TIFF images.

#include <stdio.h>
#include <stdlib.h>
#include <math.h>
#include "tiff.h"

unsigned char IntelOrdr;

extern FILE *Efp;

/////////////////////////////  ReadFxdHdr  \\\\\\\\\\\\\\\\\\\\\\\\\\\
//
// Reads the eight-byte, fixed position TIFF header. FileOffs is set
// to number that marks the beginning of the IFD (tag entries).
//
int ReadFxdHdr(FILE *fp, unsigned long *FileOffs)
{
  TIFFHEADER TIFFHdr;                 // Structure to hold the header

  fseek(fp, 0L, SEEK_SET);                       // Go to top of file
  fread(&TIFFHdr, sizeof(TIFFHEADER), 1, fp);    // Read header
```

```
    // Set global decoding flag to use correct byte ordering
    IntelOrdr = (TIFFHdr.ByteOrder == INTELBYTES) ? 1 : 0;

    if (!IntelOrdr)                    // If not Intel byte ordering,
      SwapWordOrder(&TIFFHdr.Version);        // swap byte order

    if (TIFFHdr.Version != TIFFVERSION)      // Check TIFF version
      return TIFFFORMATNOTSUPPORTED;

    // "Offset" tells where the IFD (tag entries) starts
    if (!IntelOrdr) SwapLongOrder(FileOffs);
    *FileOffs = TIFFHdr.Offset;
    fseek(fp, *FileOffs, SEEK_SET);
    return 1;
}


//////////////////////////// ReadTags \\\\\\\\\\\\\\\\\\\\\\\\\
//
// Copies the information in the tags to the IMAGEINFO structure.
// It assumes that the file pointer is pointing at the number
// of tags in the file.
//
int ReadTags(FILE *fp, IMAGEINFO *ImInfo)
{
  unsigned int i, j;
  unsigned int Val;
  unsigned int NumTags;             // Number of tags in the IFD
  TAGENTRY Entry;                   // A tag entry
  unsigned long FilePos;            // File position

  ReadWord(fp, &NumTags);
  for (i=0; i<NumTags; i++) {
    ReadTag(fp, &Entry);             // Read one tag entry at a time
    switch(Entry.Tag) {
      case TGBITSPERSAMPLE:          // Bits per sample
        if (Entry.DataType != TIFFSHORT)
          return TIFFFORMATNOTSUPPORTED;
        if (Entry.Length == 1)
          ImInfo->BitsPerSample = (int)Entry.Offset;
        else if (Entry.Length == 3)
          // Note: This really isn't correct. The code should
          // verify that the three actual numbers--at the
          // Entry.Offset location in the file--equal 8. For
          // simplicity, we'll assume that they do.
          ImInfo->BitsPerSample = 8;
        break;
      case TGCOMPRESSION:            // Compression flag
        if (Entry.DataType != TIFFSHORT || Entry.Length != 1)
          return TIFFFORMATNOTSUPPORTED;
```

```
        ImInfo->Compression = (int)Entry.Offset;
break;
    case TGSAMPLESPERPIXEL:      // Samples per pixel
      if (Entry.DataType != TIFFSHORT || Entry.Length != 1)
        return TIFFFORMATNOTSUPPORTED;
      ImInfo->SamplesPerPixel = (int)Entry.Offset;
      break;
    case TGROWSPERSTRIP:
      // This tag isn't used so it can be removed; however,
      // the field is required
      if ((Entry.DataType != TIFFSHORT &&
        Entry.DataType != TIFFLONG) || Entry.Length != 1)
        return TIFFFORMATNOTSUPPORTED;
      break;
    case TGSTRIPOFFSETS:          // Strip file offsets
      if (Entry.DataType != TIFFSHORT &&
        Entry.DataType != TIFFLONG) {
        return TIFFFORMATNOTSUPPORTED;
      }
      ImInfo->NumStrips = (int)Entry.Length; // Number of strips
      // Allocate memory to hold the file pointers that point
      // to where each strip begins in the file
      ImInfo->StripOffsets = (unsigned long *)malloc
        (sizeof(unsigned long)*ImInfo->NumStrips);
      if (ImInfo->StripOffsets == NULL) {
        return OUTOFMEMORY;
      }
      if (ImInfo->NumStrips == 1) {
        // Only one strip length, so the value is in the
        //  Offset field
        ImInfo->StripOffsets[0] = Entry.Offset;
      }
      else {  // The strip offsets are stored later in the file
        FilePos = ftell(fp);  // Remember where the file is now
        // Skip ahead to the list of strip offsets
        fseek(fp, Entry.Offset, SEEK_SET);
        // Read the strip offset. It may be stored as either a
        // long or short.
        if (Entry.DataType == TIFFLONG)
          for (j=0; j<ImInfo->NumStrips; j++)
            ReadULong(fp, &ImInfo->StripOffsets[j]);
        else {
          for (j=0; j<ImInfo->NumStrips; j++) {
            ReadWord(fp, &Val);
            ImInfo->StripOffsets[j] = Val;
          }
        }
        // After reading the strip offsets, go back to the
        // last tag read
```

```
                fseek(fp, FilePos, SEEK_SET);
              }
              break;
          case TGSTRIPBYTECOUNTS:        // Strip lengths
            if (Entry.DataType != TIFFSHORT &&
              Entry.DataType != TIFFLONG)
              return TIFFFORMATNOTSUPPORTED;
            ImInfo->NumStrips = (int)Entry.Length;
            ImInfo->StripLengths = (unsigned long *)malloc
              (sizeof(unsigned long)*ImInfo->NumStrips);
            if (ImInfo->StripLengths == NULL) {
              free(ImInfo->StripOffsets);
              return OUTOFMEMORY;
            }
            // There is only one strip length so value is in Offset
            if (ImInfo->NumStrips == 1)
              ImInfo->StripLengths[0] = Entry.Offset;
            else { // The strip offsets are stored later in the file
              FilePos = ftell(fp);   // Remember where the file is
              // Skip ahead to the list of strip bytes. This
              // routine can read long or word strip lengths.
              fseek(fp, Entry.Offset, SEEK_SET);
              if (Entry.DataType == TIFFLONG)
                for (j=0; j<ImInfo->NumStrips; j++)
                  ReadULong(fp, &ImInfo->StripLengths[j]);
              else {
                for (j=0; j<ImInfo->NumStrips; j++) {
                  ReadWord(fp, &Val);
                  ImInfo->StripLengths[j] = Val;
                }
              }
              // After reading the strip lengths, go back to the
              // last tag read
              fseek(fp, FilePos, SEEK_SET);
            }
            break;
        default: break;  // Ignore the other tags
      }
    }
    return 1;
}


//////////////////////////// ReadStrips \\\\\\\\\\\\\\\\\\\\\\\\\\
//
// Reads the image's strips in the file using an 8K buffer.
// If a strip is bigger than the buffer, it uses multiple reads.
//
int ReadStrips(FILE *fp, IMAGEINFO *ImInfo, unsigned char huge *Im)
{
```

```
unsigned int i, j, k, NumPieces, MaxStripLen=8192;
unsigned long p;
unsigned char *Buffer;

// Allocate memory to hold the buffer
Buffer = (unsigned char *)malloc(MaxStripLen);
if (Buffer == NULL) return OUTOFMEMORY;

// There should be a four-byte NULL after the tag entries, but
// we'll skip it and go straight to the image. Read the image
// strip by strip.
p = 0;
for (j=0; j<ImInfo->NumStrips; j++) {
  // Go to where the stip begins
  fseek(fp, ImInfo->StripOffsets[j], SEEK_SET);
  // Calculate how many times the 8k buffer must be used
  // to read the whole strip
  NumPieces = (double)ImInfo->StripLengths[j] / MaxStripLen;
  for (i=0; i<NumPieces; i++) {
    if (fread(Buffer, 1, MaxStripLen, fp) != MaxStripLen)
      break;
    for (k=0; k<MaxStripLen; k++, p++)
      Im[p] = Buffer[k];   // Copy the strip to the image
  }
  // Read any remaining bytes in the strip
  NumPieces = (unsigned int)
    (ImInfo->StripLengths[j] % MaxStripLen);
  if (NumPieces != 0) {
    if (fread(Buffer, 1, NumPieces, fp) != NumPieces) break;
    for (i=0; i<NumPieces; i++, p++)
      Im[p] = Buffer[i];   // Copy the strip to the image
  }
}
free(Buffer);
return 1;
}


///////////////////// ReadGrayTIFFImage \\\\\\\\\\\\\\\\\\\\\
//
// Reads a grayscale image from a TIFF file. The Im array
// must be large enough to hold the image. Call GetTIFFImageInfo
// to retrieve the size of the image so that you can allocate
// memory for it.
//
int ReadGrayTIFFImage(FILE *fp, unsigned char huge *Im)
{
  unsigned long FileOffs;      // Running offset in file
  IMAGEINFO ImInfo;
  int Err;
```

```
  // Read the fixed header
  if ((Err=ReadFxdHdr(fp, &FileOffs)) != 1)
    return Err;

  // Copy the information in the tags to the ImInfo structure
  if ((Err=ReadTags(fp, &ImInfo)) != 1)
    return Err;

  // Check whether you are reading the correct image type
  if (ImInfo.BitsPerSample != 8 ||
      ImInfo.Compression != NOCOMPRESSION ||
      ImInfo.SamplesPerPixel != 1) {
    Err = TIFFFORMATNOTSUPPORTED;
  }
  else
    Err = ReadStrips(fp, &ImInfo, Im);   // Read the strips
  free(ImInfo.StripOffsets);
  free(ImInfo.StripLengths);
  return Err;
}


////////////////////////  ReadRGBTIFFImage \\\\\\\\\\\\\\\\\\\\\\\
//
// Reads an RGB image from a TIFF file. Call GetTIFFImageInfo
// first to get the size of the image so that you can allocate
// memory for it.
//
int ReadRGBTIFFImage(FILE *fp, unsigned char huge *Im)
{
  unsigned long FileOffs;      // Running offset in file
  IMAGEINFO ImInfo;
  int Err;

  // Read the fixed header
  if ((Err=ReadFxdHdr(fp, &FileOffs)) != 1)
    return Err;

  if ((Err=ReadTags(fp, &ImInfo)) != 1)  // Read each tag entry
    return Err;

  // Check whether you are reading the correct image type
  if (ImInfo.BitsPerSample != 8 ||
      ImInfo.Compression != NOCOMPRESSION ||
      ImInfo.SamplesPerPixel != 3) {
    Err = TIFFFORMATNOTSUPPORTED;
  }
  else
    Err = ReadStrips(fp, &ImInfo, Im);   // Read the strips
  free(ImInfo.StripOffsets);
```

```
    free(ImInfo.StripLengths);
    return Err;
}


//////////////////////// GetTIFFImageInfo \\\\\\\\\\\\\\\\\\\\\\\\
//
// Reads the TIFF file's header to determine how many pixels are
// in the image. It also sets ImType to 1 if it's a grayscale
// image and 2 if it's an RGB image.
//
int GetTIFFImageInfo(FILE *fp, int *ImWd, int *ImHt, int *ImType)
{
    int Err;
    unsigned int i;
    unsigned int NumTags;       // The number of tags in the file
    TAGENTRY Entry;             // A tag entry
    unsigned long FileOffs;     // File offset

    // Read the fixed header
    if ((Err=ReadFxdHdr(fp, &FileOffs)) != 1)
        return Err;

    *ImWd = -1;    *ImHt = -1;    *ImType = -1;
    fseek(fp, FileOffs, SEEK_SET);
    ReadWord(fp, &NumTags);
    for (i=0; i<NumTags; i++) {
        ReadTag(fp, &Entry);            // Read one tag entry at a time
        switch(Entry.Tag) {
            case TGIMAGELENGTH:                    // Image length tag
                if ((Entry.DataType != TIFFSHORT &&
                    Entry.DataType != TIFFLONG) || Entry.Length != 1)
                    return TIFFFORMATNOTSUPPORTED;
                *ImHt = (int)Entry.Offset;
                break;
            case TGIMAGEWIDTH:                     // Image width tag
                if ((Entry.DataType != TIFFSHORT &&
                    Entry.DataType != TIFFLONG) || Entry.Length != 1)
                    return TIFFFORMATNOTSUPPORTED;
                *ImWd = (int)Entry.Offset;
                break;
            case TGPHOTOMETRICINTERPRETATION:      // Image type tag
                if (Entry.DataType != TIFFSHORT || Entry.Length != 1)
                    return TIFFFORMATNOTSUPPORTED;
                *ImType = (int)Entry.Offset;
                break;
            default: break;  // Ignore the other tags
        }
    }
    if (*ImWd == -1 || *ImHt == -1 || *ImType == -1)
```

```
      // Didn't find all the basic information to read the file
      return TIFFFORMATNOTSUPPORTED;
    return 1;
  }


  ///////////////////////// GetImageInfo \\\\\\\\\\\\\\\\\\\\\\\\\
  //
  // Retrieves the width, height, and image type of the image in
  // a TIFF file. Returns 0 if it can't read the TIFF format.
  //
  int GetImageInfo(char *Path, int *ImWd, int *ImHt, int *ImType)
  {
    FILE *fp;

    if ((fp=fopen(Path, "rb")) == NULL)
      return 0;

    if (GetTIFFImageInfo(fp, ImWd, ImHt, ImType) != 1) {
      fclose(fp);
      return 0;
    }
    fclose(fp);
    return 1;
  }


  /////////////////////////// ReadImage \\\\\\\\\\\\\\\\\\\\\\\\\\\
  //
  // Primary, high-level routine to read an RGB or grayscale TIFF
  // image. Call GetImageInfo first to get the size of the image
  // so that you can properly allocate memory for it.
  //
  int ReadImage(char *Path, unsigned char huge *Im)
  {
    FILE *fp;
    int ImWd, ImHt, ImType, RetVal=1;

    if ((fp=fopen(Path, "rb")) == NULL)
      return 0;

    if (GetTIFFImageInfo(fp, &ImWd, &ImHt, &ImType) < 0) {
      fclose(fp);
      return 0;
    }

    if (ImType == 1) {
      // The photometric interpretation field says that
      // this file is potentially a grayscale image
      if (ReadGrayTIFFImage(fp, Im) < 0)
```

```
      RetVal = 0;
  }
  else if (ImType == 2) {
    // This file is an RGB image
    if (ReadRGBTIFFImage(fp, Im) <= 0)
      RetVal = 0;
    return RetVal;
  }
  else
    RetVal = 0;;  // Image type not supported
  fclose(fp);
  return RetVal;
}

////////////////////////// WriteTag \\\\\\\\\\\\\\\\\\\\\\\\\\
//
// Writes a single tag to the output file. It assumes that the
// file pointer is already pointing to the location where the
// tag is to be placed.
//
int WriteTag(FILE *fp, unsigned int Tag, unsigned int DataType,
  unsigned long Len, unsigned long Offs)
{
  TAGENTRY Entry;

  Entry.Tag = Tag;
  Entry.DataType = DataType;
  Entry.Length = Len;
  Entry.Offset = Offs;
  fwrite(&Entry, sizeof(TAGENTRY), 1, fp);  // Write the tag
  return 1;
}

////////////////////////// WriteFxdHdr \\\\\\\\\\\\\\\\\\\\\\\\\\
//
// Writes the eight-byte fixed header to the top of a file
//
int WriteFxdHdr(FILE *fp)
{
  TIFFHEADER TIFFHdr;

  TIFFHdr.ByteOrder = INTELBYTES;
  TIFFHdr.Version = TIFFVERSION;
  // Start IFD after TIFF header
  TIFFHdr.Offset = sizeof(TIFFHEADER);
  fwrite(&TIFFHdr, sizeof(TIFFHEADER), 1, fp); // Write header
  return 1;
}
```

```
/////////////////////  WriteRGBTIFFHeader  \\\\\\\\\\\\\\\\\\\\\
//
//  Writes a header for a 24-bit, RGB image
//
int WriteRGBTIFFHeader(FILE *fp, unsigned long ImWd,
  unsigned long ImHt, unsigned long StripSize)
{
  unsigned long FileOffs;      // Running offset in file
  unsigned long NextIFD;       // Pointer to next IFD
  unsigned long StartOfStrip;
  unsigned long Numerator = 75L;  // 75 dpi
  unsigned long Denominator = 1L;
  int NumTagEntries = 14;      // 14 tag entries for the file
  unsigned int StripsPerImage, i;
  unsigned long LastStripLen;
  unsigned int RowsPerStrip;
  unsigned int Val;
  unsigned long Size;

  RowsPerStrip = (unsigned int)(StripSize / (ImWd * 3));
  if (RowsPerStrip == 0) {   // A strip can't be smaller
    return 0;                // than a row
  }
  Size = ImWd * ImHt * 3L;
  StripsPerImage = (unsigned int)(Size / StripSize + Size % StripSize);

  WriteFxdHdr(fp);

  FileOffs = sizeof(TIFFHEADER);
  // Build the IFD as a list of tag
  // entries. FileOffs is initially set to the location after
  // the tags. This calculation accounts for the eight-byte TIFF
  // header, the two bytes that specify the number of tag entries,
  // the tag entries themselves, and a four-byte null terminator
  // at the end of the IFD.
  FileOffs += sizeof(int) + sizeof(long) +
            NumTagEntries * sizeof(TAGENTRY);
  // Write the number of tag entries
  fwrite(&NumTagEntries, sizeof(int), 1, fp);
  // Append the tag entries to the file. These are organized in
  // ascending order.
  WriteTag(fp, TGNEWSUBFILETYPE, TIFFLONG, 1L, 0L);

  WriteTag(fp, TGIMAGEWIDTH, TIFFSHORT, 1L, ImWd);

  WriteTag(fp, TGIMAGELENGTH, TIFFSHORT, 1L, ImHt);

  // The three RGB bytes are saved with 8 bits each
  WriteTag(fp, TGBITSPERSAMPLE, TIFFSHORT, 3L, FileOffs);
```

```
// Update location of next free location in file
FileOffs += 3L * sizeof(short);

// A value of 1 signals that no compression is used
WriteTag(fp, TGCOMPRESSION, TIFFSHORT, 1L, 1L);

// Pixels are stored as consecutive RGB values
WriteTag(fp, TGPHOTOMETRICINTERPRETATION, TIFFSHORT, 1L, 2L);

// Save the file offsets for each image strip later in the
// file. This assumes that there is more than one strip.
// If the image fits into one strip, you'll need to change
// this so that it saves the strip offset in the Offset
// field of the tag entry structure.
WriteTag(fp, TGSTRIPOFFSETS, TIFFLONG, StripsPerImage,
              FileOffs + 4L * sizeof(unsigned long) +
              StripsPerImage * sizeof(unsigned long));
WriteTag(fp, TGSAMPLESPERPIXEL, TIFFSHORT, 1L, 3L);

WriteTag(fp, TGROWSPERSTRIP, TIFFLONG, 1L, RowsPerStrip);

// Save the image strip lengths later in the file. This
// assumes that there is more than one strip. If there isn't,
// you'll need to save the strip in the Offset field of the tag.
WriteTag(fp, TGSTRIPBYTECOUNTS, TIFFLONG, StripsPerImage,
  FileOffs+4L*sizeof(unsigned long));

WriteTag(fp, TGXRESOLUTION, TIFFRATIONAL, 1L, FileOffs);
FileOffs += sizeof(unsigned long) * 2L;

WriteTag(fp, TGYRESOLUTION, TIFFRATIONAL, 1L, FileOffs);
FileOffs += sizeof(unsigned long) * 2L;

// The image data is stored as RGBRGBRGB...
WriteTag(fp, TGPLANARCONFIGURATION, TIFFSHORT, 1L, 1L);

WriteTag(fp, TGRESOLUTIONUNIT, TIFFSHORT, 1L, 2L);

NextIFD = 0L;  // There aren't any more tags. Write four zeros.
fwrite(&NextIFD, sizeof(unsigned long), 1, fp);

// Write the sizes of the RGB samples that the bits per sample
// tag was set to point to
Val = 8;
fwrite(&Val, sizeof(short), 1, fp);
fwrite(&Val, sizeof(short), 1, fp);
fwrite(&Val, sizeof(short), 1, fp);

// Write the XRESOLUTION value. It's a rational number which
```

```
    // consists of two unsigned longs: a numerator and denominator.
    fwrite(&Numerator, sizeof(unsigned long), 1, fp);
    fwrite(&Denominator, sizeof(unsigned long), 1, fp);

    // Now write the YRESOLUTION rational number
    fwrite(&Numerator, sizeof(unsigned long), 1, fp);
    fwrite(&Denominator, sizeof(unsigned long), 1, fp);

    // Next, write the sizes of the image strips. The strip lengths
    // are stored as unsigned longs. Handle the last strip as a
    // special case. It may not be as long as the others.
    LastStripLen = ((unsigned long)ImWd * (unsigned long)ImHt * 3L) -
        ((unsigned long)StripSize * (StripsPerImage-1));
    if (LastStripLen == 0) {
      // If LastStripLen is 0, then StripSize evenly divides
      // into the image so that all strips will be the same length
      LastStripLen = StripSize;
    }
    // Write lengths of each strip
    for (i=0; i<StripsPerImage-1; i++)
      fwrite(&StripSize, sizeof(unsigned long), 1, fp);
    // Now add in last strip length
    fwrite(&LastStripLen, sizeof(unsigned long), 1, fp);
    // Add in strip lengths from above to the file offset
    FileOffs += sizeof(unsigned long) * StripsPerImage;

    // Calculate where the image strips will start in the file
    StartOfStrip = FileOffs + sizeof(unsigned long) * StripsPerImage;

    // First image strip starts at FileOffs, next strip starts
    // at StartOfStrip+StripSize, and so on
    for (i=0; i<StripsPerImage; i++) {
      fwrite(&StartOfStrip, sizeof(unsigned long), 1, fp);
      StartOfStrip += StripSize;
    }
    return 1;
}


/////////////////////// WriteGrayTIFFHeader \\\\\\\\\\\\\\\\\\\\\\\
//
// Writes a TIFF header in preparation for storing a grayscale
// image. StripSize should be at least large enough to hold
// a single image row.
//
int WriteGrayTIFFHeader(FILE *fp, unsigned long ImWd,
  unsigned long ImHt, unsigned long StripSize)
{
  unsigned long FileOffs;          // Running offset in file
  unsigned long NextIFD;           // Pointer to next IFD
```

```
unsigned long StartOfStrip;
unsigned long Numerator = 75L;     // Display at 75 dpi
unsigned long Denominator = 1L;
int NumTagEntries = 14;            // 14 tag entries in file
unsigned int StripsPerImage, i;
unsigned long LastStripLen;
unsigned int RowsPerStrip;
unsigned long Size;

RowsPerStrip = (unsigned int)(StripSize / ImWd * 3);
if (RowsPerStrip == 0) {    // A strip can't be smaller
  return 0;                 // than a row
}
Size = ImWd * ImHt;
StripsPerImage = (unsigned int)(Size / StripSize + Size % StripSize);

WriteFxdHdr(fp);
FileOffs = sizeof(TIFFHEADER);

// Build the IFD as a list of tag
// entries. FileOffs is initially set to the location after
// the tags. This calculation accounts for the eight-byte TIFF
// header, the two bytes that specify the number of tag entries,
// the tag entries themselves, and a four-byte null terminator
// at the end of the IFD.
FileOffs += sizeof(int) + sizeof(long) +
            NumTagEntries * sizeof(TAGENTRY);

// Write the number of tag entries
fwrite(&NumTagEntries, sizeof(int), 1, fp);
// Append the tag entries to the file
WriteTag(fp, TGNEWSUBFILETYPE, TIFFLONG, 1L, 0L);

WriteTag(fp, TGIMAGEWIDTH, TIFFSHORT, 1L, ImWd);

WriteTag(fp, TGIMAGELENGTH, TIFFSHORT, 1L, ImHt);

WriteTag(fp, TGBITSPERSAMPLE, TIFFSHORT, 1L, 8L);
// No compression
WriteTag(fp, TGCOMPRESSION, TIFFSHORT, 1L, 1L);
// Set to grayscale format
WriteTag(fp, TGPHOTOMETRICINTERPRETATION, TIFFSHORT, 1L, 1L);
// The strip offsets are stored later in the file
WriteTag(fp, TGSTRIPOFFSETS, TIFFLONG, StripsPerImage,
  FileOffs + 4L * sizeof(unsigned long) +
  StripsPerImage * sizeof(unsigned long));
// Okay for grayscale and color palette images
WriteTag(fp, TGSAMPLESPERPIXEL, TIFFSHORT, 1L, 1L);
```

```
WriteTag(fp, TGROWSPERSTRIP, TIFFLONG, 1L, RowsPerStrip);
// The strip lengths are saved later in the file
WriteTag(fp, TGSTRIPBYTECOUNTS, TIFFLONG, StripsPerImage,
    FileOffs+4L*sizeof(unsigned long));

WriteTag(fp, TGXRESOLUTION, TIFFRATIONAL, 1L, FileOffs);
FileOffs += sizeof(unsigned long) * 2L;

WriteTag(fp, TGYRESOLUTION, TIFFRATIONAL, 1L, FileOffs);
FileOffs += sizeof(unsigned long) * 2L;
// Image data is stored on one contiguous plane
WriteTag(fp, TGPLANARCONFIGURATION, TIFFSHORT, 1L, 1L);
// Use inch resolution
WriteTag(fp, TGRESOLUTIONUNIT, TIFFSHORT, 1L, 2L);

NextIFD = 0L;  // There aren't any more IFDs
fwrite(&NextIFD, sizeof(unsigned long), 1, fp);

// Write out the values that were set aside by using
// the offsets earlier. Write the XRESOLUTION rational
// number, which consists of two unsigned longs.
fwrite(&Numerator, sizeof(unsigned long), 1, fp);
fwrite(&Denominator, sizeof(unsigned long), 1, fp);

// Now write the YRESOLUTION rational number
fwrite(&Numerator, sizeof(unsigned long), 1, fp);
fwrite(&Denominator, sizeof(unsigned long), 1, fp);

// Next, write the sizes of the image strips. The strip lengths
// are stored as unsigned longs. Handle the last strip as a
// special case. It may not be as long as the others.
LastStripLen = ((unsigned long)ImWd * (unsigned long)ImHt) -
    ((unsigned long)StripSize * (StripsPerImage-1));
if (LastStripLen == 0) {
  // If LastStripLen is 0, then StripSize divides evenly into
  // the image and all strips will be the same length
  LastStripLen = StripSize;
}
// Write the lengths of each strip
for (i=0; i<StripsPerImage-1; i++)
  fwrite(&StripSize, sizeof(unsigned long), 1, fp);
fwrite(&LastStripLen, sizeof(unsigned long), 1, fp);
// Add in strip lengths from above to the file offset
FileOffs += sizeof(unsigned long) * StripsPerImage;

// Update FileOffs which points to where the image data starts.
// The image data will start immediately after a series of
// strip offsets.
StartOfStrip = FileOffs + sizeof(unsigned long) * StripsPerImage;
```

```
  // First image strip starts at FileOffs, next strip starts
  // at StartOfStrip+StripSize, and so on
  for (i=0; i<StripsPerImage; i++) {
    fwrite(&StartOfStrip, sizeof(unsigned long), 1, fp);
    StartOfStrip += StripSize;
  }
  return 1;
}

//////////////////////////// SwapWordOrder \\\\\\\\\\\\\\\\\\\\\\\\\
//
// Swaps the two bytes in a 16-bit word
//
void SwapWordOrder(unsigned int *Word)
{
    unsigned char *Byte = (unsigned char *)Word;
    unsigned char Tmp;

    Tmp = Byte[1];
    Byte[1] = Byte[0];        // Move first byte to second
    Byte[0] = Tmp;            // Move second to first byte
}

//////////////////////////// SwapLongOrder \\\\\\\\\\\\\\\\\\\\\\\\\
//
// Swaps the bytes in a 32-bit integer
//
void SwapLongOrder(unsigned long *Long)
{
    unsigned char *Byte = (unsigned char *)Long;
    unsigned char Tmp;

    Tmp = Byte[3];
    Byte[3] = Byte[0];        // Move first byte to fourth
    Byte[0] = Tmp;            // Move fourth byte to first
    Tmp = Byte[2];
    Byte[2] = Byte[1];        // Move second byte to third
    Byte[1] = Tmp;            // Move third byte to second
}

//////////////////////////// ReadTag \\\\\\\\\\\\\\\\\\\\\\\\\\\\\\\
//
// Reads a tag entry. Swaps the bytes if the file was written
// using a non-Intel format.
//
int ReadTag(FILE *fp, TAGENTRY *Entry)
{
  int t = fread(Entry, sizeof(TAGENTRY), 1, fp); // Read tag
  if (t == 1) {                  // If read operation was successful,
```

```
  if (!IntelOrdr) {           // swap the byte ordering if they
    SwapWordOrder(&Entry->Tag);          // were written with
    SwapWordOrder(&Entry->DataType);    // a non-Intel format
    SwapLongOrder(&Entry->Length);
    SwapLongOrder(&Entry->Offset);
    if (Entry->DataType == TIFFSHORT && Entry->Length == 1)
      // Take only the two most significant bytes
      Entry->Offset = Entry->Offset >> 16;
  }
  return 1;
}
  return 0;
}


/////////////////////////  ReadWord  \\\\\\\\\\\\\\\\\\\\\\\\\
//
// Reads a 16-bit word from a file. Swaps the bytes if the file
// was written using a non-Intel format.
//
int ReadWord(FILE *fp, unsigned int *Val)
{
  int t = fread(Val, sizeof(unsigned int), 1, fp); // Read tag
  if (t == 1) {                // If read operation was successful,
    if (!IntelOrdr)            // swap the byte ordering if the
      SwapWordOrder(Val);      // word was not written with an
    return 1;                  // Intel machine
  }
  return 0;
}


/////////////////////////  ReadULong  \\\\\\\\\\\\\\\\\\\\\\\\\
//
// Reads a 32-bit long value. Swaps the bytes if the file was
// written using a non-Intel format.
//
int ReadULong(FILE *fp, unsigned long *Val)
{
  int t = fread(Val, sizeof(unsigned long), 1, fp); // Read tag
  if (t == 1) {                // If read operation was successful,
    if (!IntelOrdr)            // swap the byte ordering if the
      SwapLongOrder(Val);      // word was not written with an
    return 1;                  // Intel machine
  }
  return 0;
}
```

Image Processing
Essentials

Most photographers would say that creating a good photograph often requires as much skill in the darkroom as it does with the camera. The same is true for computer imaging. In fact, if you spend much time at all working with images on your computer, you'll soon want what amounts to a digital darkroom. In this chapter, we'll focus on the essential routines that every imaging workbench should include. For instance, we'll build functions for changing the contrast of images, rotating images, zooming in on a portion of an image, and more.

WORKING WITH IMAGES

The ray tracer, discussed earlier in this book, generates digital images. To the computer, these images are no different than any other digital image. However, a more common way to get an image into a computer is to use a frame grabber or scanner. Frame grabbers typically capture and digitize images from a video camera. Scanners, on the other hand, digitize still images or printed pages.

Most of the image processing techniques we'll discuss in this chapter are particularly useful for improving the quality of images captured with a frame grabber or scanner. Frame grabbers, for instance, typically capture low-quality, low-resolution, images. Therefore, additional processing to enhance the image is often required. Realize, however, that you can apply the techniques presented here to any image, whether it is real or synthetically generated.

AN IMAGE PROCESSING TOOLKIT

The rest of this chapter presents a variety of image processing functions. Each of these routines is included in the IMTOOLS.C source file at the end of this chapter. Table 11.1 describes each of these functions.

Generally, the routines in IMTOOLS.C support only grayscale images. But with a few additional steps, you can enhance the routines so that they completely support 24-bit color images. The organization of the images is the problem here: grayscale images are arranged sequentially, but 24-bit images are a bit more complicated. The RAY tracer sets forth one possible configuration that we've been using. That is, the image pixels are stored in consecutive order as red, green, and blue triples. Unfortunately, organizing 24-bit color images as RGB triples is not the most convenient arrangement for image processing. Often, it is better to have the color components stored in separate image planes. With the planar approach, you can usually use the same code to process grayscale images and 24-bit color images. You just have to call the basic image processing function three times—once for each color plane. Since our color images have the RGB components intertwined, however, we must add special code to process them.

The IMTOOLS.H header file defines a standard image type, **IMAGE**, using the following **typedef**:

```
typedef unsigned char huge* IMAGE
```

Table 11.1 Functions included in IMTOOLS.C.

Function	Description
Average	Averages 3-by-3 groups of pixels
BrightenIm	Adds a value to each pixel
Colorize	Converts a grayscale image to 24-bit color
ColorToGray	Converts a 24-bit color image to grayscale
ContrastEnhance	Stretches the histogram of an image to improve the image's contrast
GammaCorr	Gamma corrects the pixels in an image
Histogram	Returns a grayscale image's histogram
MirrorXIm	Flips an image about its center column
MirrorXYIm	Flips an image about its diagonal, effectively rotating the image 90 degrees
MirrorYIm	Flips an image about its center row
ResizeIm	Resizes an image
SharpenIm	Enhances the edges in an image
ZoomIm	Zooms in or out of a portion of an image

The images are declared as huge arrays so they can be over 64K and the compiler will generate the proper indexing code for us. This comes with a heavy cost, however. Huge pointers are twice the size of far pointers and therefore noticeably slower. The benefit, of course, is that they're easy to use. If you use far pointers, for instance, you'll have to watch for crossing segment boundaries. Huge pointers take care of this for you automatically.

Using Histograms

You and I can look at an image and instantly tell whether it is too dark or has sufficient contrast, but how can a computer make these distinctions? One technique is to enlist a *histogram*. A histogram is a graph that plots the number of times each intensity level occurs in an image. Figure 11.1, for instance, shows a grayscale image and its histogram. The intensity values that form the major peak in the histogram correspond to the background in the image. This makes sense, since the background occupies a major portion of the image.

The **Histogram** function in IMTOOLS.C places an image's histogram information into an array. The array should contain one entry for each possible gray level. For instance, the following statements allocate memory for a single histogram array:

```
unsigned int* Hist;
Hist = (unsigned int *)malloc(256*sizeof(unsigned int));
```

The **malloc** statement allocates 256 cells in the **Hist** array—the correct number for a typical grayscale image. The image is declared as an **unsigned int** array so that the pixel frequency count can reach 32,767. If there are more pixels than this, the histogram values will not be accurate.

Figure 11.1 A histogram plots the number of times each gray level occurs.

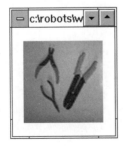
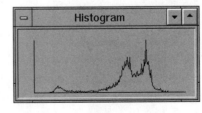

The **Histogram** function increments the **Hist** array counter for each intensity encountered:

```
for (I=0; I<256; I++)
  Hist[I] = 0;
for (J=0; J<ImHt; J++) {
  Offset = J * ImWd;
  for (I=0; I<ImWd; I++)
    Hist[InIm[I+Offset]]++;
}
```

The **ImWd** and **ImHt** variables refer to the image's width and height, respectively.

After the **Histogram** function terminates, the **Hist** array contains a frequency count for each possible gray level. Low values indicate that there are few pixels in the image with their gray levels and large values specify popular pixels.

Contrast Enhancement

Quite often, images captured with a frame grabber have poor contrast. The pixel intensities are bunched together and don't extend across the full range of possible intensity values. Figure 11.2, for example, shows a low contrast image and its histogram. Notice that there are a lot of pixels that have a mid-range of values but very few are completely black or white.

We can correct this by using the **ContrastEnhance** function. The **ContrastEnhance** routine in IMTOOLS.C implements a simple contrast enhancement algorithm that sets all pixels above and below specified values to black or white, then scales the remaining pixels so they encompass the full range of possible intensities. Figure 11.3 shows the image in Figure 11.2 and its new histogram after the image's contrast is enhanced.

Figure 11.2 A low-contrast image does not typically use the full range of possible gray levels.

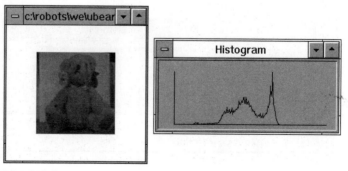

Figure 11.3 The image in Figure 11.2 after contrast enhancement.

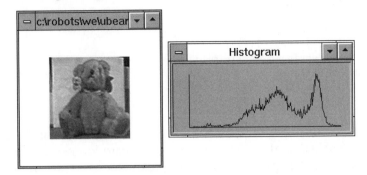

The contrast-enhanced image is placed in the **OutIm** array that is passed into the **ContrastEnhance** function. You're responsible for allocating memory for **OutIm** before calling **ContrastEnhance** . However, if you set **OutIm** to the **InIm** image array, you'll overwrite **InIm** with the contrast-enhanced image.

Brightness Adjustment

Another common problem with images is that they are too dark. An effective way to brighten these images is to add a value to each pixel with the **BrightenIm** function. Figure 11.4 shows an image before and after its pixel intensities have been shifted by 30 gray levels.

Figure 11.4 The image on the right is a brightened version of the left image.

Here's the complete **BrightenIm** function:

```
for (J=0; J<ImHt; J++) {
  Offset = J * ImWd;
  for (I=0; I<ImWd; I++) {
    Tmp = (unsigned int)InIm[Offset+I] + Val;
    OutIm[Offset+I] = (Tmp > 255) ? 255 : (unsigned char)Tmp;
  }
}
```

BrightenIm simply sequences through the image, adding the value in **Val** to each pixel. Along the way, it takes special care to ensure that the gray levels don't exceed 255, the maximum allowable intensity in an image.

Reducing Noise

Many images captured with a frame grabber contain a noticeable amount of *noise*. The noise appears as random pixels that are a few gray levels higher or lower than they should be. Because these pixels are sprinkled throughout the image, the noise is often referred to as *salt-and-pepper* noise.

One way to reduce noise is to average groups of neighboring pixels. The **Average** function in IMTOOLS.C, for instance, replaces each pixel value with the average of itself and its eight connecting neighbors, as illustrated in Figure 11.5.

A drawback to **Average** is that it blurs the image a bit. Sometimes, this won't be noticeable. However, if you need a lot of sharpness, **Average** may not work very well.

Sharpening an Image

The **SharpenIm** function in IMTOOLS.C can sometimes improve the sharpness of an image. It is particularly useful for enhancing images that are slightly out of focus or taken with a jittery camera.

Basically, **SharpenIm** magnifies the strength of the edges in the image by operating on 3-by-3 portions of the image at a time. The two **for** loops shown here perform this operation:

```
for (J=1; J<ImHt-1; J++) {
  Offset = J * ImWd;
  PrevCol = (unsigned int)InIm[Offset];
  for (I=1; I<ImWd-1; I++) {
    Pix = Offset + I;
    Intermed = 4 * (unsigned int)InIm[Pix] +
      (unsigned int)InIm[Pix] - (unsigned int)InIm[Pix+1] -
      PrevCol - (unsigned int)InIm[Pix+ImWd] -
      (unsigned int)PrevRow[I];
```

```
Intermed = abs(Intermed);
if (Intermed > 255) Intermed = 255;
PrevCol = (unsigned int)InIm[Pix];
PrevRow[I] = InIm[Pix];
OutIm[Pix] = (unsigned char)Intermed;
```

As you look through this code, you may notice that it's somewhat complicated by the temporary array **PrevRow** and the variable **PrevCol**, which ensure that the function will work properly if the result image array, **OutIm**, is the same as the input image, **InIm**. They're required because the 3-by-3 window uses values in the input image that are on the previous row and column. If these pixel values were modified earlier by the **for** loops, the current result would be incorrect. This would occur if the input and output images were the same.

There's one caveat to the **SharpenIm** function: the function will probably increase the salt-and-pepper noise in an image.

Figure 11.5 The Average function replaces each pixel with the average of nine neighboring pixels.

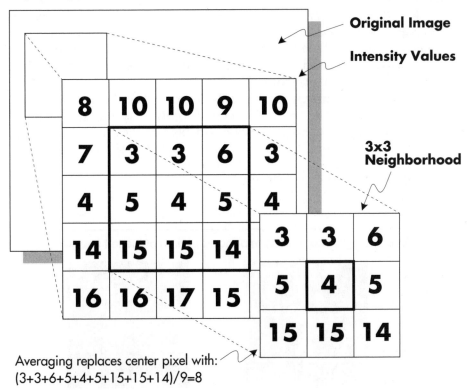

Averaging replaces center pixel with:
$(3+3+6+5+4+5+15+15+14)/9=8$

Zooming and Resizing Images

The **ResizeIm** function stretches or compresses an image horizontally or vertically. It's useful for changing the size of an image array. The real workhorse behind **ResizeIm**, however, is the **ZoomIm** function. It stretches or compresses a *portion* of an image horizontally or vertically. If you call **ZoomIm** twice, once for each direction, you can zoom in or out of an image, as shown in Figure 11.6.

ZoomIm takes six parameters, as its function prototype suggests:

```
void ZoomIm(IMAGE InIm, int CurrLen, int InStep, IMAGE OutIm,
  int NewLen, int OutStep);
```

The first two parameters are the input image and its length in the direction that the image is being operated on. The third parameter is set to 1 if the image is being zoomed horizontally. If the image is being manipulated vertically, however, the third parameter is set to the width of the image. The fourth and fifth parameters specify the output image and its new dimension. The last parameter is similar to the third, except that it is set to the output image's width if the image is being stretched vertically.

When you zoom in on an image, the code spreads each input pixel across multiple output pixels. If you're compressing the image, multiple pixels in the input image are combined to produce each output pixel. Of course, the code is complicated by the fact that fractional parts of pixels may be used in the compression or zooming process.

How does **ZoomIm** work? Basically, it accumulates input pixels until there are enough to generate an output pixel. **ZoomIm** has four key variables that keep track of this process. The **Scale** variable specifies how the input pixels relate to the output pixels, and is calculated using this simple equation:

```
Scale = (double)NewLen / CurrLen;
```

Figure 11.6 The right image is an expanded portion of the left image.

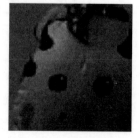

The **Scale** variable tells the code how many input pixels are required for each output pixel. The **InAmt** and **UseAmt** variables keep track of how much of the current input and output pixels have been processed. And finally, the **Accum** variable maintains a running weighted sum of the input pixel's intensity levels.

The following **if** statement is where most of the work is done:

```
if (InAmt < UseAmt) {
  Accum += Val * InAmt;     // Add in weighted contribution
  UseAmt -= InAmt;
  InAmt = 1.0;
  I += InStep;
}
else {  // Input pixel is not completely used in current pixel
  Accum += Val * UseAmt;
  OutIm[Pixel] = Accum * Scale;
  Pixel += OutStep;
  Accum = 0;
  InAmt -= UseAmt;
  UseAmt = 1 / Scale;
}
```

The top portion of the statement is used when more input pixels need to be added together to create a complete output pixel. The **else** part of the statement is used when enough input pixels have been accumulated and it's time to generate an output pixel. A **while** loop wraps around the **if** statement, ensuring that enough pixels are generated for the output image.

Mirroring and Rotating Images

Rotating an image takes special care. The problem is that, as you rotate the image, the input pixels spread across several pixels in the output image. One technique is to scan through the output image and apply a rotation matrix to determine what input pixel should be placed in the current output pixel. Realize that if you perform this operation in the opposite direction—starting with the input image—you may get holes in the output image. In addition, you must interpolate pixel values to produce a good image.

IMTOOLS.C takes a far simpler approach. Instead, it includes three additional functions you can use to flip and rotate images: **MirrorYIm**, **MirrorXIm**, and **MirrorXYIm**. These three routines flip an image horizontally, vertically, or about the image's diagonal, respectively. In effect, **MirrorXYIm** rotates an image 90 degrees counterclockwise.

Since each routine is similar, let's focus on **MirrorYIm**. The **MirrorYIm** function swaps each row with its mirrored row. In other words, the first image row is swapped with the last, the second row is exchanged with the second to the last row, and so on. Here's the code that performs these steps:

```
void MirrorYIm(IMAGE Im, int ImWd, int ImHt)
{
  unsigned long I, J, K, Offset, Offset2;
  unsigned char Tmp;

  for (J=0, K=ImHt-1; J<ImHt/2; J++, K--) {
    Offset = J * ImWd;
    Offset2 = K * ImWd;
    for (I=0; I<ImWd; I++) {
      Tmp = Im[Offset2+I];
      Im[Offset2+I] = Im[Offset+I];
      Im[Offset+I] = Tmp;
    }
  }
}
```

Notice that the function overwrites the original image. This is different than many of the other routines in IMTOOLS.C. Figure 11.7 shows an image before and after it was flipped with the **MirrorYIm** function.

Converting a Color Image to Grayscale

The **ColorToGray** function converts a 24-bit RGB image to grayscale. Each pixel in the grayscale image is calculated as the average of the red, green, and blue intensities of the corresponding pixel in the color image. Here's the complete function:

```
void ColorToGray(IMAGE InIm, IMAGE OutIm, int ImWd, int ImHt)
{
  unsigned long I, J, Offset;

  for (J=0; J<ImHt; J++) {
    Offset = J * ImWd;
    for (I=0; I<ImWd; I++) {
      OutIm[I+Offset] = ((unsigned int)InIm[(I+Offset)*3] +
        (unsigned int)InIm[(I+Offset)*3+1] +
        (unsigned int)InIm[(I+Offset)*3+2]) / 3;
    }
  }
}
```

Colorizing an Image

Many low-cost frame grabbers can only produce grayscale images. However, with the **Colorize** function, you can add a touch of color. This routine was used, for instance, to generate the RGB image of the wood grain used in

Figure 11.7 The MirrorYIm function flips images, as shown on the right.

Chapter 5's kitchen scene: a grayscale photograph of a wood venire finish was captured, then the image was colorized by multiplying the grayscale pixel values with red, green, and blue multipliers.

The red, green, and blue multipliers range between 0 and 1. If you want a red image, for instance, you'd set the red multiplier to a value close to 1 and the green and blue components close to 0. The nested **for** loops in **Colorize** apply these multipliers to the grayscale value in the input image:

```
for (J=0; J<ImHt; J++) {
  Offset = J * ImWd;
  for (I=0; I<ImWd; I++) {
    OutIm[(I+Offset)*3] = InIm[I+Offset] * Red;
    OutIm[(I+Offset)*3+1] = InIm[I+Offset] * Green;
    OutIm[(I+Offset)*3+2] = InIm[I+Offset] * Blue;
  }
}
```

Notice that the output image is assumed to be large enough to hold a 24-bit version of the input image and is organized as RGB triples. Also, realize that **Colorize** operates on a whole image.

Gamma Correction

Although you may never have noticed, your computer monitor actually darkens the colors that it displays. Fortunately, as long as you only display your images on your monitor, you'll never have to worry about this. However, if you print out your images on a high-quality color printer, your images will probably look different. Most likely, the colors will look lighter than they did on the screen. To solve this problem, you must use *gamma correction*, which can be performed by raising each pixel to a particular power, (Gamma):

```
NewPixelValue = (OldPixelValue)Gamma
```

The value of Gamma controls the gamma correction. If Gamma is greater than 1, the image is darkened. If it falls between 0 and 1, the image is lightened.

Many monitors require a gamma correction of about 2.2. In other words, if you take a scanned image or a list of true RGB values and plot them on the screen, they'll appear darker than they should. To solve this problem, you can use the equation listed earlier with a Gamma value of 2.2. The **GammaCorr** function performs this operation for you.

If, on the other hand, you've developed your images interactively using what you've been seeing on the monitor, many of the colors will be too light when you print them on a color printer. You can correct this by setting Gamma to about 0.45.

These values, however, are only guidelines. Not all monitors require the same amount of gamma correction, so it may take some trial and error to get the right values for your equipment.

The following statements are extracted from **GammaCorr** and reveal how simple the process of gamma correction is:

```
for (J=0; J<ImHt; J++) {
  Offset = J * Offset;
  for (I=0; I<ImWd; I++) {
    Offset2 = (Offset + I) * 3;
    Res = pow((double)InIm[Offset2], Val);
    OutIm[Offset2] = (Res > 255) ? 255 : (unsigned char)Res;
    Offset2++;
    Res = pow((double)InIm[Offset2], Val);
    OutIm[Offset2] = (Res > 255) ? 255 : (unsigned char)Res;
    Offset2++;
    Res = pow((double)InIm[Offset2], Val);
    OutIm[Offset2] = (Res > 255) ? 255 : (unsigned char)Res;
  }
}
```

Notice that the function assumes that the input and output images are 24-bit RGB organized as RGB triples.

Testing **IMTOOLS.C**

The IMTEST.C program listed immediately after this section puts a handful of the routines in IMTOOLS.C through their paces. The program is written as a DOS application and runs in 320-by-200, 256-color mode. You'll need to supply a 256-color or 24-bit PCX image file.

The name of the PCX file is passed to the program as its sole command-line argument. The source code disk includes the file COMPUTER.PCX, which is a 128-by-128 grayscale image. It's small size is an advantage if you have a slow computer.

The program performs various image processing operations on the image you supply. The operations are performed one at a time, with the results displayed after each step. You must press a key between operations to proceed to the next.

The program begins by reading the image in the PCX file into the **Im1** image array. If the image is a 24-bit image, it's converted to a grayscale image. This image is then displayed on the screen. Realize that the image is clipped to the screen if it is wider or taller than 320 by 200. IMTEST's second step is to expand or reduce the image's size to a 128-by-128 image using the **ResizeIm** function. This new image is copied to the **Im** array and **Im1** is freed. Next, the program enhances the image using **SharpenIm** and rotates it 90 degrees counterclockwise using **MirrorXYIm**.

To build IMTEST, you must compile and link IMTEST.C with IMTOOLS.C, GRPHICS.C, and PCXTOOL.C. Because of the amount of memory IMTEST requires, you should compile the program in the large memory model. To run the program and analyze the COMPUTER.PCX image, you must type the following command at the DOS prompt:

```
imtest computer.pcx
```

Here's the complete TESTIM.C program:

```
// IMTEST.C: Tests a variety of the image processing tools in
// IMTOOLS.C. Compile with the large memory model. Link with
// the files GRPHICS.C, PCXTOOL.C, and IMTOOLS.C.

#include <stdio.h>
#include <stdlib.h>
#include <math.h>
#include "grphics.h"
#include "pcxtool.h"
#include "imtools.h"

#define SCREENHT 200        // The pixel height of the screen
#define SCREENWD 320        // The pixel width of the screen

FILE *Infp;
IMAGE Im1, Im;
int Wd, Ht;

int ReadImage(FILE *Infp, IMAGE *Image, int *ImWd,
   int *ImHt, int *BytesPerPixel);
void DisplayIm(IMAGE Im, int ImWd, int ImHt, int ImType);

int main(int argc, char *argv[])
{
```

```
unsigned long I, J, Offset, Offset2;
int b, Err;

if (argc != 2) {
  printf("imtest <pcx_image_file>\n");
  exit(1);
}
Infp = fopen(argv[1], "rb");
if (Infp == NULL) {
  printf("Could not open %s.\n", argv[1]);
  exit(1);
}
if ((Err=ReadImage(Infp, &Im1, &Wd, &Ht, &b)) < 0) {
  printf("Failed to read the PCX image: %s.\n", argv[1]);
  printf("Error code: %d\n", Err);
  exit(1);
}
// If the image is a 24-bit color image, convert it
// to a grayscale image. It will overwrite the original
// image with the grayscale version and leave the end of
// the image array unused.
if (b == 3) {    // 3 bytes per pixel
  ColorToGray(Im1, Im1, Wd, Ht);
  b = 1;
}
if (SetupDisplay(M320x200x256 | COLORPALETTE)) {
  DisplayIm(Im1, Wd, Ht, b);    // Display the current image
  // Resize the image so that it is now 128 by 128 pixels.
  // If the image is the same size, the following steps
  // effectively copy the image in Im1 to the Im array.
  Im = (IMAGE)farmalloc(128L*128L);
  if (Im == NULL) {
    printf("Out of memory.\n");
    EndDisplay();
    exit(1);
  }
  ResizeIm(Im1, Wd, Ht, Im1, 128, 128);
  DisplayIm(Im1, Wd, 128, 1);  // Display the new image
  // Copy the resized image to the Im array
  for (J=0; J<128; J++) {
    Offset = J * Wd;
    Offset2 = J * 128;
    for (I=0; I<128; I++)
      Im[Offset2+I] = Im1[Offset+I];
  }
  farfree(Im1);    // Free the original image's memory
  Wd = 128;    Ht = 128;    b = 1;
  DisplayIm(Im, Wd, Ht, b);  // Display the new image
```

```
    getch();
    SharpenIm(Im, Im, Wd, Ht); // Enhance the edges in the
    DisplayIm(Im, Wd, Ht, b);  // image
    getch();
    MirrorXYIm(Im, Wd, Ht);     // Rotate the image counter-
    DisplayIm(Im, Wd, Ht, b);  // clockwise 90 degrees
    EndDisplay();
  }
  fclose(Infp);
  farfree(Im);
  return 0;
}

///////////////////////// ReadImage \\\\\\\\\\\\\\\\\\\\\\\\\\\\\
//
// Reads the image from the specified PCX file
//
int ReadImage(FILE *Infp, IMAGE *Image, int *ImWd,
  int *ImHt, int *BytesPerPixel)
{
  PCXHEADER PCXHdr;
  unsigned char *Row;
  IMAGE Im;
  unsigned long I, J, ImSize;

  if (!ReadPCXHeader(Infp, &PCXHdr))  // Read the header
    return -1;
  if (!IsValidPCX(&PCXHdr)) // Does the header say the
    return -2;              // image is the right type?
  // Extract the image dimensions from the header
  GetPCXInfo(&PCXHdr, ImWd, ImHt, BytesPerPixel);
  ImSize = (unsigned long)(*ImWd) *
    (unsigned long)(*ImHt) * (unsigned long)(*BytesPerPixel);
  Im = (IMAGE)farmalloc(ImSize);
  if (Im == NULL) return -3;          // Not enough memory
  // Allocate memory for one image row
  Row = (unsigned char *)malloc((*ImWd)*(*BytesPerPixel));
  if (Row == NULL) return -4;         // Not enough memory
  for (J=0; J<*ImHt; J++) { // Read each image row
    if (!GetPCXRow(Infp, Row, PCXHdr.NPlanes,
      PCXHdr.BytesPerRow, *ImWd)) {
      free(Row);
      return -5;                // Could not read the image
    }
    // Copy the row to the image
    for (I=0; I<*ImWd*(*BytesPerPixel); I++)
      Im[J*(*ImWd)*(long)(*BytesPerPixel)+I] = Row[I];
  }
```

```
    free(Row);
    *Image = Im;
    return 1;
}


//////////////////////////// DisplayIm \\\\\\\\\\\\\\\\\\\\\\\\\\\
//
// Displays an image of the size ImWd by ImHt at the top-right
// of the screen. The image is clipped to the dimensions of the
// screen.
//
void DisplayIm(IMAGE Im, int ImWd, int ImHt, int ImType)
{
  unsigned long I, J, Offset;

  for (J=0; J<ImHt && J<SCREENHT; J++) {
    Offset = J * ImWd;
    for (I=0; I<ImWd && I<SCREENWD; I++) {
      if (ImType == 3)
        PutPixel(0, I, J,
          Im[(Offset+I)*3], Im[(Offset+I)*3+1], Im[(Offset+I)*3+2]);
      else
        PutPixel(0, I, J,
          Im[Offset+I], Im[Offset+I], Im[Offset+I]);
    }
  }
}
```

• IMTOOLS.H

```
// IMTOOLS.H: Header file for IMTOOLS.C.

#ifndef IMTOOLSH
#define IMTOOLSH

// Images are defined as huge pointers
typedef unsigned char huge* IMAGE;

// Function prototypes
void ResizeIm(IMAGE InIm, int ImWd, int ImHt, IMAGE OutIm,
  int OutWd, int OutHt);
void ZoomIm(IMAGE InIm, int CurrLen, int InStep,
  IMAGE OutIm, int NewLen, int OutStep);
int SharpenIm(IMAGE InIm, IMAGE OutIm, int ImWd, int ImHt);
void Colorize(IMAGE InIm, IMAGE OutIm, int ImWd, int ImHt,
  float Red, float Green, float Blue);
void ColorToGray(IMAGE InIm, IMAGE OutIm, int ImWd, int ImHt);
void MirrorXIm(IMAGE Im, int ImWd, int ImHt);
```

```
void MirrorYIm(IMAGE Im, int ImWd, int ImHt);
void MirrorXYIm(IMAGE Im, int ImWd, int ImHt);
void BrightenIm(IMAGE InIm, IMAGE OutIm, int ImWd, int ImHt,
  int Val);
int Average(IMAGE InIm, IMAGE OutIm, int ImWd, int ImHt);
void Histogram(unsigned int *Hist, IMAGE InIm,
  int ImWd, int ImHt);
int ContrastEnhance(IMAGE InIm, IMAGE OutIm,
  int ImWd, int ImHt, int LowVal, int HiVal);
void GammaCorr(IMAGE InIm, IMAGE OutIm, int ImWd, int ImHt,
  double Val);

#endif
```

• IMTOOLS.C

```
// IMTOOLS.C: A collection of image processing tools.

#include <math.h>
#include <stdlib.h>
#include "grphics.h"
#include "imtools.h"

//////////////////////////// ResizeIm \\\\\\\\\\\\\\\\\\\\\\\\\\
//
// Copies and resizes the image in InIm, which is ImWd by ImHt
// in size, to the OutIm array, which is OutWd by OutHt in size.
//
void ResizeIm(IMAGE InIm, int InWd, int InHt, IMAGE OutIm,
  int OutWd, int OutHt)
{
  unsigned long I;

  for (I=0; I<InHt; I++)  // Stretches image horizontally
    ZoomIm(&InIm[I*InWd], InWd, 1, &OutIm[I*InWd], OutWd, 1);
  for (I=0; I<OutWd; I++) // Stretches image vertically
    ZoomIm(&OutIm[I], InHt, InWd, &OutIm[I], OutHt, InWd);
}

//////////////////////////// ZoomIm \\\\\\\\\\\\\\\\\\\\\\\\\\\\
//
// Zooms in on a portion of an image in one dimension. CurrLen
// is the current dimension's length. NewLen is to be the new
// length. The ratio of these two values determines how much
// the input image is stretched or compressed. InStep and
// OutStep are set to 1 to stretch or compress the image
// horizontally. To stretch or compress an image vertically,
// set InStep to the width of the input image and OutStep to
```

```
// the pixel width of the output image.
//
void ZoomIm(IMAGE InIm, int CurrLen, int InStep, IMAGE OutIm,
  int NewLen, int OutStep)
{
  unsigned long I=0, Pixel=0;
  float Accum=0, Val, Scale, InAmt=1.0, UseAmt;

  Scale = (double)NewLen / CurrLen;
  UseAmt = 1 / Scale;
  // Compute the output pixels
  while (Pixel < (unsigned long)NewLen*OutStep) {
    // Linearly interpolate the current image pixel
    Val = InAmt * InIm[I] + (1.0-InAmt) * InIm[I+InStep];
    // Use what's in InAmt. However, there still isn't enough
    // to make up a whole output pixel.
    if (InAmt < UseAmt) {
      Accum += Val * InAmt;      // Add in weighted contribution
      UseAmt -= InAmt;
      InAmt = 1.0;
      I += InStep;
    }
    else {  // Input pixel is not completely consumed in current pixel
      Accum += Val * UseAmt;
      OutIm[Pixel] = Accum * Scale;
      Pixel += OutStep;
      Accum = 0;
      InAmt -= UseAmt;
      UseAmt = 1 / Scale;
    }
  }
}


/////////////////////////// SharpenIm  \\\\\\\\\\\\\\\\\\\\\\\\\\\
//
// Enhances the edges in an image by subtracting the Laplacian
// from the image. The edges of the image are not affected. The
// function allocates memory to hold one row of the image. If
// there is not enough memory to hold the image, the function
// returns with a value of 0. Otherwise, it will return 1.
//
int SharpenIm(IMAGE InIm, IMAGE OutIm, int ImWd, int ImHt)
{
  unsigned long I, J, Offset, Pix;
  unsigned int Intermed, PrevCol;
  unsigned char *PrevRow;

  // Allocate memory to hold the last row of the image processed
  PrevRow = (unsigned char *)malloc(ImWd);
```

```
    if (!PrevRow) return 0;  // Not enough memory
    // Copy the top row of the image to the PrevRow array
    for (I=0; I<ImWd; I++) {
      PrevRow[I] = (unsigned int)InIm[I];
      OutIm[I] = InIm[I];
      OutIm[(ImHt-1)*ImWd+I] = InIm[(ImHt-1)*ImWd+I];
    }
    for (I=0; I<ImHt; I++) {
      Offset = I * ImWd;
      OutIm[Offset] = InIm[Offset];
      OutIm[Offset+ImWd-1] = InIm[Offset+ImWd-1];
    }
    // Edges of the image are left unchanged
    for (J=1; J<ImHt-1; J++) {
      Offset = J * ImWd;
      PrevCol = (unsigned int)InIm[Offset];
      for (I=1; I<ImWd-1; I++) {
        Pix = Offset + I;
        Intermed = 4 * (unsigned int)InIm[Pix] +
          (unsigned int)InIm[Pix] - (unsigned int)InIm[Pix+1] -
          PrevCol - (unsigned int)InIm[Pix+ImWd] -
          (unsigned int)PrevRow[I];
        Intermed = abs(Intermed);
        if (Intermed > 255) Intermed = 255;
        PrevCol = (unsigned int)InIm[Pix];
        PrevRow[I] = InIm[Pix];
        OutIm[Pix] = (unsigned char)Intermed;
      }
      PrevRow[0] = InIm[Offset];
      PrevRow[ImWd-1] = InIm[Offset+ImWd-1];
    }
    free(PrevRow);
    return 1;
}


////////////////////////// Colorize \\\\\\\\\\\\\\\\\\\\\\\\\\
//
// Converts a grayscale image (InIm) to a color image by
// multiplying each pixel times the red, green, and blue
// components passed in. The values of the color components
// should be between 0 and 1.
//
void Colorize(IMAGE InIm, IMAGE OutIm, int ImWd, int ImHt,
  float Red, float Green, float Blue)
{
  unsigned long I, J, Offset;

  for (J=0; J<ImHt; J++) {
    Offset = J * ImWd;
```

```
    for (I=0; I<ImWd; I++) {
      OutIm[(I+Offset)*3] = InIm[I+Offset] * Red;
      OutIm[(I+Offset)*3+1] = InIm[I+Offset] * Green;
      OutIm[(I+Offset)*3+2] = InIm[I+Offset] * Blue;
    }
  }
}


///////////////////////// ColorToGray \\\\\\\\\\\\\\\\\\\\\\\\\\\
//
// Creates a grayscale image from a 24-bit RGB image
//
void ColorToGray(IMAGE InIm, IMAGE OutIm, int ImWd, int ImHt)
{
  unsigned long I, J, Offset;

  for (J=0; J<ImHt; J++) {
    Offset = J * ImWd;
    for (I=0; I<ImWd; I++) {
      OutIm[I+Offset] = ((unsigned int)InIm[(I+Offset)*3] +
        (unsigned int)InIm[(I+Offset)*3+1] +
        (unsigned int)InIm[(I+Offset)*3+2]) / 3;
    }
  }
}


///////////////////////// MirrorXIm \\\\\\\\\\\\\\\\\\\\\\\\\\\
//
// Flips a grayscale image about its center row. Note: this
// function overwrites the original image with the flipped image.
//
void MirrorXIm(IMAGE Im, int ImWd, int ImHt)
{
  unsigned long I, J, K, Offset;
  unsigned char Tmp;

  for (J=0; J<ImHt; J++) {
    Offset = J * ImWd;
    for (I=0, K=ImWd-1; I<ImWd/2; I++, K--) {
      Tmp = Im[Offset+K];
      Im[Offset+K] = Im[Offset+I];
      Im[Offset+I] = Tmp;
    }
  }
}


///////////////////////// MirrorYIm \\\\\\\\\\\\\\\\\\\\\\\\\\\
//
// Flips a grayscale image about its center column. Note: this
```

```
// function overwrites the input image with the flipped image.
//
void MirrorYIm(IMAGE Im, int ImWd, int ImHt)
{
  unsigned long I, J, K, Offset, Offset2;
  unsigned char Tmp;

  for (J=0, K=ImHt-1; J<ImHt/2; J++, K--) {
    Offset = J * ImWd;
    Offset2 = K * ImWd;
    for (I=0; I<ImWd; I++) {
      Tmp = Im[Offset2+I];
      Im[Offset2+I] = Im[Offset+I];
      Im[Offset+I] = Tmp;
    }
  }
}


//////////////////////////// MirrorXYIm \\\\\\\\\\\\\\\\\\\\\\\\\\\\
//
// Flips a grayscale image about its diagonal, which effectively
// rotates the image 90 degrees counterclockwise. Note: this
// function overwrites the original image with the flipped image.
//
void MirrorXYIm(IMAGE Im, int ImWd, int ImHt)
{
  unsigned long I, J, C, Offset, Offset2;
  unsigned char Tmp;

  for (J=0; J<ImHt; J++) {
    Offset = J * ImWd;
    for (I=0; I<J; I++) {
      Offset2 = I * ImWd + J;
      Tmp = Im[Offset2];
      Im[Offset2] = Im[Offset+I];
      Im[Offset+I] = Tmp;
    }
  }
}


//////////////////////////// Average \\\\\\\\\\\\\\\\\\\\\\\\\\\\\\
//
// Averages 3-by-3 neighborhoods of pixels in a grayscale image.
// The function allocates one row of temporary storage. If this
// allocation fails, the function returns 0. Otherwise, it
// returns 1. The borders of the image are not changed.
//
int Average(IMAGE InIm, IMAGE OutIm, int ImWd, int ImHt)
```

```
{
  IMAGE PrevRow;
  unsigned long I, J, Offset, Pix;
  int Ave, PrevCol;

  // Allocate memory to hold the last row of the image processed
  PrevRow = (unsigned char *)malloc(ImWd);
  if (!PrevRow) return 0;  // Not enough memory
  // Copy the top row of the image to the PrevRow array
  for (I=0; I<ImWd; I++) {
    PrevRow[I] = (unsigned int)InIm[I];
    OutIm[I] = InIm[I];
    OutIm[(ImHt-1)*ImWd+I] = InIm[(ImHt-1)*ImWd+I];
  }
  for (I=0; I<ImHt; I++) {
    Offset = I * ImWd;
    OutIm[Offset] = InIm[Offset];
    OutIm[Offset+ImWd-1] = InIm[Offset+ImWd-1];
  }
  // Edges of the image are left unchanged
  for (J=1; J<ImHt-1; J++) {
    Offset = J * ImWd;
    PrevCol = (unsigned int)InIm[Offset];
    for (I=1; I<ImWd-1; I++) {
      Pix = Offset + I;
      Ave = ((int)PrevRow[I-1] + (int)PrevRow[I] +
        (int)PrevRow[I+1] + PrevCol + (int)InIm[Pix] +
        (int)InIm[Pix+1] + (int)InIm[Pix+ImWd-1] +
        (int)InIm[Pix+ImWd] + (int)InIm[Pix+ImWd+1]) / 9;
      PrevCol = InIm[Pix];
      PrevRow[I] = InIm[Pix];
      OutIm[Pix] = (unsigned char)Ave;
    }
    PrevRow[0] = InIm[Offset];
    PrevRow[ImWd-1] = InIm[Offset+ImWd-1];
  }
  free(PrevRow);
  return 1;
}


///////////////////////// Histogram \\\\\\\\\\\\\\\\\\\\\\\\\
//
// Returns the histogram of a grayscale image. You must allocate
// space for the histogram array before calling this routine.
// Therefore, to allocate a histogram array large enough to
// hold 256 gray levels, use:
// hist = (unsigned int *)malloc(NUMBEROFGRAYLEVELS*sizeof(int));
//
void Histogram(unsigned int *Hist, IMAGE InIm, int ImWd, int ImHt)
```

```
{
  unsigned long I, J, Offset;

  for (I=0; I<256; I++)
    Hist[I] = 0;
  for (J=0; J<ImHt; J++) {
    Offset = J * ImWd;
    for (I=0; I<ImWd; I++)
      Hist[InIm[I+Offset]]++;
  }
}


///////////////////// ContrastEnhance \\\\\\\\\\\\\\\\\\\\\\\
//
// Stretches the histogram of the image in order to improve the
// contrast. This function cuts out all pixels below LowVal and
// above HiVal and then stretches the remaining pixels in the
// histogram so that they are evenly distributed across the
// image. This function currently only works with grayscale
// images.
//
int ContrastEnhance(IMAGE InIm, IMAGE OutIm,
  int ImWd, int ImHt, int LowVal, int HiVal)
{
  unsigned long I, J, Offset, Pix;
  float Scale;

  Scale = 255.0 / (float)(HiVal - LowVal);
  for (J=0; J<ImHt; J++) {
    Offset = J * ImWd;
    for (I=0; I<ImWd; I++) {
      Pix = Offset + I;
      if (InIm[Pix] < LowVal)
        OutIm[Pix] = 0;
      else if (InIm[Pix] > HiVal)
        OutIm[Pix] = 255;
      else
        OutIm[Pix] = (unsigned char)
          (Scale * (float)(InIm[Pix] - LowVal));
    }
  }
  return 1;
}


//////////////////////// BrightenIm \\\\\\\\\\\\\\\\\\\\\\\\
//
// Adds a value to each pixel in a grayscale image
//
```

```
void BrightenIm(IMAGE InIm, IMAGE OutIm, int ImWd, int ImHt,
   int Val)
{
  unsigned long I, J, Offset;
  unsigned int Tmp;

  for (J=0; J<ImHt; J++) {
    Offset = J * ImWd;
    for (I=0; I<ImWd; I++) {
      Tmp = (unsigned int)InIm[Offset+I] + Val;
      OutIm[Offset+I] = (Tmp > 255) ? 255 : (unsigned char)Tmp;
    }
  }
}


///////////////////////////// GammaCorr \\\\\\\\\\\\\\\\\\\\\\\\\\
//
// Applies a gamma correction to an RGB image. Set Val between
// 0 and 1 to lighten the image and greater than 1 to darken it.
// To gamma correct for an image that looks good on a monitor,
// a good value to use is 0.45. The function assumes that the
// image is an RGB image.
//
void GammaCorr(IMAGE InIm, IMAGE OutIm, int ImWd, int ImHt,
  double Val)
{
  unsigned long I, J, Offset, Offset2;
  double Res;

  for (J=0; J<ImHt; J++) {
    Offset = J * ImWd;
    for (I=0; I<ImWd; I++) {
      Offset2 = (Offset + I) * 3;
      Res = pow((double)InIm[Offset2], Val);
      OutIm[Offset2] = (Res > 255) ? 255 : (unsigned char)Res;
      Offset2++;
      Res = pow((double)InIm[Offset2], Val);
      OutIm[Offset2] = (Res > 255) ? 255 : (unsigned char)Res;
      Offset2++;
      Res = pow((double)InIm[Offset2], Val);
      OutIm[Offset2] = (Res > 255) ? 255 : (unsigned char)Res;
    }
  }
}
```

Morphing Magic

Without even being aware of it, you're probably already familiar with the image processing technique we'll discuss in this chapter. Its results are so stunning that it's become a favorite special effect in many motion pictures, including *An American Werewolf in London, Willow,* and *Terminator II.*

This astounding bit of imaging magic is called *morphing.* Morphing gives the illusion of one object magically being transformed into another. In this chapter, you'll learn how to build an application you can use to create your own morphing movies.

How Morphing Works

In its simplest form, morphing takes two different objects and generates a sequence of images in which the first object is seemingly transformed into the second. For you to accomplish this transformation, two actions usually need to occur, as illustrated in Figure 12.1. First, the starting and ending frames are stretched, compressed, or warped, so that the shapes of the two objects are similar. Second, these intermediate, warped frames are blended together so that they gradually change from the first image to the second, producing a smooth transition.

Warping Images

Warping the starting and ending images is a key part of morphing. There are a variety of methods we can choose from to perform this step. We'll use a technique in which we define a set of triangles for the two images and

Figure 12.1 The process of morphing two images.

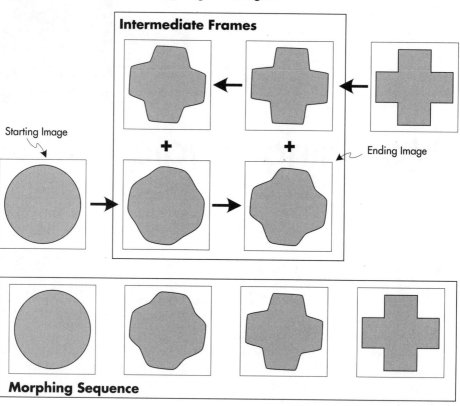

gradually warp them so the shape of the starting triangles match the ending ones and vice versa. Of course, as each triangle is warped, the image within it is warped too. Figure 12.2, for example, shows how a simple mesh pattern of four triangles might generate two intermediate frames.

When morphing an image, however, two sets of intermediate images are effectively created. One set is of the starting image being warped into the shape of the ending image, the other set is of the ending image being warped into the starting frame. The locations of the intermediate triangles are interpolated from the positions of the starting and ending meshes.

Mapping Images

After a morphing program generates the intermediate triangles, it must determine what to paint inside each triangle. Each pixel is calculated from a combination of corresponding pixels in the starting and ending images. Therefore, the first

Figure 12.2 Using triangles to warp an image.

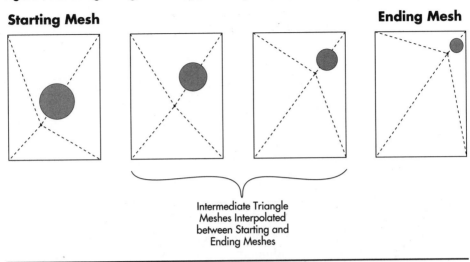

Intermediate Triangle
Meshes Interpolated
between Starting and
Ending Meshes

step is to determine which point in the starting image and ending image corresponds to the pixel being rendered. The next step is to blend the colors of these two points. Usually, a morphing program interpolates between each pair of colors and scales them so that initially the intermediate images favor the starting image and then gradually the ending frame.

CREATING A SIMPLE MORPHING PROGRAM

The rest of this chapter focuses on MORPH, a simple morphing program. MORPH takes two images and their corresponding mesh patterns and generates a series of intermediate, morphed images. When you play these images back, you'll have your own "movie" of one object transforming into another. The primary source file for MORPH is MORPH.C, which is listed at the end of this chapter. Like RAY, the program uses WINSHELL.C, discussed in Appendix C, enabling you to compile it for DOS or Windows.

Controlling the MORPH Program

To keep things simple, MORPH.C does not provide a sophisticated user interface. Instead, it reads the names of the image files that it is to use and their triangular meshes from a text file. Figure 12.3 illustrates the format of this control file.

The first two lines in the file list the filenames of the starting and ending image files, respectively. The third line specifies the root filename to use for the

---

Figure 12.3 The format of the control file that MORPH uses.

```
Starting Image Filename
Ending Image Filename
Output Name
Number of Morphed Images
Number of Triangles in Mesh

Triangle 1's Vertices for Starting Image
Triangle 2's Vertices for Starting Image
                    ⋮
Triangle N's Vertices for Starting Image
Triangle 1's Vertices for Ending Image
Triangle 2's Vertices for Ending Image
                    ⋮
Triangle N's Vertices for Ending Image
```

---

morphed image files. Next is the number of morphed images to generate—including the starting and ending images—followed by the number of triangles in the mesh pattern. The remainder of the file lists the vertices of the two sets of triangles. The first set is the starting image's mesh pattern and the last set is the ending image's.

Initializing the Morphing Process

The **Setup** function gives you a high-level view of the initialization that MORPH requires. Most importantly, **Setup** calls **ReadMeshFile** to process the control file and read the starting and ending triangle meshes. These are placed into the **STris** and **ETris** arrays, which are defined as arrays of **TRIANGLE** structures. Each **TRIANGLE** structure holds three pairs of x and y image coordinates that specify the vertices of a triangle, and is defined as:

```
typedef struct {
  POINT2 p[3];      // A triangle has three vertices
} TRIANGLE;
```

The **POINT2** structure is also defined in MORPH.C, and holds a single (x,y) coordinate pair. The top-left coordinate in an image is (0,0) and the bottom right is (**ImWd**-1,**ImHt**-1). And finally, **ImWd** and **ImHt** are the pixel width and height of the image.

Setup also reads the starting and ending images into the **SIm** and **EIm** arrays. Currently, MORPH only reads and writes grayscale and 24-bit RGB PCX image files.

Generating Images

After the initialization is performed MORPH calls the **GenImage** function to launch the morphing process. **GenImage** contains a **for** loop that generates **NumFrames** of morphed images. Within the **for** loop, the code calls the **Warp** function to create each intermediate frame, display the result, then write the image to a PCX file.

The output filename is built from three components. First, the root of the filename, which is read from the control file and stored in the **OutFilename** variable, forms the base of the filename. Second, the current frame number is appended to the root name so that each frame's filename is unique. Finally, the PCX extension is added to complete the filename. Therefore, if **OutFilename** is set to the string "OUT," the first frame is stored as OUT0.PCX, the second as OUT1.PCX, and so on. Therefore, if you specify that MORPH should generate three frames, you'll get three image filenames: OUT0.PCX, OUT1.PCX, and OUT2.PCX.

Moving the Triangle Patches

The **Warp** function calculates the positions of the intermediate triangles required to generate the intermediate, warped frames. This is performed by linearly interpolating between the vertices of corresponding triangles in the starting and ending meshes. The interpolated positions of the triangles are based on the ratio of the current frame number to the number of frames to generate. This value is stored in the variable **Pcent**:

```
float Pcent = (float)FrameNum / (float)NumFrames;
```

The function loops through each of the triangles, calculates the positions of the intermediate triangles, then places the results in the **ITris** array:

```
for(I=0; I<NumTris; I++) {  // Process each triangle
  for (J=0; J<3; J++) {       // Process each triangle vertex
    ITris[I].p[J].x = STris[I].p[J].x +
      (ETris[I].p[J].x - STris[I].p[J].x) * Pcent;
    ITris[I].p[J].y = STris[I].p[J].y +
      (ETris[I].p[J].y - STris[I].p[J].y) * Pcent;
  }
}
```

Finally, **Warp** calls **GenIntImage** to apply the triangle mesh to the starting and ending images and generate the intermediate frame.

Morphing the Images

The **GenIntImage** function is the routine that actually performs most of the morphing. The function accepts a hefty 11 arguments and probably appears a bit challenging at first. Table 12.1 lists and defines each of the arguments.

The **OutIm** variable, which is set to the morphed image, is the only output of **GenIntImage**. The image is rendered using the intermediate triangle mesh, **ITris**. The goal of **GenIntImage**, therefore, is to determine what colors to display in each part of the triangles in **ITris**.

To accomplish this, it uses a *scanline algorithm*. A scanline algorithm operates the same as a fill operation. That is, it starts at the top of each triangle and scans each row in the image from left to right until the whole triangle has been filled or operated on. By operating in pixel coordinates, the scanline algorithm can be relatively fast and efficient.

Here's an overview of what **GenIntImage** does:

```
For each intermediate triangle
    For each point in each of the intermediate triangles
        Determine what point in the starting image corresponds to the current point
        Determine what point in the ending image corresponds to the current point
        Interpolate between the colors of these two points
        Set the current pixel in the intermediate frame to the interpolated color
```

You'll find three nested **for** loops in **GenIntImage**: the outer loop visits each triangle in the intermediate triangle mesh, the middle **for** loop scans each image row of the triangle, and the inner **for** loop visits each column in the rows. The scanline algorithm starts at the vertex with the smallest y value and continues to the vertex with the largest y value. Within these rows, it scans from

---

Table 12.1 Arguments Passed to GenIntImage.

Parameter	Description
NumTris	Number of triangles in the triangle meshes
ITris	List of intermediate triangles
STris	List of starting triangles
ETris	Ending triangles
SIm	Starting image
EIm	Ending image
OutIm	Morphed image
ImWd	Pixel width of the image
ImHt	Pixel height of the image
Bytes	Number of bytes per pixel
Pcent	Percent to apply to interpolated colors

Figure 12.4 A scanline algorithm is used to paint each intermediate triangle.

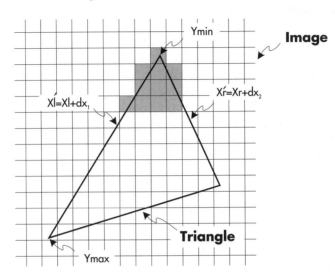

the left extent, **Xl**, to the right extent, **Xr**, as shown in Figure 12.4. The **Xl** and **Xr** variables are incrementally calculated by adding the slope of the triangle's edges to the previous row's extents. The slope of each side of the triangle is calculated in the function **CalcSideSlopes** and stored in the **Sides** array.

Determining a Point in a Triangle

Calculating each pixel of the **OutIm** array is a two step process: first, **GenIntImage** must determine what points in the starting and ending images correspond to the current point in the intermediate triangle. The solution is to use *Barycentric coordinates*, illustrated in Figure 12.5. Given a point P within a triangle, you can divide the triangle into three smaller triangles, U, V, and W. The Barycentric coordinate is a triple (u,v,w) coordinate calculated from the ratio of the area of each of these triangles with the original triangle's area. Mathematically, this is expressed as:

$$u = \frac{\text{Area U}}{\text{Area T}} \qquad v = \frac{\text{Area V}}{\text{Area T}} \qquad w = \frac{\text{Area W}}{\text{Area T}}$$

The **GenIntImage** function determines what (u,v,w) coordinate corresponds to the current scanline point. The code then determines what image points in the starting and ending images correspond to the same Barycentric coordinate.

Figure 12.5 A point (x,y) within a triangle can also be expressed as a Barycentric coordinate (u,v,w).

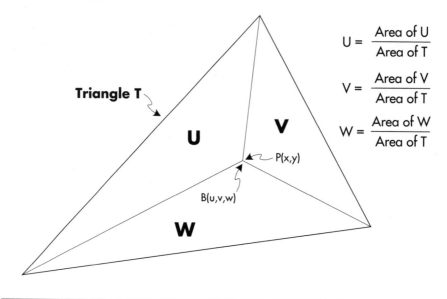

$$U = \frac{\text{Area of U}}{\text{Area of T}}$$

$$V = \frac{\text{Area of V}}{\text{Area of T}}$$

$$W = \frac{\text{Area of W}}{\text{Area of T}}$$

To keep the code relatively efficient, only the Barycentric coordinates of the endpoints of a scanline are explicitly calculated. The code interpolates the (u,v,w) coordinates for those in between. Therefore, the function **PointToBary**, which converts an (x,y) coordinate to (u,v,w) space, is only called at the end of each scanline. The **BaryToPoint** function is provided to convert a Barycentric coordinate to an x,y image location.

Generating the Output Color

Once MORPH has the two pixels in the starting and ending images that correspond to the current point being calculated, it blends their colors together. We could compute a simple average; however, instead **GenIntImage** linearly interpolates between these two colors. The value of **Pcent**, which is based on the frame number, scales the colors so that initially the starting image contributes more to the intermediate image, then gradually the ending image becomes more significant. This produces a gentle fade of the images.

Realize that **GenIntImage** only generates points in the output image where the intermediate triangle mesh is defined. Therefore, if you want to generate a complete image, the starting and ending mesh patterns must cover the whole image.

Compiling MORPH

You can compile MORPH for DOS or Windows. If you want to build MORPH as a DOS application, you must compile and link MORPH.C with GRPHICS.C and PCXTOOL.C, using the large memory model. If you want to run MORPH as a Windows application, you must also link these files with WINSHELL.C and define the compilation macro **FORWINDOWS**. Of course, you'll need a Windows-capable compiler to generate a Windows version of the application. Note that as a DOS application, MORPH displays its intermediate results in 320x200 256-color mode.

Using MORPH

MORPH requires one command-line argument: the name of the control file. The following control file, TEST.MOR, lists the points that generate the sequence shown in Figure 12.6:

```
cactus.pcx
zebra.pcx
out
10
17

0    0      51  51      0  199
0    0      99  15      51  51
0    0      199  0      99  15
199  0      99  15      148  54
199  0      148  54     199  199
99   15     51  51      90  51
99   15     90  51      110  53
99   15     110  53     148  54
51   51     64  126     0  199
51   51     64  126     99  199
64   126    0  199      99  199
51   51     90  51      99  199
90   51     110  53     99  199
110  53     148  54     99  199
148  54     138  126    99  199
148  54     138  126    199  199
138  126    99  199     199  199

0    0      71  97      0  199
0    0      104  58     71  97
0    0      199  0      104  58
199  0      104  58     131  97
199  0      131  97     199  199
104  58     71  97      72  97
104  58     72  97      130  97
```

104 58	130 97	131 97
71 97	56 143	0 199
71 97	56 143	104 199
56 143	0 199	104 199
71 97	72 97	104 199
72 97	130 97	104 199
130 97	131 97	104 199
131 97	144 143	104 199
131 97	144 143	199 199
144 143	104 199	199 199

To create these images, type MORPH TEST.MOR at the DOS prompt.

The TEST.MOR file transforms the image of the cactus in the file CACTUS.PCX into a zebra, located in ZEBRA.PCX. In all, it generates ten frames, which are named OUT0.PCX, OUT1.PCX, OUT2.PCX, and so on. You can use a modified version of the PLAYBACK program in Chapter 6 to view this morphed sequence. Specifically, you'll need to change PLAYBACK.C so that it reads PCX images.

Figure 12.6 A portion of the morphed sequence generated using TEST.MOR.

Morphing Tips

Like ray tracing, creating impressive morphed sequences is definitely an art. Here are a few tips to help you out:

1. Morph only one pair of objects at a time.

2. Pick your mesh points so they correspond to comparable features in the initial and final images. For instance, if you morph one face to another, define mesh points for each person's eyes.

3. Place your mesh points on important features in the images.

4. Use images with an identical, constant background. If you want a backdrop, you can always overlay your morphed sequence onto the background.

5. Use initial and final images that have similar lighting and have their objects in the same basic location or orientation.

6. Generally, the more triangles you use the better the morphing will be.

• MORPH.C

```c
// MORPH.C: Morphs two images together.

#include <stdio.h>
#include <string.h>
#include <stdlib.h>
#include <math.h>
#include "grphics.h"
#include "pcxtool.h"

typedef struct {
   float x, y;          // The x and y coordinates of a point
} POINT2;

typedef struct {
   POINT2 p[3];         // A triangle has three vertices
} TRIANGLE;

typedef struct {        // Scan conversion data for a side
   float x, y;          // Current scan x coordinate
   float dx;            // The x slope component of a side
} SIDE;

// Image pointers for a starting, ending, and OutIm
// image. The three images are assumed to be the same type.
typedef unsigned char huge* IMAGE;
IMAGE SIm, EIm, OutIm;
int ImWd, ImHt;         // Pixel width and height of an image
int Bytes;              // Number of bytes per color
TRIANGLE *STris;        // Starting triangle mesh
```

```
    TRIANGLE *ETris;       // Ending triangle mesh
    TRIANGLE *ITris;       // Intermediate triangle mesh
    int NumTris;           // Number of triangles in each mesh
    int NumFrames;         // The number of frames to generate,
                           // including the starting and ending frames
    char SFilename[80];    // Starting image filename
    char EFilename[80];    // Ending image filename
    char OutFilename[80];  // Base name of output files
    unsigned char Palette[768];
    int VMode;


    // Function prototypes:
    void GenIntImage(int NumTris, TRIANGLE ITris[],
      TRIANGLE STris[], TRIANGLE ETris[], IMAGE SIm,
      IMAGE EIm, IMAGE OutIm, int ImWd, int ImHt, int Bytes, float Pcent);
    void DisplayIm(int hDC, IMAGE Im, int ImWd, int ImHt, int Bytes);
    void Warp(int FrameNum, int NumFrames, int NumTris,
      TRIANGLE *STris, TRIANGLE *ETris, TRIANGLE *ITris,
      IMAGE SIm, IMAGE EIm, IMAGE OutIm, int ImWd, int ImHt, int Bytes);
    int ReadMeshFile(char *Filename);
    int SaveImage(int I, IMAGE Im, int ImWd, int ImHt, int Bytes);
    int ReadPCX(char *FileName, IMAGE *Im, int *ImWd,
      int *ImHt, int *Bytes);
    void BaryToPoint(float U, float V, float W,
      TRIANGLE *Tri, POINT2 *p);
    void PointToBary(POINT2 *V1, POINT2 *V2, POINT2 *V3, POINT2 *P,
      float *U, float *V, float *W);
    float Area(POINT2 *P1, POINT2 *P2, POINT2 *P3);


    /////////////////////////////  main  \\\\\\\\\\\\\\\\\\\\\\\\\\\

    #if !defined(FORWINDOWS)
    int main(int argc, char *argv[])
    {
      if (argc != 2) {
        printf("MORPH: Morphs two images\n");
        printf("Usage: morph <command_file>\n");
        exit(1);
      }
      // Set the default video mode to 320x200x256 so that
      // it uses a color palette. This field only affects the
      // program if it is compiled as a DOS application.
      VMode = M320x200x256 | COLORPALETTE;
      Setup(argv[1]);
      if (SetupDisplay(VMode)) {
        GenImage(0);
        EndDisplay();
        Cleanup();
      }
```

```
    return 0;
}
#endif

////////////////////////////// Setup \\\\\\\\\\\\\\\\\\\\\\\\\\
//
// Sets up default values for variables
//
void Setup(char far *Str)
{
  if (Str == NULL)
    exit(1);
  if (!ReadMeshFile(Str)) {
    printf("Failed to read mesh file: %s.\n", Str);
    return;
  }
  // Read the starting and ending images to morph between
  if (ReadPCX(SFilename, &SIm, &ImWd, &ImHt, &Bytes) < 0) {
    printf("Failed to read starting image: %s.\n", SFilename);
    return;
  }
  if (ReadPCX(EFilename, &EIm, &ImWd, &ImHt, &Bytes) < 0) {
    printf("Failed to read ending image: %s.\n", EFilename);
    return;
  }
  OutIm = (IMAGE)farmalloc((unsigned long)ImWd*ImHt*Bytes);
  if (!OutIm) {
    printf("no memory\n");
    return;
  }
}

////////////////////////////// Cleanup \\\\\\\\\\\\\\\\\\\\\\\\\\
//
// Performs any cleanup actions
//
void Cleanup()
{
  farfree(OutIm);
}

////////////////////////////// GenImage \\\\\\\\\\\\\\\\\\\\\\\\\\
//
// This is the main entry point for the ray tracing code. If
// compiled as a DOS application, the hDC parameter is not used.
// In Windows, hDC is a handle to the device context to draw on.
//
void GenImage(int hDC)
{
```

```
    int I;

    for (I=0; I<=NumFrames; I++ ) {
      Warp(I, NumFrames, NumTris, STris, ETris, ITris,
        SIm, EIm, OutIm, ImWd, ImHt, Bytes);
      DisplayIm(hDC, OutIm, ImWd, ImHt, Bytes);
      SaveImage(I, OutIm, ImWd, ImHt, Bytes);
    }
}


///////////////////////////// Warp \\\\\\\\\\\\\\\\\\\\\\\\\\\\\
//
// Calculates the intermediate mesh coordinates that are used to
// warp the starting and ending images
//
void Warp(int FrameNum, int NumFrames, int NumTris,
  TRIANGLE *STris, TRIANGLE *ETris, TRIANGLE *ITris,
  IMAGE SIm, IMAGE EIm, IMAGE OutIm, int ImWd, int ImHt, int Bytes)
{
  float Pcent = (float)FrameNum / (float)NumFrames;
  int I, J;

  // Interpolate the locations of the intermediate triangles
  // for the current image frame
  for(I=0; I<NumTris; I++) {  // Process each triangle
    for (J=0; J<3; J++) {     // Process each triangle vertex
      ITris[I].p[J].x = STris[I].p[J].x +
        (ETris[I].p[J].x - STris[I].p[J].x) * Pcent;
      ITris[I].p[J].y = STris[I].p[J].y +
        (ETris[I].p[J].y - STris[I].p[J].y) * Pcent;
    }
  }
  // Generate the intermediate image by scan converting the
  // intermediate triangles
  GenIntImage(NumTris, ITris, STris, ETris,
    SIm, EIm, OutIm, ImWd, ImHt, Bytes, Pcent);
}


//////////////////////// DisplayIm \\\\\\\\\\\\\\\\\\\\\\\\\\\\
//
// Displays an image on the screen
//
void DisplayIm(int hDC, IMAGE Im, int ImWd, int ImHt, int Bytes)
{
  int X, Y;
  IMAGE Color = Im;

  if (Bytes == 1) {   // Grayscale image
    for (Y=0; Y<ImHt; Y++)
```

```
      for (X=0; X<ImWd; X++) {
        PutPixel(hDC, X, Y, *Color, *Color, *Color);
        Color++;
      }
  }
  else {          // RBG image
    for (Y=0; Y<ImHt; Y++)
      for (X=0; X<ImWd; X++) {
        PutPixel(hDC, X, Y, *Color, *(Color+1), *(Color+2));
        Color+=3;
      }
  }
}


////////////////////////// ReadMeshFile \\\\\\\\\\\\\\\\\\\\\\\\\\
//
// Reads the program's parameters and mesh coordinates from a file
//
int ReadMeshFile(char *Filename)
{
  FILE *fp;
  int I, J;

  if ((fp=fopen(Filename, "r")) == NULL)
    return -1;    // Failed to read input file
  fscanf(fp, "%s", SFilename);  // Starting image filename
  fscanf(fp, "%s", EFilename);  // Ending image filename
  fscanf(fp, "%s", OutFilename);// Output image filename
  fscanf(fp, "%d", &NumFrames); // Number of frames to create
  fscanf(fp, "%d", &NumTris);   // Number of triangles in a mesh
  NumFrames-;
  // Allocate memory for the starting, intermediate, and ending
  // meshes. The intermediate mesh will be filled later.
  STris = (TRIANGLE *)malloc(NumTris*sizeof(TRIANGLE));
  ETris = (TRIANGLE *)malloc(NumTris*sizeof(TRIANGLE));
  ITris = (TRIANGLE *)malloc(NumTris*sizeof(TRIANGLE));
  if (ITris == NULL) {
    printf("Couldn't allocate mesh for %d triangles.\n",
      NumTris);
    fclose(fp);
    exit(1);
  }
  // Read the starting mesh coordinates
  for (I=0; I<NumTris; I++)
    for (J=0; J<3; J++)
      if (!fscanf(fp, "%f%f", &STris[I].p[J].x,
        &STris[I].p[J].y))
          return -2;
  // Read the ending mesh coordinates
```

```
    for (I=0; I<NumTris; I++)
      for (J=0; J<3; J++)
        if (!fscanf(fp, "%f%f", &ETris[I].p[J].x,
          &ETris[I].p[J].y))
            return -2;
    fclose(fp);
    return 1;
}

///////////////////////// SaveImage  \\\\\\\\\\\\\\\\\\\\\\\\\\
//
// Saves an image to a PCX file
//
int SaveImage(int I, IMAGE Im, int ImWd, int ImHt, int Bytes)
{
  FILE *fpout;
  char Filename[80];
  int J;

  if (Bytes == 1)   // Create a grayscale palette
    for (J=0; J<256; J++) {
      Palette[J*3] = J;
      Palette[J*3+1] = J;
      Palette[J*3+2] = J;
    }
  sprintf(Filename, "%s%d.pcx", OutFilename, I);
  if ((fpout=fopen(Filename, "wb")) == NULL)
    return -1;
  WritePCXImage(fpout, (unsigned char *)Im, ImWd, ImHt, Bytes, Palette);
  fclose(fpout);
  return 1;
}

///////////////////////// ReadPCX  \\\\\\\\\\\\\\\\\\\\\\\\\\
//
// Reads a PCX image file
//
int ReadPCX(char *FileName, IMAGE *Im, int *ImWd,
  int *ImHt, int *Bytes)
{
  FILE *fp;
  PCXHEADER PCXHdr;  // PCX file header
  unsigned char *ImRow;
  IMAGE Tmp;
  unsigned long X, Y, Offset;

  if ((fp=fopen(FileName, "rb")) == NULL)
    return -1;
  if (!ReadPCXHeader(fp, &PCXHdr)) { // Read the header
```

```
    fclose(fp);
    return -2;
  }
  if (!IsValidPCX(&PCXHdr)) {// Does the header say the image is
    fclose(fp);
    return -2;
  }
  // Extract the image dimensions from the header
  GetPCXInfo(&PCXHdr, ImWd, ImHt, Bytes);
  Tmp = (IMAGE)farmalloc((unsigned long)(*ImWd)*(*ImHt)*(*Bytes));
  if (Tmp == NULL) {
    printf("Failed to allocate memory for Wd=%d Ht=%d\n",
      *ImWd, *ImHt);
    fclose(fp);
    return -3;
  }
  ImRow = (unsigned char *)malloc(*ImWd*(*Bytes));
  if (ImRow == NULL) {      // Allocate a buffer to retrieve
    fclose(fp);             // one image row at a time
    return -3;
  }
  for (Y=0; Y<*ImHt; Y++) {  // Read each image row
    Offset = Y * (*ImWd)*(*Bytes);
    if (!GetPCXRow(fp, ImRow,
      PCXHdr.NPlanes, PCXHdr.BytesPerRow, *ImWd)) {
      free(Tmp);
      free(ImRow);
      fclose(fp);
      return -4;
    }
    // Copy the image row to the actual image array
    for (X=0; X<*ImWd*(*Bytes); X++)
      Tmp[Offset+X] = ImRow[X];
  }
  // Note: If there is a palette, it is ignored because
  // the image is assumed to be a grayscale or RGB image
  *Im = Tmp;
  free(ImRow);
  fclose(fp);
  return 0;
}

//////////////////////////// CompareUV  \\\\\\\\\\\\\\\\\\\\\\\\\\\\
//
// Comparison function that is used to sort a triangle's vertices
//
int CompareUV(const void *U, const void *V)  {
  if (((POINT2*)U)->y < ((POINT2*)V)->y)
    return -1;
```

```
      if (((POINT2*)U)->y > ((POINT2*)V)->y)
        return 1;
      if (((POINT2*)U)->x > ((POINT2*)V)->x)
        return 1;
      return 0;
    }


    //////////////////////// CalcSideSlopes  \\\\\\\\\\\\\\\\\\\\\\\
    //
    // Calculates the slopes of the three sides of a triangle
    //
    void CalcSideSlopes(TRIANGLE *Tri, SIDE Sides[])
    {
      float dx;
      float dy = Tri->p[1].y - Tri->p[0].y;
      if (dy != 0) {
        dx = Tri->p[1].x - Tri->p[0].x;
        Sides[0].dx = dx / dy;
        Sides[0].x = Tri->p[0].x;
        Sides[0].y = Tri->p[0].y;
      }
      dy = Tri->p[2].y - Tri->p[0].y;
      if (dy != 0) {
        dx = Tri->p[2].x - Tri->p[0].x;
        Sides[1].dx = dx / dy;
        Sides[1].x = Tri->p[0].x;
        Sides[1].y = Tri->p[0].y;
      }
      dy = Tri->p[2].y - Tri->p[1].y;
      if (dy != 0) {
        dx = Tri->p[2].x - Tri->p[1].x;
        Sides[2].dx = dx / dy;
        Sides[2].x = Tri->p[1].x;
        Sides[2].y = Tri->p[1].y;
      }
    }


    // The Tris arrays hold the triangles to warp using a scanline
    // process. The vertices in the triangles must be sorted in y
    // and x. The vertices of the triangles are labeled as follows:
    //                     p0
    //                    /  \
    //                   /    \
    //          Side 0  /      \  Side 1
    //                 /        \
    //               p1 —— p2
    //                   Side 2
    //
```

```
// NumTris is the number of triangles in the meshes. STris
// is the beginning triangle mesh and ETris is the ending mesh.
// ITris is the intermediate mesh currently being displayed.
//
void GenIntImage(int NumTris, TRIANGLE ITris[],
  TRIANGLE STris[], TRIANGLE ETris[], IMAGE SIm,
  IMAGE EIm, IMAGE OutIm, int ImWd, int ImHt, int Bytes, float Pcent)
{
  int YMin, YMax, Y, I, J, Xl, Xr, X, TransitionAt;
  SIDE Sides[3];
  int LeftEdge, RightEdge;  // These variables select the side to use
  unsigned char SRed, SGreen, SBlue, ERed, EGreen, EBlue;
  POINT2 Pt, OldPt, V1, V2, V3;
  float U, V, W;
  unsigned long Pixel;

  for (I=0; I<NumTris; I++) {
    V1 = ITris[I].p[0];
    V2 = ITris[I].p[1];
    V3 = ITris[I].p[2];
    // Sort the vertices in the triangle
    qsort(&ITris[I].p[0], 3, sizeof(POINT2), CompareUV);
    // Get the top, leftmost coordinate. The vertices are assumed
    // to be sorted so this will be the p[0] vertex.
    YMin = ITris[I].p[0].y + 0.5;
    YMax = ITris[I].p[2].y + 0.5;  // Bottom-right vertex
    if (YMin < 0) YMin = 0;
    if (YMax >= ImHt) YMax = ImHt-1;
    CalcSideSlopes(&ITris[I], Sides);
    // Triangles can be scan converted in four special cases.
    // The first case is if the top of the triangle is horizontal.
    if (ITris[I].p[0].y == ITris[I].p[1].y) {
      LeftEdge = 1;   // Side 1 is the left edge of the triangle
      RightEdge = 2;  // Side 2 is the right edge of the triangle
      TransitionAt = YMax + 1;  // Don't transition to another edge
    }
    // The bottom edge of the triangle is horizontal
    else if (ITris[I].p[1].y == ITris[I].p[2].y) {
      LeftEdge = 0;   // Side 0 is the left edge of the triangle
      RightEdge = 1;  // Side 1 is the right edge of the triangle
      TransitionAt = YMax + 1;  // Don't transition to another edge
    }
    else {
      // These are the remaining triangle cases
      if (ITris[I].p[1].x == ITris[I].p[2].x &&
          ITris[I].p[0].x == ITris[I].p[1].x) {
        continue;   // Don't paint this triangle
      }
```

```
    else if ((ITris[I].p[0].x >= ITris[I].p[1].x &&
       ITris[I].p[2].x > ITris[I].p[1].x) ||
       (ITris[I].p[0].x-(ITris[I].p[0].y-ITris[I].p[1].y)*
       (ITris[I].p[2].x-ITris[I].p[0].x) /
       (ITris[I].p[2].y-ITris[I].p[0].y) >= ITris[I].p[1].x)) {
      LeftEdge = 0;              // Set which side is the left and
      RightEdge = 1;             // right edges of the triangle
    }                            // for the current scanline
    else {
      LeftEdge = 1;
      RightEdge = 0;
    }
    // Switch edges when you reach vertex 1
    TransitionAt = ITris[I].p[1].y;
  }
  Sides[LeftEdge].x = Sides[LeftEdge].dx *
    (YMin - Sides[LeftEdge].y) + Sides[LeftEdge].x;
  Sides[RightEdge].x = Sides[RightEdge].dx *
    (YMin - Sides[RightEdge].y) + Sides[RightEdge].x;
  for (Y=YMin; Y<=YMax; Y++) {
    Xl = Sides[LeftEdge].x + 0.5;
    Xr = Sides[RightEdge].x + 0.5;
    if (Xl < 0) Xl = 0;
    if (Xr >= ImWd) Xr = ImWd - 1;
    if (Xl <= Xr) {
      Pt.y = Y;
      for (X=Xl, J=0; X<=Xr; X++, J++) {
        Pt.x = X;
        // Determine the barycentric coordinate for the
        // current point in the intermediate mesh
        PointToBary(&V1, &V2, &V3, &Pt, &U, &V, &W);
        // Find the pixel in the starting image that
        // corresponds to the point (U,V,W)
        BaryToPoint(U, V, W, &STris[I], &OldPt);
        // Retrieve the corresponding color in the starting image
        Pixel = (unsigned long)OldPt.y * ImWd + OldPt.x;
        if (Bytes == 1)
          SRed = SIm[Pixel];    // Use the red field for grayscale
        else {
          Pixel *= 3;
          SRed = SIm[Pixel];
          SGreen = SIm[Pixel+1];
          SBlue = SIm[Pixel+2];
        }
        // Find the pixel in the ending image that
        // corresponds to the point (U,V,W)
        BaryToPoint(U, V, W, &ETris[I], &OldPt);
```

```
        // Retrieve the corresponding color in the ending image
        Pixel = (unsigned long)OldPt.y * ImWd + OldPt.x;
        if (Bytes == 1)
          ERed = EIm[Pixel];  // Use the red field for
        else {                     // grayscale images
          Pixel *= 3;
          ERed = EIm[Pixel];
          EGreen = EIm[Pixel+1];
          EBlue = EIm[Pixel+2];
        }
        // Calculate pixel location in output image to paint
        Pixel = (unsigned long)Y * ImWd + X;
        // Copy the morphed color to the OutIm image
        if (Bytes == 1)
          OutIm[Pixel] = SRed + (ERed-SRed) * Pcent;
        else {
          Pixel *= 3;
          OutIm[Pixel] = SRed + (ERed-SRed) * Pcent;
          OutIm[Pixel+1] = SGreen + (EGreen-SGreen) * Pcent;
          OutIm[Pixel+2] = SBlue + (EBlue-SBlue) * Pcent;
        }
      }
    }
  }
  // Calculate the starting and ending coordinates of the
  // next row's strip in the current triangle
  Sides[LeftEdge].x += Sides[LeftEdge].dx;
  Sides[RightEdge].x += Sides[RightEdge].dx;
  if (TransitionAt <= Y-0.5) {
    // This situation handles the case when the scanline
    // reaches point 1. A new left edge or right edge is
    // then used for the scanning. This never occurs for
    // triangles that have a horizontal side.
    if (!LeftEdge) {
      LeftEdge = 2;  // Use side 2 as the left edge now
      Sides[LeftEdge].x = Sides[LeftEdge].dx *
        (Y + 0.5 - Sides[LeftEdge].y) + Sides[LeftEdge].x;
    }
    else {
      RightEdge = 2; // Use side 2 as the right edge now
      Sides[RightEdge].x = Sides[RightEdge].dx *
        (Y + 0.5 - Sides[RightEdge].y) + Sides[RightEdge].x;
    }
    TransitionAt = YMax + 1;  // It shouldn't transition again
  }
    }
   }
  }
}
```

```
////////////////////////// BaryToPoint \\\\\\\\\\\\\\\\\\\\\\\\\\\
//
// Calculates the image coordinate that corresponds to the barycentric
// coordinate (u,v,w)
//
void BaryToPoint(float u, float v, float w, TRIANGLE *Tri, POINT2 *p)
{
    p->x = u * Tri->p[0].x + v * Tri->p[1].x + w * Tri->p[2].x + 0.5;
    p->y = u * Tri->p[0].y + v * Tri->p[1].y + w * Tri->p[2].y + 0.5;
}


////////////////////////// Area \\\\\\\\\\\\\\\\\\\\\\\\\\\\\\\\\\
//
// Calculates the signed area of a triangle
//
float Area(POINT2 *P1, POINT2 *P2, POINT2 *P3)
{
  return P1->x * (P2->y - P3->y) -
    P2->x * (P1->y - P3->y) + P3->x * (P1->y - P2->y);
}


////////////////////////// PointToBary \\\\\\\\\\\\\\\\\\\\\\\\\\\
//
// Calculates the barycentric coordinate (u,v,w) of a point P
// inside the triangle (V1,V2,V2)
//
void PointToBary(POINT2 *V1, POINT2 *V2, POINT2 *V3, POINT2 *P,
  float *U, float *V, float *W)
{
  float TriArea;

  TriArea = Area(V1, V2, V3);
  *U = Area(P, V2, V3) / TriArea;  // Area of u / triangle's area
  *V = Area(V1, P, V3) / TriArea;  // Area of v / triangle's area
  *W = Area(V1, V2, P) / TriArea;  // Area of w / triangle's area
}
```

Vector Operations

Although you don't have to understand the math behind the numerous vector operations sprinkled throughout this book, you'll want to be comfortable with them if you plan on modifying the programs that rely on them. This appendix describes VECTOR.C, a vector toolkit that several of the programs in this book use. The VECTOR.C source file and its header file, VECTOR.H, are listed at the end of this appendix. Table A.1 lists the functions included in VECTOR.C. Figure A.1 graphically displays what each of these routines do.

WORKING WITH VECTORS

The VECTOR.H header file defines the **VECTOR** type to represent a single vector:

```
typedef struct {
  float x, y, z;
} VECTOR;
```

Table A.1 Vector operations Included in VECTOR.C.

Function	Description
Add	Adds two vectors together
Cross	Calculates the cross product of two vectors
Divide	Divides each component of a vector by a number
Dot	Calculates the dot product of two vectors
Mag	Returns the magnitude of a vector
Normalize	Normalizes a vector
Subtract	Subtracts two vectors component by component

The x, y, and z fields in the **VECTOR** structure typically store a three-dimensional point or the direction of a ray. For example, Figure A.2 shows a ray located at (1,2,2) that has the direction vector (0,2,1).

Realize that a vector has length and direction. The **Mag** function returns the length of a vector. It accepts a single vector as a parameter and returns the

Figure A.1 The VECTOR.C toolkit supports a handful of vector operations.

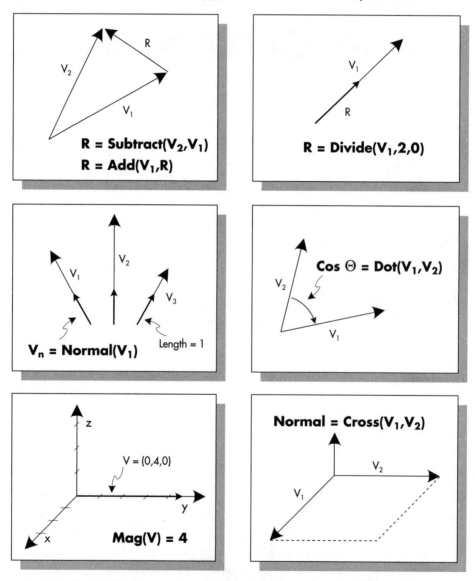

Figure A.2 You can represent a ray using a location and direction vector.

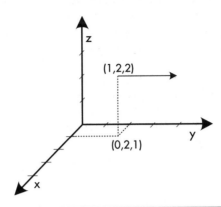

---

length of the vector as a floating point value. In contrast, the **Normalize** function scales each of the components in a vector by the vector's magnitude. This effectively puts different vectors on the same scale. Normalizing vectors is particularly useful when you want to compare their directions.

Vector Operations

This section briefly describes each of the remaining routines in VECTOR.C. The **Subtract** function takes two vectors as parameters and subtracts each of the vectors' fields. Here's the complete **Subtract** routine:

```
VECTOR Subtract(VECTOR *V1, VECTOR *V2)
{
  VECTOR D;

  D.x = V1->x - V2->x;
  D.y = V1->y - V2->y;
  D.z = V1->z - V2->z;
  return D;
}
```

As you look at the vector subtraction example in Figure A.1, notice that the vectors must be oriented with respect to each other, as shown. The **Add** function is similar, except that it adds the fields of two vectors. The **Divide** function is also straightforward: It divides each of a vector's components by a single value. The result is a second, shorter vector if the divisor is greater than 1.

The **Dot** and **Cross** functions are a bit less intuitive. The **Dot** routine calculates the dot product of two vectors. It multiplies and adds together each of the components of two vectors. For instance, if there are two vectors **V1** and **V2**, the dot product can be calculated as:

```
D = V1.x * V2.x + V1.y * V2.y + V1.z * V2.z;
```

The result of a dot product is a scalar value—a single number. A dot product of two normalized vectors with the same location is particularly useful because it yields the cosine of the angle between the two vectors. You'll see the ray tracing code exploit this fact time and time again in this book.

As its name implies, the **Cross** function computes the cross product of two vectors. Like a dot product, it multiplies the components of two vectors together, however, in a more complicated fashion. Here's the complete **Cross** function:

```
VECTOR Cross(VECTOR *V1, VECTOR *V2)
{
  VECTOR C;

  C.x = V1->y * V2->z - V2->y * V1->z;
  C.y = V1->z * V2->x - V2->z * V1->x;
  C.z = V1->x * V2->y - V2->x * V1->y;
  return C;
}
```

As you can see, the cross product returns a vector. In particular, the calculated vector is perpendicular to the plane that contains the other two vectors. You can determine the direction of the normal using the right-hand rule. Imagine your right hand's index finger aligning to **V1**, and your other fingers sweeping toward **V2**. Your thumb will point in the direction of the normal. The cross product, therefore, is particularly useful at calculating a normal vector. Again, the cross product is a common graphics operation.

• VECTOR.H

```
// VECTOR.H: Header file for VECTOR.C.

#ifndef VECTORH
#define VECTORH

typedef struct {
  float x, y, z;
} VECTOR;

// Functions included in VECTOR.C:
float Mag(VECTOR *V);
VECTOR Subtract(VECTOR *V1, VECTOR *V2);
```

```
VECTOR Add(VECTOR *V1, VECTOR *V2);
VECTOR Cross(VECTOR *V1, VECTOR *V2);
VECTOR Divide(VECTOR *V, float Num);
void Normalize(VECTOR *V);
float Dot(VECTOR *V1, VECTOR *V2);
#endif
```

• VECTOR.C

```
// VECTOR.C: A collection of vector operations.

#include <math.h>
#include <stdlib.h>
#include "vector.h"


/////////////////////////// Mag \\\\\\\\\\\\\\\\\\\\\\\\\\\\
//
// Calculates the magnitude of the vector V
//
float Mag(VECTOR *V)
{
  return sqrt(V->x * V->x + V->y * V->y + V->z * V->z);
}


/////////////////////////// Subtract \\\\\\\\\\\\\\\\\\\\\\\\\\\\
//
// Subtracts the two vectors V1 and V2
//
VECTOR Subtract(VECTOR *V1, VECTOR *V2)
{
  VECTOR D;

  D.x = V1->x - V2->x;
  D.y = V1->y - V2->y;
  D.z = V1->z - V2->z;
  return D;
}


/////////////////////////// Add \\\\\\\\\\\\\\\\\\\\\\\\\\\\
//
// Adds the two vectors V1 and V2
//
VECTOR Add(VECTOR *V1, VECTOR *V2)
{
  VECTOR D;

  D.x = V1->x + V2->x;
  D.y = V1->y + V2->y;
  D.z = V1->z + V2->z;
```

```
    return D;
}


//////////////////////////// Cross  \\\\\\\\\\\\\\\\\\\\\\\\\\\\
//
// Calculates the cross product of the two vectors V1 and V2
//
VECTOR Cross(VECTOR *V1, VECTOR *V2)
{
  VECTOR C;

  C.x = V1->y * V2->z - V2->y * V1->z;
  C.y = V1->z * V2->x - V2->z * V1->x;
  C.z = V1->x * V2->y - V2->x * V1->y;
  return C;
}


//////////////////////////// Divide  \\\\\\\\\\\\\\\\\\\\\\\\\\\\
//
// Divides the scalar number (Num) into the vector V
//
VECTOR Divide(VECTOR *V, float Num)
{
  VECTOR Result;

  if (Num != 0) {
    Result.x = V->x / Num;
    Result.y = V->y / Num;
    Result.z = V->z / Num;
  }
  return Result;
}


//////////////////////////// Normalize  \\\\\\\\\\\\\\\\\\\\\\\\\\\\
//
// Normalizes the vector V
//
void Normalize(VECTOR *V)
{
  float D = sqrt(V->x * V->x + V->y * V->y + V->z * V->z);
  if (D != 0) {
    V->x = V->x / D;
    V->y = V->y / D;
    V->z = V->z / D;
  }
}
```

```
/////////////////////////// Dot \\\\\\\\\\\\\\\\\\\\\\\\\\\\
//
// Calculates the dot product of the two vectors V1 and V2
//
float Dot(VECTOR *V1, VECTOR *V2)
{
  return V1->x * V2->x + V1->y * V2->y + V1->z * V2->z;
}
```

A Graphics Toolkit

T he GRPHICS.C toolkit, listed at the end of this appendix, provides all the graphics primitives that the programs in this book require. The GRPHICS.C package provides functions to set the video mode, paint a pixel, and control the colors that are displayed. For the greatest flexibility, the toolkit is also designed so you can use it with both DOS and Windows. We'll focus on the DOS-specific code here and wait until Appendix C to discuss how it supports Windows.

SETTING THE MODE

One of the first things any graphics program must do is set the display mode. The **SetupDisplay** function in GRPHICS.C provides this service. **SetupDisplay** takes a single parameter that corresponds to one of the constants provided in GRPHICS.H and listed in Table B.1.

For instance, on a standard VGA card you can switch to the 320x200, 256-color mode using the statement:

```
SetupDisplay(M320x200x256);
```

Table B.1 The modes supported by GRPHICS.C.

Constant	Value	Description
M320x200x256	1	320x200x256 color mode
M640x480x256	2	640x480x256 color mode
M640x480x32K	3	640x480 32K color mode
M800x600x32K	4	800x600 32K color mode

You'll need a Super VGA to support the other display modes. Further, the 32K-color modes are written for graphics adapters based on the Tseng Labs chipset, and are equipped with a Sierra Hicolor DAC.

In addition to specifying the display resolution, you can configure your system to display grayscale or color pixels by ORing the **COLORPALETTE** or **GRAYSCALEPALETTE** constant with **SetupDisplay**'s parameter. By default, the GRPHICS toolkit displays images exclusively with grayscale pixels. To select a range of colors, you could use:

```
SetupDisplay(M320x200x256 | COLORPALETTE);
```

The **SetupDisplay** function sets the video mode using BIOS interrupt 0x10 (hexadecimal). **SetupDisplay**'s parameter selects the mode that is passed to the interrupt. The modes available are listed in the **Modes** array, which is also defined in GRPHICS.C. Realize that **SetupDisplay** does not try to verify that the requested mode is supported by your hardware.

You can also use **SetupDisplay** to return to text mode by passing it the constant **MTEXT**. Alternatively, you can use the **EndDisplay** function, which waits for a key press and then exits graphics mode.

SETTING A PIXEL

The **PutPixel** routine in GRPHICS.C displays a single pixel on the screen. The last three of the function's six parameters specify the red, green, and blue components of the color to display. The actual color that is displayed, however, depends on the capabilities of your graphics adapter and the color mode you've specified in **SetupDisplay**. The second and third parameters specify the column and row of the pixel. The top left of the screen is the pixel (0,0). **PutPixel**'s remaining parameter is an integer value that is ignored in DOS; however, in Windows it's used to specify the display context. Appendix C describes this further. The following statement, for example, sets the pixel at column 20 and row 10 to red:

```
PutPixel(0, 19, 9, 255, 0, 0);
```

PutPixel writes directly to the video memory, which begins at A000:0000 for each of the supported modes. Fortunately, all these modes organize memory linearly. That is, the top left of the screen corresponds to the address A000:0000 and the bottom right of the screen is the largest address supported in the video mode.

The 320x200 mode has the simplest organization to follow. Each pixel corresponds to one byte in video memory. Therefore, the top left of the screen corresponds to the address A000:0000 and the bottom right to A000:FFFF. Notice that the full screen fits into one segment. Writing to the screen is accomplished by assigning a value to the desired memory location. The following statements, for instance, would set the top-left pixel on the screen to white:

```
unsigned char far* Screen = (unsigned char far *)0xA0000000L;
*Screen = 255;
```

The other modes are slightly more complicated because they stretch across several segments. Therefore, before the code can write the desired pixel value to the screen's memory, it must select the proper memory bank by setting a segment register on the graphics adapter. This is accomplished by writing the upper bits of the pixel address to the port 0x3CD:

```
WriteSeg = Pixel / 65536L;   // There are 64K pixels/segment
outp(0x3CD, WriteSeg);       // Set the segment register
```

The 32K color modes add another twist. In these modes, each pixel consumes two bytes of memory. Notice that the code uses an integer pointer in the video memory to compensate for the two-byte memory arrangement. Actually, only the lower 15 bits of each two bytes are used to specify the color. Five bits each are used for the red, green, and blue color components. In contrast, the 256-color modes use 6 bits per color.

WORKING WITH COLORS

Some modes, such as the 256 color modes, can simultaneously display only a small portion of the colors that they are able to generate. In these modes, the graphics adapter uses a palette of colors to list those that are currently available. Fortunately, the palette is programmable.

By default, the GRPHICS toolkit sets the palette to a list of grayscale colors. Actually, it only sets the palette entries 64 through 127 to shades of gray. The 64 gray levels are produced by defining equal intensities of red, green, and blue that vary from 0 to 63. Only 64 shades of gray are possible because 6 bits of resolution are only available in 256-color modes. Here's the code that creates the grayscale palette:

```
(void)outp(WRITE_PIXEL, 64); // Start writing at palette index 64
for (i=0; i<64; i++) {
  (void)outp(WRITE_PIXEL+1, i);
  (void)outp(WRITE_PIXEL+1, i);
  (void)outp(WRITE_PIXEL+1, i);
}
```

Later, when you paint a pixel using **PutPixel**, the color is mapped to the grayscale values listed in the palette. The grayscale palette is useful when you don't know the range of colors you need to display.

GRPHICS.C manages color palettes in a completely different manner. Instead of spelling out all the colors available and then allowing your code to use them, the palette is built as you make calls to **PutPixel**. In other words, initially the color palette is empty. Then as you make calls to **PutPixel**, each new color is added to the palette. The function **SetPaletteColor** determines whether the pixel color is already in the palette. If it isn't, the function adds it in. If the palette is full, however, the closest matching color is used instead. Building a palette on the fly like this is not really that efficient, but it does allow our ray tracer to effortlessly display an image as the program is rendering it.

Realize that 32K and 24-bit color modes don't use palettes. The colors are specified directly using the red, green, and blue components passed to **PutPixel**. You'll have to step up to Windows, however, if you want to use a 24-bit graphics mode, since GRPHICS.C doesn't support them.

SUPPORTING C AND C++ COMPILERS

Besides providing a set of graphics primitives, the GRPHICS.C toolkit also includes a handful of statements that compensate for some of the differences between Microsoft and Borland compilers. For instance, Borland uses a header file named ALLOC.H, while Microsoft's comparable file is called MALLOC.H. GRPHICS.C uses the **__TURBOC__** compilation constant, defined by Borland's compilers, to select the proper code.

If you need to modify the programs in this book to work with another compiler, you may want to restrict your changes to GRPHICS.H, so you don't have to make numerous changes throughout the code.

• GRPHICS.H

```
// GRPHICS.H: This header file provides support for DOS and
// Windows graphics programs.
#ifndef GRPHICSH
#define GRPHICSH

// Set up the header files based on whether the program is being
// compiled as a DOS or Windows application and the compiler used
#if defined(FORWINDOWS)   // For Windows applications:
#include <windows.h>
#else                     // For DOS applications:
#include <conio.h>        // Used by some applications
#endif
#include <stdlib.h>
#ifdef __TURBOC__
#include <alloc.h>        // Include for farmalloc
#else                     // Assume Microsoft C
#include <malloc.h>
```

```
#include <time.h>
time_t _grphicstime;
#define randomize() srand((unsigned)time(&_grphicstime));
#define farmalloc(bytes) halloc(bytes,1)
#define farfree hfree
#endif
// Define a series of macros that define some of
// the functions used in Windows and DOS
#if defined(FORWINDOWS)   // For Windows applications:
#define DECLARE_HDC ;     // Generate a null statement
#else                     // For DOS applications:

#define MTEXT             0        // Text mode
#define M320x200x256      1        // 320x200x256-color mode
#define M640x480x256      2        // 640x480x256-color mode
#define M640x480x32K      3        // 640x480 32K-color mode
#define M800x600x32K      4        // 800x600 32K-color mode
#define COLORPALETTE      0x80     // Use a color palette
#define GRAYSCALEPALETTE 0x00 // Use gray scale palette
                                   // (VGA default)
extern int ScrnMode;               // Video mode

unsigned int SetPaletteColor(unsigned char Red,
  unsigned char Green, unsigned char Blue);
void SetVGAPalette(unsigned char Red, unsigned char Green,
  unsigned char Blue);
void SetVGA64Palette(void);
#endif

extern int ImWd, ImHt;    // Resolution of output image
extern float AspectRatio; // Aspect ratio of the screen; Y/X
// The following are used by both DOS and Windows applications
void GenImage(int hDC);
int SetupDisplay(int Mode);
void EndDisplay(void);
void PutPixel(int HDC, int X, int Y, unsigned char Red,
  unsigned char Green, unsigned char Blue);
void Setup(char far *Str);// The application must define these
void Cleanup(void);       // two functions

#endif
```

• GRPHICS.C

```
// GRPHICS.C: Various functions used to support DOS and Windows
// graphics programs.
#if !defined(FORWINDOWS)
#include <dos.h>
```

```c
#include <stdlib.h>
#endif
#include "grphics.h"

int ScrnMode;                   // The current screen mode
int ScrnWd, ScrnHt;             // The current screen's width and height
unsigned int MaxColor;          // Maximum color index available
unsigned int ScrnSeg=0;         // Current video segment
unsigned char UseColorPalette;  // Nonzero if palette holds colors
int NextPaletteNdx;             // Next free location in color palette
float AspectRatio = 1.0;        // Aspect ratio of screen
struct MODE {           // Contains information about a video mode
  int ModeVal;          // Mode register value
  int Wd;               // Width of mode
  int Ht;               // Height of mode
  float AspectRatio;    // Aspect ratio of mode
};
struct MODE Modes[5] = {
  {0x03, 0,   0,   1},    // Text mode, 80x25 color
  {0x13, 320, 200, 1.33}, // 320x200x256; 256 colors
  {0x2E, 640, 480, 1},    // 640x480x256
  {0x2E, 640, 480, 1},    // Tseng 640x480 32K colors
  {0x30, 800, 600, 1.1}   // Tseng 800x600 32k colors
};
#if !defined(FORWINDOWS)
// A logical palette that is used to add palette entries when
// true 256-color images are displayed
struct PALETTECOLOR {           // A palette entry has red, green,
  unsigned r, g, b;             // and blue components
};
struct PALETTECOLOR LogPalette[256];  // A logical color palette
#endif

/////////////////////////// SetupDisplay \\\\\\\\\\\\\\\\\\\\\\\\\
//
// In a DOS application, initialize the graphics system
//
int SetupDisplay(int Mode)
{
#if !defined(FORWINDOWS)
  union REGS Regs;

  ScrnMode = Mode & 0x7F;
  ScrnWd = Modes[ScrnMode].Wd;
  ScrnHt = Modes[ScrnMode].Ht;
  ScrnSeg = 0;   UseColorPalette = 0;   NextPaletteNdx = 0;
  switch(ScrnMode) {
    case MTEXT:
    case M320x200x256:
```

```
    case M640x480x256:
      Regs.x.ax = Modes[ScrnMode].ModeVal; // AH = 0x00 AL = mode
      int86(0x10, &Regs, &Regs);
      MaxColor = (ScrnMode == MTEXT) ? 0 : 255;
      if (Mode & COLORPALETTE) {
        UseColorPalette = 1;
        SetVGAPalette(0, 0, 0);    // Set the background color black
      }
      else if (Mode & MTEXT) return;
      else                       // Use a gray scale palette
        SetVGA64Palette(); // Create gray scale palette
      break;
    case M640x480x32K:
    case M800x600x32K:
      // Set AX to 0x10F0 to select the Hicolor mode
      Regs.x.ax = 0x10F0;   // AH = 0x10  AL = 0xF0
      Regs.x.bx = Modes[ScrnMode].ModeVal;
      int86(0x10, &Regs, &Regs);
      MaxColor = 32767;     // 32K modes don't have a palette
      break;
    default:
      return 0;             // Return failure flag
  }
  AspectRatio = Modes[ScrnMode].AspectRatio;
#endif     // Don't do anything if compiling for Windows
  return 1;
}


/////////////////////////// EndDisplay \\\\\\\\\\\\\\\\\\\\\\\\\
//
// In a DOS application, wait for a keypress and then exit
// graphics mode
//
void EndDisplay(void)
{
#if defined(FORWINDOWS)
#else
  getch();                // Wait for a keypress
  SetupDisplay(MTEXT);    // Set the display to color text mode
#endif
}


/////////////////////////// PutPixel \\\\\\\\\\\\\\\\\\\\\\\\\\\
//
// Writes a pixel to the screen. Supports 32K-color mode for
// Tseng Labs ET-4000 chipset equipped with a Sierra Hicolor DAC.
//
void PutPixel(int hDC, int X, int Y, unsigned char Red,
  unsigned char Green, unsigned char Blue)
```

```
  {
#if defined(FORWINDOWS)
  SetPixel(hDC, X, Y, PALETTERGB(Red,Green,Blue));
#else
  unsigned long Pixel;
  unsigned char WriteSeg;
  unsigned int far *ScreenPtr;
  unsigned char far *VGAScreenPtr;
  unsigned int Color;

  if (MaxColor == 255) {
    // Convert RGB value to a black and white value. The 12 comes from
    // the fact that we are taking the average of three values
    // and only six bits of each color component are used. Thus,
    // they are also divided by four.
    if (UseColorPalette)   // Add color to palette if there is room
      Color = SetPaletteColor(Red, Green, Blue);
    else    // Use a grayscale value
      Color = (Red + Green + Blue) / 12 + 64;
    Pixel = X + (long)Y * ScrnWd;
    if (ScrnMode == M640x480x256) {
      WriteSeg = Pixel / 65536L;  // There are 64K pixels/segment
      outp(0x3CD, WriteSeg);     // Set the segment register
    }
    FP_SEG(VGAScreenPtr) = 0XA000;
    FP_OFF(VGAScreenPtr) = (unsigned int)(Pixel & 0xFFFF);
    *VGAScreenPtr = Color;        // Set the pixel's color
  }
  else {                        // 32K colors
    Color = ((Red/8 & 31)<<10) | ((Green/8 & 31)<<5) | (Blue/8 & 31);
    // Compute the pixel location in memory. Note: There are
    // two bytes per pixel.
    Pixel = (X + Y * (unsigned long)ScrnWd) * 2;
    // Determine which 64k segment the pixel is in
    WriteSeg = Pixel / 65536L;
    if (WriteSeg != ScrnSeg) {
      outp(0x3CD, WriteSeg);         // Set the segment register
      ScrnSeg = WriteSeg;            // Remember the segment
    }
    FP_SEG(ScreenPtr) = 0XA000;
    FP_OFF(ScreenPtr) = (unsigned int)(Pixel & 0xFFFF);
    *ScreenPtr = Color;         // Set the pixel's color
  }
#endif
}


#if !defined(FORWINDOWS)
```

```
//////////////////////// SetVGA64Palette \\\\\\\\\\\\\\\\\\\\\\\\
//
// Sets the DAC registers of the VGA 320x200 mode directly.
// 64 gray levels starting at palette location 64 are set to
// various shades of gray. These are the colors used to display
// an image. None of the other palette locations are affected.
//
#define  WRITE_PIXEL  0x3c8    // Write pixel address reg on VGA

void SetVGA64Palette(void)
{
  int i;

 (void)outp(WRITE_PIXEL, 64); // Start writing at palette index 64
  for (i=0; i<64; i++) {
    (void)outp(WRITE_PIXEL+1, i);
    (void)outp(WRITE_PIXEL+1, i);
    (void)outp(WRITE_PIXEL+1, i);
  }
}


//////////////////////// SetVGAPalette \\\\\\\\\\\\\\\\\\\\\\\\
//
// Sets one of the colors in the physical and logical palettes
//
void SetVGAPalette(unsigned char Red, unsigned char Green,
  unsigned char Blue)
{
  (void)outp(WRITE_PIXEL, NextPaletteNdx);
  (void)outp(WRITE_PIXEL+1, Red/4);
  (void)outp(WRITE_PIXEL+1, Green/4);
  (void)outp(WRITE_PIXEL+1, Blue/4);
  LogPalette[NextPaletteNdx].r = Red;
  LogPalette[NextPaletteNdx].g = Green;
  LogPalette[NextPaletteNdx].b = Blue;
  NextPaletteNdx++;
}


//////////////////////// SetPaletteColor \\\\\\\\\\\\\\\\\\\\\\\\
//
// If the color does not already exist in the palette, then
// add it in if there is room. If there isn't any more
// room in the palette, then use the closest matching color.
//
unsigned int SetPaletteColor(unsigned char Red,
  unsigned char Green, unsigned char Blue)
{
  int i, MinNdx;
```

```
unsigned long MinDist, Dist;
unsigned int DistR, DistG, DistB;

// See if the color is already in the logical palette
for (i=0; i<NextPaletteNdx; i++)
  // If it is, use its palette color
  if (LogPalette[i].r == Red && LogPalette[i].g == Green &&
    LogPalette[i].b == Blue)
    return i;
// The color isn't in the palette. Is there room to add it?
if (NextPaletteNdx >= 256) {
  i = 0;                    // If there isn't room for a
  MinNdx = 0;               // new color, use the closest
  MinDist = 0xffff;         // matching color
  for (i=0; i<256; i++) {
    DistR = abs(LogPalette[i].r - Red);
    DistG = abs(LogPalette[i].g - Green);
    DistB = abs(LogPalette[i].b - Blue);
    Dist = (DistR + DistG + DistB) / 3;
    if (MinDist > Dist) {
      MinDist = Dist;
      MinNdx = i;
    }
  }
  return MinNdx;
}
else {
  SetVGAPalette(Red, Green, Blue);
  // Return the index of the color just added to the palette
  return NextPaletteNdx-1;
}
}
#endif
```

Working with Windows

Many of the programs in this book are designed to support both DOS and Windows. The advantages of Windows are that you don't have to worry about low-level graphics support and you have access to more than 640K of your computer's memory. The WINSHELL.C file, listed at the end of this appendix, enables your programs to run under Windows. WINSHELL acts as a bridge between your application and Windows by creating and managing a window that your application can draw in. Your code is responsible for generating and painting inside the window. This appendix describes WINSHELL's internals, and explains how you can use the Windows shell with the programs in this book or your own custom applications.

OVERVIEW OF **WINSHELL**

WINSHELL is a miniature Windows program that pops up a single window and calls your code to display an image in it. The shell provides only two functions: **WinMain** and **ShellWndProc**. The **WinMain** function acts as the **main** function for the Windows program. It creates the window and sets up a message loop to capture the window's messages. The windows' messages are processed within WINSHELL's **ShellWndProc** routine. Specifically, **ShellWndProc** traps for three messages: **WM_CREATE**, **WM_DESTROY**, and **WM_PAINT**. The **WM_CREATE** message occurs just before the window is created, **WM_PAINT** signals the code to paint the interior of the window, and **WM_DESTROY** occurs just before the window is closed. WINSHELL does not draw anything in the window; this is the responsibility of your code.

Using WINSHELL

An application that uses WINSHELL must supply three routines: **Setup**, **GenImage**, and **Cleanup**. The **Setup** routine should perform any initialization that your application requires, **GenImage** should display an image in the window, and **Cleanup** should perform any last-minute actions. In addition, you should remove your code's **main** function since WINSHELL provides one compatible with Windows. You can selectively accomplish this by placing the following two lines around your **main** function:

```
#if defined(FORWINDOWS)
#endif
```

Then when you define the **FORWINDOWS** constant, the **main** function will not be compiled. The **WinMain** routine creates the window that is displayed and calls the **Setup** function.

Preparing for Windows

The **Setup** function performs all the initialization that your program requires, such as opening files, allocating memory, and so on. However, minimally **Setup** should set the two integer variables **ImWd** and **ImHt** to the desired pixel width and height of the window. For instance, if you want to render a 200x200 image, **ImWd** and **ImHt** should be set to 200. Your application is also responsible for defining the two integer variables **ImWd** and **ImHt**.

The **Setup** function accepts a single string parameter. This parameter points to the command-line argument passed to the application when it is launched. The RAY and MORPH programs, for instance, use this argument to specify a file the programs use to read any options.

Displaying an Image

Your application is responsible for painting inside the window that WINSHELL creates. You should place this code in a function called **GenImage**. WINSHELL will call **GenImage** one time to display an image in the window. You should call **PutPixel** in GRPHICS.C to paint the pixels in the window. The sole parameter to **GenImage** is a handle to the screen's device context. It should be passed to the **PutPixel** function provided in GRPHICS.C.

A major portion of the **WM_PAINT** code creates and maintains a bitmap copy of the window. The bitmap is useful when the window must be repainted. The bitmap is used to repaint the window rather than calling **GenImage** again. For a time-consuming ray tracing application, this function is more than a convenience; it's a necessity.

The bitmap is created within the **WM_PAINT** code the first time it is executed and is freed when the **WM_DESTROY** message is encountered. An important assumption of the code is that the image is no larger than the dimensions of the window.

Working with Colors

Colors are passed to the **PutPixel** function as 24-bit triples. Of course, not all graphics adapters can display 24-bit images. Fortunately, Windows takes care of this for us, since GRPHICS.C uses the **PALETTERGB** macro when specifying colors of a pixel. You'll find a call to it in the **SetPixel** routine within **PutPixel**.

The **PALETTERGB** macro displays the specified color in 24-bit or 32K modes. In a 256-color mode, **PALETTERGB** uses one of the colors in a palette that WINSHELL creates. This logical palette supplies your program with 64 shades of gray. Windows ignores the logical palette in 32K and 24-bit color modes, since these modes don't use palettes.

The logical palette is created when the **WM_CREATE** message is encountered, which occurs as the window is displayed. Similarly, when the window is removed from the screen, your application encounters the **WM_DESTROY** message, and the memory associated with the palette is freed.

COMPILING FOR WINDOWS

To compile your programs for Windows, you must have a Windows-capable compiler such as Borland C++. In addition, you must define the compiler macro **FORWINDOWS** and compile and link your application with WINSHELL.C and GRPHICS.C using a large memory model. You may also need to provide a Windows definition file when you link your program; although with some compilers, such as Borland C++, you do not have to do so.

• WINSHELL.C

```
// WINSHELL.C: A Windows shell for ray tracing and image display.
// Link with your graphics application so that it can run
// under Windows. Your program must supply the three functions:
// Setup(), GenImage(), and Cleanup(). Make sure to define the
// macro constant FORWINDOWS when compiling your application.
#include <windows.h>
#include <string.h>
#include "grphics.h"

char far CommandLine[80];
long FAR PASCAL ShellWndProc(HWND, UINT, WPARAM, LPARAM);
```

```
//////////////////////////// WinMain \\\\\\\\\\\\\\\\\\\\\\\\\\
//
// The main function for the Windows application
///
int PASCAL WinMain(HANDLE hInstance, HANDLE hPrevInstance,
 LPSTR lpszCmdLine, int cmdShow)
{
  HWND hWnd;
  MSG Msg;
  WNDCLASS WndClass;

  // The Setup function, supplied by your application, performs
  // any initialization that may be required. Its parameter is
  // the command-line string passsed to the program.
  Setup(lpszCmdLine);
  if (!hPrevInstance) {
    WndClass.lpszClassName = "SHELL:MAIN";
    WndClass.hInstance = hInstance;
    WndClass.lpfnWndProc = ShellWndProc;
    WndClass.hIcon = LoadIcon(NULL, IDI_APPLICATION);
    WndClass.hCursor = LoadCursor(NULL, IDC_ARROW);
    WndClass.hbrBackground = GetStockObject(BLACK_BRUSH);
    WndClass.lpszMenuName = NULL;
    WndClass.style = CS_HREDRAW | CS_VREDRAW;
    WndClass.cbClsExtra = 0;
    WndClass.cbWndExtra = 0;
    RegisterClass(&WndClass);
  }
  hWnd = CreateWindow("SHELL:MAIN", "", WS_OVERLAPPEDWINDOW,
    CW_USEDEFAULT, 0, ImWd, ImHt, NULL, NULL, hInstance, NULL);
  ShowWindow(hWnd, cmdShow);
  while (GetMessage(&Msg, 0, 0, 0)) {
    TranslateMessage(&Msg);
    DispatchMessage(&Msg);
  }
  return 0;
}


//////////////////////////// ShellWndProc \\\\\\\\\\\\\\\\\\\\\\\
//
// Handles the messages for the window
//
long FAR PASCAL ShellWndProc(HWND hWnd, UINT Msg, WPARAM wParam,
  LPARAM lParam)
{
  int NumColors, i;
  static LPLOGPALETTE LogPal;    // The logical palette
  static HPALETTE hLogPal;       // A handle to the logical palette
```

```
    PAINTSTRUCT ps;              // A paint structure
    RECT rect;                   // A rectangle
    HDC hDC;                     // Handle to the screen's context
    HCURSOR hOldCursor;          // Handle to the current cursor
    static HDC MemDC;            // Memory device context
    static HBITMAP hBitmap;      // Handle to a bitmap
    static BOOL First = TRUE;    // TRUE for the first WM_PAINT message

switch(Msg) {
  case WM_CREATE:   // Called when the window is created
    // Create a logical palette that contains 64 shades of gray
    // for 256-color modes. The palette is ignored by 32K and
    // 24-bit color modes.
    NumColors = 64;
    LogPal = (LPLOGPALETTE)farmalloc(sizeof(LOGPALETTE) +
      sizeof(PALETTEENTRY) * (NumColors-1));
    LogPal->palVersion = 0x300;
    LogPal->palNumEntries = NumColors;
    for (i=0; i<64; i++) {
      LogPal->palPalEntry[i].peRed = i*4;     // Define 64
      LogPal->palPalEntry[i].peGreen = i*4;   // shades of
      LogPal->palPalEntry[i].peBlue = i*4;    // gray
      LogPal->palPalEntry[i].peFlags = 0;
    }
    hLogPal = CreatePalette(LogPal);
    break;
  case WM_DESTROY:            // Called when the window is removed
    farfree(LogPal);
    DeleteObject(hLogPal);  // Free the logical palette
    DeleteObject(hBitmap);  // Free the bitmap
    Cleanup();  // Supplied by your application to perform cleanup
    PostQuitMessage(0);     // Post a quit message
    break;
  case WM_PAINT:     // Paints the interior of the window
    // Paints the scene to the screen and then copies it to a
    // bitmap so the window can be rapidly refreshed
    hDC = BeginPaint(hWnd, &ps);       // Initiate the window update
    GetClientRect(hWnd, &rect);        // Get the window's dimensions
    SelectPalette(hDC, hLogPal, 0);    // Use the logical palette's
    RealizePalette(hDC);               // colors, if it is supported
    MemDC = CreateCompatibleDC(hDC); // Create a memory device context
    if (First) {
      // The first time through, call your application's GenImage
      // function to generate and display the image. Then copy
      // the image to a bitmap so that if the window must be
      // repainted, the bitmap can be used to update the screen.
      hBitmap = CreateCompatibleBitmap(hDC, ImWd, ImHt);
      SelectObject(MemDC, hBitmap);
```

```
            SelectPalette(MemDC, hLogPal, 0);   // Use the logical
            RealizePalette(MemDC);                 // palette in the bitmap
            // Initialize the bitmap to black
            PatBlt(MemDC, 0, 0, ImWd, ImHt, BLACKNESS);
            // Switch to the hourglass cursor
            hOldCursor = SetCursor(LoadCursor(NULL, IDC_WAIT));
            // GenImage is supplied by your application to display
            GenImage(hDC);            // the image in the window
            // Copy the screen to the bitmap
            BitBlt(MemDC, 0, 0, ImWd, ImHt, hDC, 0, 0, SRCCOPY);
            SetCursor(hOldCursor); // Restore the cursor
            First = FALSE;           // Don't call GenImage a second time
          }
        else {                    // Display the bitmap in the window
          SelectObject(MemDC, hBitmap);
          BitBlt(hDC, 0, 0, ImWd, ImHt, MemDC, 0, 0, SRCCOPY);
          }
        DeleteDC(MemDC);          // Free the memory device context
        EndPaint(hWnd, &ps);  // End of the painting
        break;
      default:                    // Pass other messages on
        return DefWindowProc(hWnd, Msg, wParam, lParam);
    }
    return 0L;
}
```

Index

24-bit true color, 43, 388
256-color mode, 42–43, 385, 387
32,768 colors, 42, 387, 388

A

A1 vector, 11–12, 15
A2 vector, 11–12, 15
A3 vector, 11–12, 15
AddFog function, 78–79
AddLight function, 80, 131
AddObject function, 72, 140
Ambient keyword, 142
Ambient light, 25–26
    calculating, 26, 32
    definition of, 26
    setting, 142
    values of, 26
Animate array, 201
ANIMATEAT constant, 201, 204
ANIMATEFROM constant, 201, 203
ANIMATEOBJLOC constant, 201, 204
ANIMATE structure, 201
Animation
    defining, 204–205
    file names and, 206
    language support, 204–206
    maximum objects, 201
    number of frames, 205
    number of objects, 201
    playing back, 207
    steps of, 200–203
    supporting, 200–204
    types of, 201
    updating objects, 203–204
    viewer position, 205
Antialiasing, 81–83
Antialiasing keyword, 141
AppendFrameNumber function, 206
AspectRatio function, 13–14
At keyword, 141
At point
    definition of, 3–4
    setting, 12
Average function, 336

B

Background color, 141
Background keyword, 141
Background variable, 46
BALLS.SDF, 207–209
Base vector, 11
BeginGroup keyword, 139
Bitmap image, 396–397
Blended colors, 187–189
Blend keyword, 188
Blue color component, 6
Bounding boxes
    dimensions of, 85
    hierarchy of objects, 85
    intersecting with a ray, 85
    reasons for using, 83
    supporting, 84, 86–87
BoundingBoxObj class, 84
BrightenIm function, 335–336
Brightness adjustment, 335–336
Bump mapping, 218

C

C language, 55, 59, 388
C++ language
  compiling with, 388
  converting to C, 59
  using, 55–56
Camera model, 2–3
CenterV variable, 13
Checker keyword, 182
Checker pattern, 176–177
  color of, 183
  defining, 182–183
  mapping, 177
  repeating, 176
Cleanup function, 10
  description of, 10, 396
  RAY's, 72
  using, 10
Cloud keyword, 227
Clouds
  creating, 233, 236
  ellipsoids and, 233
  texture function, 226
  three-dimensional model, 231–233
  transparency, 231–232
  two-dimensional model, 225–228
  types of, 225
CLOUDS.SDF, 227
CLOUDS1.SDF, 233
Color components, 6
Colorize, 340–341
Color keyword, 142
Color palette, 386
COLORPALETTE constant, 10, 43, 386
Colors
  determining, 2, 31
  specifying, 6, 40
ColorToGray function, 340
COLOR typedef, 6, 46
Compression, 274–275
ComputeLight function, 9, 32–35
  calling, 39
  description of, 32

  parameters of, 32
  return value, 40
  source code, 51–53
ComputeNormal function
  CylinderObj's, 71
  description of, 58
  EllipsoidObj's, 69
  RectangleObj's, 63
  TriangleObj's, 67
ComputeT function, 58
ComputeTForPlane function, 9, 19, 49
ComputeTForSphere function, 9, 20–22, 49–50
Cone keyword, 142
ConeLight class
  angle of, 76
  definition, 74, 129
Cone light source
  angle of, 76
  default angle, 77
  description of, 73
  direction, 75
  setting, 142
Contouring, 42
ContrastEnhance function, 334–335
Contrast enhancement, 334–335
CosAlpha variable, 35
CurrStep variable, 201, 204
Cycloid functions, 216
Cylinder, *See also* CylinderObj class
  equation of, 70
  mapping to, 181–182
Cylinder keyword, 142
CylinderObj class
  definition of, 69–70
  description of, 69
  dimensions of, 70
  normal, 71–72

D

Derived object types, 57–58
DetermineNormal function, 24, 38, 50–51

DeterminePattern function
  calling, 174
  colors used, 174, 176
  purpose of, 59
  setting, 174
  using, 174
Diffuse keyword, 142
Diffuse light, 25–26
  calculating, 27, 32–34
  definition of, 26
  values of, 27
Directed keyword, 142
DirectedLight class
  definition of, 75, 129
  description of, 75
Directed light source
  description of, 73
  direction of, 75
  power of, 76
  setting, 142
Direction variable, 75–76
Direction vector, 11
DirectPow variable, 75–76
Dir keyword, 142
DMax variable, 78
DMin variable, 78
DOS
  compiling for, 40–41
  setting the graphics mode, 42–43
  versus Windows, 43
DSRT1.ODF, 251
DSRTMTN.SDF, 251–252

E

Ellipsoid, *See also* EllipsoidObj class
  equation of an, 68
  mapping to, 180–181
  normal of, 69
Ellipsoid keyword, 142
EllipsoidObj class
  description of, 68
  definition of, 68

intersecting a ray with, 69
  normal, 69
EndDisplay function, 10, 386
EndGroup keyword, 139
Eye coordinates, 11–12

F

FindClosestIntersection function, 9,
    22–23, 38, 50
Floating point calculations, 45
Fog
  color of, 79
  implementation, 78–79
  model of, 78
FogMin variable, 78
FogMax variable, 79
FORWINDOWS constant, 41, 45,
    396–397
Fourier series, 225
Fractals, 237–246
  randomness, 245–246
  three-dimensional, 238–239
  two-dimesional, 238
Frame grabber, 331
FrameNum variable, 203
FreeObjects function, 72–73
From keyword, 141
From point
  definition of, 2–4
  location of, 11–12
  setting, 12
  using, 11

G

Gamma correction, 341–342
GenImage function,
  RAY's, 92
  SIMPLRAY's, 9–10, 48
  using, 10, 396
GENMTN.C, 247–249, 257–265
GENSWEEP.C, 146, 167–171
GetMaxGradient function, 244

GetToken function, 136–137
Glass
    sample, 146–147
    wavy, 222–224
GLASS.ODF, 149
GLASS.SDF, 146–147
Graphics
    using a color palette, 10, 386–387
    using a grayscale palette, 10, 387
    setting the mode, 10, 42–43,
        385–386
    Windows and, 43
Graphics adapters, 42
    colors of, 42–43, 387
    resolutions of, 42
Gray levels, 42, 387
GRAYSCALEPALETTE constant, 43, 386
Green color component, 6
Grouping objects
    bounding boxes, 85–87
    scene description language, 139–140
GroupList variable, 140
Group variable, 58, 85
GRPHICS.C, 16, 389–394
GRPHICS.H, 388–389

H

hDC variable, 40
Highlights, 25
Histogram function, 333–334
Histograms, 333–334
HorizonOffset variable, 187
Huge arrays, 332–333

I

Images
    determining colors in, 5
    dimensions of, 141
    memory organization, 276
Image file directory, 296
Image mapping, *See* Mapping images
ImageNdx variable, 58, 176

Image plane
    definition of, 3–4
    projecting rays through, 5
Image processing, 331–354
    brightness adjustment, 335
    colorizing, 340
    color reduction, 340
    contrast enhancement, 334–335
    gamma correction, 341–342
    grayscale images, 340
    histograms, 333–334
    mirroring images, 339–340
    reducing noise, 336
    resizing an image, 338–339
    rotating an image, 339
    sharpening an image, 336–337
    zooming an image, 338–339
Images array, 185
Image sequences, *See* Animation
IMAGE structure, 184
IMAGE typedef, 332
ImHt variable, 12, 334, 396
IMTOOLS.C
    functions in, 332
    header file, 346–347
    overview, 332
    source code, 347–354
    testing, 342–343
IMTOOLS.H, 346–347
ImWd variable, 12, 334, 396
Include keyword, 143
Initial rays, 11
Inline functions, 56
InShadow function, 36–38, 51
Intel byte-ordering, 294–295
Intensity function, 80
Intersecting a ray and an object
    finding the closest intersection, 22
    intersecting a ray and plane, 19

J

Jagged edges, *See* Antialiasing

K

Keywords, 134–135
KITCHEN.SDF, 189–198
kt variable, 81

L

LastObj variable, 73
LastRow variable, 82
LEFTPAREN constant, 136
LFw variable, 75
Light
   ambient, 25–26, 29–30
   calculating, 29
   diffuse, 25–26, 29–30
   multiple light sources, 30
   scaling, 34, 77–78
   specular, 25, 28–30
   types of, 25–30
LightFactor function, 75–77
Light keyword, 142
LIGHT structure, 6
Lighting model, *See also* ComputeLight
     function
   applying, 32–35
   calculating the, 29
   definition of, 5
   description of, 25–29
   enhanced, 73
Light rays
   behavior of, 2
   description of, 2
Lights array, 80
LIGHTS.CPP, 130–131
LIGHTSCALE contstant, 45
LIGHTS.H, 128–130
Light sources
   color of, 75
   cone, 73, 76–77
   description of, 2
   directed, 73, 75–76
   distance to, 34
   hierarchy of, 74
   location of, 75
   multiple, 30, 80
   point, 73–75
   scaling, 75
   types of, 73
LIGHT typedef, 9, 27, 46
LMax variable, 78
LMin variable, 78
Loc keyword, 142
Logical palette, 388, 397
LZW compression, 299

M

M300x200x256 constant, 10, 43, 385
M300x200x32K constant, 43, 385
M640x480x256 constant, 43, 385
M800x600x256 constant, 43, 385
Major axis, 62
MapImage function, 183–184
Map keyword, 186
Mapping a pattern, 174
   rectangle, 178
   surface, 174
Mapping images, 183–187
MapToUV function
   coordinate space, 175
   cylinders, 181–182
   ellipsoids, 180–181
   overriding, 175
   purpose of, 59
   rectangles, 178–179
   spheres, 180–181
   triangles, 179
Marble texture, 228–229
Math coprocessor, 45
Matte surfaces, 26, 29
MAXLEVEL variable, 36, 45, 53
MAXOBJECTS constant, 72
MaxT0 variable, 58
Midpoint displacement, 237
Mirrored surfaces, 29
Mirroring an image, 339

MirrorXIm function, 339
MirrorXYIm function, 339
MirrorYIm function, 339–340
Mode keyword, 140–141
MORPH.C
    compiling, 363
    controlling, 357–358
    determining points in a triangle, 361
    generating images, 359, 362
    initializing, 358
    overview, 357
    tips for generating, 365
    using, 363
    working with triangles, 359
Morphing
    introduction, 355–356
    mapping images, 355
    program, 357–363
    tips, 365
    warping images, 355
Motorola byte-ordering, 294–295
Mountains
    bounding boxes, 246–247
    designing, 249–250
    fractals and, 237–238
    generating, 239–250
    levels of recursion, 241
    natural appearing, 237–238
    randomness, 245–246
    rock color, 244
    roughness, 250
    scale of, 241, 250
    snow line, 244
    specifying, 240–241
    steepness, 244

N
NDotL variable, 34
Nested objects, 86–87
NO constant, 29
NoPattern function
    description of, 59

Normal
    direction of, 38–39
    of a plane, 16, 23
    of a rectangle, 63
    of a sphere, 24
Normalize function, 24
NormalN variable, 34
NumFrames keyword, 205
NumImages variable, 185
NumObjToAnimate variable, 202
NumWaveCenters variable, 219

O
Object hierarchy in RAY.C, 57
Object-oriented programming, 56–57
Object class
    constructor, 58
    default settings, 58
    definition, 57
    description of, 56–57
    member functions, 58
Object properties, 5
Objects array, 9, 46, 72
Obscuring objects, 31
OBJECTS.CPP, 107–128
OBJECTS.H, 104–107
OBJECT typedef, 7–8, 26–27, 46
OutFilename variable, 144
Overloading operators, 56

P
PALETTERGB macro, 397
Parametric equations, 17
Parser, 136–140
    nested commands, 138
    processing a file, 137–138
    processing parameters, 138
    reading tokens, 136–137
    strings, 137
PARSERA.C, 266–269
PARSERA.H, 265–266
PARSER.CPP, 149–167

PathFrom keyword, 205
PathTo keyword, 205
PATTERNHT constant, 177
PATTERNWD constant, 177
PatternOnSurface function, 176
Patterns, *See also* Textures
   blended colors, 187–188
   checker pattern, 176–177
   non-checker patterns, 177
PCX files
   color palette, 272
   compression, 274–275
   decoding a file, 275
   encoding a file, 274–275
   header, 272–273
   overview, 271
   toolkit, 275–281
PCXHEADER typedef, 276–277
PCXTOOL.C, 275–281
   file types supported, 276
   functions in, 277
   image size, 278
   initializing a header, 277–278
   overview, 275–276
   processing a palette, 279
   reading an image, 280–281
   reading the header, 276–278, 280
   source code, 286–292
   testing, 282–283
   version supported, 273
   writing a header, 278
   writing an image, 278–279
PCXTOOL.H, 285–286
Perspective projection, 3–4
Pixels, 3, 386
Planes, 8, 16–19
   equation of, 16
   examples of, 16
   intersecting with a ray, 18
   normal of, 16, 23
   parametric equation, 18
   specifying, 16–17

PLAYBACK program
   description of, 207
   source code, 209–214
Point keyword, 142
PointLight class
   definition of, 74, 128–129
   description of, 7, 74
Point light source, 73
Points, 8
PrevColor variable, 82
PrevList variable, 140
Procedural texture, 174
ProcessFile function, 139
Projected rays, 11
PutPixel function, 16, 40
   colors and, 387–388, 396–397
   parameters of, 40, 386
   specifying colors with, 40

Q

Quadratic formula, 20

R

Random numbers, 245–246
RAY.CPP program
   adding an object, 72, 142
   animation, 199–214
   antialiasing, 141
   background, 141
   bounding boxes, 83–87
   compiling, 144
   features in, 55
   files in, 56
   freeing objects, 72–73
   graphics mode, 141
   image size, 141
   lighting model, 73
   light sources, 80, 142
   number of objects, 72–73
   object hierarchy, 57
   objects supported, 57
   overview, 56

saving an image, 143
source code, 89–104
textures, 173–198
translucent objects, 80–81
using, 144
viewing parameters, 141
world model, 72
RAY.H, 87–89
Ray tracing,
  backwards analysis, 2
  definition, 1–2
  description of, 2, 5
  levels of, 36
  image coordinates, 13
  initial rays, 11
  specifying rays, 11
  testing for intersections, 16
ReadObjectTerms function, 139
Rectangles, *See also* RectangleObj class
  mapping, 178–179
  projecting, 62
Rectangle keyword, 142
RectangleObj class
  definition of, 59
  description of, 59–60
  extents of, 60–61
  intersecting with, 61
  location of, 60
  mapping to the surface, 178–179
  normal of, 60, 63
  specifying a, 60
Recursive levels, 36
Red color component, 6
Reflected light, 2
Reflecting ray, 28, 31, 34
  calculating the, 34–36
  equation of, 34
RepositionObjects function, 204
ResizeIm function, 338
Resizing an image, 338–339
Resolution
  color, 42, 385–387
  display, 42

image, 141
Resolution keyword, 141
RightV variable, 13
ROAD.SDF, 253–257
ROADMTN.ODF, 252
RockGradient keyword, 245
Room lighting, 26
Rotating an image, 339
Run-length encoding, 274–275

S

Salt-and-pepper noise, 336
SaveTo keyword, 143
ScaleLight function, 77–78, 130
Scanner, 331
Scene description language, *See also*
    RAY.CPP
  case sensitivity, 134
  comment style, 136
  description of, 133–136
  errors, 140
  example commands, 135
  grouping objects, 139–140
  keywords, 134–135
  nesting files, 143
  parser, 136–140
  using, 140–144
SetConeLightAngle function, 76, 131
SetEye function, 11–12, 54
SetLightDirection function, 131
SetLightParams function, 139
SetObjectParams function, 139
SetPixel function, 397
SetupDisplay function
  default action, 386
  description of, 10
  using, 386
Setup function, 396
Shadows, *See also* InShadow function
  description of, 31
  determining if in, 33–34, 36–38
SHAPES.SDF, 145–146
SharpenIm function, 336–337

Sibling variable, 58, 85
SIMPLRAY.C, 5–54
   Cleanup function, 48
   compiling, 40–41
   data structures in, 6–9
   default mode, 43
   description of, 5
   EndDisplay function, 10
   field of view, 47
   generating rays, 10
   GenImage function, 9–11, 48
   image size, 12, 14, 44
   initialization, 10
   levels of recursion, 45
   main function, 9–10, 47
   modifying, 44–45
   objects in, 7–9, 44
   output of, 41
   overview, 9–10
   plotting pixels, 16
   setting graphics mode, 10, 42–43
   Setup function, 10, 44, 47
   source code, 45–54
   TraceRay function, 15
   tracing rays, 10
   viewer location, 44
   world model of, 44
Sky color, 250–251
Specular highlight,
   description of, 28
   size of, 29
Specular light, 25, 28–29
   calculating, 28, 34–35
   definition of, 28
   range of, 28
Sphere, 8, *See also* SphereObj class
   equation of, 20
   intersecting with a ray, 21–22
   mapping to, 180–181
   normal of, 24
   parameteric equation, 20
   precomputing values, 21
Sphere keyword, 142

SphereObj class, 67
SpreadAngle keyword, 142
SpreadPower keyword, 142
STEP structure, 200
Super VGA
   color resolution, 42
   colors available, 42
   resolution of, 42
Surface mapping, 174–175
Surface of revolution, 146
SVGA, see Super VGA
Swept surfaces, 146–149

T

TESTIM.C, 343–346
TESTPCX.C, 283–285
TESTTIFF.C
   compiling, 308
   description of, 306–308
   running, 308
   source code, 309–312
Text mode, 386
Textures
   bump mapping, 218
   cylinders, 181–182
   ellipsoids, 180–181
   images and, 184
   marble, 228–229
   objects with, 59
   procedural, 174
   rectangles, 176–179
   spheres, 180–181
   supporting, 173–197
   triangles, 179
   water, 215–224
ThreeDCloudPattern function, 231–232
TIFF.C
   color images, 305
   functions in, 300
   grayscale images, 305
   image size, 303
   processing tags, 302–303
   reading a header, 300–301

reading the image, 303–304
source code, 315–330
testing, 306–308
writing a header, 305–306
writing an image, 306
TIFF files
byte ordering, 294–295
classes of files, 294
components of, 294
compression, 299
image organization, 299
overview, 293–294
tags, 296–298
toolkit, 299–308
types of data, 298
TIFF.H, 313–315
TraceRay function, 10–11, 15, 36, 38,
53–54
Translucent objects, 80–81
Transparency function, 80–81
Transparency keyword, 142
Transparent objects, *see* Translucent
objects
Triangle, *See also* TriangleObj class
mapping to, 179
points inside, 63
Triangle keyword, 142
TriangleObj class
definition of, 67
description of, 63–67
dimensions of, 63
intersecting a ray, 63–66
normal, 67
points inside a triangle, 63–65
rendering, 63–67
True color, 43
TwoDCloudPattern function, 226

U

UInc variable, 13
Unit vectors, 11, 14
Up keyword, 141

UpV variable, 13
Up vector
definition of, 3–4
setting, 12

V

VECTOR.C, 9
functions in, 377
source code, 381–383
VECTOR.H, 380–381
Vector operations, 377–383
addition, 378–379
cross product, 378–379
division, 378–379
dot product, 378–379
magnitude, 378
normal, 378
normalize, 379
subtraction, 378–379
Vectors, 8, 377–378
VECTOR typedef, 8, 377
VGA, 385–387
Video memory, 386–387
Viewer
animating, 205
line of sight, 2
position, 12, 141
Viewing angle, 3–4
VInc variable, 13
Virtual functions, 58–59

W

WATER1.SDF, 221–222
Water
model of, 215–218, 224
normal of, 219–220
waves, 216
WaterObj class, 218
Waves
animating, 217–218
creating, 219
frequency of, 219

model of, 216
number of, 219
Windows
   256-color mode and, 43
   bitmaps and, 396–397
   colors in, 43, 397
   compiling for, 41, 397
   defining FORWINDOWS, 41
   hDC variable, 40
   logical palette, 397
   supporting messages, 395
   versus DOS, 43

WinMain function, 396
WINSHELL.C, 41, 395–400
WM_CREATE, 395
WM_DESTROY, 395
WM_PAINT, 395–396
World model, 5, 15, 72
WorldToScreen function, 231

Z

ZoomIm function, 338
Zoom operation, 338–339

Disk Order Form

If you want to avoid typing in the programs in this book, you can order the *Advanced Graphics Companion Disk*. This disk includes all the source code and sample images presented in the book, ready for you to experiment with.

To receive your disk, fill out the form below (or write the information on a separate sheet of paper) and mail it along with $15 in check or money order to Robots Etc, P.O. Box 122, Tempe, AZ 85280. Make checks payable to Robots Etc.

For phone orders or furthur information, call (602) 966-0695 or fax (602) 966-0769. The image files used in this book are also available free of charge on the Robots Etc BBS (9600 Baud, N,8,1) at (602) 966-9905.

• •

Please send me _____ copies of the *Advanced Graphics Companion Disk* at $15 each. Make checks payable to Robots Etc. (Checks must be in U.S. funds drawn on a U.S. bank.)

Diskette Size: ❑ 5-1/4" (1.2MB)   ❑ 3-1/2" (720K)

_____

Name

_____

Address

_____

City   State   Zip

_____

Country   Telephone

Send to: Robots Etc, P.O. Box 122, Tempe, AZ 85280
Please allow 2-4 weeks for delivery.

John Wiley & Sons, Inc., is not responsible for orders placed with Robots Etc.

READ THE MAGAZINE
OF TECHNICAL EXPERTISE!

Published by The Coriolis Group

For years, Jeff Duntemann has been known for his crystal-clear, slightly-be-mused explanations of programming technology. He's one of the few in computer publishing who has never forgotten that English is the one language we all have in common. Now he's teamed up with author Keith Weiskamp and created a magazine that brings you a selection of readable, practical technical articles six times a year, written by himself and a crew of the very best technical writers working today. Michael Abrash, Tom Swan, Jim Mischel, Keith Weiskamp, David Gerrold, Brett Glass, Michael Covington, Peter Aitken, Marty Franz, Jim Kyle, and many others will perform their magic before your eyes, and then explain how *you* can do it too, in language that you can understand.

If you program under DOS or Windows in C, C++, Pascal, Visual Basic, or assembly language, you'll find code you can use in every issue. You'll also find essential debugging and optimization techniques, programming tricks and tips, detailed product reviews, and practical advice on how to get your programming product finished, polished and ready to roll.

Don't miss another issue—subscribe today!

☐ 1 Year $21.95   ☐ 2 Years $37.95

☐ $29.95 Canada; $39.95 Foreign   ☐ $53.95 Canada; $73.95 Foreign

Total for subscription _____
Arizona orders please add 6% sales tax _____
Total due, in US funds _____

Send to:
PC TECHNIQUES
7721 E. Gray Road, #204
Scottsdale AZ 85260

Name _____
Company _____
Address _____
City/State/ZIP _____
Phone _____

Phone (602) 483-0192
Fax   (602) 483-0193

VISA/MC # _____   Expires _____

Signature for charge orders _____